The English
"Loathly Lady" Tales

THE ENGLISH "LOATHLY LADY" TALES

BOUNDARIES, TRADITIONS, MOTIFS

Edited by
S. Elizabeth Passmore
and Susan Carter

STUDIES IN MEDIEVAL CULTURE XLVIII

Medieval Institute Publications
Kalamazoo, Michigan

Library of Congress Cataloging-in-Publication Data

The English "Loathly Lady" tales : boundaries, traditions, motifs / edited by S. Elizabeth Passmore and Susan Carter.
   p. cm. -- (Studies in medieval culture ; 48)
Includes bibliographical references and index.
ISBN 978-1-58044-123-0 (alk. paper) -- ISBN 978-1-58044-124-7 (pbk. : alk. paper)
   1. English poetry--Middle English, 1100-1500--History and criticism. 2. Women in literature. 3. Metamorphosis in literature. 4. Counseling in literature. 5. Sovereignty in literature. 6. Gower, John, 1325?-1408. Confessio amantis. 7. Chaucer, Geoffrey, d. 1400. Wife of Bath's tale. 8. Gawain (Legendary character)--Romances--History and criticism. 9. Romances, English--History and criticism. 10. Ballads, English--England--History and criticism. I. Passmore, S. Elizabeth, 1963- II. Carter, Susan, 1947-
PR317.W66E54 2007
821'.1093522--dc22

               2007036844

    ISBN 978-1-58044-123-0 (casebound)
    ISBN 978-1-58044-124-7 (paperbound)

Printed in the United States of America
1 2 3 4 5 C P 5 4 3 2 1

CONTENTS

ACKNOWLEDGMENTS

Any project requires the proffering of a great deal of gratitude to a great many people; however, an essay collection bears a unique relationship to these acknowledgments, primarily because of the communal quality of the project. The editors would like first of all to thank each and every one of the contributors to the collection, who have been models of the perfect collaborators. We especially are grateful to Russell Peck and R. F. Yeager for their initial and continuing enthusiasm as well as for the element of *auctorité* which contributions from such eminent scholars would bring to any collection, and certainly to ours. Susan Carter also acknowledges her gratitude to Stephanie Hollis, whose mentoring first sparked her interest in the field of medieval literature, and to E. Ruth Harvey, who supervised her doctoral thesis.

Patricia Hollahan, managing editor at Medieval Institute Publications, deserves a round of applause for her large part in bringing this essay collection to the world. She has been a wonderful help throughout the process. Her initial excitement about the project and her unwavering patience in dealing with two novices in the editing process have borne us through the many twists and turns to publication. The anonymous reader she selected must also be thanked for generally positive comments. Finally, we are grateful for Heather Padgen, who has worked with diligence, energy, efficiency, and enthusiasm to take us through the final stages and into hard copy.

We would also like to extend our gratitude to some people whose assistance is not immediately obvious. C. David Benson and Derek Pearsall both helped immensely by their suggestions for contributors, which led us to seek out Russell Peck and R. F. Yeager. Peter Beidler's graciousness is most appreciated, for his offer to sponsor and preside over our first Medieval Congress session on the Loathly Lady tales in 2002. Emmanuel Manalo has been a supportive employer to Susan, enabling that tricky index to see the light of day.

We thank each other. It would be hard to imagine, and more difficult to find, two collaborators more suited to working together. Each has inspired the other in many ways throughout the course of this project, and the balanced nature of our talents has, we believe, contributed to the creation of a collection which will offer much to the flowering of scholarship on the Loathly Lady tales.

Finally and not at all least, Susan thanks her most cherished companion for his support throughout the course of the project. Neale Johnson (whose name sounds the same as Níall's) is Susan's hero, who helps her to get out of the woods and into the castle, court, and feast.

Abbreviations

BJRL	*Bulletin of the John Ryland's Library*
CR	*Chaucer Review*
DIAS	Dublin Institute for Advanced Studies
EC	*Études Celtiques*
EETS	Early English Text Society
EHR	*English Historical Review*
ELH	*English Literary History*
JRMMRA	*Journal of the Rocky Mountain Medieval and Renaissance Association*
LSE	*Leeds Studies in English*
MAE	*Medium Ævum*
MLN	*Modern Language Notes*
MLR	*Modern Language Review*
MRTS	Medieval and Renaissance Texts and Studies
NM	*Neuphilologische Mitteilungen*
PMLA	*Publications of the Modern Language Association*
PQ	*Philological Quarterly*
RC	*Revue Celtique*
RIA	Royal Irish Academy
SAC	*Studies in the Age of Chaucer*
SN	*Studia Neophilologica*

SP   *Studies in Philology*

YES   *Yearbook of English Studies*

PREFACE

Since creation stories always hold some fascination, we thought we would share the story of the creation of this collection. The two of us first met and conceived of our Loathly Lady collection at the 2000 Kalamazoo Medieval Congress. It was Susan's first visit, and she was overwhelmed by the choices of exhilarating sessions but knew that she must attend the session on gendered hags and monsters at which Elizabeth presented a paper on the monstrous images of the Irish and English Loathly Ladies. Susan was in the final stages of completing her thesis on the Loathly Lady motif, and Elizabeth was beginning one on the same topic when we met.

Finding that someone else is working on your thesis topic is always alarming. We met warily but also quickly realized that we were attracted to the Loathly Lady for the same reasons and that it was exciting to meet someone else who was focusing on the same material. Soon enough, we discovered that our approaches, styles, and conclusions were quite different; we could be friends. We happily ran through why we had chosen this subject for several years work—the motif sits on an intersection of national politics and gender issues; it contests gender roles, being transgressively sexually active; the shape-shifting body defies codified ideals of female beauty, undermining the objectification of women through appearance; the hag also gives advice and is a woman who is always right. And she is not textually reproved for this. The medieval motif spreads from the Irish material (which held a great deal of Elizabeth's interest) to Arthurian legend, into ballads, and through to the canon with Gower's and Chaucer's surprisingly distinctive versions. Other shape-shifting figures such as the lamia connect, as well. Susan had originally hoped to follow the motif to the present time, through the Romantics and into modern movies, although she had in fact stopped her thesis at Spenser's Duessa, with more than enough to discuss. Our interest in the shape-shifter herself meant that it was a real pleasure to find another enthusiast.

So we ritualistically allayed any fears of treading on each other's patch by concurring that our approaches were quite different and moved through the suspicion of a conflict of interest to a celebration that we would be wonderfully useful to each other. Susan was impressed by Elizabeth's dedicated study of Old Irish and her insistence on working with the Irish material in its original language. Having worked through her own thesis, Susan felt that she had unfolded some of the implications of the motif, following from those earlier scholars—G. H. Maynadier, Sigmund Eisner, Francis J. Child, and others—who had done the detective work of locating and recording cross-cultural connections. It seemed to us that there was much more to be said about this motif than had been covered. Elizabeth was clearly expanding on this detective work, venturing into the wilderness of the Old Irish genealogies to bring forth genuinely new knowledge.

We agreed that some time in the future we should co-edit a collection of essays on the motif itself, probably in the context of the medieval English tales, since this was an area of mutual interest and knowledge. Elizabeth began the process of getting this collection together over the next couple of years, first soliciting the interest of Peter G. Beidler and the Texas Medieval Association to preside over and sponsor a Medieval Congress session in 2002 on the Irish and English tales behind "The Wife of Bath's Tale." At this session, Elizabeth and Susan joined with Elizabeth Biebel-Stanley to present contrasting but complementary views of the Loathly Lady. In 2003, Elizabeth sponsored and presided over a session at the same conference called, simply, "The Loathly Lady Tales," which included several other essays that appear in our collection. Along the way, we have found a community of scholars with similar interests in this provocative motif. The wide range of views revealed through the essays in this collection shows just how promiscuous the Loathly Lady is as a generator of ideas. You doubtless bring some of your own to this volume.

Introduction

S. Elizabeth Passmore and Susan Carter

The Loathly Lady, that shape-shifter who is loathsome at first, and at last is lovely to all, is the manifestation of a concept, created out of ideas. Whereas some literary motifs such as the tyrant, the beggar, and the crone have equivalents in the real world, the Loathly Lady is a creature of the imagination. Yet she is not merely a whimsical fantasy. In the earliest extant versions, the Irish sovereignty hag tales, her excessive body allegorizes the nature of sovereignty; the Loathly Lady is the shape of success in power contestation. Because the vehicle of the allegory is gendered, however, and because the motif's fictional flesh is sexually active, these ideas about control are entangled with personal power politics. These factors make the motif curiously promiscuous, an intersection of ideas that generates other ideas, sometimes unexpectedly, always provocatively, as this collection of essays demonstrates. Ambivalence is at the core of the Loathly Lady figure. Our multifarious readings take shape from the motif herself.

This volume concentrates on the medieval English Loathly Lady tales, written a little later than the Irish tales, and developing the motif as a vehicle for social ideology. Geoffrey Chaucer's "Wife of Bath's Tale" and John Gower's "Tale of Florent" are the better known of the English Loathly Lady tales, but "The Wedding of Sir Gawain and Dame Ragnelle," the balladic versions—"The Marriage of Sir Gawain" and "King Henry" (and even "Thomas of Erceldoune")—all use shape-shifting female flesh to convey ideas about the nature of women, about heterosexual relations, and about national identity. One of our agendas with this collection of essays is to promote the non-canonical Loathly Ladies as worthwhile subjects for scholarly consideration.

Yet although the English Loathly Lady is our primary quarry here, Elizabeth Passmore's identification of the twin aspects of the Irish sovereignty hag's influence over the Irish hero enables her to start this series of articles by showing that not only is prophecy important in the Irish narratives, but counsel has always been part of the Loathly Lady's function. The Celtic tales are thus our starting point for an investigation of the English tales, and the influential role of the Loathly Lady is our entrance ticket to discussion of the motif. Previous scholarship has focused on the fact that the sovereignty goddess reveals herself to the true king, that is, the king who is foreseen as fated to the throne. The goddess represents the kingdom—Ireland itself—and she seeks union with the youth prophesied to be king. But Passmore shows that, for contemporary political reasons, the earliest Irish tales emphasize the advice that the Loathly Lady gives to the chosen candidate. Merely being the "true" king is not all it takes; the youth must also follow the hag's instructions. Passmore investigates the role the Loathly Lady has as counselor to the hero, a role which the motif carries with her into the English tales and one which has much in common with the popular medieval "mirrors for princes" genre of advice literature. The English Loathly Lady romances become miniature "mirrors for princes," demonstrating through "tales of wonder" their authors' ideas about the need for rulers, whether kings or lords, to accept good counsel. Starting with her distinction between prophecy and advice in the Irish tales, Passmore demonstrates how the two canonical English tales, Chaucer's and Gower's, and even the Gawain tales, develop the theme of advice. A good king or knight must be able to take it.

R. F. Yeager expands upon the theme of advice with a precise dissection of the personal and political levels of Gower's "Tale of Florent." He first speculates on this Loathly Lady tale's placement in the *Confessio Amantis*'s Book I as part of Genius's lesson against Pride that particularly reproves "murmur and complaint." Yeager considers the collection of stories with which "The Tale of Florent" is grouped for what they suggest about Gower's strategy for his Loathly Lady tale. Specifically, the image of Nebuchadnezzar's statue with its four ages shows a regressive historical model, in whose context "The Tale of Florent" is set in the Brass Age, dislocated from the Arthurian setting of the other English versions; by distancing the tale in this way, Gower is able to mask his political critique in order to avoid the consequences of speaking frankly. Full investigation of the scope of two key words, *strengthe* and *vois*, used in the tale in relation to Florent's struggle to silence his inner murmuring and complaining, enables Yeager to locate the political in the fairy tale in the shape of Gower's implicit advice for, especially, England's barons to support their sovereign.

Yet Yeager takes his reading further than a skillful revelation of advice to king, barons, and individual reader based on the adventures of the hero rather than the motif of the hag. He also contextualizes "The Tale of Florent" in terms of the three occasions when Gower would have witnessed foreign queens in the process of acquiring sovereignty in the English court and thus being absorbed into the familiar. Acknowledging that it is impossible to know whether Gower was aware that the shape-shifting Loathly Lady has her roots in an Irish Sovereignty myth, or whether he connected this to the transform-ative rituals of queenly coronation, Yeager nonetheless indicates Gower's sensitivity to the sovereignty connections of his source. While demonstrating Gower's hermeneutics, Yeager insists that there clearly is a political dimension in all the "Loathly Lady" narratives which follows from the idea inherent in the Irish tales (particularly evident in Níall's sexual enthusiasm) that willing obedience is rewarded by redemptive transformation. Good rule is thus liberating.

Elizabeth M. Biebel-Stanley's essay begins where Yeager's ends, with consideration of queenship and female power in relation to the Irish sovereignty theme, specifically in relation to the Wife of Bath and her tale. Biebel-Stanley charts topical political intention by demonstrating that the sovereignty theme reflects a woman's role as advisor that would have compelled Chaucer's medieval audience to associate "The Wife of Bath's Tale" with Richard II's queen, Anne of Bohemia, rather than with the king himself. She discusses the significance of the Irish tales to the English and uses New Historicist methods to argue that if the Loathly Lady can reform a rapist, a good queen can reform an unruly king through her counsel, with their people benefiting from their dual rule. Biebel-Stanley's essay identifies in the advice role of the Loathly Lady the reflection of a specifically feminine—and historical—face.

Motivated, like Biebel-Stanley, by the sense that the Loathly Lady somehow promotes female power, and yet focusing predominantly on the motif rather than the function of the hag, Susan Carter speculates on the way that virginity or its absence is surprisingly unimportant across the spectrum of Loathly Ladies. Linguistically inspecting the sheets of the marriage bed in "The Wife of Bath's Tale" (in particular) for evidence as to whether there can be identified a hymen in the "old wyf"s reconfigured flesh, Carter investigates the lack of distinction between sexually experienced and virginal hags. Suspecting that obsession with virginity arises from the societal commodifi-cation of the female body, Carter concludes that this motif is much more interested in women getting what they want than in whether or not they are virginal. Her sense is that a recuperation of female volition is just one of the ways that the motif collapses gender role boundaries.

Russell A. Peck's essay on "The Tale of Florent" takes a more holistic approach to the Loathly Lady narratives by rooting the mythic power of the Loathly Lady motif within classical and folkloric traditions. Arguing that John Gower created the basic narrative of the English Loathly Lady tales as we know it by drawing upon traditional oral materials, Peck observes that such tales of enchantment are likely to have emerged from vernacular folk traditions, and that, in their new literary context, they often are used subversively as an expression of "maternal power." Peck points out that Gower is sometimes said to be a friend of women in the *Confessio Amantis*, often as a result of his use of folk devices that empower women, for example through emphasis on their ability to give good advice, to show compassion, and to redeem masculine presumption. Mythic precedents begin Peck's contextualization and establish the psychological resonances of the shape-shifting female. He broaches the interface between the literary and the folkloric, applying Greimas's narratological theories as well as recent scholarship on the fairy tale and folklore to anatomize the English medieval tales.

Peck considers both the political and the personal: he cites the historical and highly political staging of an interlude (a *spiel*) during one of King Edward I's "Round Tables," around 1299, in which a Loathly Damsel takes part in a scene meant to inspire the knights present to commit themselves to military support. The *spiel* is thus multiply performative, an entertainment that instates obligation. Peck argues that, like Edward, Gower exploits folk motifs for political ends in his Loathly Lady tale. But Gower's objectives also address the psychological domain of the inner subject, exemplified in the "double bind" in which Florent finds himself, keeping his word both to Branchus's relatives and to the Loathly Lady herself. Gower's mode is folkloristic: understated, down to earth, with the authenticity of the voice of the people. The configuration of Loathly Lady motifs which Gower activates resonates with matriarchal power that may be traced back to the most ancient of myths, and speaks of personal transformation. Peck's illumination of how the folkloric functions within the English Loathly Lady tales of canonical literature (particularly in reference to Gower) addresses one of the aims of this collection, which is to collapse the boundaries between high and low cultures. The motif bridges and breaches these boundaries, resisting categorization, and our selection of essays follows her model.

Continuing discussion of the relationship between literature and folklore by launching from Carl Lindahl's interest in the power exerted by the orality of some Loathly Lady versions, Paul Gaffney uses Roland Barthes's narratological theory of *histoire* and *discours* to show why the noncanonical versions have such strong appeal: Gaffney proposes that the less fixed the meaning of a *discours*, the more evocative it can be. Whereas the canonical versions of Chaucer and Gower control the *discours* carefully, aiming at what Chaucer identifies as "the best sentence and moost solas" (*Canterbury Tales*, I.798), the noncanonical versions, the balladic and the folkloric, have a less intentive direction. Less control frees the *histoire* to the shape of the reader's imagination. Folk literature offers strength of its own, alternative to the strength of elite culture literature. Gaffney thus satisfyingly locates why this motif is so provocative both within and without courtly literature.

If Gaffney provides a logical argument as to why the forms that emerge from orality have a power of their own that defies their lower status within the canonical hierarchy, Stephanie Hollis puts pressure on the boundaries between high and low literary forms by investigating the potential of the lacunae in "The Marriage of Sir Gawain": into this gap, she speculates a logical development of the *histoire* in accordance with the ballad's specific interests. Hollis sets up her case by outlining the distinctive and original aspects of the "Marriage" author's handling of the plot in comparison with "The Wedding of Sir Gawain and Dame Ragnelle." Reading carefully around the lacunae, she considers and refutes other critics, notably Thomas Hahn and Thomas J. Garbáty, insisting instead on a reading that credits the ballad with more design than previously has been acknowledged. Hollis shows that the "Marriage" broadens the scope of courtesy from an exclusive aristocratic code to a universal principle, so that respect and good-natured kindness might encompass even a woman whose appearance breaches social expectations so extremely as the Loathly Lady's.

Mary Edwards Shaner's essay concentrates on reclaiming another balladic Loathly Lady tale, the "King Henry" ballad first recorded in the late eighteenth century but presumed to have medieval origins. Shaner demonstrates that theory can be profitably applied to Loathly Lady ballads by taking a Jungian approach to reading "King Henry." She uses the Jungian idea that the object of human psychological development is a wholeness achieved by the integration of the *animus* and the *anima*. Henry, out hunting, exemplifies the *animus*, the masculine principle. Shaner equates Henry's progression through to his symbolic death when he lies down with a fearsome "fiend that dwells in Hell," to a Jungian syzygy, whereby his acceptance of the *anima*, the female principle, heals both king and hag: him into joy, her into beauty. The *animus* must acknowledge the existence of the *anima*, giving it permission to be itself in order for it to find its own beauty, and to transform itself from something feared by the masculine into something that can be loved. The *anima* has the agentive role in pushing the king into union. His Loathly Lady's unreasonable demands prove good for King Henry, enabling him to be made whole by giving himself over to the female principle and finding union.

Also interested in female agency as well as in the element that rape adds to the Loathly Lady *histoire*, Lynn M. Wollstadt attentively compares "The Wife of Bath's Tale" with the ballad "The Knight and the Shepherd's Daughter." Both narratives are built upon rape, punishment, and reward concerning a woman who is not what she appears. Wollstadt proposes that the ballad echoes "The Wife of Bath's Tale" much more closely in both substance and message than any other Loathly Lady analogue. Applying ballad theory to her interpretation, Wollstadt proposes that women singers may well have recognized the same contradictions in the happy union between rapist and victim that modern literary critics do. The differences between the oral and broadside versions further suggest that male and female singers, authors, and audiences might have considered the basic tale quite differently according to their gender. Ultimately, both "The Knight and the Shepherd's Daughter" and "The Wife of Bath's Tale" reflect dual interpretations, offering narratives of male subjugation to female authority that seemingly reinforce masculinist hegemony. Regardless of the stories' endings, however, the bulk of each balladic text focuses on the punishment of the rapists. This focus may well explain the ballad's appeal to generations of women singers, just as it explains the relish with which the Wife of Bath tells her tale. Wollstadt thus finds a link between the Wife of Bath and the feminine balladic tradition that accounts for the ambiguity of the tale's ultimate message regarding gender and power. The ambivalence Wollstadt locates is the dynamic that allows scholarly differences of interpretation regarding "The Wife of Bath's Tale" as to which gender holds more sway at closure, and whether the tale is for or against female control.

Such ambivalence is inherent to the Loathly Lady, and Mary Leech considers the interpretive potential that exists through a discrepancy found in the conclusion to "The Wedding of Sir Gawain and Dame Ragnelle." Through theories of social order and disorder, particularly in the works of Mikhail Bahktin and anthropologist Mary Douglas, along with notions of feminine roles within medieval society, Leech explores the contradiction inherent in the idealized world of Arthur and argues that the ending of "The Wedding of Sir Gawain and Dame Ragnelle" registers the tenuous nature of civilized authority. In other words, Ragnelle must die, having shown the

Arthurian court its own flaws. Alive, she would remain a constant reminder of her own superiority in saving Arthur's life as well as of the debt he owed her. In death, however, she is sanctified—she can be praised and flattered, but can no longer make demands. By transforming Ragnelle into an iconic ideal of femininity, the poet reaffirms masculine authority through the very one who had demonstrated the inconsistencies and defects of the patriarchal social structure.

While Leech peers into the void of ambivalence at the end of the "Wedding," Ellen M. Caldwell approaches a similar problem differently, questioning whether the Loathly Lady, who initially appears to exercise female sovereignty, does in fact offer a message of empowerment for women. She shows that the Loathly Lady oscillates between using her ugly old intelligence or being happily and vacuously beautiful. Caldwell locates the problem in the fact that when the loathly women become beautiful, they revert to their conventional roles, seemingly losing their power. In general terms, it is only when a Loathly Lady is loathsome and "ungendered," that is, outside of her female role, that she is beyond male control. Then she is sought after, not as a sexual object but as the source of special powers, the provider of advice and superior knowledge. Thus, the happy ending of beauty and union that makes Dame Ragnelle desirable as a woman returns her to a woman's subordinate position. Neither beauty or feminine brains can truly penetrate the homosociality of the Arthurian court.

Our consideration of the medieval English Loathly Lady tales engages with a myriad of concerns, including anxieties about virginity and sex, power and assimilation, beauty and beastliness. Our essays investigate both the visual effects of the motif of the Loathly Lady and her varying, yet often associated, functions, particularly those which connect her role to issues of contemporary politics. We attend to folkloric as well as literary applications of the motif, reclaiming some of the lesser-known Loathly Lady narratives from comparative scholarly neglect. The Loathly Lady and her tales are many-shaped. So too are our readings of her.

THE ENGLISH
"LOATHLY LADY" TALES

Through the Counsel of a Lady
The Irish and English Loathly Lady Tales and the "Mirrors for Princes" Genre

S. Elizabeth Passmore

While the medieval Irish and English Loathly Lady versions have long been connected to each other through the motif of the transforming hag-beauty,[1] little attention has been paid to the nonphysical aspects of the relationship between the hero and lady in these tales, particularly to the unique role the Loathly Lady has as a counselor to the protagonist. The theme of instruction and advice, however, connects the Irish and English narratives as strongly as the visual motif of the Loathly Lady. The Irish Loathly Lady tales depict the sovereignty goddess instructing the king-candidate on how to take the kingship for which he proves his qualifications in the course of each narrative.[2] The English protagonists, unlike the Irish ones, lack some essential interior quality which they require in order to fulfill their noble roles, and the English Loathly Lady guides the hero to this goal through the advice that she gives. The counselor role of the Loathly Lady is determined by the readiness of the protagonist to attain kingship, whether that be interpreted literally or symbolically.[3] She offers "formative instruction" to the exemplary Irish protagonist and "transformative advice" to the imperfect English protagonist.[4] The Loathly Lady's counsel is, moreover, inspired by "mirrors for princes" literature such as *Audacht Morainn* for the Irish texts and Thomas Hoccleve's *Regiment of Princes* for the English ones.[5] The medieval "mirrors for princes" genre of advice literature had long been in existence, with the Irish narrative possibly representing the earliest western European example of the genre.[6] In England, vernacular compositions of "mirrors for princes" were increasingly popular with aristocratic readers in the late fourteenth to the mid-fifteenth centuries.[7] In this essay, I demonstrate how the Loathly Lady's role as counselor connects the Irish and English narratives and supports the relationship discussed by various scholars of the similarity in the visual images of the Loathly Lady motif.[8]

The Irish tales, through an emphasis on either prophecy or counsel, illuminate not only the Loathly Lady's role as counselor but also the changing role of the poet-historian in Irish culture. Through the sovereignty goddess's instruction, Níall and Lugaid, the protagonists of the kingship tales, attain kingship as the poets implicitly demonstrate contemporary eleventh- and twelfth-century political requirements for rulership. T. M. Charles-Edwards, in *Early Christian Ireland,* divides qualifications for succession for early medieval Irish kings into three distinct parts, including "the *febas,* personal excellence."[9] The emphasis on prophecy in the Irish texts, the Irish poet's tool for conveying his approval of a king-candidate, is also possibly an extension of an earlier emphasis on counsel, exemplified by the *Audacht Morainn.*[10] This seventh-century text is in the form of counsel from a *fili* to a king and explicates the characteristics a good king should display, including justice in the form of the *fír flaithemon,* the "ruler's truth," a concept which determined, in part, that the behavior of the king would directly affect the well-being of his subjects and his realm.[11] That the *Audacht Morainn* specifically conveys the advice of a poet to a king reinforces the Irish poet's early connection to the theme of counsel.

The role of the poet was affected by changes in the eleventh and twelfth centuries in kingship in Ireland, after the brief high kingship attained by Brían Borumha in the early eleventh century. At the same time, the changes in the depiction of the goddess—connected to the status of the poet—illustrate a gradual shift in ideas about kingship from the over-king/client-king concept to conform more closely to the continental vision of kingship exemplified in the feudal bond between king and knight. Kingships were collapsing, with more powerful kings becoming ever more powerful and lesser kings losing ground, and consideration of kingship in the Irish texts reflects some changes in the understanding of the concept of rule between the period of Viking invasions after the eighth century and the Anglo-Norman invasion of 1171.

In contrast, the English texts make the connection of kingship to knighthood through shared chivalric concerns. In England, though the country was ruled by one king only, that king became increasingly reliant on the goodwill of the barons and lords who formed his council (and those barons and lords, themselves, ruled the tenants on their own lands).[12] Without loyal supporters, the king was subject to the whims of the wealthy and powerful in his country, sometimes with deadly results, as can be proven by the outcomes of the reigns of Richard II and Henry VI, the rulers of

England at the time of the composition of the English Loathly Lady tales. Those who provided support needed to feel that the king took heed of wise advice. The popularity of advice literature for rulers at this time is proof of the perceived need to counsel the king in relation to the well-being of the country as a whole.

Counsel and kingship have long been connected in advisory texts like the "mirrors for princes," where the role of the poet is that of counselor to a king. The poet in Ireland, however, was able to attain an equally high status in society as the king; this was not true of the English poet. In contrast to the Irish poet's status and profession as propagandist for the ruler, the English poet's status relied on a more diffused patronage from the nobility.[13] Geoffrey Chaucer, John Gower, and Thomas Hoccleve were never employed by the Crown specifically for the purpose of creating works of literature, though their close connections with the Ricardian and Lancastrian courts are demonstrable.[14] An important point about the theme of counsel in late medieval English literature is that writers needed to take great care in considering how to go about critiquing those on whose patronage they depended. As Judith Ferster comments in *Fictions of Advice*, the dangers inherent in explicit criticism of the king and government were widespread and often led to the use of "camouflaged texts" to convey critique in the form of "mirrors for princes": "Advice can become critique, and the audience for the work may include not only the prince to whom it is nominally addressed, but his subjects as well."[15]

Ferster discusses the "mirrors for princes" themselves, while I further argue that one common way the advisory purpose of a text could be disguised was to submerge the criticism in a pleasant and entertaining format, such as romances like the English Loathly Lady tales. However, as Ferster also notes, "if the critique is disguised well enough to 'fool' the government, there is no guarantee that it can be understood correctly by a wider audience, including us."[16] In other words, a romance or ballad might be written so entertainingly that any recognition of it as a potentially critical or even advisory text might be submerged. One example of this might be the ending of "The Wedding of Sir Gawain and Dame Ragnelle," when the poet mentions his current sojourn in prison and his plea for help from, especially, that "veray King Royalle" (line 847), God in heaven. This comment has rarely been regarded in scholarship, but its purpose could be to induce the reader or listener to think more carefully about the poet's presentation of the other king in the romance—King Arthur—and his poor treatment of Sir Gromer Somer Joure, the disgruntled knight who confronts the king with his woes.[17] By submerging critique in his work such a way, a poet could both entertain and inform with less personal danger as to how his words might be interpreted.

Ferster further explains that many "mirrors for princes" echo the biblical injunction to obtain as many forms of advice as possible (Prov. 24:6). The English Loathly Lady texts reflect this injunction, for the protagonists go on lengthy quests to seek advice about the answer to the question of what women most desire. Chaucer's rapist-knight travels throughout the land speaking with everyone he sees, and "The Tale of Florent" clearly shows Florent consulting with his advisors, though they are unsuccessful at helping him.[18] In the Gawain texts, Sir Gawain even convinces King Arthur to bring along a book to fill with the responses he receives.[19] Although the procedure does not actually work for these knights, the attempt to learn what the general population believes has some similarities to the "mirror for princes" advice to rulers to gain counsel from a number of sources.[20] It is significant that the protagonists encounter the English Loathly Lady and her counsel only after having sought advice unsuccessfully elsewhere. The Loathly Lady, however, is able to give appropriate advice to the protagonist. Hoccleve, in the *Regiment*, also specifies that the king should not disregard the advice of those of lower birth (lines 4880–93). Furthermore, the counsel of the Loathly Lady to the knight, after their marriage, underscores the need for the knight to follow advice. For example, the "pillow lecture" of Chaucer's "olde wyf" in "The Wife of Bath's Tale" uses the language of "mirrors for princes" manuals to explain to the knight the nature of true nobility: specifically, her insistence that behavior, not birth, identifies "gentillesse" is also propounded by the "mirrors."[21]

Geraldine Barnes, in *Counsel and Strategy*, argues for a wider though more implicit application of counsel than does Ferster, extending the topic of advice thoroughly into the genre of Middle English romance: "The process of counsel often has independent thematic significance in Middle English romance, as a means of measuring royal and knightly competence."[22] While Barnes's interpretation of counsel does not specifically highlight the advice from "mirrors for princes," as did Ferster, her examination of counsel in Middle English romance validates my own argument. Barnes discusses the historical significance of counsel in the relationship between the English king and his vassals; such counsel was important since the Anglo-Saxon period, but it becomes a difficult problem in the thirteenth and fourteenth centuries when the king and his barons could not agree on how much (or how little) the king should be expected to pay attention to the advice he received.[23] In fact, this ongoing argument became so heated that late medieval complaint poetry often brought up the idea that the king should seek advice widely: "In the late fourteenth and early fifteenth century, the notion that a king should heed the advice of all his subjects becomes a repeated theme in the poetry of complaint, while the 'problem of counsel' is a major issue in the literature of late fifteenth-century social comment."[24]

Two examples of such complaint poems are "Richard the Redeless" and "Mum and the Sothsegger," both written soon after the deposition of Richard II, during the reign of Henry IV. Barnes, however, instead discusses several English romances from the thirteenth and fourteenth centuries to demonstrate her point, identifying a distinctively English attitude in the use of counsel in romance narratives, an attitude which, she believes, is "a reflection of the feudal tradition of *consilium et auxilium* as well as a more topical reminder of the royal-baronial conflicts of the thirteenth and fourteenth centuries."[25] Barnes's work, along with Ferster's, allows me to connect the concept of kingship to the theme of counsel through the Loathly Lady's position as advisor to the protagonist. Barnes points out that the role of counselor was often reserved for one of advanced age,[26] and the English Loathly Lady, in fact, appears to function in the narratives as a type of the aged counselor, for she often gives advice to the hero while in her loathsome, rather than lovely, form. While most of the advisors that Barnes discusses are male, she demonstrates that, sometimes, women function in the romances as political advisors, such as Goldeboru in *Havelok* and Rymenhild in *King Horn*.[27] Barnes also points to the popularity of the theme of the hero's education in European romance, and, here again, the English Loathly Lady (as teacher and advisor to the hero) exemplifies the forms.[28]

The time period during which the English Loathly Lady tales were written, the late fourteenth century (for Gower's and Chaucer's tales) to the mid-fifteenth century (for the Gawain romance and ballad), was a period during which advice to rulers was particularly necessary. Both Richard II and Henry VI, kings during the period of time these tales were composed, were problematic rulers.[29] Furthermore, many of the problems in the reigns of Richard II and Henry VI had to do directly with the role of advisors, good and bad, and especially with each ruler's need for good counsel. Additionally, the deposition of Richard II by Henry of Lancaster ensured that Henry IV, and even his son, Henry V, were both concerned with the need to consider seriously the role and identity of the king.[30] Likewise, the English Loathly Lady's role as advisor to the hero emphasizes the real need for good counsel. This essay will demonstrate how the counselor role of the Loathly Lady in the Irish and English texts is inspired by the "mirrors for princes" genre in general—though for different reasons and to different effects. Overall, the role of the Loathly Lady as counselor connects the narratives through the themes of kingship and counsel rather than only through the shape-shifter motif.

The Irish kingship tales exist in two different forms, the Níall tales and the Lugaid tales, but in five different versions. These tales demonstrate different levels of emphasis on either prophecy or advice given by the sovereignty goddess. Due to space limitations, however, I will concentrate in this article on the variation in emphasis as revealed in the Níall tales alone.[31] The advice-giving role of the sovereignty goddess is of particular importance for understanding the future role of the English Loathly Lady as counselor. The initial political significance of the Irish kingship tales relates to the demonstration of the candidate's ability to follow counsel as well as to possess certain qualifications and characteristics of kingship. The transition from an emphasis on advice in the earlier tales to prophecy in the later tales can partly be explained by the changing role of the poet in Irish society. Written by monastically educated poets, the earlier narratives emphasize pagan prophetic powers which is, perhaps, understandable. Depicting the goddess as advisor rather than oracle was perhaps more palatable to Christian writers. However, in the twelfth century, the monastic position of the *filid* (the poet-historian) was contested due to church reforms, and the poet moved out of the monastic environment to form a secular class of poet-historians. With this change in environment, a greater emphasis on prophecy became paramount in order to demonstrate the social importance of the class of poets who authored these kingship tales. The later change to prophecy from an emphasis on advice submerges but does not eliminate the thematic significance of the Loathly Lady as counselor when the theme reappears in the English narratives.

The earliest Níall tale, a three-hundred-line poem called "Echtra mac Echdach Mugmedóin," dates from the early eleventh century and was written by Cúan Ua Lothcháin, court poet of Máel Sechnaill II, son of Domnaill and king of Tara from 980 to 1022.[32] The poem was composed to promote the candidacy of Máel Sechnaill II, who became king of Míde (Meath) in the late tenth century. To understand the advisory role of the sovereignty goddess in this poem, we must look closely at the interactions between the Irish Loathly Lady and the protagonist, Níall.[33] In this narrative, Níall's ability to follow the formative instruction of the goddess is crucial to the success of his candidacy. The goddess's counseling of Níall begins after her transformation when she tells Níall to go to Tara and meet there with all the chiefs of

Ireland. To emphasize the importance of his actions, she admonishes him: "ná coillder do thréngissi" (let not thy mighty vows be broken [stanza 54]). The goddess details her instructions and explanations at length, informing Níall that he is the heir of Tara because he was not dissuaded by her monstrous appearance: "In gráin atchess duit arm' gnúis ar báig niarni do drúis, / at adbar flatha Temra fo mbiat catha comlebra" (The fearsomeness in my face thou sawest, since it repelled not thy desire, thou art the princely heir of Tara, 'neath which shall be long extended battalions [stanza 55]). Níall's actions, not this prophecy, indicate his suitability for rulership, but the goddess's instructions demonstrate for him how he can grasp that rule for which he is qualified. The goddess warns him that his brothers will find trouble via the draught of water for which they had all searched (only Níall being successful): "Mescfaitir do bráthir de" (Trouble awaits thy brothers therefrom [stanza 58]), with the implication being that it will be that much simpler for Níall to become king in their stead.[34] She instructs Níall to return to the "úarboithe" (hunting-booth) and requests from each of his brothers a "cuinnig" (boon) that Níall should be allowed "i ndáil fer talman sunn so labrad lá is aidchi rempo" (to speak before them day and night, at a gathering of the men of this land [stanzas 58–59]). This is the most significant passage in the goddess's advice; if Níall follows her instructions, he will be enabled to take the right of the eldest to be the first one to speak in the company of all the court—he will obtain seniority over all of his brothers in a legal sense, even though he is quite young (stanzas 11–12), and this seniority will pave the way for him to take the kingship as well.[35]

The goddess thus instructs Níall point-by-point on the way in which he should gain the kingship. It is insufficient for him to be prophesied to be the rightful king, nor is it sufficient for him to demonstrate his qualifications through tests. In addition to these proofs of candidacy, he must also carefully follow the steps delineated by the goddess in order to grasp the kingship to which he has a right through the prophecy and his abilities. Though one might assume that the existence of the prophecy heralding Níall as rightful king would be enough to make him king in reality, the goddess reveals here that Níall must behave in certain ways in order to bring his prophecy to fulfillment. The significance of the goddess's instructions in contrast to her prophecy distinguishes Ua Lothcháin's version from the later prose "Echtra," discussed below, in which the prophecy holds equal power with the counsel of the goddess to determine how Níall finally becomes king.

The prose "Echtra" was written at some point in the early years of the twelfth century by an anonymous writer, about a hundred years after the

poetic "Echtra" was composed.[36] This narrative, while still conveying a sense
that Níall himself controls the outcome of his destiny, unfolds equally to the
prophecies and counsel of the druid-poet, Torna, and of the sovereignty
goddess. One possibility for this difference may relate to the later composition
of this version and the historical redefinition attempts of the *filid* which had
begun by this time in Irish society. The ability to relate true prophecies was
important to the position of the *filid*, perhaps never more so than after the
poet-historian class became part of the secular rather than the monastic
world, and the straddling of poet's roles is reflected in the narrative's equal
weight given to both prophecy and counsel. Torna the poet foretells the story
of Níall's life soon after the hero's birth. Much later in the narrative, after her
physical transformation to beauty, the goddess explains that "Misi in Flaithius"
(I am the Sovranty), in response to Níall's question, and she provides Níall with
counsel as well as a prophecy and an explanation (para. 15).[37] The goddess
prophecies that if Níall follows her directions, kingship and power will follow
him and his descendants, except for two of his brother Fiachra's descendants
("Dathi 7 Ailill Molt") and "oenrigh a Mumain .i. Brian Boruma" (one king
out of Munster, namely Brian of the Tribute [para. 16]).[38] She describes the
nature of kingship and how Níall's courage has indicated his qualifications:
"amail adcondarcais misi co granna connda aduathmar artús 7 alaind
fadeoid, is amlaid sin in flaithius, uair is annam fogabar he cen chatha 7 cen
chongala, alaind maisech immorro ria nech e fodeoid" (as thou hast seen me
loathsome, bestial, horrible at first and beautiful at last, so is the sovranty; for
seldom it is gained without battles and conflicts; but at last to anyone it is
beautiful and goodly [para. 16]). Kingship, in other words, is never easily
obtained; rather, a potential ruler must demonstrate his ability to accept all
its qualities, both the negative and the positive.

The goddess's formative instruction to Níall is as detailed as her
prophecy, and her counsel recalls the "mirrors for princes" advice to kings as
well as Irish succession laws about seniority and its place in the choice of a
future king: "Eirig do saigid do braithrech ... 7 ber usce lat.... Acht chena na
tabair-seo in t-usce dod braithrib co tucad aisceda dait .i. co tucud a
sindsirrdacht duid, 7 co ro thocba th'arm ed lama uas a n-armaib seom" (Go
now to thy brothers ... and take water with thee.... Howbeit, give not the
water to thy brothers until they make gifts to thee, to wit, seniority over them,
and that thou mayst raise thy weapon a hand's breadth over their weapons
[para. 16]). The Loathly Lady is explicit about Níall's need to obtain the
official right to the seniority from his brothers before he speaks, rather than

simply speaking before them. Her additional instruction to have him raise his weapon higher than theirs is another indication of superiority.[39] Her admonition that he use the water to elicit clear promises from his brothers is an acknowledgment of the need for a ruler to negotiate with his subjects.[40] The goddess's counsel to Níall, and his obedience to her instruction, help to fulfill the initial prophecy of his kingship. Without the goddess's counsel, Níall would not have had the wisdom to gain the kingship; the formative instructions give him clear assistance.

The latest Níall poem, "Tarrnig in sealsa ag Síl Néill," dates from about 1191, written by an unknown poet on behalf of the kingship of Cathal Croibhdhearg Ó Conchubhair, who was king of Míde from 1189 to 1224.[41] The discussion between the goddess and Níall is, in this version, greatly expanded in comparison with the two previous narratives; however, counsel plays an unusual role in this text. What is most obvious about the narrative initially is the clearly expanded role of prophecy. The goddess makes specific prophecies about historical kings of the twelfth century, for the poem carefully demonstrates the validity of the rule of a descendant of Níall's eldest brother, Brían, rather than himself. The sovereignty goddess, upon Níall's arrival at her fountain, warns him:

> Dámad duit, a fhir engaig,
> a uí Thuathail a Temraig,
> nocha béra can luach lat
> uisce tonnglas mo thiprat.

> (Even you, o one who has been foretold, o descendant of Tuathal from Tara, you shall not bring away with you without payment the clear-surfaced water of my well [stanza 25].)

With these words, the goddess indicates both that Níall's existence (and future kingship) had been foretold and that he still must follow the same rules as other candidates for kingship, for the water of her well symbolizes the kingship itself. Níall must perform certain actions in order to fulfill the prophecy, but the goddess hints at these only after the protagonist cannily shows he is ready to bargain for the water. He points out that he has no silver or gold and no intention of giving away the cup belonging to his father the king: "ní thibar duit tar a chenn / cuach Echach airdríg Éirenn" (I shall not give you in exchange for it the cup of Eochaid the high-king of Ireland [stanza 26]).[42] The cup of Eochaid symbolizes his father's kingship, and he is right to refuse to trade that rule for his own: for Níall, possession of his father's cup indicates only his genealogical qualifications for kingship, not that he will necessarily benefit from them. Though unwilling to trade this particular object, however, he does not simply depart from the goddess as did Fergus and his other siblings. His resolve proves his determination as well as his exemplary abilities. In response, the Loathly Lady tells Níall:

> Dámad let in cuach do-chím
> do shloinnis-se ón airdríg
> bad ferr lim caemthach colla
> let, a laedán Liatroma.

> (Even if you owned the cup I see which you name as the high-king's I would sooner have sexual union with you, o pith of Liatroim [stanza 27].)

She validates Níall's prior refusal by acknowledging that he cannot give away a cup that does not belong to him. Furthermore, she reveals that, even if the cup is a symbol of Níall's genealogical qualifications, as indicated above, he must do more to attain kingship than simply show these physical qualifications for kingship. In addition, he must prove his courage by overlooking her fearsome appearance and grasping hold of her as a symbol of kingship in both its fearsome aspects (of wars and battles) and its loveliness (of power and riches). The implication is that the cup (the right to rule) will one day be Níall's, yet he must still prove his capability for the position its ownership implies, that is, the kingship.[43]

Beyond these tests and prophesies for Níall, however, "Tarrnig" reveals the goddess as counselor to a king but not (as in the poetic and prose "Echtra") to Níall, the legendary king-candidate. Rather, she specifies at the poem's conclusion that a new king is about to appear—Cathal Croibhdhearg—the historical king for whom the text was written:

> Naí mbliadna 'cus trícha trén
> remes in Chroibdeirg, ní chél,
> mór cliath, mór cuire ro cherb
> co toracht in laech láimderg.

> Náram léic uada im aenar,
> toisc dá mbia in Banba i mbaegal,
> in t-airdrí ceirtbrethach cáid;
> bidam senóir in tan táir.

(Nine and thirty years is the age of In Croibderg—I shall not conceal it; many bands will have fought many battles before the red-handed warrior arises. May the noble high-king of the rightful judgments not let me depart from him in single state, an event whereby Ireland will be endangered; I shall be old by the time he will come.)[44]

She advises Cathal to sleep with her, and to do so quickly; if he does not, the whole country will suffer. Since the text postdates the Anglo-Norman invasion of 1171 by about a generation, the sense of urgency in the goddess's words is a signal for the historical king himself to take charge of the increasingly serious political situation. The goddess's counsel moves outside of the text to address the king-candidate for whom the poem was actually composed, departing from her earlier role as instructor of the legendary Níall but continuing her counselor role to a king, this one from contemporary twelfth-century Ireland.

The English narratives, though not overtly written for political propaganda as were the Irish tales, reveal their implicit political nature partly by expanding the counselor role of the Loathly Lady. The English Loathly Lady's counsel of the protagonist is essential for his quest's success, as she advises the hero on the inner qualities he needs to be an effective leader. The protagonist of the English texts possesses the outer attributes of chivalric knighthood but must overcome some interior deficiency through the Loathly Lady's transformative advice before he can be truly considered noble.[45]

John Gower's "Tale of Florent" and Geoffrey Chaucer's "Wife of Bath's Tale" were both written during the latter part of Richard II's reign in the late fourteenth century. Richard II had been dogged by bad counsel and criticisms of his court throughout the latter part of the 1380s, culminating in the Wonderful Parliament of 1386 and the Merciless Parliament of 1388, when several of his key advisors and members of his inner circle were either exiled or put to death.[46] The 1390s witnessed the king becoming even more autocratic and distanced from good counsel, especially after the death of Richard II's first queen, Anne of Bohemia, in 1394. Both Gower's and Chaucer's tales were written during this period, from the late 1380s to the early 1390s, when Richard II's behavior and choice of counsel was heavily criticized. As we know, Richard II's reign ended in disaster in 1399, when he was deposed by the efforts of Henry of Derby (later King Henry IV) and later killed while imprisoned in the Tower of London. Gower's and Chaucer's Loathly Lady texts cannot, of course, reflect these later disastrous events because of the earlier dates of their composition; however, they do appear to indicate a

strong concern with counsel, and the Loathly Lady plays a significant
advisory role which might profitably be considered in relation to the
mediatory role acceptable for a medieval queen such as Anne of Bohemia.[47]
Gower's tale appears in a collection, the *Confessio Amantis*, the overall theme
of which is kingship, particularly Book VII, which has often been described
as following the "mirrors for princes" genre.[48] Chaucer's tale, in contrast,
appears initially to have little relationship to kingship; however, "The Tale
of Melibee" has been argued to be a "mirror for princes," and the pillow lecture
may also be interpreted as a "mirror for princes," for reasons mentioned above
and delineated below.[49]

Those scenes in "The Tale of Florent" in which the protagonist deals
directly with the Loathly Lady illuminate the similarity between the lady's
comments and "mirrors" such as Hoccleve's *Regiment*, which suggests that a
lord should seek counsel for everything he does: "It needful is to do by conseil
ay" (line 4860). On Florent's first encounter with the Loathly Lady, she points
out his need for counsel and, particularly, for her counsel:

> Thou hast on honde such a game,
> That bot thou be the betre avised,
> Thi deth is shapen and devised,
> That al the world ne mai thee save,
> Bot if that thou my conseil have.
> (lines 1542–46)

The key word in this passage is *conseil*, in that the knight must, according to
the Loathly Lady, prepare to accept her advice in order to save his life.[50]
Florent, desperately hoping for some way to save his life, offers to give her
whatever she requests: "'What thing,' quod he, 'that thou wolt axe'" (line
1555). A better payment the hag cannot imagine, but she now requests a more
formal pledge of his agreement, "Thou schalt me leve such a wedd, / That I
wol have thi trowthe in honde / That thou schalt be myn housebonde" (lines
1558–60). *Wedd* is used here to mean "pledge," but the fact that *wedd* can also
mean "to marry"—and is used as such a little later in the narrative—implies
that the pun is meant to convey a greater significance than is yet obvious.[51]
Florent initially rejects the offer, suggesting instead a variety of possessions:
land, income, game reserves, farmland. The hag, though (betraying her origins
as a sovereignty goddess of land), is uninterested. Finally, "this yonge lusti
knyht" agrees that, if it transpires that only her advice would save him, he
would marry her. His agreement is carefully conditional, in that he will only
marry her if he can find no other way to save his life: "And thus his trowthe

he leith to wedde" (line 1588).[52] The Loathly Lady, with this assurance of her reward, agrees that "if eny other thing / Bot that thou hast of my techying" would save him, she would release him from this bond (lines 1591–92). She then gives Florent her "conseil," admonishing him to listen carefully to what she says.

Like the Irish goddesses, Florent's Loathly Lady appears capable of prophetic vision, in that she knows exactly what he must do to succeed and exactly what he will encounter upon his return to Branchus's family. Because of her foreknowledge, she knows he will not hold back from what he thinks is his best effort, yet she is also aware that only her counsel will save him:

> And elles this schal be my lore,
> That thou schalt seie, upon this molde
> That alle wommen lievest wolde
> Be soverein of mannes love:
> For what womman is so above,
> Sche hath, as who seith, al hire wille;
> And elles may sche noght fulfille
> What thing hir were lievest have.
> (lines 1606–13)

To save his life, Florent must follow the lady's "lore," just as the Irish protagonist, Níall, had to follow the clear instructions of the goddess he encountered.

A move ahead to another significant scene in the text will indicate how the Loathly Lady's counsel is capable of transforming the protagonist, just as she transforms herself physically. After the wedding, when the couple is left alone in their bed, the hag becomes quite gleeful while Florent sinks deep into depression: "His body myhte wel be there, / Bot as of thoght and of memoire / His herte was in purgatoire" (lines 1774–76). In the introduction to his edition of the *Confessio Amantis*, Russell Peck discusses Gower's use of theories of memory, particularly those of Augustine, to show that memory functions in Gower's text as a way of keeping people aware of who they are.[53] In relation to the bedroom scene, these medieval theories of memory likewise indicate that Florent has wholly forgotten who he is: he exists as a physical shell representing conformity to the public code of chivalry rather than to an internal code of honor. He wallows in the misery of committing to his public oath without embracing the internal implications of that oath. The narrative reaches its climax with this encounter in the marriage bed. Florent has behaved thus far as a knight intent on preserving his honor so as to avoid public shame but now must address the issue of private honor in the face of what repulses him. Although Florent had earlier pondered keeping the marriage secret by putting the Loathly Lady in seclusion on an island, his marriage vows require him to comply with her wishes. Yet, for all the necessity of compliance, the knight does not appear to be particularly willing to act companionably (lines 1780–85). The passage mentions that "thei were abedde naked" (line 1781) and Peck's gloss defines this as "amorously in bed" though it is hard to imagine the knight feeling amorous toward the Loathly Lady at this juncture. Instead, Florent turns his back on the Loathly Lady so that he will not have to look on such a "fole wyht" (line 1785).[54]

Yet the Loathly Lady will not allow Florent either to wallow in his despair or to reject the implications of his oaths to "wedd." The moments before her physical transformation are described carefully and with a great attention to detail, perhaps to emphasize the significance of her transformative counsel:

> The chambre was al full of lyht,
> The courtins were of cendal thinne,
> This newe bryd which lay withinne,
> Thogh it be noght with his acord,
> In armes sche beclipte hire lord,
> And preide, as he was torned fro,
> He wolde him torne ageinward tho;
> "For now," sche seith, "we ben bothe on."
>   (lines 1786–93)

The lighted chamber, the fine, thin bed curtains, and the revolting hag verbally elevated to the "newe bryd" who lies within the bed create an image of beauty, contrasting with Florent's deep despair. Everything about the scene is lovely and sweet, except for the unresponsive husband and the ugly, yet demonstrative, wife. While the reader can be easily distracted in this scene by the appearance of the Loathly Lady, the key point is that she refuses to accept Florent's unresponsiveness as final. Instead, she lectures him on his obligations to her because of his marriage vows:

> And he lay stille as eny ston,
> Bot evere in on sche spak and preide,
> And bad him thenke on that he seide,
> Whan that he tok hire be the hond.
>   (lines 1794–97)

Finally, Florent understands, through the Loathly Lady's transformative advice, the significance and implications of his promises: "He herde and understod the bond, / How he was set to his penance" (lines 1798–99). Though Florent continues to consider his marriage in terms of penance (and "purgatoire"), this moment marks a significant point in the text, for the hag's counsel finally makes Florent realize the significance of the marriage "wedd"—a bond quite as significant as the pledge he had made long before to be true to the codes of chivalry. Convinced at last, Florent turns to look at the Loathly Lady and is rewarded by the vision of her transformation, as he "syh a lady lay him by / Of eyhtetiene wynter age, / Which was the faireste of visage / That evere in al this world he syh" (lines 1802–5).[55] Florent's enlightenment under the Loathly Lady's counsel is made literal in the physical transformation of her flesh.

The learning process is not yet complete, however, for the transformed heroine now "seith that for to wynne or lese / He mot on of tuo thinges chese" (lines 1809–10), and Florent's choices are similar to those given in the Gawain texts, which are discussed below: "Wher he wol have hire such on nyht, / Or elles upon daies lyht" (lines 1811–13).[56] The wording of the choice is briefer than in the other English texts, but the implications are clear. If the shape-shifting lady is beautiful during the day, all the world can admire her loveliness and admire him for having obtained such a lovely wife. His public reputation would be increased, along with his public honor, and he would have, in effect, what he had earlier thought he wanted—an easy way to keep her loathsomeness secret from the world, one rather simpler than leaving her on a deserted island (as he had contemplated in line 1578). But if Florent chooses to enhance his public honor with her public beauty, she would be a hag at night when they would share their bed. Into the complicated nature of this choice comes the fact that Florent has only just realized the importance of upholding his marital vows to avoid being—even privately—dishonored and shamed by either breaking his pledge or paying his marriage debt to a loathsome wife. Florent, at the beginning of the poem, sought "fame," but public reputation (he now realizes) does not indicate true virtue. In effect, his choice revolves around whether he prefers to retain the public perception of honor which he now knows to be incomplete, or whether he would accept the public perception of dishonor while privately keeping his vows.

Florent is overcome yet again by confusion about his choices:

And he began to sorwe tho,
In many a wise and caste his thoght,

Bot for al that yit cowthe he noght
Devise himself which was the beste.
                    (lines 1814–17)

He cannot determine the best choice (whether she should be lovely or loathly during the day or night) because each possibility represents only one of two things, both of which he now deems important: public honor and private honor. Clearly, he wants enjoyment as well, but he can only both fulfill his desire for public reputation and honor his private oaths (exemplified by his marriage bond) if the Loathly Lady becomes lovely both in public and in private. While Florent agonizes over his dilemma, the lady "that wolde his hertes reste, / Preith that he sholde chese algate" (lines 1818–19). As Florent's counselor, the Loathly Lady is genuinely concerned about his internal debate; possibly, she is willing to counter his answer as does the Loathly Lady in the Gawain ballad discussed below, as long as he gives her a choice with which she can work. Finally, after much agonizing, Florent hands the decision over to her as one which he simply cannot make, "And what as evere that ye seie, / Riht as ye wole so wol I" (lines 1830–31). His decision, as the shape-shifting woman explains to him, signifies that he has given her the sovereignty in the relationship by giving her the responsibility to make the decision: "For of this word that ye now sein, / That ye have mad me soverein" (lines 1833–34).[57] Furthermore, because he has made her sovereign, her destiny has been fulfilled,

That nevere hierafter schal be lassed
Mi beauté, which that I now have,
Til I be take into my grave;
Bot nyht and day as I am now
I schal alwey be such to yow.
                    (lines 1836–40)[58]

   Florent's Loathly Lady, through her transformative advice, has carefully guided the knight to a new recognition of the importance of keeping his vows, whether public or private. The concept of justice, so important in the "mirrors," is here exemplified by the total commitment to one's oaths that the Loathly Lady advises.[59] Through her counsel, Florent's ability to be a good lord and knight is enhanced; by following the lady's advice, he develops beyond his initial identity as a knight interested only in gaining the "fame of worldes speche" to become one concerned wholly with keeping honor, regardless of how private.

Turning now to Chaucer's "The Wife of Bath's Tale," we witness another Loathly Lady's even more dramatic ability to counsel and transform a knight. During their initial encounter in the wood, the "olde wyf" both encourages the knight's confidence by pointing out that "olde folk kan muchel thyng" (line 1004) and assures him of his safety, for none would "dare seye nay of that I shal thee teche" (line 1019), thereby defining herself clearly as the aged counselor of which Barnes spoke.[60] Later, after their private wedding, when the couple is left alone in their marriage bed, the Loathly Lady's role as advisor expands and develops further (lines 1086–97). While the hag responds to the knight's dismay, offering to amend her "gilt," she seems amused by his attitude: "His olde wyf lay smylynge everemo, / And seyde, 'O deere housbonde, benedicitee! / Fareth every knyght thus with his wyf as ye?'" (lines 1086–88). The education of the rapist-knight begins at this point, as she reminds him that she had saved his life and "yet ne dide I yow nevere unright" (line 1093); ultimately, the knight is shown true mercy by being given every opportunity to learn from her counsel.

The knight responds with complaints about the Loathly Lady's appearance, age, and low class status, and the order of his complaints are revealed, as the scene unfolds, to be of great significance. When his "wyf" asks if all this is the reason for his agitation, and he responds, "Ye, certeinly ... no wonder is!" her own response implies a certain amount of magical power on her part: "'Now, sire,' quod she, 'I koude amende al this, / If that me liste, er it were dayes thre, / So wel ye myghte bere yow unto me'" (lines 1104–8). Since she presumably could not change herself without magical power, what is the significance of her promise? If she has the power to transform herself, what benefits do her appearance and social condition provide that she would wish to remain as she appears? It seems clear that, by showing the rapist-knight how badly he errs in his preconceived notions about appearance, age, and wealth, she demonstrates her desire to re-educate and to transform the protagonist through her counsel in the "pillow lecture" which follows. This lecture contains, moreover, a number of points also dealt with in contemporary "mirrors for princes," such as in Hoccleve's *Regiment of Princes*.[61] Where Hoccleve's "mirror" emphasizes not only the necessity to seek counsel from all possible advisors, no matter who they be, he also delineates, through separate sections devoted to each theme, the need for such noble qualities as pity and justice.[62] In addition, his digression on women—in a section about peace—appears to owe some of its inspiration to "The Wife of Bath's Tale" and "The Tale of Florent," for he discusses the "desire" of women to have "maistrie" of their husbands, and he interprets this partly as the influence of their counsel.[63]

The importance of the "pillow lecture" to the transformation of the knight is significant and, therefore, requires a thorough discussion of the words of the "olde wyf." The "wyf" begins with a discussion of true "gentillesse," during which she describes the difference between inherited nobility and true nobility, the latter being determined by behavior rather than birth:

> Looke who that is moost vertuous alway,
> Pryvee and apert, and moost entendeth ay
> To do the gentil dedes that he kan;
> Taak hym for the grettest gentil man.
>   (lines 1113–16)

The "wyf" admonishes the knight that his perception of nobility as an inherited quality is erroneous, for true nobility resides in one's actions, not in one's ancestors. One may appear to be noble because of one's social status, but in fact, it is through one's actions—whether publicly acknowledged or only privately seen—that one's true character is revealed, a point also made in "Florent." Clearly, the knight is ignoble according to this definition, for he behaved badly from the very beginning of the poem, first by raping the young maiden he saw and perhaps, too, by being so openly rude to the "olde wyf" due to her appearance and apparent low class status.[64]

Chaucer's Loathly Lady further explains that nobility descends from Christ only, not from one's ancestors. Even though an ancestral line can give us "al hir heritage" (line 1119), it cannot bequeath the ancestor's "vertuous lyvyng" (line 1122) which caused them to be called gentlemen in the first place and "bad us folwen hem in swich degree" (line 1124). Nobility is first bestowed on people because their actions are so noteworthy that they deserve recognition, but when a noteworthy person has children and grandchildren and on, those descendants merely acquire the label of nobility from their ancestor without necessarily being worthy of the implications of that label.[65] Only by claiming Christ as our ancestor and seeking to emulate his ways can we truly obtain nobility, and this has nothing to do with society's method of determining class status. Rather, by claiming nobility from Christ, a princess and a peasant can be considered equally noble. Furthermore, the Loathly Lady adds, if nobility really were a physical thing, planted in a certain family, then both in private and in public the members of this family could not avoid behaving nobly (lines 1133–38), for they would be incapable of vice. The point here about both private and public nobility recalls the similar connection made in "Florent" and reinforces the significance of the Loathly Lady's lesson. The "olde wyf" proves with her examples the true ignobility of the knight, for his villainous deed of rape would be rendered impossible were nobility actually inherited like material goods and family reputation.

Furthermore, through her anecdote about fire, which burns brightly regardless of whether or not it is seen (lines 1139–49), the Loathly Lady demonstrates that a person can be noble even in the middle of nowhere. True nobility does not require acknowledgment or recognition in order to exist (the lesson, incidentally, that Florent had learned under the influence of the Loathly Lady). Although she concludes this first part of her lecture by revealing that she herself, being of "so lough a kynde" (line 1101) could attain nobility by living sinlessly and virtuously, in actuality, most of her lecture concentrates on the important point that inherited nobility—like the knight's—is irrelevant when the so-called nobleman behaves villainously—as did the knight. The situation is turned upside down, so that the knight is a churl whereas the raped maiden and Loathly Lady are noble.[66]

Next the "wyf" addresses her poverty, which she herself had referred to in front of the court when she acknowledged that she, "be foul, and oold, and poore" (line 1063). While the knight had only implied his objection to her lack of funds through his comment that she is a peasant, she begins her counsel against distaste for poverty with the example of Christ who himself chose to live in voluntary poverty. This point, supported by Seneca and others, forms one of her two arguments. The other involves collectively all the positive traits of being poor, including that it enables one to recognize one's true friends, teaches wisdom and patience, brings one closer to God, and eliminates the fear of being attacked by thieves when traveling. The "olde wyf" then turns to her final discussion, concerning old age,[67] and she draws here on common knowledge, rather than written authority. Again, she has only two major points, that noblemen such as the knight claim that people should respect the elderly, and that, because old age tends not to attract people, he need not ever fear that she might be unfaithful to him.[68]

Her closing comment, "[b]ut nathelees, syn I knowe youre delit, / I shal fulfille youre worldly appetit" (lines 1217–18), recalls the beginning of the lecture, in which the Loathly Lady had claimed she could fix all the rapist-knight's complaints in just three days. This, then, completes the circle of the discussion begun by that previous promise. The hag finally presents a choice—the wording of which is unique to Chaucer—to the knight:

"Chese now," quod she, "oon of thise thynges tweye:
To han me foul and old til that I deye,
And be to yow a trewe, humble wyf,
And nevere yow displese in al my lyf,
Or elles ye wol han me yong and fair,
And take youre aventure of the repair[69]
That shal be to youre hous by cause of me,
Or in som oother place, may wel be.
Now chese yourselven, wheither that yow liketh."
                                        (lines 1219–27)

Whereas in the other English tales the Loathly Lady had the knight choose whether she should be beautiful at night or during the day (a question of public honor or private enjoyment), the question in Chaucer's tale apparently revolves around faithfulness. However, as the lecture of the "olde wyf" demonstrates, nobility is revealed through behavior, not appearance, which can be deceptive. Therefore, the question becomes one of exterior versus interior honor: in other words, is his wife's noble appearance (exteriority) or her noble behavior (interiority) of more importance to the knight? The wording of this final question demonstrates the necessity for the knight to acknowledge the validity of the arguments of the Loathly Lady regarding whether nobility is proven by action alone. The truly noble—and honorable—choice (and wife) would account for noble behavior, not merely the appearance of nobility.

    The rapist-knight's initial reaction to the Loathly Lady's question is somewhat ambiguous: "This knight avyseth hym and sore siketh" (line 1228). While often interpreted to mean that he painfully sought the answer to her question, the line also implies that he painfully sought his conscience. He appears more disturbed at his realization that she is correct than at the dilemma before him, but at last he calls her his "lady and my love, and wyf so deere," and he gives himself over to her "wise governance" to decide which choice would "be moost plesance / And moost honour to yow and me also" (lines 1228–33). He has taken her counsel and has demonstrated his ability to discern the correct course of action, which in this case is to defer to the Loathly Lady.[70] The "wyf" first asks him for further clarification about his offer to her: "'Thanne have I gete of yow maistrie,' quod she, / 'Syn I may chese and governe as me lest?'" (lines 1236–37). With his assurance granted, she responds, then, that she will be both beautiful and good to him, "'[k]ys me,' quod she, 'we be no lenger wrothe, / For, by my trouthe, I wol be to yow bothe— / This is to seyn, ye, bothe fair and good'" (lines 1239–41). Far from

being a reward for poor behavior, the conclusion here demonstrates the
Loathly Lady's acknowledgment that the knight has finally learned his lesson
about appropriate behavior, one which has taken him over a year and on a
journey throughout the land to learn.[71] The fact that she also compares her
beauty to that of noblewomen—"any lady, emperice, or queene"—emphasizes
that her arguments have revolved around, primarily, the behavior of the
upper classes (line 1246). The Loathly Lady's counsel about noble behavior
has taught the knight to understand true nobility, which is demonstrated
through one's actions, not by one's birthright. Through the transformative
advice of the "olde wyf" (counsel which, like that in the "mirrors for princes,"
teaches proper princely behavior), the knight finally learns the importance of
behaving nobly.

The final two tales, the romance and ballad of Sir Gawain, King Arthur,
and their adventures with the Loathly Lady, were possibly both written
during the reign of Henry VI, around 1450. The opening sections of "The
Wedding of Sir Gawain and Dame Ragnelle" and "The Marriage of Sir
Gawain" indicate immediately the significance of understanding proper
qualities of a good ruler. In both, King Arthur encounters a disgruntled
knight who he had, in the past, divested of his land: the king must address the
challenges of Sir Gromer (in "Wedding") and the Baron (in "Marriage"), and
he does so eventually with the help of his favorite knight, Sir Gawain, and
with the counsel of the Loathly Lady. Through the transformative advice of
the Loathly Lady, the "twinned heroes" of these tales (King Arthur and Sir
Gawain) embrace the qualities of a good ruler. These protagonists represent
two different sides of one figure, for the narrative raises the issue of the
qualities of all good kings by focusing on one king's shortcomings and one
knight's loyalties, and it resolves the issue by emphasizing the common
chivalric ideals of both kings and knights.[72]

The narrator of the mid-fifteenth-century romance, "The Wedding of Sir
Gawain and Dame Ragnelle," immediately draws attention to kingship, for
the protagonist at the beginning of the tale is King Arthur and, only after he
calls on Sir Gawain to help him out of his troubles, does the function of the
protagonist revert to that knight.[73] By the time King Arthur first encounters
the Loathly Lady in this narrative, both Arthur and Gawain had already
sought counsel from everyone in the land (as is recommended in such
"mirrors" as Hoccleve's *Regiment*).[74] The Loathly Lady, a woman named Dame
Ragnelle, tells him straightforwardly that "thy lyfe is in my hand" (line 256)
and warns the king that none of the answers he and Gawain had collected in
their books are correct. Without her help, he will surely die: "Thou wenyst I

knowe nott thy councelle, / Butt I warn the, I knowe itt every dealle. / Yf I
help the nott, thou art butt dead" (lines 264–66). However, she also promises
that "for thy lyfe I make warrauntyng" (line 268) if the king would only agree
to grant her "butt one thyng" (line 267). Though Arthur calls her "Lady,"
even "fayre," he is otherwise not very chivalrous to the Loathly Lady, telling
her in no uncertain terms that "of thy wordes I have great dispyte; / To you
I have no nede" (lines 271–72). He is indignant that she claims he possesses
entirely useless information about the desire of women and rejects the
concept that she might be of any help. His initial refusal to take counsel from
the Loathly Lady reflects back to "The Tale of Florent," in which that
Loathly Lady, too, had assured Florent that he required her counsel for his
success.[75] Finally, though, the king appears to change his mind, and he does
so in the verbal terms of the "desyre" of the "Lady" with whom he speaks,
showing his curiosity about her information and his acceptance of her
terms.[76] In just this first encounter with the Loathly Lady, the king begins to
transform, from a ruler incapable of accepting good counsel, to one who is
receptive to all forms of advice (as a ruler should be, according to Hoccleve's
Regiment and other "mirrors for princes" manuals).

After their second meeting, Dame Ragnelle sends the king on his way,
advising him to inform the knight, Sir Gromer, of everything she has said
about the desires of women and that the knight will "curse her fast that itt
[him] taughte" (line 435). After successfully resolving his debt to Sir Gromer,
Arthur returns to Dame Ragnelle, who now reminds him of his promise.[77]
The unlikely couple ride into "Karlyle" together, with Dame Ragnelle riding
boldly beside the king: "Into the courte she rode hym by; / For no man wold
she spare, securly— / Itt likyd the Kyng fulle ylle" (lines 518–20). This scene
is significant, for it indicates Dame Ragnelle's refusal to behave as anything
less than the equal of the king. Dame Ragnelle, as King Arthur's advisor,
perceives herself as his equal in status. While Dame Ragnelle may appear
initially to be merely a revolting old woman who ignores the accepted
etiquette of the court of King Arthur, her position as counsel to the king gives
her the right (though she may be the only one to recognize this right) to ride
by the king's side as his equal.

After the marriage between Sir Gawain and Dame Ragnelle, the setting
shifts to the shared chamber of Gawain and Ragnelle, where the Loathly
Lady tells Gawain, her new advisee (and the other half of the hero-doubling
in this tale), that he should show her his courtesy in bed, since "with ryghte
itt may nott be denyed" (line 631). Unfortunately, one leaf is missing from the
manuscript, a leaf which contained about seventy lines between the events of

the wedding feast and the bedroom scene.[78] The narrative resumes at the end
of the Loathly Lady's lecture to the knight about how he should behave
toward her: "A, Sir Gawen, syn I have you wed, / Shewe me your cortesy in
bed; / With ryghte itt may nott be denyed" (lines 629–31). Dame Ragnelle
upbraids Sir Gawain for not kissing her, pointing out that, were she beautiful,
he would surely act otherwise: "Butt of wedlock ye take no hed" (line 634).
She asks him at least to kiss her "for Arthours sake" (line 635), and, in
response, Sir Gawain—like Níall in the prose "Echtra" to the sovereignty
goddess—claims, "'I wolle do more / Then for to kysse, and God before!' /
He turnyd hym her untille" (lines 638–40). Turning, he observed "the fairest
creature / That evere he sawe, withoute mesure" (lines 641–42). The first
challenge overcome, Dame Ragnelle now offers him a choice, because her
"beawty wolle nott hold" (line 658), which of the two appearances he would
prefer: whether he would have her be "fayre on nyghtes / And as foulle on
days to alle men sightes, / Or els to have me fayre on days / And on nyghtes
on the fowlyst wyfe" (lines 659–62). The lady offers Sir Gawain either the
honor of the public sphere (by which she would perform duties as a sort of
"trophy wife") or happiness in the private sphere (with her beauty by his side
at night, when no one else could witness it). With the first choice, the
court—the public—would believe the knight had the most beautiful of
women for his wife, and he would be honored for this illusion. If he chooses
the second option, however, he may lose honor in the public sphere because
members of the court would perceive her as foul and rude and would,
perhaps, respect him less for possessing such an undesirable wife.

   Sir Gawain's confusion is the more understandable when one realizes
that what he, and any other knight of the court, truly desires is honor at once
in both the public and the private spheres. This is a key revelation, in fact, for
the world of the court, of chivalry and the knighthood in general, is based
wholly on the acquisition of honor in the public sphere.[79] Yet this scene
clearly reveals a human need for fulfillment in the private sphere as well as
the public. Ultimately, Sir Gawain is incapable of choosing which sphere is
more important to him, for he understands already that, in fact, both spheres
must be satisfied. Sir Gawain's own words reveal this dilemma clearly:

> To have you fayre on nyghtes and no more,
> That wold greve my hartt ryghte sore,
> And my worshypp shold I lese.
> And yf I desire on days to have you fayre,
> Then on nyghtes I shold have a simple repayre.
>   (lines 670–74)[80]

Gawain acknowledges here that her loathliness during the day would lose him "worshypp," though her loathliness at night would cause him personal distress. Finally, Gawain decides only that he cannot choose which would be best, because he sees both positive and negative in each choice.[81] The knight hands over the choice to Dame Ragnelle's wise counsel: "Butt do as ye lyst nowe, my Lady gaye. / The choyse I putt in your fyst" (lines 677–78). He goes even further by giving her everything he possesses, and the lady accepts graciously all that he offers, telling him that she will remain "fayre and bryghte" (line 689) as long as she lives, both by day and by night. The following morning when the "new" Ragnelle is reintroduced to the court, she initially appears to have been silenced like many medieval romance heroines after marriage.[82] She does speak up, however, to notify the king "fayre and welle / How Gawen gave her the sovereynté every delle, / And whate choyse she gave to hym" (lines 775–77). This action is significant, for it highlights that Dame Ragnelle recognizes the necessity of making public all promises and deals.[83] Private promises are made binding only when made public, a view which reflects backward to the Irish goddess's instructions for Níall. Moreover, Dame Ragnelle does not cease to counsel after her transformation, for she advises the king (appealing to his "gentilnes") to be a "good lord" to Sir Gromer. For his part, the king accepts this counsel graciously, promising to do so for her sake (lines 811–16). Both king and knight have interiorized the need to seek and accept counsel.

The ballad "The Marriage of Sir Gawain," though damaged and incomplete,[84] has the same basic plot as the "Wedding" and also clearly demonstrates the Loathly Lady's role as advisor to the king and to Sir Gawain in two different scenes. When the king and Loathly Lady first meet in the woods, the lady is eager to greet Arthur, but the king is rendered speechless in surprise at her mutantlike appearance and forgets the niceties of conversation (lines 65–68). The lady wonders what kind of knight he is, that he will not speak to her, and assures him that, despite her ugliness, he need not be worried about her:

> "What knight art thou," the lady sayd,
> "That will not speak to me?
> Of me be thou nothing desmayd
> Tho I be ugly to see."
>
> (lines 69–72)

The lady's expectation of chivalric behavior from a knight indicates her connection with the aristocracy (which is later confirmed anew by her comment that her father is an "old knight" who married a "younge lady" (lines 175, 177). She points out that she greeted him courteously but he refuses to do the same, even though she might be able "to ease thee of thy paine" (line 76). With the Loathly Lady's help, Arthur's life and his kingdom are preserved and, in exchange, Sir Gawain agrees to marry the loathsome woman.

Unfortunately missing from the manuscript are both the wedding and the lady's transformation, but the Loathly Lady's role as advisor to Gawain is evident in the bedroom scene when she manages to coerce Gawain into answering her question "correctly," about whether he would like her beautiful during the day or at night. She rejects his first response (that he would prefer her beauty to himself), exclaiming that she would be too ashamed to be seen in public (lines 163–66).[85] Though the "Marriage" Loathly Lady appears in general to be a rather more subdued character than the lively Dame Ragnelle, she can clearly be quite forceful as is demonstrated by her interaction here with the protagonist. The transformed lady tells Gawain to choose whether he "wilt have me in this liknesse / In the night or else in the day" (lines 42–43), and Gawain's initial answer, he discovers, is the wrong one:

To have thee fowle in the night
When I with thee shold play;
Yet I had rather, if I might,
Have thee fowle in the day.
                    (lines 159–62)

He would prefer to have her beautiful at night, for his own enjoyment, and "fowle" during the day, when she would be in the company of others. This Gawain cares extraordinarily little for the opinion of the court or for public honor generally. Regardless of Gawain's desires, though, the lady influences his choice by objecting strenuously to his initial response. The Loathly Lady's reaction here recalls the kind of "informal influence" which Helen Maurer discusses in relation to Henry VI's queen, Margaret of Anjou (but which is applicable to all late medieval English queens).[86] A late medieval queen, Maurer explains, might not have institutional power at her disposal, but she could shape policy by influencing those around her, particularly her husband, the king. Hoccleve, too, comments in the *Regiment* on the power of women's influence over their husbands.[87] As in the "Wedding," the "Marriage" Loathly Lady's concerns relate to public honor, for she would be profoundly embarrassed at having to appear in public looking as ugly as she does. However, she also differs in her reaction from Dame Ragnelle, who appeared entirely unconcerned about the opinions of others.[88] The "Marriage" Loathly Lady responds with dismay:

> "What! When lords goe with their feires," shee said,
> "Both to the ale and wine?
> Alas! Then I must hyde my selfe,
> I must not goe withinne."
>
> (lines 163–66)

She would feel compelled to hide herself in her rooms when the lords and ladies of the court gather together for social occasions.[89] She is upset at the idea that she would be perceived as "fowle," even if Sir Gawain knew of her beauty at night. More importantly, this shape-shifter is the only English Loathly Lady to tip the protagonist's hand: when he gives her the "wrong" answer to her question of choice, she gives him another chance to make the correct choice. Though generally one of the quietest of the hag-ladies, this "lady in red scarlet" is also one of the most forthright, since she forces the "correct" choice out of the knight. After seeing her negative response, Gawain claims his first response was "but a skill" (line 168), and he assures her, then, that "because thou art my owne lady, / Thou shalt have all thy will" (lines 169–70), thereby repeating the response which had saved the king's life earlier.

The lady blesses Gawain and tells him that "[f]or as thou see me att this time, / From henceforth I wil be" (lines 173–74). The choice appears to have been a trick, since the only correct answer Gawain could give is to let the lady choose. If he chooses at all, she can only be beautiful part of the time, because this is the stipulation of the question. However, she desires this option as little as he does. If he lets her make the final choice, on the other hand, she is not bound by the question of choice to one appearance or the other but can choose the appearance of beauty all the time. With her guidance, then, the Loathly Lady convinces the knight of the correct choice; happiness can be attained by both of them as long as the knight acknowledges the need to be counseled by the Loathly Lady. Moreover, in this, the latest of the Loathly Lady tales, the Loathly Lady's counsel is most transformative for the king, who saves his kingdom—literally—by following her advice.

The communications between the Loathly Lady and the protagonist in each of these different tales reveals one commonality—that the Loathly Lady acts as a primary counselor to the hero, either through formative instruction or transformative advice. She determines whether he possesses the necessary qualities for a good ruler, and, if not, she shows him how to behave more properly in order to gain those qualities he requires. "Ruler" here is, of course, defined loosely as either a "king" or as a "knight." In the Irish tales, the protagonist will literally become a king, following the precepts in the anonymous *Audacht Morainn*, whereas in the English narratives, the hero is often a knight lacking certain necessary interior qualities, such as those discussed in Hoccleve's *Regiment* and other "mirrors for princes," which he needs to develop to be considered truly fit for rulership. Often the virtues the knight in question lacks are those which focus on one's private and personal life in contrast to a public perception of honor.

Moreover, the Irish narratives move from a clear emphasis on advice over prophecy to a greater reliance on prophecy than on counsel, whereas the English tales consistently feature advice and counsel with little interest in prophetic powers. During the late fourteenth and fifteenth centuries in England, many complaint poems and other courtly narratives, such as the romances discussed here, were used to convey implicitly certain political views about the importance of good counsel and the necessary qualities for a good ruler. The English Loathly Lady romances become miniature "mirrors for princes," demonstrating through apparent whimsy their authors' ideas about the necessity for rulers, whether kings or lords, to accept good counsel and to demonstrate their nobility through wise actions and measured behavior.

NOTES

1. The association dates back to Whitley Stokes's 1892 edition and translation of a short tale in the *Cóir Anmann* collection about the sons of King Dáire, all named Lugaid, and their encounters with a hideous hag, the Irish sovereignty goddess. See Stokes, "The Marriage of Sir Gawain," p. 399; Maynadier, *Wife of Bath's Tale*; and Eisner, *Tale of Wonder*.

2. On the topic of the sovereignty goddess, see Mac Cana, "Aspects of the Theme of King and Goddess." This relationship between king and goddess indicates an early belief in sacral kingship which is found throughout the Indo-European world. On this topic, see Aguirre, "Riddle," pp. 273–82; and Coomaraswamy, "Loathly Bride," pp. 391–404. Katharine Simms points out that "[t]he fundamental theory underlying such literary references is that right order in society can only flourish under the rule of the right king. The peaceful succession of property from father to son, the due fulfilment of contracts, security from outside attack, fertility in man and beast, increase of crops,

clement weather, absence of disease, are all secured if the land herself, or the local goddess of sovereignty, is 'married' to a true king" (*From Kings to Warlords*, p. 21).

3. For a definition of knighthood as encompassing the nobility in general, see Wilson, *English Nobility*, pp. vii, 14–19.

4. These are terms that I have developed in order to distinguish between the kinds of counsel the Loathly Ladies offer to the protagonists. I have denoted the Irish Loathly Lady's counsel as formative instruction, for with it she guides the protagonist's strategy to gain kingship through her step-by-step instruction. The English Loathly Lady's counsel, on the other hand, is that of transformative advice, for by way of it she attempts to improve the hero's interior understanding of chivalric duty.

5. See Kelly, *Audacht Morainn*, for a discussion of this "mirrors for princes" text which was likely first composed in the seventh century but survives in several manuscripts dating from the twelfth to the eighteenth centuries (pp. xx–xxxiii). See also Hoccleve, *Regiment*.

6. See Binchy, *Celtic and Anglo-Saxon Kingship*, pp. 9–10.

7. See Manzalaoui, *Secretum Secretorum*, and Ferster, *Fictions*.

8. See Maynadier, *Wife of Bath's Tale*; Eisner, *Tale of Wonder*; Coomaraswamy, "Loathly Bride," pp. 391–404; Shenk, "Liberation," pp. 69–77; Aguirre, "Riddle," pp. 273–82; and Vasta, "Chaucer, Gower, and the Unknown Minstrel," pp. 395–418.

9. The remaining parts are "the bare genealogical qualification" and "a direct political competition between the leading candidates." See Charles-Edwards, *Early Christian Ireland*, pp. 90–92. On Irish kingship, see Byrne, *Irish Kings and High-Kings*, p. 74; Jaski, *Early Irish Kingship*, pp. 143–70.

10. See Passmore, "Loathly Lady Transformed," pp. 66–120.

11. See Charles-Edwards, *Early Christian Ireland*, pp. 138–41, and McCone, *Pagan Past*, pp. 127–29, pp. 141–42.

12. About king's councils and their composition, see Barnes, *Counsel and Strategy*, pp. 1–3. In the fourteenth and fifteenth centuries, "the king's council was developing into an institution that had great power in the royal administration, especially when the king was incapable of ruling or incapacitated" (Ferster, *Fictions*, p. 2).

13. See Green, *Poets and Princepleasers*, p. 205.

14. Green, *Poets and Princepleasers*, argues that "there seems to have been no obvious connection between the nature of their [the poets'] professional employment and the fact that they were men of letters," although he later acknowledges that "[t]he number of poets employed in the familia regis cannot be dismissed as an historical accident; the rituals of literary commission, dedication, and presentation cannot have been quite meaningless. Obviously literature in the court occupied some kind of ill-defined no man's land somewhere between a job and a hobby" (p. 12).

15. Ferster, *Fictions*, p. 4.

16. Ferster, *Fictions*, p. 4.

17. See "The Wedding of Sir Gawain and Dame Ragnelle," in Hahn, *Sir Gawain*, pp. 41–80. About Arthur's treatment of Sir Gromer (and the Baron), see Rogers,

"'Illuminat vith lawte,'" pp. 94–111. Also see Donnelly, "Aristocratic Veneer," pp. 321–43, and Forste-Grupp, "Woman Circumvents the Laws," pp. 105–22.

18. In "The Wife of Bath's Tale," the knight "seketh every hous and every place / Where as he hopeth for to fynde grace" (lines 919–20). In "The Tale of Florent," see especially that "[t]he wiseste of the lond" were sent for (line 1493) and later, "he his privé conseil nam / Of suche men as he moste troste" (lines 1738–39). All quotations of "The Wife of Bath's Tale" are from Benson, *The Riverside Chaucer*; all quotations from "The Tale of Florent" are from Peck's edition of the *Confessio Amantis*.

19. See "Wedding," especially Gawain's suggestion: "And I shalle also ryde anoder waye / And enquere of every man and woman and gett whatt I may / Of every man and womans answere; / And in a boke I shalle theym wryte" (lines 187–90).

20. See, for example, Hoccleve, *Regiment*, line 4870: "what every man seith wel herkne and heere."

21. See Manzalouai, *Secretum Secretorum*, p. 218 and 220–21, for comments on this topic in advice manuals. For discussions about the "olde wyf's" point that "gentillesse" is not inherited, see Brewer, "Class Distinction in Chaucer," pp. 290–305; Coghill, *Chaucer's Idea*, p. 15; Saul, "Chaucer and Gentility," pp. 41–45. The fact that the figure of a king is virtually absent from this text (King Arthur appears only to relinquish to his queen the position as judge of the rapist-knight), effectively transforming the knight into the only male power in the story (and one desperately in need of transformative advice), supports the possibility of viewing the pillow lecture as inspired by "mirror for princes."

22. Barnes, *Counsel*, pp. xi–xii.

23. Barnes, *Counsel*, p. xii.

24. Barnes, *Counsel*, p. xi.

25. Barnes, *Counsel*, xii.

26. Barnes, *Counsel*, p. ix.

27. Barnes, *Counsel*, p. 15.

28. Barnes, *Counsel*, p. x.

29. For discussions of Richard's kingship, see Saul, *Richard II*, pp. 366–404, as well as Mathew, *Court of Richard II*, pp. 146–60 and Gillespie, *Age of Richard II*. On Henry VI, see Watts, *Henry VI and the Politics of Kingship*, and Wolffe, *Henry VI*. On kingship, see Renna, "Kingship in the Fourteenth Century," pp. 13–21.

30. On this subject, see Castor, *The King, the Crown, and the Duchy of Lancaster*; Leland, "The Oxford Trial of 1400," pp. 165–89; and Strohm, *England's Empty Throne*, pp. 173–95.

31. I am, therefore, omitting discussion here of the greater emphasis on prophecy than advice in the two Lugaid tales (*Cóir Anmann* and "Carn Máil") since it is the theme of counsel, not of prophecy, which primarily connects the Irish to the English tales (in conjunction, of course, with their link through the visual image of the Loathly Lady.)

32. This poem was translated and edited by Joynt, "Echtra mac Echdach Mugmedóin," pp. 91–111.

33. I would like to point out here that only rarely do Irish scholars use the term "Loathly Lady," which is a commonplace in discussions of these tales by English scholars. Stokes, however, did use this term in his 1892 article pointing out the connection between the English and Irish tales through the transformation motif. The sovereignty goddess's first words to Níall in the poetic "Echtra" are an admonition that "dó deog deccair" (the wondrous draught) will be "ná bad séim ... cen chéim dó 'na comlepaid" (not easy for him ... unless he should come and share her couch [stanza 47]). The goddess's words only make sense in relation to the traditional concept of sovereignty and the king binding the land together in a symbolic relationship.

34. Literally, as Joynt, "Echtra," notes, "there shall be confusion to thy brothers from it" (p. 107, n. 4). The relationship here between the drinking of intoxicating beverages and their effect highlights the difference between Níall and his brothers, as the goddess makes a point of assuring Níall that his own drink will be smooth, but his brothers will be cast into confusion from the same beverage. In other words, Níall's brothers are simply incapable of becoming kings. The passage thus emphasizes the political nature of the poem, in that the descendants of Níall are more appropriate choices for kingship than the descendants of his brothers. Pointing out the inadequacies of the brothers is not, however, the goddess's immediate point here.

35. The poet appears to mention Níall's exact age when he says "nóiblíadnach" (after nine years [stanza 11]), and "[h]i cind nói mblíadan n-ergnaid céttichtain Néill do Themraich" (At the end of nine prosperous years was Níall's first coming to Tara; [stanza 12]). See also Kelly, *Guide to Early Irish Law*, who admits that it is not clear at what age fosterage usually ended, although there is some indication that a boy would finish his fosterage at the age of seventeen (p. 88). Unfortunately, this does not explain the age of Níall being given as nine in the poetic "Echtra"; it may be poetic license, perhaps an allusion to Níall's nickname, "Nóigíallach" (of the Nine Hostages), or a way of connecting Níall to another famous Irish boy-hero—Cú Chulainn—who came to the court of Ulaid at a very young age and performed heroic feats that would have been impressive for an adult. Alternatively, the poet merely implies that nine are the prosperous years of Níall's tutelage under Torna before they return to the Hill of Tara.

36. See Stokes, "Echtra mac Echach Muigmedóin," pp. 172–73, pp. 190–203, and also O'Grady, "Echtra mac n-Echach," pp. 368–73. The author elaborates on the characters of Torna the Poet, who saved the infant Níall from a certain death, and Sithchenn the druid-smith, who appeared as an unnamed smith in the poetic "Echtra."

37. Stokes, "Echtra," p. 200, n. 6. Interactions between the hero and the Loathly Lady in the prose "Echtra" differ from the poetic "Echtra," as can be demonstrated from the beginning of their discussions in paragraph 14 of the prose version. Níall at last seeks water and finds the well with its guard, and his response to the hag's demands is wholehearted: "'Laigfead lat la taeb poici do thabairt fri taeb.' Tairnid fuirri iarsin 7

dobeir poic di" ("Besides giving thee a kiss, I will lie with thee!" Then he throws himself down upon her and gives her a kiss). The hag immediately becomes quite beautiful "[a]ntan immorro ro shill fuirri" (when he looked at her) and "ni raibi forsin domun ingen bid chaime tachim nó tuarascbail inda si" (not a damsel whose gait or appearance was more loveable than hers! [para. 14]). About the translation of *flaithius* as "sovranty," see Bollard's article arguing against a connection between the Irish and English tales on this account ("Sovereignty," pp. 41–57). Bollard refutes the connection between the French/German/Welsh tales and the English and Irish versions (p. 45): I disagree with some, though certainly not all, of Bollard's interpretations.

38. See Stokes's note, "Echtra," p. 201, n. 1: "Son of Cennétig, slain at Clontarf (Cluain-tarbh) A.D. 1014." Brían Borumha defeated Máel Sechnaill II, Cúan Ua Lothcháin's king, in the early eleventh century. See also Ó Corráin, *Ireland Before the Normans*, pp. 120–31.

39. See Jaski, *Early Irish Kingship*, pp. 113–42, for seniority rules in Irish succession laws.

40. My thanks to Susan Carter for pointing out that the kind of cunning negotiation the goddess recommends here suggests the advice in the early modern "mirror for princes," Machiavelli's *Prince*. Carter notes that "she is teaching him the Machiavellian principle that you should use one advantage of power to get greater advantages. So she is advising on skills in leadership, not only in moral behavior.... This really interests me in prefiguring that Machiavellian ethos of being aggressive in gaining ascendancy, and to my way of thinking this is a sophistication of the Níall tales" (personal correspondence, 12 February 2004). See also Ferster's discussion of Machiavelli (*Fictions*, pp. 160–73). Also see the *Audacht Morainn*, which recommends, along the same lines, "Apair fris, nach frithfholuth rodn-dligther to-rata, na aurnaidm ara-rona ro-sá" (Tell him, let him give any reciprocal service which is due from him, let him enforce any bond which he should bind [stanza 30]).

41. See Ó Cúiv, "Cathal Croibhdhearg," pp. 157–74.

42. Incidentally, Níall refers to the goddess in this stanza as "a ben dífhregra dímór" (a woman who has no match for size), which serves as the first overall size indicator of the hag in the poem. Previously, in stanza 22, her hand was described as "féithig fata fortuaig" (long sinewy and very emaciated), the only other indicator of the figure's size.

43. See Low, *Celtic Christianity*, pp. 47–48.

44. Ó Cúiv, "Cathal," p. 167 and 171: stanzas 52–53.

45. For a more comprehensive discussion of the English protagonist, see Passmore, "The Loathly Lady Transformed," pp. 121–73.

46. See Ferster, *Fictions*, pp. 85–86 and 175–76, on the actions of the Parliaments and the king.

47. See the essays by Elizabeth Biebel-Stanley ("Sovereignty Through the Lady") and R. F. Yeager ("Politics of 'Strengthe' and 'Vois'") in the present volume. On Anne of Bohemia, also see Saul, *Richard II*, who comments that Queen Anne's "interventions

were for the most part confined to acts of intercession" (p. 455), yet "[f]rom the beginning of the 1390s there is evidence that Anne was earning the respect of the English political elite" and "[h]ad she lived she might have emerged as a figure of considerable political stature" (p. 456). Compellingly, when she died, "on the epitaph composed for her tomb Richard chose to honour his wife for her skill in settling disputes" (p. 456). Also see Green, *Poets and Princepleasers*, pp. 161–66. About the mediatory role of medieval queens, see Maurer, *Margaret of Anjou*, pp. 10–13; Parsons, "Family, Sex, and Power," pp. 1–11; and Strohm, "Queens as Intercessors," in which Strohm argues that Chaucer's images of noblewomen, "move beyond intercessory images pleasing to autocracy in order to produce ideas of queenship that argue for the tempering of kingly power by good advice" (p. 119).

48. Ferster, *Fictions*, p. 3.

49. Staley Johnson, "Inverse Counsel," pp. 137–55.

50. See Watts, *Henry VI and the Politics of Kingship*, pp. 16–17, for the importance of counsel in rulership during the late Middle Ages.

51. See Olsen, "*Betwene Ernest and Game*," especially chapter 2, in which Olsen demonstrates that more interpretations about the purpose of each of Gower's tales is possible than the ones indicated in the Latin glosses and through Gower's characters (pp. 19–31).

52. The word *wedde* here again means "pledge," as it did above.

53. Gower, *Confessio Amantis*, pp. 12–13. Also see Carruthers, *Book of Memory*, and Yates, *Art of Memory*, for medieval theories about the importance and uses of memory.

54. This scene recalls the poor young maidens who were forced into marrying men three or four times their age during this historical time period. Florent's distress highlights what their own reactions must have been, more so than the other Loathly Lady tales.

55. Russell Peck writes in the introduction to his edition of the Prologue and Books I and VIII of the *Confessio Amantis* about the concept of time (past to present to future) and how Gower draws on Augustine's thoughts about time as "movement": the present really does not exist, for it is always either the future or the past. In the sense of time as perceived through Augustine, therefore, a life happens in a moment, and an eighteen-year-old girl is instantly an ancient, ugly woman. See *Confessio Amantis*, p. 3, n. 8.

56. The implication is, of course, that "such" is the Loathly Lady in her beautiful guise and that she will be ugly for one twelve-hour period each day.

57. This is, of course, a direct reversal of the concept of sovereignty (*fláithius*) in the Irish stories, in which the goddess bestows sovereignty on the king-candidate, not the other way around. See Bollard, "Sovereignty," who deems this an example of the lack of connection between the Irish and English texts. I would suggest, rather, that the change in meaning of "sovereignty" and in its application is suggestive only of the changes in cultural attitudes from Ireland to England, from the twelfth century to the fourteenth.

58. This passage indicates that the Loathly Lady still remains under an enchantment, though it differs from the previous one: unless she dies quite young, she will always appear to be the eighteen-year-old that she is at that time. Line 1840, however, gives a slightly different implication to her assurance of everlasting beauty, when she adds, "I schal alwey be such to you." I interpret this line to mean that, while she may not always be exactly as she appears at that moment, Florent will always perceive her to look just as beautiful as she is at present. Similarly, in Chaucer's tale, it can be interpreted that the rapist-knight merely *perceives* the woman as ugly but finally recognizes her real beauty.

59. Hoccleve, *Regiment*, devotes a section to the topic of justice (lines 2465–772) and also discusses, generally, the importance of keeping one's oaths (lines 2217–18, 2332–38, 4800–4882).

60. See Barnes, *Counsel and Strategy*, pp. ix and 15. See also Curtius, *European Literature*, pp. 101–5, on the motif in late classical writings of the old / young woman. Curtius suggests that "the phenomenon of rejuvenation ... symbolizes a regeneration wish of the personality" (p. 105), yet he does not address the role of the Loathly Lady in particular. Moreover, his Jungian suggestions that such a motif belongs to "the stock of archaic proto-images in the collective unconscious" and "correspond[s] to the language of dreams" do not address the function nor the significance of her counsel to the protagonist while she is in an old and unattractive form.

61. See, for example, what Hoccleve has to say about pity, a virtue which the ignoble knight lacks but must develop. It signifies "good wil inward of debonaire herte / And outward speeche, and werk of man to fonde / To helpe him that men seen in mescheef smerte. / Men seelde him seen into wikkid deeth sterte / That pitous is, but they haveth cruel deeth / Often, whos crueltee cruelly steeth" (lines 2998–3003). Suggestively, one must demonstrate this virtue in three ways, through inner emotion but also through speech and action, and the possession of such a virtue can be literally lifesaving, according to Hoccleve.

62. Other themes addressed in separate sections in the *Regiment* include mercy, patience, generosity, and peace.

63. Though Hoccleve initiates this discussion with a derogatory—yet unsurprising—reference to the mistake of listening to women's counsel (because of Eve's counsel to Adam), he recovers from the diatribe with an open apology to women and a long, involved "defense" (which might not be entirely ironic) of their "worthynesse," particularly as advisors to their husbands (lines 5090–5194).

64. About the knight's behavior, see Townsend, "Chaucer's Nameless Knight," who actually views him somewhat positively: "He is the kind of young fellow who can commit rape and still be the darling of the ladies" (p. 2). A more intuitive view is that of Roppolo, "Converted Knight," who characterizes him as "a selfish, proud, and morally blind knight" (p. 263) and as an "impatient, discourteous, and unhappy Knight" (p. 267), with an overall comment that "the Knight's character is anything

but admirable" (p. 267). See also McKinley, "Silenced Knight," pp. 361–63, about the lecture and the choice.

65. This point might well have resonated with Chaucer's audience, for it raises the unpleasant specter of Richard II's own grandfather (Edward II), who had been deposed partly because of his alleged manipulation by bad counselors. More explicitly, Richard II's close relationship with Robert de Vere, until the latter's self-exile in 1388, was resented by the king's other magnates almost as greatly as was the power of Edward II's close companion, Piers Gaveston. See Saul, *Richard II*, pp. 121–22.

66. The order of the complaints which the knight has against the Loathly Lady is also turned upside-down. He had complained that she was "so loothly, and so oold also, / And thereto comen of so lough a kynde" (lines 1100–1101), yet she first addresses his complaint about her "lough" birth. Next, she addresses poverty and, finally, her elderly status. Never does she address, in her lecture, his complaint about her "loothly" appearance—this complaint she introduces only at the end, when she gives him the option to have her "yong and fair" but potentially dishonorable, or foul and old but a "trewe, humble wyf" (lines 1220–24). Classical theories of rhetoric demand that the most important point be made last; if these theories are applied to the knight's complaint, the most important part of his complaint is her class status, a complaint which she reverses to address first in her lecture to him. See Minnis, *Medieval Theory of Authorship*, pp. 147–49. Perhaps, by addressing both nobility of action and beauty at the same time in her offer of a choice (with which she concludes her lecture), the Loathly Lady tests the knight's ability to understand the overall significance of her lecture, which is that nobility is found in actions, not in appearance or ancestry. This point seems to be the most important of the lecture and, by extension, of the entire tale.

67. Note that she spends less and less time on each topic. On "gentillesse," she spoke sixty-seven lines in all; on "poverte," twenty-nine lines; and on "elde," only nine lines.

68. See Cooke, "Nice Young Girls," pp. 219–28. Cooke comments about this part of the lecture that the Loathly Lady, while "appearing to remind the knight that nobles should honour old people," uses the term *fader* to indicate how that respect should be offered, thereby suggesting "that only old men, and not old women, should be treated with respect" (p. 226).

69. *Repair* is glossed as "resort, visitors" in the *Riverside Chaucer* (Benson, p. 121).

70. Hoccleve, *Regiment*, says that one should seek counsel from others, but that one should also be able to decide by oneself what counsel one should take: "Also yee been at your eleccioun / To do or leve it as yourselven leste. / If it be good, impresse it in the cheste / Of your memorie and executith it; / If it nat be, to leve it is a wit" (lines 4896–4900). Barnes, *Counsel and Strategy*, claims that the real indication of a hero's attainment of maturity is when he can distinguish good counsel from bad (pp. 14–15).

71. As Roppolo, "Converted Knight," comments, "To deserve the coming happy ending, the Knight must change" (p. 267).

72. See Hoccleve, *Regiment* (lines 3924–26), about how a good king reveals himself to be equally a good knight. See also Watts, *Henry VI*, on the similarity of virtues required for both kings and knights (p. 35).

73. This romance exists only in Bodleian Library MS 11951 (formerly Rawlinson C.86), which dates to the sixteenth century. Frederic Madden (1839) describes the manuscript as "very carelessly written" by a scribe with a "negligent hand" (Hahn, *Sir Gawain*, p. 44). One leaf of the romance is missing after line 628, so that the part of the story after the wedding and before the bedroom scene is lost. The manuscript, which contains thirty-five items in all, also contains Chaucer's "The Clerk's Tale" and "The Prioress's Tale," as well as some Latin verses lamenting the death of Edward IV. This manuscript also indicates the type of literature popular in the mid- to late fifteenth century. See Griffiths, "Re-examination," pp. 381–88.

74. See, for instance, Hoccleve's suggestions to seek counsel from the poor as well as the rich and from the young as well as the old (*Regiment*, lines 4880–93 and 4942–63).

75. See Watts, *Henry VI*, in which he discusses the importance of counsel for effective kingship, as shown in "mirrors" (pp. 15–16 and 21–22). Taken along with this scene in "Wedding," Watts's contention implies that King Arthur lacks the appropriate behavior for a good king. See also Mary Leech's discussion on the subject of Arthur's unkingly actions in her article "Why Dame Ragnelle Had to Die" in the present volume.

76. Through his interest, he is perhaps also showing that he is capable of learning the necessary virtues of a king.

77. Curiously, even Arthur's response to Dame Ragnelle brings up the topic of counsel, with himself as advisor, revealing perhaps that he still needs to learn to accept counsel for himself: "So ye wol be rulyd by my councelle, / Your wille then shalle ye have" (lines 504–5). The Loathly Lady, however, recognizes clearly that, if she is ruled by the king's own counsel, she would not be getting her "wille" after all, and she refuses outright to concede to him. The lesson to be learned here is for the king to accept counsel, not for the counselor to be led by the king's will.

78. Hahn, *Sir Gawain*, p. 64.

79. See, in this respect, Hahn's comment concerning lines 656–61, about Chaucer's version being more obvious about the "public vs. private male enjoyment of the lady's sexual attractions" (*Sir Gawain*, p. 78). I believe, however, "male enjoyment" is not all there is to the choice. See also Keen, *Chivalry*, pp. 7–8, and Mathew, *Court of Richard II*, p. 118.

80. Hahn glosses *A simple repayre* as "dismal relations" (*Sir Gawain*, p. 65).

81. Incidentally, Gawain's difficulty in deciding here, similar to Florent's pained decision-making in "The Tale of Florent," indicates a rather more advanced thought process than one might usually expect from a romance. See Barnes, *Counsel and Strategy*, p. 14. See Hanning, *Individual*, about the concept of the self in French romance; and Barron, *English Medieval Romance*, pp. 177–78, about the transitions in the genre from France to England.

82. See Hudson, "Construction of Class, Family, and Gender," pp. 76–94.

83. Furthermore, the poet's final plea for help (lines 841–52) raises the question of whether the text can be construed as an implicit criticism of a fifteenth-century king, probably Henry VI, whereby King Arthur's contrasting treatment of Sir Gromer and Sir Gawain has some real significance for the poet's own situation. Also, the emphasis on public perception here, which differs from the message in Gower's and Chaucer's tales, may have some relevance for the poet's own situation. In other words, perhaps the poet was the recipient of a private promise from the king, a promise which was not kept and which, because of its neglect, now has landed the poet in prison. While speculative, this suggestion may connect the text to contemporary difficulties in Henry VI's rule, especially since the romance is widely accepted to have been composed around 1450, after Henry VI's marriage to Margaret of Anjou but before Henry's protracted illness of 1453, the aftereffects of which eventually moved the country into civil war. See Maurer, *Margaret of Anjou*, pp. 77–79.

84. This ballad exists only in British Library Additional MS 27879, also called the Percy Folio manuscript. The manuscript was compiled around 1650, and it contains a number of "popular" texts, many of which are dated by their language to the late Middle Ages. The first part of the manuscript contains Arthurian ballads and romances, but any systematic ordering of the texts rapidly breaks down. Bishop Thomas Percy (1729–1811) of Dromore, Ireland, writes at the beginning of the manuscript that he found the "scrubby, shabby, paper" book "lying dirty on the floor under a Bureau in the Parlour" of his friend, Humphrey Pitt of Shiffnal in Shropshire, "being used by the maids to light the fire" (qtd. in Hahn, *Sir Gawain*, p. 311).

85. I would like to thank Susan Carter for pointing out that this ballad is the only version in which the knight himself actually attempts to give an answer to the Loathly Lady's question (though it is the wrong one), and that he then chivalrously revises his answer to accommodate his wife's expressed preference. As Carter commented, this is "quite a likeable picture of Gawain" (personal correspondence, 23 February 2003).

86. See Maurer, *Margaret of Anjou*, pp. 10–13.

87. See Hoccleve, *Regiment*, lines 5108–19.

88. See, for example, Dame Ragnelle's response to Queen Guenevere's suggestion that she marry early in the morning so as to avoid witnesses: "I wol be weddyd alle openly, / For with the Kynge suche covenaunt made I. / I putt you oute of dowte, / I wolle nott to churche tylle Highe Masse tyme / And in the open halle I wolle dyne, / In myddys of all the rowte" (lines 575–80). In the face of Ragnelle's strong resolve, the queen can only agree, though she insists she was thinking solely of Ragnelle's honor. Yet Ragnelle is equally confident on that point, too: "Ye, as for that, Lady, God you save. / This daye my worshypp wolle I have, / I telle you withoute boste" (lines 584–86).

89. Hahn glosses line 166 as that the Loathly Lady must not go "into the hall (public space)" (*Sir Gawain*, p. 368).

WORKS CITED

Aguirre, Manuel. "The Riddle of Sovereignty." *MLR* 88 (1993), 273–82.

Barnes, Geraldine. *Counsel and Strategy in Middle English Romance*. Rochester, N.Y.: Brewer, 1993.

Barron, W. R. J. *English Medieval Romance*. New York: Longman, 1987.

Benson, Larry D., gen. ed. *The Riverside Chaucer*. 3rd ed. Boston: Houghton Mifflin, 1987; repr. Oxford: Oxford University Press, 1988.

Binchy, D. A. *Celtic and Anglo-Saxon Kingship*. Oxford: Clarendon Press, 1970.

Bollard, J. K. "Sovereignty and the Loathly Lady in English, Welsh, and Irish." *LSE* 17 (1986), 41–59.

Brewer, D. S. "Class Distinction in Chaucer." *Speculum* 43 (1968), 290–305.

Byrne, Francis John. *Irish Kings and High-Kings*. Dublin: Four Courts, 2001.

Carruthers, Mary J. *The Book of Memory: A Study of Memory in Medieval Culture*. Cambridge: Cambridge University Press, 1994.

Castor, Helen. *The King, the Crown, and the Duchy of Lancaster: Public Authority and Private Power, 1399–1461*. Oxford: Oxford University Press, 2000.

Charles-Edwards, T. M. *Early Christian Ireland*. Cambridge: Cambridge University Press, 2000.

Coghill, Nevill. *Chaucer's Idea of What Is Noble*. Oxford: Oxford University Press, 1971.

Cooke, Jessica. "Nice Young Girls and Wicked Old Witches: The 'Rightful Age' of Women in Middle English Verse." In *The Court and Cultural Diversity*, ed. Evelyn Mullally and John Thompson, pp. 219–28. Cambridge: Brewer, 1997.

Coomaraswamy, Ananda K. "On the Loathly Bride." *Speculum* 20 (1945), 391–404.

Curtius, Ernst R. *European Literature and the Latin Middle Ages*. Trans. Willard R. Trask. 1948; repr. Princeton: Princeton University Press, 1967.

Donnelly, Colleen. "Aristocratic Veneer and the Substance of Verbal Bonds in *The Weddynge of Sir Gawen and Dame Ragnell* and *Gamelyn*." *SP* 94 (1997), 321–43.

Eisner, Sigmund. *A Tale of Wonder: A Source Study of "The Wife of Bath's Tale."* Wexford, Ire.: John English, 1957.

Ferster, Judith, *Fictions of Advice: The Literature and Politics of Counsel in Late Medieval England* (Philadelphia: University of Pennsylvania Press, 1996).

Forste-Grupp, Sheryl L. "A Woman Circumvents the Laws of Primogeniture in *The Weddynge of Sir Gawen and Dame Ragnell*." *SP* 99 (2002), 105–22.

Gillespie, James L., ed. *The Age of Richard II*. New York: St. Martin's, 1997.

Goodman, Anthony. "King Richard's Councils." In *Richard II*, ed. Goodman and Gillespie, pp. 59–82.

Goodman, Anthony, and James Gillespie, eds. *Richard II: The Art of Kingship*. Oxford: Clarendon Press, 1999.

Gower, John. *Confessio Amantis*. Ed. Peck, Russell A. Vol. 1. Kalamazoo, Mich.: Medieval Institute Publications, 2000.

Green, R. F. *Poets and Princepleasers: Literature and the English Court in the Late Middle Ages.* Toronto: University of Toronto Press, 1980.

Griffiths, J. J. "A Re-examination of Oxford, Bodleian Library, MS Rawlinson.C.86." *Archiv für das Studium der Neueren Sprachen und Literaturen* 219 (1982), 381–88.

Hahn, Thomas, ed. *Sir Gawain: Eleven Romances and Tales.* Kalamazoo, Mich.: Medieval Institute Publications, 1995.

Hanning, R. W. *The Individual in Twelfth-Century Romance.* New Haven: Yale University Press, 1977.

Hoccleve, Thomas. *The Regiment of Princes.* Ed. Charles R. Blyth. Kalamazoo, Mich.: Medieval Institute Publications, 1999.

Hudson, Harriet E. "Construction of Class, Family, and Gender in Some Middle English Popular Romances." In *Class and Gender in Early English Literature,* ed. Britton J. Harwood and Gillian R. Overing, pp. 76–94. Bloomington: Indiana University Press, 1994.

Jaski, Bart. *Early Irish Kingship and Succession.* Dublin: Four Courts, 2000.

Joynt, Maud, trans. and ed. "Echtra mac Echdach Mugmedóin." *Ériu* 4 (1910), 91–111.

Keen, Maurice. *Chivalry.* New Haven: Yale University Press, 1984.

Kelly, Fergus, ed. and trans. *Audacht Morainn.* Dublin: DIAS, 1976.

——. *A Guide to Early Irish Law.* Dublin: DIAS, 1998.

Leland, John L. "The Oxford Trial of 1400: Royal Politics and the County Gentry." In *Richard II*, ed. Goodman and Gillespie, pp.165–89.

Low, Mary. *Celtic Christianity and Nature: Early Irish and Hebridean Traditions.* Edinburgh: Edinburgh University Press, 1996.

Mathew, Gervase. *The Court of Richard II.* New York: Norton, 1969.

Mac Cana, Proinsias. "Aspects of the Theme of King and Goddess in Irish Literature." Parts 1–3. *EC* 7 (1955–56), 76–114, and 356–413; *EC* 8 (1958–59), 59–65.

Manzalaoui, M. A., ed. *Secretum Secretorum: Nine English Versions.* Vol. 1. EETS, o. s. 276. Oxford: Oxford University Press, 1977.

Maurer, Helen E. *Margaret of Anjou: Queenship and Power in Late Medieval England.* Rochester, N.Y.: Boydell, 2003.

Maynadier, G. H. *"The Wife of Bath's Tale": Its Sources and Analogues.* London: Nutt, 1901.

McKinley, Kathryn L. "The Silenced Knight: Questions of Power and Reciprocity in the 'Wife of Bath's Tale.'" *CR* 30 (1996), 359–78.

McCone, Kim. *Pagan Past and Christian Present in Early Irish Literature.* Naas, Ire.: An Sagart, 1990.

Minnis, A. J. *Medieval Theory of Authorship: Scholastic Literary Attitudes in the Later Middle Ages.* 2nd ed. Philadelphia: University of Pennsylvania Press, 1988.

Ó Corráin, Donnchadh. *Ireland Before the Normans.* Dublin: Gill, 1980.

Ó Cúiv, Brian, trans. and ed. "A Poem Composed for Cathal Croibhdhearg Ó Conchubhair." *Ériu* 34 (1984), 157–74.

O'Grady, Standish Hayes, trans. and ed. "Echtra mac n-Echach." In *Silva Gadelica 1–31*, pp. 368–73. Vols. 1–2. 1892; repr. New York: Lemma, 1970.

Olsen, Alexandra Hennessey. *"Betwene Ernest and Game": The Literary Artistry of the "Confessio Amantis."* New York: Lang, 1999.

Parsons, John Carmi. "Family, Sex, and Power: The Rhythms of Medieval Queenship." In *Medieval Queenship*, ed. J. C. Parsons, pp. 1–11. New York: St. Martin's, 1993.

Passmore, S. Elizabeth. "The Loathly Lady Transformed: A Literary and Cultural Analysis of the Medieval Irish and English Hag-Beauty Tales." PhD diss., University of Connecticut, Storrs, 2004.

Renna, Thomas. "Kingship in the Fourteenth Century." *Michigan Academician* 14 (1981), 13–21.

Rogers, Gillian. "'Illuminat vith lawte, and with lufe lasit': Gawain Gives Arthur a Lesson in Magnanimity." In *Romance Reading on the Book,* ed. Jennifer Fellows, Rosalind Field, Gillian Rogers, and Judith Weiss, pp. 94–111. Cardiff: University of Wales Press, 1996.

Roppolo, Joseph P. "The Converted Knight in Chaucer's 'Wife of Bath's Tale.'" *College English* 12 (1950), 263–69.

Shenk, Robert. "The Liberation of the 'Loathly Lady' of Medieval Romance." *JRMMRA* 2 (1981), 69–77.

Simms, Katharine. *From Kings to Warlords: The Changing Political Structure of Gaelic Ireland in the Later Middle Ages.* Woodbridge: Boydell, 1987.

Saul, Nigel. "Chaucer and Gentility." In *Chaucer's England: Literature in Historical Context,* ed. Barbara Hanawalt, pp. 41–45. Minneapolis: University of Minnesota Press, 1992.

———. *Richard II.* New Haven: Yale University Press, 1997.

Staley Johnson, Lynn. "Inverse Counsel: Contexts for the *Melibee.*" *SP* 87 (1990), 137–55.

Stokes, Whitley, trans. and ed. "Echtra mac Echach Muigmedóin." *RC* 24 (1903), 172–73, 190–203.

———. "The Marriage of Sir Gawain." *Academy* 41 (1892), 399.

Strohm, Paul. *England's Empty Throne: Usurpation and the Language of Legitimation, 1399–1422.* New Haven: Yale University Press, 1998.

———. "Queens as Intercessors." In *Hochon's Arrow: The Social Imagination of Fourteenth-Century Texts,* pp. 95–119. Princeton: Princeton University Press, 1992.

Townsend, Francis G. "Chaucer's Nameless Knight." *MLR* 49 (1954), 1–4.

Vasta, Edward. "Chaucer, Gower, and the Unknown Minstrel: The Literary Liberation of the Loathly Lady." *Exemplaria* 7 (1995), 395–418.

Watts, John. *Henry VI and the Politics of Kingship.* 1996; repr. Cambridge: Cambridge University Press, 1999.

Wilson, Chris Given. *The English Nobility in the Late Middle Ages: The Fourteenth-Century Political Community.* London: Routledge, 1987.

Wolffe, Bertram. *Henry VI.* 1981; repr. New Haven: Yale University Press, 2001.

Yates, Francis A. *The Art of Memory.* Chicago: University of Chicago Press, 1984.

The Politics of *Strengthe* and *Vois* in Gower's Loathly Lady Tale

R. F. Yeager

Because it is the nearest extant analogue to Chaucer's "Wife of Bath's Tale" and a prominent member of the "Loathly Lady group," "The Tale of Florent" is among the best known of the many narratives in John Gower's Middle English poem, the *Confessio Amantis*. It occurs in Book I, lines 1407–1861, and at 453 lines it is one of Gower's longer exempla. The subject of Book I is Pride, to which Genius—Gower's priest of Venus and the confessor of Amans, from whom the poem takes its title—attributes "minstres five ful diverse."[1] "Florent" is intended to illuminate Inobedience, the second of these Ministers of Pride, by illustrating an alternative to "Murmur and Compleignte" (CA I.1345), a subspecies of Inobedience ultimately destructive of lovers' hopes, and (Gower suggests, when found at large in society) a threat to the longevity of the state.

"Florent" is thus a cautionary tale on several levels. Appropriately, its suitability within Gower's framing fiction, the examination of the behavior of the lover Amans toward his lady, has drawn the most critical attention: the tale has first to speak its part amid Gower's larger imaginative enterprise before the presence of other discourses can be acknowledged.[2] And at this "Florent" is notably successful. Set alongside Chaucer's version, Gower's tale appears "a simple story simply told"—as indeed it is, and purposely.[3] Gower has no Wife of Bath for whom to script self-revelation, and he keeps his eye squarely monitoring the more modest narrative range demanded by his larger plan.[4] In the *Confessio*'s thrifty fictive economy Genius seeks to register a lesson for Amans's betterment as lover and as man, a quite basic task that excludes *a principio* significant complexities of character from the *personae* of the tales. Genius and Amans, themselves the most rounded figures in the poem, never—despite some charming moments—threaten to step out of their frame into near-reality, as some readers have felt the Wife of Bath to do. They are both allegorical in conception, and at bottom remain so—even Amans at the poem's end, when he has accepted from Venus his new "identity" as the old man John Gower, and his black rosary for prayer, "por reposer."[5]

It is important in reading all of Gower's works, however, never to confuse a simple style with simplicities of implication. Of this his "Tale of Florent" offers a case in point. The key term (always, for Gower in the *Confessio* and to large degree in his ballade sequences) is undoubtedly "scale": adapting the parts, usually by thoughtful retention of a few well-chosen details from more abundant descriptions in his sources, to benefit a decorum both unifyingly pervasive and flexibly suggestive. For "Florent" (as for "The Wife of Bath's Tale"), we have no certain source for comparison. (Each has been variously cited as originary to the other, but this merely begs the question.)[6] Nevertheless, wherever Gower found his story—and as I shall argue subsequently, it was unlikely to have been in a manuscript of Chaucer's—we can be confident that he trimmed it to fit his purpose, or purposes, since while "The Tale of Florent" decorously negotiates amongst the several narratives of Book I without untoward self-assertion, it is for all that a barbed instrument with several simultaneous targets in view.

In the process of that trimming, Gower effectively obscured the origins of "Florent," but it is quite clear that his decision to insert it into Book I must have been thoughtfully made. Regardless of whether we take to be true the commission that Gower reports (in manuscripts of the so-called "first recension") was issued him on the Thames by Richard II, that "Som newe thing I scholde boke / That he himself it mihte loke" (CA Pro. 51–52), and so conclude that Gower expected the king as his primary audience; or whether it was for Gower merely a trope, another way of saying "A boke for Engelondes sake" (CA Pro. 24), as he put it in later versions—the narratives to be included in his poem's first book could only have been deeply considered. They were, after all, the first of a great many more in the subsequent seven books of the *Confessio* to which a reader of any status or sort could anticipate devoting a good deal of time to absorb, and if they fell flat, the bulk of Gower's labor might be put aside unsampled. This, for any writer—but perhaps most for a self-conscious moralist like Gower, who wrote in order to effect social change—would have been unthinkable, the worst possible outcome. It is therefore useful to look briefly at the collection of stories with which "Florent" is grouped, for what they suggest about what Gower's strategy might have been, for his Loathly Lady tale.

All, of course, in one way or another illustrate types of Pride—but given the inclusivity of the sin, finding exempla to do so, to this degree or that, is scarcely a tall order. What is more interesting is imagining the library whence Genius, quick to point out he is himself a reader, went for the tales of Book I. Most he pulled down from his classics shelf—not surprising, perhaps, if Gower had any intention of establishing Genius' fictive credibility as emissary of a Roman goddess. "Acteon" and "Medusa," the first two he tells, Genius says he got from "Ovide the Poete," "in Metamor" (CA I.386, 389).[7] There follows "The Prudence of the Serpent," based on Psalm 58, but unlike the two prior tales, left unattributed.[8] Yet in context it too has a classical feel, perhaps because it seems a kind of logical extension of the Medusan coiffure; nor does Gower's narration carelessly betray its biblical origin. "The Tale of the Sirens," found "in the tale of Troie" (CA I.483), directly claims its classical heritage—and from the reader's perspective at this point, it matters not a jot that Genius cribbed from Guido, and not Homer *pro se.* [9] The next tale, "Mundus and Paulina," is from Josephus, whom Gower knew as a Jew but primarily as a Roman; his "Croniqe" (CA I.759), *Antiquities*, might have well been shelved near Ovid, in Genius' imaginary library.[10] Most importantly, however, Gower puts us firmly in Rome with the tale's opening:

> It fell be olde daies thus,
> Whil themperour Tiberius
> The Monarchie of Rome ladde,
> Ther was a worthi Romein hadde
> A wif, and sche Pauline hihte.
>   (CA I.761–65)

After "Mundus and Paulina" comes "The Trojan Horse"—Benoît de Sainte-Mor this time, but it matters only academically[11] and after that, "The Tale of Florent." Before looking more closely at what this means, however, we should finish noting Genius' selections for the rest of Book I. Following "Florent" it's back to the classics for "The Tale of Capaneus" (probably from Statius),[12] then the "Trump of Death," set in "Hungarie" (CA I.2022)—despite taking place "be olde daies" (CA I.2023), very openly *not* classical[13]—but immediately followed by "Narcissus," from Ovid again.[14] Then comes "Albinus and Rosemund," Albinus being "the ferste of alle" "Of hem that we Lombars now calle" (CA I.2460, 2459), and so a marginally classical figure;[15] "Nebuchadnezzar's Punishment" ("in the bible his name is bore," *CA* I.2788) comes next;[16] and the book concludes with "The Tale of the Three Questions," for which no proven source has been identified.[17]

With particular relevance to "The Tale of Florent," salient among the several noteworthy things about this congeries is the clear effort Gower made to situate his narratives historically. Without exception, they are said to have taken place in the past—in most cases, the ancient past. (Genius' tooth for classical literature is in this regard predictive.) Gower executes several strategies to establish the idea that his material in Book I is the product of antiquity. When his sources are well known and old, he names them—Ovid's "Metamor," "the tale of Troie" (*CA* I.483), "the bible" (*CA* I.2788); more often, he implies age by referring to his stories as gleaned from unnamed "Croniques" (the tales "Mundus and Paulina," "Florent," "Capaneus," and "Three Questions" fit this category);[18] or he will state directly that the narrative events took place "be olde daies."[19] Beyond these, for the reader with ready Latin, he sometimes dates the tales in the marginal or interlinear rubrics (Florent's uncle is, for example, identified in one such as the Roman emperor Claudius);[20] and for the memorious, who also read the Prologue with care, there is Gower's anthropomorphic "time line," the monstrous statue of Nebuchadnezzar's dream as interpreted by Daniel, whose gold head and neck Gower tells us represent the ancient world until the defeat of Babylon by the Persians; its silver arms and breast, the Persians until Alexander; its brass stomach to the knees, the Greeks and Romans; its steel legs and a bit of the feet, post-Imperial and Christian Rome, including the Lombards, Charlemagne, and the "Alemans;" and the predominantly clay feet, the years since, through the present day.[21]

While Gower's reasons for doing all of this may have been as various as his techniques, we can assume with confidence that two at least were present in his mind. The first, very probably, in importance was to establish the authority of his poem. Gower must have been—for him—unusually concerned about authority in the Prologue and Book I because as far as we know the *Confessio Amantis* was his initial foray in English verse. Prior to this, he had written in French (the *Mirour de l'Omme*, and ballades) and in Latin (most, if not all, of the *Vox Clamantis*, and perhaps some shorter pieces), both languages with recognized "authority" of their own requiring no justification as media in which to communicate serious ideas poetically.[22] English in the 1380s when Gower no doubt started the *Confessio* had a less solid *a priori* claim as a language to be listened to about important matters—and perhaps we can glimpse Gower's uncertainty about his project in the Latin verses heading sections, and the running Latin prose commentary he wrote to direct interpretation of the tales.[23] Both assert the authority of *Latinitas*, in the presence of the language itself, and visually, by suggesting that Gower's English poem is one among that category of works meriting commentary.[24] Not insignificantly, all such texts were written in Latin. It's as if, at first at least, the apparatus was a kind of lifeline for him, connecting his risky new venture with the certitudes of Latin poetic, just in case. No doubt in that light we should see as well the predominant effort to classicize the *Confessio* outright—the Roman deities of the frame narrative, the insistent "antiquity" of Genius' stories, even when (as in the case of "Florent") their sources are demonstrably "modern."

The second reason we can guess that Gower had in mind for setting his narratives in the past is frankly political, and goes to the heart of Gower's goal for his poem.[25] This he states more clearly in the so-called "Henrician" Prologue found in the best later manuscripts.[26] Recalling "daies olde" when "Wrytinge was beloved evere / Of hem that weren virtuous" (CA Pro. 38–39) because it preserved honorable deeds for posterity's emulation, and condemned for all time "tho that deden thanne amis / Thurgh tirannie and crualte" (CA Pro. 48–49), Gower reveals his kinship with that precise kind of antique writer. He, although a mere "burel clerk,"[27] will "wryte a bok / After the world that whilom tok / Long tyme in olde daies passed" (CA Pro. 53–55), on the subject of "The world which neweth every dai" (CA Pro. 59)—a world which, unfortunately, "is now lassed / In worse plit than it was tho" (CA Pro. 56–57). The political intentions of the *Confessio* could not be more directly stated; but in times of "worse plit" direct critiques—especially in English, which choice ensured the broadest possible readership—of those responsible for "tirannie and crualte" could be risky, in Gower's view. He says as much in a strong comment, not insignificantly in Latin verse, following line 92 of the Prologue:

> Now Fortune leaves the blessed time of yore,
> And turns the antique customs on her wheel.
> Harmonious love begat the ancient peace,
> When yet man's face was herald of his mind:
> The air of that age shone, one-hued, with laws;
> The paths of justice then were plain and smooth.
> Now hidden hatred paints a loving face,
> And hides a time of war beneath feigned peace.

The law, chameleon-like, transforms and shifts:
In novel realms, new laws; and regions which
Were strong, through Fortune's wheel are rendered weak,
Nor there a hub of quiet do they find.[28]

Writing in times of such violence and hypocrisy, when "hidden hatred paints a loving face" and the law "chameleon-like" offers no assured protection—this from a man who often trusted the law to protect his rights in the 1360s and 1370s, and who may have been a lawyer—requires from the prudent truth-telling poet like measures of camouflage, to guard his back.[29] Hence the distancing of Genius' stories from the present, both in time and space: events which took place long ago, and/or far away, become accusations only when topically connected off the page—and connections of that kind, in a pinch, can always be denied.

In this regard it is pertinent to notice how Gower's "historical matrix"—the polychotomous giant of Nebuchadnezzar's dream—serves at once to deflect, and direct, suspicious readings of Book I. As noted above, Genius' instructional narratives are with few exceptions drawn from ancient sources. Many of these Gower makes obvious by identifying familiar ones—Ovid, the Troy story, the Bible. But in other cases, particularly where his source was not in fact either ancient or classical, the memorable matrix of the statue helps reinforce just how far distant from the present they are to be taken. Setting a tale in Rome, for example, locates its events in the "Age of Brass," some two happy removes from the present time of Clay. Lest we fear that an Albinus walks among us, we have only to recall the statue's reassuring situation of the Lombards in the "Age of Steel," a bit close to ours of Clay for thorough-going comfort, perhaps, but still completely in the past. Such moves might well blunt criticism, especially if its edge were none too sharp to begin with.

But Gower's need for self-protection would have been realized only if he had something to say indeed about the political animals of his own times; and since he did, he had to create means among the necessary obfuscation for determined or enlightened readers to pick out the message. For this, Nebuchadnezzar's statue is of great help in Book I. The same matrix of metallicized ages that signposts the regress of Gower's tales into the past also, if read head-to-foot, insists on a progression ending in the present. This is, in fact, exactly the way Daniel explicates the statue to Nebuchadnezzar—and of course, Daniel's point, like Gower's, is that this progression from golden head

to feet of clay is degenerative. Both Daniel speaking directly to Nebuchadnezzar and Gower *in propria persona* in the Prologue, before "depicting himself as
Amans,"[30] speaking directly to us as audience, have the here-and-now as their
target. The personal addresses of both underscore a fiction of an immediate
present.

Nor are the portents for the present, neither Daniel's nor Gower's, very
pretty. Anyone reading Book I with the statue's ages in mind cannot help but
observe two things. First, that Gower has been careful to include tales
representing all of the statue's ages. "Nebuchadnezzar's Punishment" is
from the "Age of Gold;" "Acteon," "Medusa," "The Sirens," "Trojan Horse,"
"Capaneus," and "Narcissus" from the "Age of Silver;" "Mundus and
Paulina," and "Florent" from the "Age of Brass;" and "Albinus and
Rosemund" from the "Age of Steel." Three tales have no specifically expressed
assignment—"Prudence of the Serpent," "Trump of Death," and "Three
Questions"—but of these, as we have noted above, "Prudence of the Serpent"
seems to go with the Silver tales by inference, leaving "Trump of Death" and
"Three Questions" accountable as representatives of the modern "Age of
Clay." For this there seems some logic beyond mere process of elimination:
despite Gower's assertion that both "Trump of Death" and "Three Questions"
take place "be olde daies" (CA I.2023; see also "be tho daies olde," CA I.3390)
and that "Three Questions" was found in a "Cronique" (CA I.3388), they are
located in kingdoms extant in the fourteenth century, Hungary ("Trump") and
Spain ("Questions"). Moreover, in the case of the "Three Questions," Gower
names the king as "Alphonse" (CA I.3393) and the knight as "Danz Petro" (CA
I.3394), both common Spanish names, of course, but also common among
Iberian rulers of Gower's day when, because of the Castilian alliance with
France and English military and matrimonial activity on the Peninsula, many
English eyes were turned toward Portugal and Spain.[31] Such elements resonate
of ours the final age, of Clay.

Second and more significant, however, is the subtler imperative of the
statue's degenerative historical pattern. Gower's assertion in the Prologue,
that the world he inhabits *in propria persona* is "[i]n worse plit than it was
tho"—that is to say, at *any* earlier age—establishes a frightening machinery
to evaluate whatever contemporary villainy one might recognize via analogy
in his tales of past times, against that ancient villainy itself. But in this of
course the conclusion is already far gone: not merely in Gower's very brief
statement in the Prologue (which, despite its blatancy, might be missed
nonetheless, or likely forgotten as the thirty-four thousand lines of the

Confessio spool out) but also, and without question, in the exceedingly memorable presence of the statue as historical reminder—a reminder indeed that Gower's manuscripts drove home in what would appear to have been an intentional illumination project, with Nebuchadnezzar's statue in center stage.[32] The testimony of Gower's Prologue is that the evil of the present far exceeds the evil of the past; that a tyrant (say) of any previous age, however wickedly condemned in the *Confessio*, must definitionally be a child in a tutu compared with the contemporary species Gower identifies through hints and analogies in his "simple" poem about love. The testimony of the statue is to make these judgments visually, vividly commemorative.

I

Against this backdrop, then, what is initially intriguing about "The Tale of Florent" is its casting as a Roman tale, a "tale of Brass." Not that Gower says it is, specifically. There is only one location mentioned in the tale proper, and that is Sicily, "Cizile" (CA I.1841). Short of that, however, he uses several strategies, as noted above, to ensure its historical location: the "be daies olde" trope, the source in a "Cronique," and most importantly the statement in the Latin prose commentary on the opening lines that "Florencius" was "tunc Imparatoris Claudi Nepos."[33] "Claudi" is of course Claudius (fl. A.D. 41–54), which leaves little doubt of which "Court" Florent was "a Courtier" (CA I.1410).

While there is no current agreement on where Gower actually found "The Tale of Florent," we can be certain it was not in a classical text. Indeed, of the many analogues to the tale, only "Florent" is set in Mediterranean Rome. Most known versions, like Chaucer's, place the Hag and the search for an answer to the question, "What do women most desire?" in Arthurian Britain.[34] Given this broad agreement (as well as the fact that, as is generally thought, Chaucer and Gower exchanged their versions between them), it is highly likely that Gower's uniqueness attests to a purposeful decision on his part to alter his sources.[35] That Gower, like Chaucer and the various anonymous authors of the "Loathly Lady group," came upon the narrative details which he remolded into his tale for the *Confessio* in an as-yet undiscovered romance seems the best guess; and in fact, Gower hints at that conclusion himself. In *Cinkante Balade* XLIII, he lists "Florent" along with "Lancelot," Tristrans," "Generides" and "Partonopé"—all heroes of well-known romances—as faithful contrasts to the deceivers with whom the poem is otherwise concerned.[36] "Florencius" in Book I's Latin commentary sounds more like a Gowerian construct than a clue to a Latin source.

Obviously the question then becomes one of motive and design. What propelled Gower to turn a probable "Sir Florent" into Florencius of Rome? The most suggestive answer is politics—or better, political critique.[37] "The Tale of Florent," in addition to its aptitude as an exemplum contrary to Pride-in-Love's branch "Murmur and Complaint," incorporates a subtext revelatory of Gower's attitudes toward sociopolitical events of the "Age of Clay," his own 1380s and 1390s. These were unusually ripe decades for murmuring and complaining in England. The so-called Peasants' Rising (a movement actually of wider discontent, swelled rather more by small landholders and townsmen than by "peasants") in 1381,[38] and continuing on through Richard II's perceived cronyism and extravagance (and consequent unpopular taxes), resulting in the Wonderful Parliament of 1386 and the Appellants' Revolt, the Merciless Parliament and the executions of the king's counselors in 1387–88, followed by Richard's quarrels with the city of London in 1392, his revenge on the Appellants (more executions and exilings) and his apparent wish to disempower the barony by 1397, the invasion of Henry Bolingbroke, Richard's eventual deposition and death and the crowning of Henry as usurper in 1399–1400: all of these things, along with Wycliffian/Lollard dissent in the Church, predations by liveried affinities on the commons, and the debilitating war with France desultorily dragging out until the truces surrounding Richard's marriage to Isabella in 1396 thrown in for good measure, amounted to two decades of rich material for a poet of Gower's apostolic sociopolitical conscience to make comment upon.[39]

The problem must have been, however, how to go about it without drawing vengeance down upon one's ears—although Gower was hardly a man lacking courage of his convictions. In the period significantly there was no angrier nor more direct social criticism (the writings of "anonymous" being a possible exception) than Gower's, who put his name to everything he wrote. But most of that sharply pointed, "name-names" critique was done in Latin, which may have been Gower's chosen hedge against too public a presence—and the *Confessio Amantis* Gower had decided to compose in English. The choice didn't altogether silence Gower's vehemence: the Prologue is full of his familiar assault on the Three Estates (CA Pro. 93–528). "Temporal Rulers," the Church, and the commons all receive their share of blame for the disintegrating times. It is, however, a criticism intentionally quite general: in the Prologue Gower is setting up the central fiction that will frame the coming poem, and laying down the connections between Amans's individual lack of *eros* and a general absence of Empedoclean *agape* that is in his view the prime cause of the world's woes. So that Amans should be an Everyman, Gower urges universal culpability for the loss of love:

> The world is changed overal,
> And therof most in special
> That love is falle into discord.
> And that I take to record
> Of every lond for his partie
> The comun vois, which mai noghte lie;
> Noght upon on, but upon alle
> It is that men now clepe and calle,
> And sein the regnes ben divided,
> In stede of love is hate guided
>
> . . . .
>
> Men sen the sor and withoute salve,
> Which al the world hath overtake.
> Ther is no regne of alle outtake,
> For every climat hath his diel.
>   (CA Pro. 119–28; 134–37)

Gower expects to elaborate on his major point throughout the vast extension of his eight-book poem—occasionally in the frame, in all of Book VII on the education of Alexander and the realms of human knowledge, and most frequently and importantly in the individual exempla Genius spins out for Amans. Having adopted a new—for him—approach to giving advice, using story instead of direct statement, Gower proposes also a new—again, for him—hermeneutics to his readers, one requiring them to find the political in the fairy tale by properly connecting the dots.

Or this is what he does, at least, in "The Tale of Florent." His first move was to decide where in the *Confessio* to include the tale itself: right up front, in the first book, with a high potential to be read, as a lesson against Pride and in particular "Murmur and Complaint." His next was to strip it of the Arthurian jacket we must assume it came in, and using all the mechanics at his disposal reposition it safely off in the Brass Age Roman past. Undoubtedly this was self-protective, to prevent our doing what comes naturally when reading the tale of the Wife of Bath: employing our accumulated foreknowledge about the moralities of Arthur's court to comprehend the objection of the queen and her ladies to the quick dispatch of a convicted rapist. Alisoun of Bath by her own admission and Guinevere in Chaucer's tale by legendary reputation share a soft spot for a hardy lad who knows what he wants. It's not the nicest moment in a reader's excursion through "The Wife of Bath's Tale," but Chaucer's understanding both of his pilgrim and of his audience's deep opinion of Guinevere (not to mention of fabliau wives in general) is what makes his extraordinary inclusion of rape as his knight's crime such a successful middle term.[40]

Viewed one way, that Arthur's court has such a queen as its heart is, ultimately, but one component of a far-reaching indictment of the whole knightly enterprise, if *chez* Arthur is as good as it gets. Gower, very likely, took it that way—nor was he alone in his broader opinion that the violence, avarice, and pride of the English knightly class at the end of the fourteenth century were a major cause of the "divisioun" which he intended to expose in the *Confessio*, and if possible, to heal. In fact, knights and their affinities were not popular in the 1380s and 1390s, among peasants, certainly, but especially among men of Gower's class, urban commercialists and lesser gentry whose voice was repeatedly heard in Parliament in these years, criticizing the empty losses and expenditures in the failing French war, and increasingly decrying the abuses fostered on them by the liveried (and hence legally exempted) affinities of the great lords.[41]

And of course, knights and barons knew how they were seen, not being altogether deaf. In such a political climate, rife with "murmur and complaint," an Arthurian tale like "Florent" could be put to many uses, depending upon one's purposes. Among Gower's there were two salient: first, a consciousness of building a sophisticated social critique over the course of a long haul, of which a probe of chivalric realities and ideals was to be a significant part, albeit one easily oversimplified and too soon vehemently rejected, along with the whole (unread) poem, by those most in need of the nuanced advice Gower expected his fully unfolded *Confessio* to proffer; and second, concomitantly, the wish to begin as soon as possible laying a foundation for the antichivalric, essentially irenic, disquisition that the *Confessio Amantis* eventually becomes.[42]

As a result, "Florent" was placed in Book I, but in disguise, displaying a Roman eagle, not an Arthurian pennon. On what, then, did Gower rely to establish his political critique? His third move may have been to leave Florent a knight. Not that he would have felt a knight in Rome to be an anachronism—that would scarcely have crossed Gower's mind; rather, the issue might have been, with any and all details potentially alterable, how to gauge the success of the Roman milieu in delaying the recognition of the tale's social commentary. Whatever the process, a knight Florent remained, in itself providing a measure of direction, whence a message from the tale might come.

Florent's knighthood, however, turns pointed in a manner characteristic of Gower. Genius offers a key to Gower's strategy in the way he lays out what will be the primary dichotomy of the tale: "Obedience in love availeth," he says, "Wher al a mannes *strengthe* faileth" (CA I.1401–2). Obedience versus strength: precisely the problematic facing the barony under Richard, successfully negotiated perhaps (particularly in Gower's view) only by John of Gaunt and his son Henry, in their radically different ways.[43] The pairing, and the slant it lends the tale, is unique among the Loathly Lady analogues. Nowhere else but in "Florent" is "strengthe," defined either as a warrior's power to resist his own death by fighting, or as that inner capacity requisite to holding his "trouthe," in any way examined.[44] Gower, however, suggests consideration of both. His Florent is the most accomplished fighter of the Loathly Lady tales, described as a man of "mochel myhte" (CA I.1412) and getting into trouble initially because of it. "Feihtende [with] his oghne hondes" he slew Branchus, who was "of his hond / The worthieste of al his lond" (CA I.1427–28; 1431–32)—and this while purposely prowling "the Marches al aboute" (CA I.1417), not hunting unarmed, as in the analogues, but on the lookout for just the kind of reputation-building combat with a worthy opponent that he finds in Branchus.[45] Florent's formidability is acknowledged by his captors, who have overwhelmed him "be strengthe," presumably of numbers (CA I.1422), but fear to kill him outright for three reasons: "his worthinesse / Of knyhthod and of gentilesse, / And how he stod of cousinage / To themperour" (CA I.1435–38). Gentility excepted, this is a list of bellicose "strengths": an attempt on Florent's life would be dangerous for what "his worthinesse" might achieve alone (he has, after all, killed Branchus, the doughtiest knight in the land, alone in a fair fight) and for the army of warriors his uncle would muster in revenge.

It is therefore through his gentility (i.e., good breeding, evidence of which is keeping "trouthe") that the "grantdame" (CA I.1445) perceives a means to neutralize Florent's combat potential. How she describes her plan is significant: she will "him to dethe winne / Al only of his oghne grant, / Thurgh strengthe of verray covenant" (CA I.1448–50). Like a kind of pernicious jujitsu both verbal and actual, the grantdame's proposition seeks to turn Florent's chief defense —his warrior's prowess—into a weapon against him, essentially by shifting the meaning of the word *strengthe* to a new linguistic field. The transformation is skillfully done. In a trice the dichotomy of the tale is invoked: "mannes [physical] strengthe" versus "Obedience," the inner power to carry through to the end what one has agreed.

Importantly, once the grantdame has shifted fields, the meaning of *strengthe* as it appears in the rest of the tale never reverts to the simply physical. We encounter the word twice more, each an important juncture of the tale. Initially it is when Florent returns to present his answer to "that olde Mone" who rehearses "the *strengthe* of al the covenant" before the assembled court (CA I.1636); the next and final time occurs after Florent and the Hag are married, when it is the "*strengthe* of matrimoine" that overpowers his reluctance to go to bed with her "naked" (CA I.1777, 1781).[46] Both times Gower makes it clear that Florent has the *physical* option to save his life and his body, but chooses the opposite: he "hath levere forto dye / Than breke his trowthe" (CA I.1511–12), implying that he could live by not going back empty-handed; and standing by the bridal bed he rejects leaving by making an "essoine," which Macaulay rightly glosses as "excuse," that he was *not able* to submit to joining her in "bedde of compaignie" (CA I.1779–80).[47] "Essoine" in the context is a telling choice, however. Strictly speaking, it is a legal term, an excuse for nonappearance in court at an appointed time.[48] Gower uses it only here in his extant English *corpus*. (It would be tempting to assume Gower needed a rhyme for "matrimoine" in the following line, but in fact, since this instance is also the only known locus where Gower uses "matrimoine" in English—and in the context "essoine" is so apt—it is likely to have been the other way around.)[49] "Essoine" is the sort of word Gower's legal experience doubtless brought him, and its presence is of a piece with the unusual legalism of the tale. Only in "The Tale of Florent," of all the versions, does the hero think to ask that the question of women's great desire be recorded ("under Seales write," CA I.1474), as proof against subsequent fraud, and only Florent signs a written version of his oath "under his seal" (CA I.1487).[50]

By rejecting the alternatives his physical capacity to be mobile in the world afford him, Florent concedes that for him, too, the meaning of *strengthe*, along with the battlegrounds whereon he must struggle, have shifted inward. No one—certainly neither Hag nor grantdame, nor even the grantdame's people now that he is free again, armed and in the imperial court—can, practically speaking, force him into jeopardy against his will. But of course Florent's lesson, to be obedient (and hence humble, too), is all about the will, requiring a silencing of murmur and complaint of the divided inner man, as well as a stoic performance from the (at least seemingly) composed outer one. On this point Gower's version is the most dramatically delineated of all the

Loathly Lady stories, including Chaucer's. "The Tale of Florent" takes us inside its protagonist's head and heart, not once but five times (i.e., *CA* I.1568–80; 1619–26; 1703–20; 1774–80; 1798–1801) to show him divided against himself, wrestling realistically with alternative solutions, all of them "practical" (e.g., that the Hag, being old, will shortly die, and he soon will be rid of her). In the end, Florent's division is so severe that "His body mihte wel be there, / Bot as of thoght and of memoire / His herte was in purgatoire." Only his determined will forces him at last to turn bodily to the Loathly Hag beside him; his mind, however, is elsewhere, gone "as it were a man in trance."

II

And for this he is rewarded, by the sight at least of the Hag-bride transformed but with, of course, the main catch still to follow. It is important for understanding Gower's purpose here that we try to approach this latter part of the tale the way Gower's readers likely did, essentially unconscious of other versions, and as a fresh story the outcome of which was still unfolding. Otherwise, it is too easy to skip to the familiar main points—Florent gives his wife the choice, this breaks her spell, and they live happily ever after—without noticing how Gower brings us there, word by word.[51] Florent's division, what he calls his "querele" within himself, has so sapped his power to think or act that at last he surrenders both to the once-loathly lady: "O ye, my lyves hele, / Sey what you list in my querele, / I not what ansuere I schal yive" (*CA* I.1821–23). Doing so, he echoes the first expression of unity found in a tale otherwise dominated by images of division, i.e., the lady's plea that he turn around to face her in bed, "'For now,' sche seith, 'we ben bothe on'" (*CA* I.1793). Florent's wish to make that come true prompts him to decision: "Thus grante I yow myn hole vois, / Ches for us bothen" (*CA* I.1828–29). For the first time since his ordeal began, Florent's quarreling inner voices are silenced at the prospect of reintegration. "Bothe on," the two will speak with a single "vois," and by this at last grow "hole."

The aptness of Florent's synecdoche of voice for self at the resolution of an exemplum opposing "Murmur and Complaint," both sins of speech, has been commented upon at least once in the past; but since *voice* is among the words of greatest significance in Gower's trilingual vocabulary, its presence here rewards a closer look.[52] It is surprising to find how often, when one examines the *loci* in his French, Latin, and English poetry, Gower uses *voice* to convey social or apocalyptic meaning.[53] To be sure, neutral examples can be cited, when *voice* means an individual's utterance, e.g., "Musique, / That techeth upon Armonie / A man to make melodie / Be vois and soun of instrument" (CA VIII.164–67) or "A basse vois tantost me dirra, 'nay'" (*Cinkante Balades* XVII.21). But—if frequency of usage be any guide—most of the time when the word *voice* occurred to Gower, it was in a context either political, or to describe divine involvement amidst human affairs. In French, for example, where Gower uses *vois/voix* twenty-six times in many thousands of lines, twenty-one times it is in one or both of those contexts—for Gower the political and the apocalyptic being often the same thing.[54] In his Latin poetry, *vox* is more common, and in contexts covering the full range of meaning. To draw firm conclusions, every instance should be looked at—a task, in the absence of a Latin concordance, as yet beyond our scope.[55] Short of that, however (and sufficient, perhaps, for present purposes) three observations suggest that the same strong association of "voice" with politics and a divine will may have existed for Gower in Latin, too. First, instances of *vox* occur preponderantly in Book I of the *Vox Clamantis*, the so-called "Visio" section describing the Peasants' Revolt, and sporadically elsewhere. (In Gower's shorter works, for example, *vox* in any form appears only three times, all in the poem "O Deus Immense," where each time, true to pattern, it means "the voice of the common people.")[56] In the *Vox Clamantis*, at the height of the bloodbath Gower describes in his dream of peasants trans-formed into beasts—passages most extremely "political" of all his writings, perhaps—*vox* clusters prominently, as the rebels-turned-animals are character-ized extensively by their terrible "voices."[57] Second, there is Gower's choice of title—*Vox Clamantis*—for this most "messianic" political poem, purposefully relating it to the warnings of John the Baptist, whom Isaiah (40:3) described as "vox clamantis in deserto."[58] And third, more importantly perhaps, there is in consequence his pointed claim to be himself the renewed "voice" of both the Baptist and John of Patmos and the Apocalypse, with the Holy Ghost solicited as his muse.[59] As Maria Wickert pointed out many years ago, Gower carefully situated himself, defining his narrative stance at the jointure of divine inspiration and political reality, to speak in the *Vox* both as inspired preacher and as descriptor and censor of social conditions and public opinion.[60] It was a stance he maintained throughout his Latin works; indeed, most of the instances of *vox*, when they are not politically charged references to the Peasants' Revolt, or expressions of the divine will, are captured in versions of "vox populi."[61] This is also true in his French work—and of his English, as, for example, in the Prologue to the *Confessio Amantis*:[62]

The world is changed overal,
And therof most in special
That love is falle into discord.
And that I take to record
Of every lond for his partie
The comun vois, which may noght lie.
                    (lines 119–24)

In fact, of the forty-three instances of *vois* in the *Confessio*, eleven are cases of "comun vois" or related forms, thirteen describe direct utterances of the divine, with five more implicitly expressed.[63]

None of this of course is evidence that the appearance of *vois* defines "The Tale of Florent" as political critique. Sometimes *vois* simply meant "voice" for Gower, as it did for everyone else. What the high statistical incidence of political and/or apocalyptic contexts in all three of Gower's languages *does* indicate, however, is a latent association of *voice* in Gower's mind with extreme political conditions requiring radical change, often effectible only by divine intervention.[64] Telling in this regard too may be the classical context Gower has so carefully prepared for the tales of the *Confessio Amantis*, Book I, including especially "Florent," which, as we have seen, he very likely found in an Arthurian source and consciously altered its venue to Rome. Gower apparently followed an identical strategy for the "Visio" in Book I of the *Vox Clamantis*—a part of that poem he may well have been writing just before, or simultaneously with, the first book of the *Confessio*.[65] The dream of the "Visio" converts contemporary England to Homeric times, renaming London "New Troy" and confining its many allusions, comparisons, and illustrative examples to Greek myth and history as Gower found them retold by Ovid. Moreover, particularly often in the *Vox Clamantis*, Book I, Gower turns to *cento*—the direct relocation of lines from his classical sources into new contexts in his poem—to further "classicize" his work for those readers who, like himself, had much of Ovid, at least, by heart.[66]

So the presence of *vois* here, as the term chosen to serve at the moment when Florent and the Hag-bride become "bothe on," thereby reuniting his divided mind and body, and—by breaking the spell cast upon her by her "Stepmoder for an hate" (*CA* I.1844)—effectively reuniting the lady with her rightful body, as well, may, along with the classicizing of this and the other tales of *Confessio*, Book I, provide us signposts toward the secondary political discourse of "The Tale of Florent." If so, we should look once more at Gower's use of *strengthe* as an even more obvious part of the process.

Strengthe, as we have seen, changes primary meanings as the tale plays out. If at first it means "physical prowess of a knight," by the end it stands for "power to carry out a promise"—a shift, in other words, from an exterior attribute to an interior one, from an act of arms to an act of will.[67] Notably Florent's decision to accept the Hag-bride's "sovereinete" (CA I.1847) renders him no less armigerously powerful than he was at first, when he slew Branchus. His "knihthode" in that sense is still intact. What *has* been demonstrated, however, is that strength of arm is not enough, neither to create a "hol" man, nor (we cannot avoid this suggestion, given the preparation Gower has made in the Prologue to connect micro- and macrocosms, the individual with the state) a peaceful and unified England from the one Gower inhabited, riven severely in the 1380s and early 1390s, replete with "Inobedience," rife with "murmur and complainte." The political message of "The Tale of Florent" is, then, on one level, that the knightly class has only to gain by ceding sovereignty to where it rightly belongs.

Here it is tempting to refine Gower's critique still further by interpreting Florent's chivalric status as indication that his class is the sole target of the tale. There is much to be said for this reading, certainly. It accords with Gower's general anti-militarism, his opposition to the French war (and consequently to the nobles who squandered public funds on it), and his distaste for the moral laxities of chivalric romance, whence the source for "Florent" no doubt came.[68] Moreover, if Gower were writing "The Tale of Florent" during or after the Appellants' Revolt of 1387–88, the need for a renunciation of inobediently employed armigerous "strengthe" and an acceptance of "sovereinete" would have a particular currency and edge, both for Gower and his readers. During this period, despite Gower's close ties with the Lancastrian house (which in any case took no leading role in the proceedings), there is little evidence that his attitude toward Richard II had turned rebellious, no more than had John of Gaunt's.[69] The sovereign endowment of the king, at least by Gower, apparently remained unquestioned. All the more reason, then, amidst the especially parlous uncertainties of those years, when the king's supporters (among them the poet Thomas Usk, friend to Chaucer and undoubtedly Gower too) were variously stripped of their possessions and exiled, imprisoned, and/or executed after summary trials under Appellant sanction, to read "The Tale of Florent" as a scarcely veiled rebuke to the Appellants and their cohort: it makes sense of Gower's search for a deep structure to present his critique in the first place.[70]

Nonetheless such a reading is, in the end, unhelpfully reductive. After composing tens of thousands of lines in French and Latin bluntly enumerating the damage done to society by the abuses of all three estates, Gower should be taken at his word, I think, that in the *Confessio Amantis* he was adopting an entirely different poetic approach, albeit without abandoning any of his familiar views.[71] If the world is tumultuous and threatening, the result of "division"—"Division, the gospell seith / On hous upon another leith, / Til that the Regne al overthrowe" (CA Pro. 966–68)—then the operant principle in the *Confessio* is reunification of all parts divided; so also is its goal. In consequence, in his English poem he submerges, but does not abandon, the familiar critique by estate—a separation which is in itself divisive—in favor of narrative exempla with the potential to address human failures common to every class. Hence the lesson of "Florent" is not merely a directive to the knightly caste. Given the extraordinary vehemence of Gower's outrage in the first book of the *Vox Clamantis*, it is impossible to imagine that the Rising of 1381 was not still vivid in his memory as he worked on the *Confessio* a few years later. The political applicability of "The Tale of Florent" extends to all whose Pride has led to Murmur and Complaint, and outright Inobedience to established sovereign rule.

What might provide us one more indication of Gower's hopes for an embracing political exemplarity in "Florent"—what may, indeed, have drawn him to the tale in the first place, when he sought but seldom among romances for poetic material—is the Loathly Lady figure herself. At the beginning, assuming its origins have indeed been correctly identified as Irish, the lady's transformation from hag to beauty was inextricably associated with issues of right rule and appropriate sovereignty.[72] In those earliest Irish versions, the Loathly Lady is no person, but an embodiment of Sovereignty itself, her request for a kiss in exchange for a drink of water a test of worthiness to rule, and her conversion to beauty an acknowledgment that the rightful king has been found.[73] Of course Gower never saw such versions—nor could he have read the Irish if he had.[74] But there clearly is vestigial in all the Loathly Lady narratives, in the idea that paradoxically willing obedience (the young warrior Níall not merely kissing the hag, but avidly embracing her when his three brothers have spurned her) reaps transformation and a liberating sovereignty in return, a political imperative deeply recessed to which Gower responded in his tale and turned to hand in his critique of contemporary English conditions.[75] Indeed, Gower's attention to such an element would seem to be quite strong: only in "Florent" of all the analogues is the Loathly Lady of royal blood—"the kinges dowther of Cizile" (line 1841). By passing her test and wedding her, Florent, precisely like Níall in the Irish tale, may come into a kingdom—a circumstance possibly circumstantial, but also possibly not.[76]

What may have drawn Gower's notice further are certain qualities of "plasticity" and "liminality" that Louise O. Fradenburg has identified in the public presence of medieval queens—qualities shared as well by the Irish figure of Sovereignty and the Loathly Lady, that establish for them all a "particularly intense association with the concepts both of division and of unity" in the state.[77] For Fradenburg, the rituals of queen-making are shape-shifting carried out on the level of spectacle.[78] Usually foreign-born and initially foreign in appearance and custom, queens acquired sovereignty via a process of "naturalization"—the complete transformation of their (sharply undesirable) "otherness" into the familiar and local through clothing change, altered hairstyles, and the substitution of emblematized equipage.[79]

Whether Gower made the connection between the roots in Irish sovereignty myth of the shape-shifting Loathly Lady in his unknown source and the transformative rituals of queenly coronation is of course beyond demonstration. Nevertheless, the process of making queens was performative and public. As a London resident Gower would have witnessed it three times: in 1396, when Richard II married Isabella of Valois; in 1372, with the marriage of John of Gaunt to Constanza of Castile, through which he assumed the royal title; and (more significantly, given the proximate date of composition of Book I of the *Confessio*) in 1382, when Richard married Anne of Bohemia. And, given that the process was heavily indebted to exchanges of queenly clothing and coiffure, it may be meaningful that in "The Tale of Florent" alone of the Loathly Lady group, significant attention (seventeen lines, 1742–59) is paid to precisely those things.[80] The "prive women" come from the court, strip off the hag's "ragges," bathe her, re-dress her "with such atyr as tho was used," and with "craft of combes brode" re-style the "hore lockes" which—in a move enhancing her miraculous emergence as a beauty at the appropriate time—she refuses to have "schore," steadfastly and without explanation preferring the "alien" style of her arrival.[81]

If, then, Gower found in the rituals of queenship valuable analogies to elements of sovereignty in his source, he might have anticipated similar responses in his readership, and crafted "Florent" to evoke them. In any case, beginning the *Confessio Amantis*, with or without a charge from his king, in the 1380s, replete as those years were with challenges to rightful rule from mob and baron both, Gower's sensitivity to whatever wider treatment of sovereignty must have been in his source is scarcely surprising. That he sought to convey something of that through his language, choosing words such as *strengthe* and *vois* with thoughtful care, is characteristic of his poetic practice, as well.

NOTES

1. *Confessio Amantis* I.583 (hereafter cited as CA, by book and line number); that is, Hypocrisy, Inobedience, Surquidry (or Presumption), Avantance (or Boasting), and Vain-Glory. All citations of Gower's work are taken from the edition of G. C. Macaulay, *Works*; "The Tale of Florent" appears in volume 2 of this edition. Citations of *Vox Clamantis* appear as VC; citations of *Mirour de l'Omme* as MO.

2. That is, if source studies and comparisons of "The Tale of Florent" with "The Wife of Bath's Tale" are excepted. For an accessible and annotated overview of criticism through 1989, see Peter Nicholson, *Annotated Index*, pp. 132–50.

3. The description is Russell Peck's; see *Kingship and Common Profit*, pp. 46–47.

4. The "different purposes" of "Florent" and the "WBT" are well presented by Beidler, "Transformations." See further Nicholson, "'Confession.'"

5. Not all readers would agree, particularly about Amans: see for example Boitani, *English Metrical Narrative*. For a recent, full-blown allegorical reading, see Simpson, *Sciences and the Self*.

6. Most current opinion has Chaucer borrowing at least some elements from Gower: see for example Fisher, *John Gower*, pp. 202–25, 292, and 296–97; Pearsall, *Canterbury Tales*, p. 87; and Hilary in her notes to the "WBT" in *Riverside Chaucer*, pp. 872–74. An impassioned case for Gower's primacy is made by Lindeboom, *Chaucer's Testament*.

7. As Macaulay has observed, Gower did not rely solely on Ovid for these narratives; other likely sources include Boccaccio's *De Genealogia Deorum*. See *Works*, 2:467–68, note to line 389. All titles of Gower's individual stories used in this essay are Macaulay's.

8. See Macaulay, *Works*, 2:468, note to line 463.

9. Macaulay, *Works*, 2:468, note to line 483.

10. Macaulay, *Works*, 2: 470, note to line 761, cites Josephus as the original, with versions borrowed successively by Hegesippus, Vincent of Beauvais, and Gower. Gower's knowledge of Hegesippus, however, is improbable, and there was no need for him to go to Vincent, as all the elements here are present in Josephus, whose work he knew; see Josephus, *Jewish Antiquities*, 9:51–59. See also Macaulay's note to line 940.

11. Macaulay, *Works*, 2:471, note to line 1077.

12. Macaulay, *Works*, 2:474, note to line 1980.

13. Macaulay, *Works*, 2:474, note to line 2021, proposes the *Vita Barlaam et Josaphat* as the most probable source.

14. Macaulay, *Works*, 2:474–75, note to line 2275.

15. Macaulay, *Works*, 2:476–77, note to line 2459, cites Paul the Deacon, *Gesta Langobardorum*, 2.28.

16. Daniel 4:33–37.

17. Macaulay, *Works*, 2:478, note to line 3153.

18. See *CA* I.759; line 1404; line 1994; line 3388.

19. That is, *CA* I.761; line 1407; line 2023; line 3390.

20. "Florencius tunc Imperatoris Claudi Nepos," opposite *CA* I.1407, margin (in Oxford MS Fairfax 3, on which Macaulay's edition is based). See Macaulay, *Works*, 2:74.

21. *CA* Pro. 595–662.

22. On the idea of necessary "auctoritas" for serious poetry, see Minnis, *Medieval Theory*, ch. 6, "Literary Theory and Literary Practice," pp. 160–210, with special reference to Gower, pp. 177–90, and further, Minnis, "*De vulgari auctoritate*," pp. 36–74.

23. Since the Latin of the *Confessio*, both verse and prose, does not always replicate the English narration, it has been suggested both that the apparatus is variously ironic, and/or not by Gower's hand. There is, however, no reasonable alternative to Gower's authorship of the Latin as well as the English, and his irony, when and if present, is simply directive in an indirect way.

24. See Minnis's discussion, *Medieval Theory*, pp. 9–72, on prologues to academic and scriptural *auctores*; and further, see Wetherbee, "Latin Structure," pp. 7–35. On what seem to have been Gower's ideas for page layout, to connect the *Confessio* with the works of *auctores* visually, see Yeager, "English, Latin, and the Text as 'Other.'"

25. As James Simpson has noted, "the amatory narratives of the *Confessio* tend inevitably to resuscitate the political discourse that the Prologue had dismissed"; see *Reform*, p. 220; and further, see his discussion of "The Elegiac" (ch. 4), especially pp. 134–46.

26. That is, Oxford Bodley MS Fairfax 3, Macaulay's base text, and "Stafford" (Huntington MS Ellesmere 26.A 17). It is called "Henrician" because in a wholly political move it is dedicated to "Henry of Lancaster" (*CA* Pro. 81–92), replacing Richard II, all references to whom have been removed.

27. That is, a "clerk of coarse cloth," or simple learning. The description is the sort of humility gesture his readers would have expected.

28. "Tempus preteritum presens fortuna beatum / Linquit, et aniquas vertit in orbe vias. / Progenuit veterem concors dileccio pacem, / Dum facies hominis nuncia mentis erat: / Legibus vnicolor tunc temporis aura refulsit, / Iusticie plane tuncque vultum depingit amoris; / Paceque sub ficta tempus ad arma tegit; / Instar et ex variis mutabile Cameliontis / Lex gerit, et regnis sunt noua iura nouis: / Climata que fuerant solidissima sicque per orbem / Soluuntur, nec eo centra quietis habent." The translation is that of Siân Echard and Claire Fanger; see *Latin Verses*, pp. 4–7.

29. See Fisher, *John Gower*, pp. 58–69, and appendix C, pp. 313–18, for Gower's legal history.

30. "[F]ingens se auctor esse Amantem": Gower's description of his practice in Latin prose lines commenting on *CA* I.60.

31. For example, Alfonso IV ruled Portugal until 1357, followed by his son Pedro I (1357–67), followed by João I of Aviz, who married Philippa, daughter of John of Gaunt in 1387; Alfonso XI ruled Castile until 1350, followed by his son Pedro I

(1350–69), whose daughters Constanza married John of Gaunt and Isabel his younger brother, Edmund of Langley; Gaunt's daughter Katherine by Constanza married Enrique III of Castile in 1388. Major English military expeditions were carried out in Iberia by Edward Black Prince (1366), Edmund of Langley (1381), and Gaunt (1387).

32. On the program for manuscript illustrations of Nebuchadnezzar's Dream, see Jeremy Griffiths, "*Confessio Amantis:* The Poem."

33. See n. 19, above, and further Yeager, "English, Latin and the Text."

34. The major English analogues are, in addition to the "WBT," "The Marriage of Sir Gawaine" (a ballad), "The Weddynge of Sir Gawen and Dame Ragnell" (a metrical romance), "King Henry" (a ballad), and "The Knight and the Shepherd's Daughter" (a ballad). See discussions by Maynadier, *Wife of Bath's Tale*; Sumner, *Weddynge of Sir Gawen*, pp. xiii–xxvi; Eisner, *Tale of Wonder*; and Ackerman, "English Rimed and Prose Romances."

35. Assessments of Gower's originality are offered by, among others, Wickert, *Studien zu John Gower*; Nicholson, "The 'Confession,'" pp. 193–204; and Yeager, *John Gower's Poetic*, pp. 123–24 and 137–40.

36. "De Lancelot si fuissetz remembré, / Et de Tristrans, com il se contenoit, / Generides, Florent, Partonopé, / Chascun de ceaux sa loialté guardoit." See Macaulay, *Works*, 1:372.

37. On the *Confessio* as a political poem, see Fisher, *John Gower:* "the subject of the *Confessio Amantis* is moral and political instruction in a ratio of about eight to five"; p. 189 and passim; Minnis, "John Gower: *Sapiens*," pp. 207–29; Olsson, *John Gower*, pp.79–82; and Simpson, n. 25, above.

38. See Dyer, "Social and Economic Background," pp. 9–42, and generally Hilton, *Bondmen Made Free*, and Dobson, *Peasant's Revolt*.

39. For events of the period see generally McKisack, *Fourteenth Century*, and Saul, *Richard II*.

40. On Chaucer's inclusion of rape in the "WBT," see the differing views of Huppé, "Rape and Woman's Sovereignty"; Dinshaw, *Chaucer's Sexual Poetics*; and Hansen, *Chaucer and the Fictions*; and further, Gravdal, "Camouflaging Rape."

41. On the commons' complaints, over liveries and other abuses, see Tuck, "Nobles, Commons and the Great Revolt," and further, Saul, *Richard II*, pp. 263–64.

42. For Gower's pacifist views, see Yeager, "*Pax Poetica.*"

43. Gaunt maintained his fealty to Richard to the end, remaining supportive when others, including his son, turned against the king; Bolingbroke, of course, solved his differences with Richard over obedience—rather as Alexander is said to have treated the Gordian knot—with the sword. On Gaunt see especially Armitage-Smith, *John of Gaunt*, pp. 341–57.

44. A conceivable exception is *Sir Gawain and the Green Knight*, but it is not strictly speaking an analogue of "Florent," though it offers interesting opportunities for comparison.

45. "King Henry" and "The Marriage of Sir Gawen and Dame Ragnell" begin with hunts; Maynadier, *Wife of Bath's Tale*, pp. 16–17, cites the "WBT" as another such, "though here we have only a knight who has been hawking;" he remarks as well that "Probably we should find the same incident in *The Marriage of Sir Gawaine*, if we had this complete." Gower has it: "And for the fame of worldes speche, / Strange aventures forto seche, / He rod the Marches al aboute" (1414–17).

46. Walter S. Phelan has called attention to the contractual similarities in Gower's use of the phrases "strengthe of covenant" and "strengthe of matremoine"; see "Beyond the Concordance," pp. 461–79, especially p. 473.

47. See Macaulay, *Works*, 3:585, s.v. "essoine." Gower's phrasing is "That he ne mot algates plie / To gon to bedde of compaignie," in which "ne mot" must carry the sense of inability, unspecified.

48. See Kurath and Kuhn, *Middle English Dictionary*, s.v. "essoine," (n), 1 (a) and 2: "any excuse or any offering of grounds for hindering or delaying action," and further, s.v. "essoinen," (v), "to excuse a person for non-appearance in court."

49. See Pickles and Dawson, *Concordance*, s.v. "essoine" and "matrimoine." Gower uses "matrimoine" and variations frequently in French, and "essoine" three times; see Yeager, West, and Hinson, *Concordance*.

50. On the legal substructures unique to "Florent," see Fisher, *John Gower*, p. 195.

51. It is important to notice, for example, that of all the known versions of the Loathly Lady's answer, only Gower's connects women's sovereignty specifically with love ("wommen lievest wolde / Be soverein of mannes love," lines 1608–9)—a point with some psychological significance. See n. 67, below.

52. See Gallacher, *Love, the Word and Mercury*, p. 90.

53. Phelan, "Beyond the Concordance," has argued for taking close account of "the variety of personal associations which an important word accumulates as the author chooses time and again in a given work." Clearly, in the case of Gower, the trilingual evidence supports much more strongly the conclusion that "the repetition of the same word in a given context reinforces the original associations and carries to the reader, unconsciously or otherwise, the context of the preceding passage" (p. 462). Phelan draws his language and theoretical matrix from the computer-aided study of Pollio, *Structural Basis*, pp. 12–14.

54. See Yeager, West, and Hinson, *Concordance*, s.v. "vois" and "voix."

55. I base my conclusions on studies preliminary to producing a full concordance of Gower's Latin poetry, a project I have now sufficiently underway to feel some confidence in the preliminary conclusions above.

56. That is, "Plebis et audire voces per easque redire" (line 54); "Nomen regale populi vox dat tibi, quale" (line 61); "Ad vocem plebis aures sapientur habebis" (line 64); see also "de clamore populi" (line 56).

57. For example, *VC* I.543–44: "Clamat vt infernos, superatque tonitrua vocis / Horrida terribilis eius ab ore sonus." A vivid example is the description of Watte Tyler as a jaybird (*graculus*, with a play on *watte* as English slang for "jay"): I.691–92: "Arboris

in summum conscendit, et oris aperti / Voce suis paribus talia verba refert;" I.701–5: "Singula turba silet, notat et sibi verba loquentis, / Et placet edictum quicquid ab ore tulit: / Vocibus ambiguis deceptam prebuit aurem;" I.711–12: "Vocis in excessu reliquos sic commouet omnes / Graculus"; I.717–24: "Auribus extensis quemcumque vocat furor ille / Audit, et ad vocem concitus vrget iter: / Sic homo tunc multus suadente furore coactus / Sepe suam posuit mestus in igne manum. / Omnes, 'Fiat ita,' proclamant vocibus altis; / Ex nimio strepitu concussus vocis eorum / Vix potui tremulos ammodo ferre pedes." Chapter 9 offers another: "Watte vocat, cui Thomme venit, neque Symme retardat;" I.797: Sepius exclamant monstrorum vocibus altis;" I.806: "Dumque canum discors vox furibunda volat;" I.816: "Vox ita terribilis non fuit vlla prius." Perhaps the contiguity of "vox" forms to the extreme cacophony of animal sounds described in these passages should be taken into account, as well. Suggestive too are the onomatopoeic grunts, roars, bellows, etc. all very pointedly, perhaps, not deemed "voices;" e.g., I.799–820.

58. "Messianic" is borrowed from Stockton, *Major Latin Works*, p. 11.

59. Gower names himself in an acronym (VC Pro. 21–24); solicits John of Patmos, "whose name [he] bears," to "govern" ("gubernet") his writing (VC Pro. 57–58); and invokes the Holy Ghost and explains that he calls the work *Vox Clamantis* because "it was conceived … by a voice crying over all things" ("Vox Clamantis, quia de voce et clamore quasi omnium conceptus est," VC II.Pro. [prose introduction]).

60. Wickert, *Studien zu John Gower*: see especially ch. 3, "*Vox Clamantis* und die mittelalterliche Predigt," pp. 65–109.

61. For example, "vox populi" (VC VI.577), "vox communis" (VC Pro.55), "in specie vox plebis" (VC VI.545), "in plebe vox est" (VC VI.1179).

62. For example, "Au vois commune est accordant" (MO, line 12725), "Sicomme dist la commune vois" (MO, line 22248), and—particularly interesting—"La vois commune dieus oya" (MO, line 10318)].

63. For example, CA Pro. 124; I.2832; I.2901; II.879; II.2874; II.3488; V.995; V.1155; V.1721; V.2351; V.2371; V.5674; VI.426; VII.2329; VII.2643; VI.2661; VII.3752; VII.3767; VII.4034; VII.4123; VII.4721; VIII.780; VIII.1342; VIII.2728. What I call "implicit" expressions are IV.3045 (Ithecus, servant of Morpheus, "which hath the vois of every soun"); V.1626 (each of the Israelites before Moses returns with the law, "A god, to whom he yaf his vois"); and VII.3060 (Foroneus, who receives Roman law from God, "Foroneus hath thilke vois"). Perhaps the two most interesting are in Book I, both describing the "vois" of the sirens singing together as "Like to the melodye of hevene" (I.494–95) which the dazzled sailors "wene it be a Paradys" (I.501–2).

64. What I am suggesting finds an analogy in Freudian descriptions of repression: see *Repression* (1915), in Strachey, *Standard Ed.*, 14:143–58, especially the concepts "repression proper" (p. 148) and the disappearance of "the idea" (p. 153); and further, *Psychopathology*, pp. 191–216, on "Symptomatic and Chance Actions." The resistance generative of the repression is political, not sexual—but Freud affirmed repression as

a commodious concept, extending beyond the merely sexual; see "A Child Is Being Beaten" (1919), *Standard Ed.*, 17:200

65. The problem of knowing when, specifically, Gower wrote anything is probably beyond solution. Early attempts by Macaulay (in the introductions to his editions), Tatlock (for the *Mirour de l'Omme*, see his *Development*, pp. 220–25), and Fisher, *John Gower*, pp. 70–134, have set the generally agreed-upon ranges for Gower's efforts. Where they differ usually is about when Gower might have begun each work (or, in the case of the ballade sequences, whether they were written together—as is probably true of the eighteen poems of the *Traitié pour les amantz marietz*—or off and on over a period of years); but at last the question turns upon Gower's revising habits. How much can we assume Gower interpolated back into "finished" passages? Uncertainty on this point clouds attempts to date the course of writing of very long poems by one or two topical references.

66. For example, VC I.349–51; 355–56: "Tegia silua ferum talem non protulit aprum, / Quamuis in Archadia maximus ille fuit: / Non ita commouit in montibus Herculis iram.... / Non aper ille ferox, agitabat quem Meleager / In memorum latebris"; I.441–48: "Dumque canis rabidi sumpsit mutate figuram, / Ipsa dolens Hecuba non ita seua fuit, / Quin magis in canibus istis furit ira, que morsus / Figere quo poterant singula membra terunt. / Tale canes, Cadmi qui dilaniare nepotem / Acteon instabant, non coluere nephas. / Ille gigas Gereon ingens, Hispannia dudum / Quem genuit." These tales are borrowed from Ovid's *Metamorphoses*. On Gower's use of *cento*, see Yeager, "Did Gower Write *Cento*?" pp. 113–32.

67. Psychologically, Florent's shift from reliance on the purely physical to inner strength evinces maturity achieved through struggle; see Neumann, "Psychic Development," pp. 57–161, whose comments apply not only to the transformation of the hag ("she reunites herself ... with the feminine in her nature. And because she does this lovingly, and for Eros, her 'old' femininity enters into a new phase. It no longer consists of the self-contained beauty of a young girl.... It is the beauty of a woman in love, who wishes to be beautiful for the beloved, for Eros, and no one else" [p. 123]) but to Florent also ("Through Psyche's sacrifice and death the divine lover is changed from a wounded boy to a man and savior, because in Psyche he finds ... the feminine mystery of rebirth through love" [p. 125]).

68. See Yeager, "*Pax Poetica*," and on Gower's somewhat complex attitudes toward romances, *John Gower's Poetic*, pp. 89–92.

69. Gower's change of mind about Richard is variously dated, from as early as 1390 (see Stow, "Richard II in John Gower's *Confessio Amantis*"), to roughly mid-decade (Nicholson, "Dedications"), to, most recently, after the usurpation in 1399 (Jones, Yeager, Dolan, Fletcher, and D'Or, *Who Murdered Chaucer?*).

70. The poet Usk was tried, condemned, and beheaded in a single day, as was former London mayor Nicholas Brembre. The king's favorites, Robert de Vere, Michael de la Pole, earl of Suffolk, both of whom fled to avoid execution, and Alexander Neville, archbishop of York, died in exile, as did Thomas Rushook, bishop

of Chichester and the king's confessor. The chamber knights Sir Simon Burley, Sir John Beauchamp, Sir John Salisbury, and Sir James Berners were executed despite, in Burley's case, the pleading of the queen on her knees. Chief Justice Robert Tresilian was dragged out of sanctuary at Westminster Abbey and beheaded. See Saul, *Richard II*, pp. 191–94.

71. That is, "Forthi the Stile of my writings / Fro this day forth I thenke change," etc.; see *CA* I.1–16.

72. On the Irish versions, and the Loathly Lady as Sovereignty, see Eisner, *Tale of Wonder*, pp. 31–44. Although elaborate guesses have been offered to explain how the early Celtic narrative could have made its way to England (see especially Maynadier, *Wife of Bath's Tale*, pp. 80–109), the transmission would have been oral, and Gower as far as we know worked almost always—if not exclusively—from written source texts. On the other hand, lacking any clear source but assuming an as-yet unknown French romance, the door must be left a little ajar to the possibility that in that source something remained of the early Irish Lady-Sovereignty association. As Eisner notes (p. 44), "As the tale was retold in Wales, Brittany, France, and finally England, some motifs were unchanged, while others were altered." Not all agree, however, with Eisner's derivation from "Níall of the Nine Hostages": Lindeboom, *Chaucer's Testament*, examines a variety of folk motifs (pp. 172–78); and see further Hartwell, *Wedding*, who argues for Low Countries influence.

73. See the discussion by Byrne, *Irish Kings*, pp. 70–86.

74. Irish versions exist in manuscript from the eleventh century; see Joynt, "Echtra mac Echdach Mugmedóin," pp. 91–111, especially pp. 101–7. Interesting Irish-English interchanges involving women, power, and miraculous transformation include abbess lives composed ca. 1100–1300: Bridget of Ireland in the *South English Legendary*, and Modwenna of Burton-on-Trent. Modwenna "is a legendary composite of several Irish figures from different centuries" whose life circulated in Latin and Anglo-Norman versions; see Wogan-Browne, "Queens, Virgins and Mothers" (qtd. on p. 23), and further Legge, *Anglo-Norman in the Cloisters*, pp. 44–45. Also of interest in regard to Gower's source is Carl Lindahl's opinion that it may have been oral; see "Oral Undertone." If that were the case, Gower could have heard a version in which the Loathly Lady figure preserved Irish elements in a new context.

75. It is a politics to which Chaucer also responded, if to a lesser degree. I have in mind here the Loathly Lady's excursus on gentility, uncomeliness, and honest poverty in the "WBT" (*Riverside Chaucer*, ed. Benson, lines 1106–1218).

76. In direct contrast is Chaucer's insistence that the hag is poor; but that insistence itself may acknowledge awareness of a royal figure in his source.

77. See Fradenberg, "Introduction: Rethinking Queenship," pp. 1–13; on plasticity, see p. 1, n. 1, especially the definition borrowed from Roberto Mangabeira Unger, as "practical opportunism and flexible work relations" carried out with "stratagems of imagination and activity"; on "what we might call 'liminal' figures—marginal to official institutions and practices of authority, though in various

ways embedded within them, or made symbolic of them" (p. 5), she borrows profitably from Victor Turner.

78. In *Sacrifice Your Love*, Fradenburg remarks further: "The value of female sovereignty as, so to speak, a means of getting attention was immense in the later Middle Ages. As aristocratic communities valorized ever more intensely the riskiness of the prestige union, the consort bore ever more clearly the value of distinctiveness, of difference from the community over which she was to reign. And yet what was at stake was precisely the conversion of her heterogeneity into an asset for homogeneity. At a time when political communities were groupifying—one might say 'nationalizing'—queens, as 'outsiders,' could represent unities transcending the realm's internal divisions. Love for that she who, *because* of her differences, could both represent the nation's status as sublime object, and be the sublime object *for* the nation, was developed partly through pageants of mourning like *The Book of the Duchess*" (p. 109). Influenced by such a mental set, reception of the Loathly Lady's eventual power garbed in such extraordinary difference of shape and feature seems both predictable and arresting.

79. See further two other essays in *Women and Sovereignty*, "Ritual and Symbol," and Zanger, "Fashioning the Body Politic."

80. Chaucer has—suggestively—only "Now wolden som men seye, paraventure, / That for my necligence I do no cure / To tellen yow the joye and al th'array / That at the feeste was that ilke day" (lines 1073–76).

81. Suggestive too of Gower's possible awareness of a Loathly Lady–queenly sovereignty resemblance is the insistence in "The Tale of Florent" (and in none of the analogues) on the nocturnal translations of the bride-to-be from the countryside into Florent's castle, and then to the wedding itself (lines 1725–32; line 1761). The contrast with the spectacle created for a new queen's entry into London is complete, and hints at purposive reversal. For Anne of Bohemia's arrival, see *The Brut*, 2:338–39, and Kipling, "Richard II's 'Sumptuous Pageants,'" p. 88. Compare with the entry of Constanza of Castile: see *Anonimalle Chronicle*, p. 69, and also the discussion of Russell, *English Intervention*, p. 175 and n. 1. An extremely perceptive reading of the "transformation" of Isabella of Valois at Ardres in 1396 from French princess to English queen, through the medium of the departed Anne of Bohemia, is given by Susan Crane: see her chapter, "Talking Garments," in *Performance of Self*, especially pp. 26–27.

WORKS CITED

Ackerman, Robert W. "The English Rimed and Prose Romances." In *Arthurian Literature in the Middle Ages: A Collaborative History*, ed. Roger Sherman Loomis, pp. 501–5. Oxford: Clarendon Press, 1959.

Anonimalle Chronicle: 1331–1381, ed. V. H. Galbraith. London: Longmans; Manchester: Green University of Manchester Press, 1927.

Armitage-Smith, Sydney. *John of Gaunt, King of Castile and Leon, Duke of Aquitaine and Lancaster, Earl of Derby, Lincoln and Leicester, Seneschal of England.* London: Constable, 1904.

Beidler, Peter, G. "Transformations in Gower's 'Tale of Florent' and Chaucer's 'Wife of Bath's Tale.'" In *Chaucer and Gower,* ed. Yeager, pp. 100–114.

Benson, Larry D., gen. ed., *The Riverside Chaucer.* Boston: Houghton Mifflin, 1987.

Boitani, Piero. *English Metrical Narrative in the Thirteenth and Fourteenth Centuries.* Trans. Joan Krakover Hall. Cambridge: Cambridge University Press, 1982.

The Brut, or The Chronicles of England. 2 vols. Ed. F. W. D. Brie. EETS, o.s. 136. London: Trübner, 1908.

Byrne, Francis John. *Irish Kings and High-Kings.* London: Batsford, 1973.

Crane, Susan. *The Performance of Self: Ritual, Clothing and Identity During the Hundred Years' War.* Philadelphia: University of Pennsylvania Press, 2002.

Dinshaw, Carolyn. *Chaucer's Sexual Poetics.* Madison: University of Wisconsin Press, 1989.

Dobson, R. B. *The Peasant's Revolt of 1381.* 2nd ed. London: Macmillan, 1983.

Dyer, Christopher. "The Social and Economic Background to the Rural Revolt of 1381." In *The English Rising of 1381,* ed. Hilton and Aston, pp. 9–42.

The Early South English Legendary. Ed. C. Horstmann. EETS, o.s. 87. London: Trübner, 1887.

Eisner, Sigmund. *A Tale of Wonder: A Source Study of "The Wife of Bath's Tale."* Folcroft, Penn.: Folcroft, 1957.

Fisher, John H. *John Gower, Moral Philosopher and Friend of Chaucer.* New York: New York University Press, 1964.

Fradenberg, Louise Olga. "Introduction: Rethinking Queenship." In *Women and Sovereignty,* ed. Fradenburg, pp. 1–13.

——. *Sacrifice Your Love: Psychoanalysis, Historicism, Chaucer.* Minneapolis: University of Minnesota Press, 2002.

——, ed. *Women and Sovereignty,* pp. 14–35. Edinburgh: University of Edinburgh Press, 1992.

Gallacher, Patrick J. *Love, the Word and Mercury: A Reading of John Gower's "Confessio Amantis."* Albuquerque: University of New Mexico Press, 1975.

Gravdal, Kathryn. "Camouflaging Rape: The Rhetoric of Sexual Violence in the Medieval Pastourelle." *Romanic Review* 76 (1985), 361–73.

Griffiths, Jeremy. "*Confessio Amantis*: The Poem and Its Pictures." In *Gower's "Confessio Amantis": Responses and Reassessments,* ed. A. J. Minnis, pp. 162–78. Cambridge: Brewer, 1983.

Hansen, Elaine Tuttle. *Chaucer and the Fictions of Gender.* Berkeley: University of California Press, 1992.

Hartwell, David Geddes. "The Wedding of Sir Gawain and Dame Ragnell: An Edition." PhD diss., Columbia University, 1973.

Hilary, Christine Ryan. "The Wife of Bath's Tale" [notes]. In *The Riverside Chaucer,* pp. 872–74.

Hilton, Rodney H. *Bondmen Made Free: Medieval Peasant Movements and the English Rising of 1381*. London: Temple Smith, 1973.

——, and Thomas H. Aston, eds. *The English Rising of 1381*. Cambridge: Cambridge University Press, 1984.

Huppé, Bernard F. "Rape and Woman's Sovereignty in the *Wife of Bath's Tale*." *MLN* 63 (1948), 378-81.

Jones, Terry, R. F. Yeager, Terry Dolan, Alan Fletcher, and Juliette D'Or. *Who Murdered Chaucer?* London: Methuen, 2003.

Josephus, Flavius. *Jewish Antiquities*. Vol. 9 of *Works*. Ed. and trans. Louis H. Feldman. Cambridge, Mass.: Harvard University Press, 1965.

Joynt, Maud. "Echtra mac Echdach Mugmedóin." *Ériu* 4 (1910), 91–111.

Kipling, Gordon. "Richard II's 'Sumptuous Pageants' and the Idea of the Civic Triumph." In *Pageantry in the Shakespearean Theatre*, ed. David M. Bergeron, pp. 83–103. Athens: University of Georgia Press, 1986.

Kurath, Hans, and Sherman Kuhn, eds. *Middle English Dictionary*. Ann Arbor: University of Michigan Press, 1952– .

The Latin Verses in the Confessio Amantis: An Annotated Translation. Trans. Siân Echard and Claire Fanger. East Lansing, Mich.: Colleagues Press, 1991.

Legge, M. Dominica. *Anglo-Norman in the Cloisters: The Influence of the Orders upon Anglo-Norman Literature*. Edinburgh: University of Edinburgh Press, 1950.

Lindahl, Carl. "The Oral Undertone of Late Medieval Romance." In *Oral Tradition in the Middle Ages*, ed. W. H. F. Nicolaisen, pp. 59–75. Binghamton, N.Y.: MRTS, 1995.

Lindeboom, B. W. *Chaucer's Testament of Love: The Impact of the "Confessio Amantis" on "The Canterbury Tales."* Amsterdam: Vrije Universiteit, 2003.

Macaulay, G. C., ed. *The Complete Works of John Gower*. 4 vols. Oxford: Clarendon Press, 1899–1902.

Maynadier, G. H. *"The Wife of Bath's Tale": Its Sources and Analogues*. London: Nutt, 1901.

McKisack, May. *The Fourteenth Century 1307–1399*. Oxford: Clarendon Press, 1959.

Minnis, A. J. "John Gower: *Sapiens* in Ethics and Politics." *MAE* 49 (1980), 207–29.

——. *Medieval Theory of Authorship*. London: Scolar, 1984.

——. "*De vulgari auctoritate*: Chaucer, Gower and the Men of Great Authority." In *Chaucer and Gower*, ed. Yeager, pp. 36–74.

Modwenna of Burton-on-Trent. *St. Modwenna*. Ed. A. T. Baker and Alexander Bell. Oxford: Blackwell, 1947.

Neumann, Erich. "The Psychic Development of the Feminine." In *Amor and Psyche: The Development of the Feminine: A Commentary on the Tale by Apuleius*, pp. 57–161. New York: Harper, 1962.

Nicholson, Peter. "The 'Confession' in Gower's *Confessio Amantis*." *SN* 58 (1986), 193–204.

——. "The Dedications of Gower's *Confessio Amantis*." *Mediaevalia* 10 (1984), 159–80.

——. *An Annotated Index to the Commentary on Gower's "Confessio Amantis."* Binghamton, N.Y.: MRTS, 1989.

Olsson, Kurt. *John Gower and the Structures of Conversion: A Reading of the "Confessio Amantis."* Cambridge: Brewer, 1992.

Parsons, John, Carmi. "Ritual and Symbol in the English Medieval Queenship to 1500." In *Women and Sovereignty,* ed. Fradenburg, pp. 60–77.

Pearsall, Derek. *The Canterbury Tales.* London: Allen and Unwin, 1985.

Peck, Russell A. *Kingship and Common Profit in Gower's "Confessio Amantis."* Carbondale: Southern Illinois University Press, 1978.

Phelan, Walter S. "Beyond the Concordance: Semantic and Mythic Structures in Gower's Tale of Florent." *Neophilologus* 61 (1977), 461–79.

Pickles, J. D., and J. L. Dawson, eds. *A Concordance to John Gower's "Confessio Amantis."* Cambridge: Brewer, 1987.

Pollio, Howard R. *The Structural Basis of Word Association.* The Hague: Mouton, 1966.

Russell, P. E. *The English Intervention in Spain and Portugal in the Time of Edward III and Richard II.* Oxford: Clarendon Press, 1955.

Saul, Nigel. *Richard II.* New Haven: Yale University Press, 1997.

Simpson, James. *Reform and Cultural Revolution: 1350–1547.* Vol. 2 of *The Oxford English Literary History* 2. Oxford: Oxford University Press, 2002.

——. *Sciences and the Self in Medieval Poetry: Alan of Lille's "Anticlaudianus" and John Gower's "Confessio Amantis."* Cambridge: Cambridge University Press, 1995.

Stockton, Eric W. *The Major Latin Works of John Gower.* Seattle: University of Washington Press, 1962.

Stow, George B. "Richard II in John Gower's *Confessio Amantis*: Some Historical Perspectives." *Mediaevalia* 16 (1993 [for 1990]), 3–31.

Strachey, James, Anna Freid, et al., ed. and trans. *The Standard Edition of the Complete Works of Sigmund Freud.* 24 vols. London: Hogarth Press and the Institute of Psychoanalysis, 1953–74.

Sumner, Laura, ed. *The Weddynge of Sir Gawen and Dame Ragnell.* Smith College Studies in Modern Languages 5.4. Northampton, Mass.: Department of Modern Languages of Smith College, 1924; repr. Folcroft, Penn.: Folcroft, 1974.

Tatlock J. S. P. *Development and Chronology of Chaucer's Works.* London: Kegan Paul, Trench, Trübner for the Chaucer Society, 1907.

Tuck, Anthony. "Nobles, Commons and the Great Revolt of 1381." In *The English Rising of 1381,* ed. Hilton and Aston, pp. 194–212.

Wetherbee, Winthrop. "Latin Structure and Vernacular Space: Gower, Chaucer and the Boethian Tradition." In *Chaucer and Gower,* ed. Yeager, pp. 7–35.

Wickert, Maria. *Studien zu John Gower.* Köln: Universitäts-Verlag, 1953; trans. Robert J. Meindl, *Studies in John Gower,* pp. 226–42. Washington, D.C.: University Press of America, 1981.

Wogan-Browne, Jocelyn. "Queens, Virgins and Mothers: Hagiographic Representations of the Abbess and Her Powers in Twelfth- and Thirteenth-Century Britain." In *Women and Sovereignty,* ed. Fradenburg, pp. 14–35.

Yeager, R. F., ed. *Chaucer and Gower: Difference, Mutuality, Exchange.* Victoria, BC: University of Victoria Press, 1991.

———. "Did Gower Write *Cento?*" In *John Gower: Recent Readings,* ed. R. F. Yeager, pp. 113–32. Kalamazoo, Mich.: Medieval Institute Publications, 1989.

———. "English, Latin, and the Text as 'Other': The Page as Sign in the Work of John Gower." *Text 3* (1987), 251–67.

———. *John Gower's Poetic: The Search for a New Arion.* Woodbridge, Suff.: Boydell and Brewer, 1990.

———, "*Pax Poetica:* On the Pacifism of Chaucer and Gower." *SAC* 9 (1987), 97–108.

———, Mark West, and Robin L. Hinson, eds. *A Concordance to the French Poetry and Prose of John Gower.* East Lansing, Mich.: Colleagues Press, 1997.

Zanger, Abby. "Fashioning the Body Politic: Imagining the Queen in the Marriage of Louis XIV." In *Women and Sovereignty,* ed. Fradenburg, pp. 101–20.

Sovereignty through the Lady
"The Wife of Bath's Tale" and the Queenship of Anne of Bohemia

Elizabeth M. Biebel-Stanley

Scholars are uncertain about the depth of Chaucer's familiarity with the Celtic tradition of mythic tales in which the Sovereignty of the Land, personified as female, confers kingship upon a worthy man through sexual coupling. Nevertheless, the presence of a similar Loathly Lady figure in "The Wife of Bath's Tale," combined with the Wife's thematic assertion of female sovereignty and some specific details of Alisoun's character, lends itself to a reading of "The Wife of Bath's Tale" as also being concerned with sovereignty with significant relevance to the reign of Richard II and Anne of Bohemia. Many scholars have constructed compelling arguments by which Alisoun's tale and her call for sovereignty assume a greater depth of meaning when the Irish tales of the Sovereignty Goddess are applied to Chaucer's text. For example, Michael Wilks sets forth an argument that reads Alisoun's romance as Chaucer's manipulation of this motif for the purpose of calling Richard II to reform.[1] However, since Alisoun's performance focuses on the condition of women, I propose that the sovereignty theme is a reflection of woman's integral role in governance that would have compelled Chaucer's medieval audience to associate Alisoun's tale not so much with kingship and Richard II but with queenship and Anne of Bohemia. Keeping in mind Louise Fradenburg's study of the potential of the romance as an instrument of change, I propose that we may read "The Wife of Bath's Tale" as a wishful vision of a movement toward a more egalitarian society.[2] The incorporation of the folk tradition of the Loathly Lady tale into Alisoun's story plays a key role in this vision.

The Celtic sovereignty tales, the source of the British Loathly Lady tales, developed from "a sacred myth" that "embodied the symbolic marriage of the sun god and earth goddess."[3] Máire Herbert observes that the sacred marriage was "a myth of agriculturally-based communities" in which "energy or natural forces, represented by the female principle, combined with social forces represented by the male principle."[4] We should now consider how this relationship corresponds to the medieval view of queenship. Fradenburg informs us that "for queens, the link between marriage and sovereignty was specially intense, since during the period it was usually by means of marriage that queens *became* queens."[5] For medieval kings, marriage contributes symbolically to what Fradenburg terms the "plasticity of gender in the field of sovereignty."[6] In marriage, the king not only symbolically marries the land (for "queens embody the unity of nation or people or land") but also acquires "a purchase on both sexes and on all the cultural functions with which they are severally associated."[7] But what of the queen? The sovereignty of queenship, however, did have distinct limitations. As Charles Wood comments, "[royal] women in the Middle Ages experienced far more sovereign success as wives and mothers than they ever did as the direct possessors of sovereignty," and John Carmi Parsons informs us that the queen's ties to intercession were symbolized in her seating arrangement to the throne: "the English queen's seat to the king's left signified her isolation from the authority symbolized by his scepter, and *vice versa* her association with qualities embodied in the verge of justice and equity held in his left hand during the coronation."[8] The attenuated power of queenship, then, resided in the so-called feminine virtues of mercy and forgiveness and did not include the more active so-called masculine realm of governing.

What is highly significant in many of the Irish Sovereignty tales is that the Loathly Lady is an active agent of her own sexuality who possesses the power to bestow her favors where she will.[9] A prime example of the lady's power is found in *Cóir Anmann*.[10] In this tale, the Loathly Lady figure sequentially offers shelter to each of King Dáire's sons. Because Lughaidh Laidhe makes "no objection to her advances,"[11] the lady transforms into a beauty and invests him with kingship. The locus of power found in the Loathly Lady figure, however, has not remained constant over time. In later versions of the sovereignty legend, the power of the woman becomes usurped: "in the early centuries of Christian conversion, clerical writers sought to promote a Christian ideology of sovereignty in which the overseer and legitimator of royal power was not the goddess but the male god of Christianity."[12] As the reduction or replacement of the role of the earth goddess figure signifies the removal of power from a feminine principle to the male-dominant hierarchy of Christianity, "The Wife of Bath's Tale" reverses this pattern. Chaucer's sole secular female narrator, who strives for sovereignty over her husbands, relates a romance in which women's sovereignty increases as the tale progresses.

In her romance, Alisoun recalls a past world in order to exemplify how change can affect society for the better. It is indeed significant that of the five Canterbury romances, Alisoun's is the sole Arthurian tale, for the Arthurian tradition contains numerous pre-Christian elements that place Alisoun's tale in a setting distinctively different from her present, the world "Of lymytours and othere hooly freres" (line 866)[13] that "has been thoroughly transformed, demystified."[14] The otherworldly references in Alisoun's tale to fairies, "the elf-queene, with hir joly compaignye" (line 860), and the "ladyes foure and twenty, and yet mo" (line 992) who magically disappear establish the alterity of this world. Here is a place of mystery where there are supernatural powers other than those of the God of Christianity. Such recollection of earlier times when other religions held more prominent roles places more emphasis on the Loathly Lady figure as Sovereignty goddess. As a Sovereignty figure, Chaucer's Loathly Lady's desire to marry the rapist-knight casts this character in the role of a king. With such royal implications in this scene of reading we can view the fictional pair as correlating to Richard II and Anne of Bohemia. If we read Alisoun's tale as possessing an historical relevance to the marriage of Richard II and Anne of Bohemia, the united couple in Alisoun's romance can represent what Fradenburg terms the "plasticity" of gender sovereignty: "gender is provisional and practicable, that is, open to changing practice."[15] Alisoun's tale may be read as ultimately calling for a change, a transcendence of traditional gender roles that is based in the sovereignty of a goddess.

The distinct need for change in the traditional gender hierarchy is made clear in the opening of "The Wife of Bath's Tale." The rape of the maiden graphically represents the imbalance of power between the sexes in male-dominated society. Nature, the locus of woman's power in the Celtic sovereignty tales, becomes violated by the masculine will as society and its masculine principle of power, represented by the knight, encroaches upon the feminine principle. What is curiously significant in the rape scene and the subsequent "clamour" (line 889) of bringing the rapist-knight to trial is that the raped maiden has no lines of direct speech. This absence is odd because an integral part of medieval law concerning rape accusations required the plaintiff to accuse the defendant directly.[16] This textual absence of the maiden's direct speech is symbolic of the way the voice of woman disappears in patriarchal society. While the maiden has been violated and rendered mute, though, her fate is not to be representative of the fate of all women.

As the romance progresses, the female characters move steadily closer to positions of power.

Although at first glance she may not seem to be a primary character in Alisoun's tale, Arthur's queen has a pivotal role. It is through her that a resurgence of woman's voice occurs. The queen's position in the male-dominant world of the civilized court, though, does not allow her to access power directly. Her speech must be qualified in order that it be deferring to the wishes of the established authority. She and her ladies "preyeden" (line 895) Arthur for the privilege to exercise power and then "thanketh" (line 899) him for humoring them. That the queen possesses the attenuated authority of intercessor through her marriage to the king is significant to the whole of Alisoun's romance and its message regarding medieval queenship, for it is through the queen's intercession for mercy that the reformation process of the rapist begins. While the death of the rapist-knight would achieve vengeance for the victim, it would not solve the problem of women's vulnerability to rape, particularly in a society where the negation of woman's will is a frequent practice. Although the death-sentence punishment for rape existed before the knight committed his crime, it did not deter him. If the knight can reform, his life need not be wasted. The queen makes sure he knows that she will not support his existence if he remains unaltered when she encourages him to "Be war, and keep thy nekke-boon from iren!" (line 906). Kind yet decidedly firm, the queen begins the reformation process of the unruly knight; however, she is not the one who can complete this process.

When the rapist-knight sets forth upon his riddle quest, he moves away from the realm of civilization and re-enters the natural world. While nature offered no safe haven for the maiden at the beginning of the text, readers now encounter a difference in the natural world. We witness a resurgence of magic and power in the vision of the dancing ladies and the appearance of the Loathly Lady. The Loathly Lady is more free to speak than the queen, for she is not hindered by the strictures of rank imposed by male-dominated society. Indeed, it is the Loathly Lady who possesses the most autonomous power of all the women in this tale, power that is appropriate for a character who has ties to an earth goddess possessing the power to confer kingship.

The Loathly Lady's selection of this knight as her husband is a significant moment in the tale. Like the earth goddess of the sovereignty legends, she has chosen the spouse that she desires and is the active agent of her sexual desire. Perhaps even more significant is that, while the lady receives the promise from the knight to acquiesce to her will in a woodland setting, she is also able to make the knight keep his promise in the courtly world of civilization. At this point in the tale, feminine power is no longer relegated to the natural world; it moves into the realm of masculine civilization. The will of the Loathly Lady is recognized when the knight places self-governance in her hands, allowing her to choose her own form and her own sexual terms. The knight's willingness to recognize the self-sovereignty of his partner yields in turn an ending that emphasizes beauty in a literal and a figurative sense: not only does the Loathly Lady transform into a lovely woman, but she does so because of the radiance of equality which she and her partner now enjoy. As a rapist, this knight displayed no worthy characteristics of a ruler. Through the queen's intercession and the Loathly Lady's tutelage, though, the rapist transforms into one who can recognize the wills of others. Wedded to one another, if this Loathly Lady reflects the Sovereignty of the Land, then the reformed knight represents her king. As the two are now one, the reformed king assumes the wisdom of his queen: can she also, then, take on his power in addition to her role of a reforming, guiding, and governing queen?

The resemblance between the Loathly Lady figure in Chaucer's work and the Celtic tradition of the sovereignty legends is not the sole signifier of a message about queenship in the Wife of Bath's performance that allows us to draw connections to Anne of Bohemia. Several details that lie within the portrait of the Wife of Bath would prompt a medieval audience to recall Anne of Bohemia and thus locate this message regarding queenship in "The Wife of Bath's Tale." While scholars are uncertain of the specific dating of Alisoun's performance, in *The Riverside Chaucer* Catherine Ryan Hilary proposes that, "a date in the early to mid 1390s seems probable and is accepted by most scholars."[17] Since Anne of Bohemia was queen until her sudden death in 1394, we can view this reading of the Wife's tale as either a subtle message on Chaucer's part about the appropriateness of a highly popular and efficient queen having more sovereignty in her own right or, if Alisoun's recital was composed in the later mid-1390s, as Chaucer's tribute to the memory and works of the deceased "Good Queen Anne."

In one of the many scholarly articles that finds symbolic relevance in Alisoun's attire, Dale Wretlind observes that Alisoun's huge hat recalls the headdress introduced to England by Anne of Bohemia in 1382.[18] Wretlind's argument is supported by the popularity of Queen Anne's voluminous head-gear among fourteenth-century women. In her account of England's queens, Agnes Strickland writes that "these formidable novelties expanded their wings on every side, till at church or procession the diminished heads of lords and knights were eclipsed by their ambitious partners. The church declared they were 'the moony tire' denounced by Ezekiel; likely enough, for they had been introduced by Bohemian crusaders from Syria."[19] This unique fashion, then, serves as a connection that would inspire Chaucer's audience to recall Queen Anne.

In addition to the bold hat, the Wife of Bath's insistence that women's voices be heard, her multiple marriages, and her disregard for the writings of Paul are all practices that reflect the Lollard movement. While literary critics argue the extent to which we can read Alisoun as a Lollard, Chaucer's text suggests that Alisoun would approve of a religious group that called for a vernacular Bible.[20] An accessible version of Holy Writ for the populace would remove the privilege of textual glossing from church authorities. Curbing this tendency to gloss would greatly appeal to Alisoun, for she has experienced far too often the way Scripture is manipulated to misrepresent women. Lollard support for women as preachers, which is in direct opposition to the injunctions of "th'apostle" (line 49) Paul, is in accord with Alisoun's desire for the voices of women to be heard. Just as literary scholars debate the Wife's ties to Lollardry, so are historians undecided as to whether or not Anne of Bohemia was herself a Lollard. What is known is that several members of her entourage were Lollards, and Anne reportedly did her best to spare them from prosecution at the hands of the Merciless Parliament. Strickland recounts the disputed rumor that at Anne's funeral Thomas of Arundel praised her for reading Scripture in the vernacular (George Fox reported this rumor to be true, while Rapin contested it).[21] The sympathy that both Chaucer's character and Anne of Bohemia held for Wycliffite tenets mark another commonality that readers can note.

A third association between Anne of Bohemia and the Wife of Bath stems from Alisoun's involvement with the textile trade. Her association with weaving connects her historically to the English Rising of 1381, the rebellious movement which, as historian Harold Hutchison comments, "was … as much an artisans' as a peasants' revolt."[22] In 1381, textile workers were extremely concerned with the "privileges of foreign merchants and the craft secrets of foreign workers."[23] While the protestors of 1381 looked to Richard as their hope, no aid from him was forthcoming. In 1382, however, royal sympathy for prisoners convicted after the English Rising was forthcoming. It was the new queen who initiated the pardon. Through dress, philosophy, and profession, then, the Wife of Bath's portrait connects to significant facets of Anne's life. When we add these details to the importance that "The Wife of Bath's Tale" places on the intercessory powers of the queen, the tie between the tale and Anne's history of intercession strengthens.

In his discussion of medieval queenship, Parsons observes the "unrecorded custom" that "called for an act of intercession at the queen's investiture,"[24] and he surmises that Anne's petition for men convicted after the English Rising was initially intended to have taken place at her consecration. That she petitioned for the pardon of these men credits her with their reprieve in the eyes of the populace. Here was a woman who used her influence to provide justice for people who had spoken out against the authority of the state. Throughout her brief reign, Anne was also successful in urging Richard to make peace with Thomas Arundel and, on another occasion, with the city of London. Andrew Taylor observes, "in her numerous acts of intercession Anne appears to have followed an analogous pattern, achieving a degree of freedom and self-expression within the social constraints of chivalric culture."[25] Just as Anne acquires power through Richard, so too does the queen work to dispense justice in Alisoun's tale. This similarity brings us to the political message that may be found in Alisoun's tale.

Both Anne of Bohemia and Arthur's queen accomplish good for society through their intercessory powers.[26] While Arthur's queen initiates the process of the knight's reformation, the autonomous Loathly Lady effects the change. As the events of the romance reveal, women can improve society. Why, then, do these women not have sovereignty in their own right? The marriage of mutual love that we witness at the end of Alisoun's romance can be read as a claim for increased power for medieval queens. A queen signifies her king's union with so-called feminine virtues such as forgiveness, temperance, and patience, admirable qualities for a king to possess that are distanced from him by the construction of gendered virtues and perhaps as well by the very nature of the king's personality. In keeping with the mutual relationship that we find in Alisoun's romance, neither partner is subjected to the other's will. The couple functions both as two individuals and as one. Just as the rapist-knight does not claim governance over his Loathly Lady bride, recollection of the Sovereignty of the Land united with her king suggests that a king should not maintain sovereignty over his queen. If a royal marriage were based on a mutual relation of power between partners, the queen's marriage to the king would invest her with access to the king's right hand of authority as well as his left hand of justice. Invested with authority to rule in addition to her power to intercede, a queen would have increased potential to bring about change in her society. If the Sovereignty of the Land can reform a rapist, a sovereign queen could reform an unruly king, and their people could only benefit from the results.

NOTES

1. Wilks, "Chaucer and the Mystical Marriage," p. 494.

2. Fradenburg, "Wife of Bath's Passing Fancy," pp. 31–58.

3. Eisner, *Tale of Wonder*, p. 31.

4. Herbert, "Goddess and King," pp. 264–65.

5. Fradenburg, "Introduction," p. 4.

6. Fradenburg, "Introduction," p. 2.

7. Fradenburg, "Introduction," pp. 5, 2.

8. Wood, "First Two Queens Elizabeth," p. 121; and Parsons, "Ritual and Symbol," p. 64.

9. Not all of the Irish tales have such an autonomous Sovereignty figure. Herbert recounts that in the eleventh-century story *Baile in Scáil*, "it is the king-god, Lug, who instructs his female companion regarding the bestowal of the drink of sovereignty.... [I]t is his action rather than that of the goddess, therefore, which ultimately decides the ruler" ("Goddess and King," p. 269). However, as Susan Carter notes in her essay "A Hymenation of Hags" in the present volume, "The two versions [of Sovereignty tales] which provide shape-changers most like Chaucer's ... are the tale of Lugaid told in the 'Carn Máil' and the *Cóir Anmann*" (p. 84).

10. See Stokes, *Cóir Anmann*, pp. 285–87, pp. 316–23.

11. Quoted in Eisner, *Tale of Wonder*, p. 18.

12. Herbert, "Goddess and Queen," p. 268.

13. All quotations from Chaucer are from *The Riverside Chaucer* and are located in Fragment III, Group D, unless otherwise indicated.

14. Fradenburg, "Wife of Bath's Passing Fancy," p. 47.

15. Fradenburg, "Introduction," p. 10, n.1.

16. In *Rape in Medieval England*, John Marshall Carter details the six steps of appeal a medieval woman needed to follow in order to accuse a man of rape, most of which involve her speaking out directly to various authorities (p. 95).

17. Hilary, "Notes," p. 864.

18. Wretlind, "Wife of Bath's Hat," p. 381.

19. Strickland, *Lives of the Queens*, p. 210.

20. In *Premature Reformation*, Hudson finds that Alisoun's stance against authority reflects the language of Wyclif (p. 393). In "The Wife of Bath and Lollardry," pp. 224–42, Blamires observes that Alisoun's love of pilgrimages and her penchant for swearing do not reflect Lollardry. In "Alys as Allegory," Martin finds that while Alisoun's preaching and her multiple marriages are reflective of Lollard practices, her pilgrimages, church offerings, and her confessional style of speech do not conform to the Lollard's ways. In *Geoffrey Chaucer*, Dillon believes Alisoun is in accord with the Lollard preference for the vernacular over Latin and their belief in education for women. Dillon also considers Alisoun to be more radical than the Lollards.

21. Strickland, *Lives of the Queens of England*, p. 221, n. 4.

22. Hutchison, *Hollow Crown*, p. 54. In "Writing Lesson of 1381," Crane observes the parallels between Alisoun's attempts to undermine authority and the struggles of the people in 1381 (pp. 201–21).

23. Hutchison, *Hollow Crown*, p. 55: "When the rebels began to march, therefore, their ranks included not merely villeins of every degree from near serf to near freeman, but poor priests, discontented artisans, idle soldiery, yeomen and free farm labourers, wage earners and craftsmen, and every man with a grievance against those in power, the law of the land, the custom of the manor, the encroachments of sheep farming lords, the privileges of foreign merchants and the craft secrets of foreign workers."

24. Parsons, "Ritual and Symbol," pp. 64, 71, n. 19.

25. Taylor, "Anne of Bohemia," p. 99.

26. Taylor, "Anne of Bohemia," p. 108, re-evaluates the associations between Queen Anne and Chaucer's Alceste in the *Legend of Good Women* on the basis of their roles as intercessors.

WORKS CITED

Benson, Larry D., gen. ed. *The Riverside Chaucer*. Boston: Houghton Mifflin, 1987.

Blamires, Alcuin. "The Wife of Bath and Lollardy." *MAE* 58 (1989), 224–42.

Carter, John Marshall. *Rape in Medieval England: An Historical and Sociological Study*. New York: University Press of America, 1985.

Crane, Susan. "The Writing Lesson of 1381." In *Chaucer's England: Literature in Historical Context*, ed. Barbara Hanawalt, pp. 201–21. Minneapolis: University of Minnesota Press, 1992.

Dillon, Janet. *Geoffrey Chaucer*. New York: St. Martin's, 1993.

Eisner, Sigmund. *A Tale of Wonder: A Source Study of "The Wife of Bath's Tale."* New York: Burt Franklin, 1957.

Fradenburg, Louise O. "Introduction: Rethinking Queenship." In *Women and Sovereignty*, ed. Fradenburg, pp. 1–13.

——. "The Wife of Bath's Passing Fancy." *SAC* 11 (1989), 31–58.

——, ed. *Women and Sovereignty*. Edinburgh: Edinburgh University Press, 1992.

Herbert, Máire. "Goddess and King: The Sacred Marriage in Early Ireland," *Women and Sovereignty*, ed. Fradenburg, pp. 264–75.

Hilary, Catherine Ryan. "The Wife of Bath's Tale [notes]." In *The Riverside Chaucer*, gen. ed. Benson, p. 872–74.

Hudson, Anne. *The Premature Reformation: Wycliffite Texts and Lollard History*. Oxford: Clarendon Press, 1988.

Hutchison, Harold F. *The Hollow Crown: A Life of Richard II*. London: Eyre and Spottiswoode, 1961.

Martin, Carol. "Alys as Allegory: The Ambivalent Heretic." *Comitatus* 21 (1990), 52–71.

Parsons, John Carmi. "Ritual and Symbol in the English Medieval Queenship to 1500." *Women and Sovereignty*, ed. Fradenburg, pp. 60–77.

Stokes, Whitley H., and E. Windisch, trans. *Cóir Anmann. (Fitness of Names)*. In vol. 2 of *Irische Texte mit Übersetzungen und Wörterbuch*, ser. 3. Liepzig: Hirzel, 1897, pp. 285–444.

Strickland, Agnes. *Lives of the Queens of England from the Norman Conquest; with Anecdotes of Their Courts*. Vol. 2. Philadelphia: Blanchard and Lea, 1853.

Taylor, Andrew. "Anne of Bohemia and the Making of Chaucer." *SAC* 19 (1997), 95–119.

Wilks, Michael. "Chaucer and the Mystical Marriage in Medieval Political Thought." *BJRL* 44 (1962), 489–530.

Wood, Charles T. "The First Two Queens Elizabeth, 1464–1503." In *Women and Sovereignty*, ed. Fradenburg, pp. 121–31.

Wretlind, Dale E. "The Wife of Bath's Hat." *MLN* 63 (1948), 381.

A HYMENATION OF HAGS

Susan Carter

Towards the climax of "The Wife of Bath's Tale," the loathsome bride concedes to her groom, "but natheless, syn I knowe youre delit, / I shal fulfille youre worldly appetit" (lines 1217–18); in the language of consenting adults, she tells him that she is willing and able to change her body to suit his tastes. But we are not told if these include a preference for virginity in his bride. Is there a hymen in that transfigured flesh? The hymen is evidence of virginity, and thus a symbol of innocence and inexperience. The Wife of Bath, who in her prologue is so persistently attentive to detail regarding sexual "thynges," withholds mention of this small but extremely significant detail.

Nonetheless, the (at least textually) absent hymen provides a useful way of assessing the loathly/lovely shape-shifting motif.[1] Some hags have them, some do not. I acknowledge from the outset that the Loathly Lady is constructed of ideas, a noumenon rather than a phenomenon. Furthermore, the ideas that shape the motif's unstable flesh are about kingship, that is, about male power, ideals of masculinity, and royal lineage. However, allegorizing ideas about masculine power through the vehicle of female flesh places sovereignty in the realm of gender power politics.[2] Virginity or its absence ought to be crucial in an allegory that involves an active female sexuality, but curiously it matters less than it might. The lack of distinction between bona fide maidens and quasi-divinities measures the motif's tendency to collapse the difference between binary opposites, between the loathly and the lovely, and between the sexually experienced and the virginal. Furthermore, the Loathly Lady motif consistently makes chastity less of an issue than female control. Thus although we cannot inspect the sheets of the marriage bed where the narrative of the Wife's tale reaches a climax, we can make use of this telling membrane to understand better the motif central to "The Wife of Bath's Tale" and the other English Loathly Lady tales.

Chaucer's is the best-known Loathly Lady. The "olde wyf" of the Wife's tale merges with the Wife who narrates her. They both actively seek husbands, "meke yonge and fresshe abedd" (line 1259). Indeed, the shape-shifter is often described as an alter ego of the Wife, or a figment of the middle-aged Wife's wish fulfilment to have back the "flour" of her sexuality (compared with the bran she must market in her old age), her youth and beauty, as well as wifely control.[3] The Loathly Lady is more than a shadow of the Wife, however. The Wife is uniquely Chaucer's compilation, albeit one he reconstructed from various misogynist diatribes,[4] but the Loathly Lady has a pedigree of her own.[5]

Although Chaucer's source for "The Wife of Bath's Tale" is not known, it is generally agreed among scholars that the earliest extant versions are found in medieval Irish literature, where the Loathly Lady's unstable body stands for the kingdom, or more specifically, the experience of kingship.[6] While the Irish Sovereignty tales must be regarded as analogues rather than sources, they exist on a time line between Chaucer's tale and the missing Ur-text, and helpfully establish the motif's meaning, so that they illuminate Chaucer's exploitation of the baggage the hag imports to his tale.[7] The two versions which provide shape-changers most like Chaucer's, given his repeated use of the word *sovereignty*, are the tale of Lugaid told in the "Carn Máil" and the *Cóir Anmann*,[8] and the tale of Níall's ascent to power, "Echtra mac Echach Muigmedóin," that is, "The Adventures of the Sons of Eochaid."[9] These provide insight as to why the transformed bride of "The Wife of Bath's Tale" probably doesn't have a hymen, and why it ultimately doesn't matter, even though this is surprising, given the anxiety surrounding virginity, and subversive, given the tradition of patriarchal ownership of female sexuality. The exciting sense that, as used by Chaucer and other medieval English writers, this medieval motif challenges deeply entrenched gender bias can be located in the earlier usage within the Irish tales.

The Irish sovereignty hag is quasi-divine.[10] In the "Carn Máil," the Loathly Lady is menacingly large, perhaps like the figure Natura which reoccurs in medieval literature.[11] The king's sons would rather "be buried under earth alive" than look upon the "obese lustful horror" (line 141).[12] The boys' thoughts of being buried alive emphasize that the hag's size suggests that her demand for sex threatens death by assimilation into her vast body; this threat is confirmed when "the sons of Dáire gave themselves over to a death of shame" (line 141). Disappearing into a monstrous woman's "bele chose" (as the Wife of Bath calls her vagina in "The Wife of Bath's Prologue," line 447) would be an ignominious death.

Lugaid Laígde agrees to attempt the task as a hero going to his fate to save his brothers, saying that it is better that his brothers should "lose" only him.[13] His use of the euphemism "lose" for his brother's experience of his death further evokes the possibility that he will disappear irretrievably into the hag's flesh. The comparison of being "lost" in the hag's body, a murkier place than under earth, demonizes female desire at the same time that it signals to the coercive monster's personification of the land: covertly expressed is the fear that the king may find himself buried in the soil of his kingdom rather than ruling over it should he not be strong enough to keep his seat on the throne. The king-to-be wins the land through his successful negotiation of its female-gendered geography, an idea that, in a later historical period, will sit in accordance with early modern colonization discourse.[14]

Yet this land personification is not passive; she advances with the alarming vigor that more usually belongs to the conqueror. The fertility implicit in youth and beauty is not privileged in the personification; instead a compelling sexuality marks her agency in mortal affairs. The sovereignty hag seems to have chosen sexual union as a kingship selection method because of the sado-erotic pleasure that this provides her (a titillation that seems to stick to the motif in later usage). Whatever the drawbacks are of troping the land as woman, and it is a commonplace to observe the problems of this from a feminist point of view,[15] the hag's rigorous agency eludes the woman-as-land trope's tendency towards downtroddenness. This is a female who knows what she wants, and will make a spectacle of herself to get it. There is no chance of a hymen in a sovereignty goddess implicated in a cyclical if not seasonal myth; it is simply wise and kingly to please her, and to be undaunted by the prospect of being lost in the fissures of her flesh.

"The Adventures of the Sons of Eochaid" has a smaller but more specifically repulsive Loathly Lady: she is pustular and has green teeth that curl back to her ears, among other defects. She is nonetheless helpfully explicit about what her many-shaped body means. She explains, "I am the Sovranty" and "as thou hast seen me loathsome, bestial, horrible at first and beautiful at last, so is the sovranty; for it is seldom gained without battles and conflicts, but at last to anyone it is beautiful and goodly."[16] When the hag is thus a personification of the land as kingdom, a quasi-goddess in the process of choosing the king, we can assume that she does not have a maiden-head, since she is on an eternal, not mortal, time span, and she reappears when the dynasty is due for reallocation, for another one-night stand, mixing pleasure with the business of deity. Níall's hag is the one who articulates the ambiguities inherent in her shape-shifting flesh, and Níall is the successful candidate for kingship because he accepts her as "many-shaped": not just beautiful in appearance, but inherently dual, or, actually, multifaceted.

It is not uncommon for land to be portrayed as a fertile young woman, or as a mother (this happens graphically in the discourse of American as well as Irish colonization); the manifestation as a hag is what complicates the Irish figures, especially since the hag is a determined sexual predator.[17] The grotesque physicality and active sexuality of the Irish sovereignty hags scramble the image of desire. Marauding through the dreamscape territory of the early Irish tales seemingly in search of a good time, the hag makes an early emblem of feminine gratification as a precondition of peace and prosperity. At the same time that the Irish material points to the need for a symbiotic relationship between land and ruler, it shows that the true king must embrace humiliation, degradation, and difficulty when survival is at stake. Although the motif is centrally concerned with political power, masculine ideals, and right rule, through the allegory of the sovereignty hag all this is predicated on the gratification of female sexuality at its most grotesque. A good king must please the shape-shifter whose monstrous desire destabilizes gender stereotypes.

Whatever source he used, this need for the male protagonist to accommodate defamiliarized feminine desire is the aspect of the tale that Chaucer employs and amplifies. As with other English Loathly Lady tales, the central quest of "The Wife of Bath's Tale" is the answer to the riddle, "What thyng is it that wommen moost desiren" (line 905), proposing that this is a worthwhile consideration; it is a life-and-death one for the knight in the tale. The Irish sovereignty hag is not confined to a happy-ever-after state of marital bliss, and she is clearly a deity figure. When sexual union is consummated, it is on her terms, which seem to be her own sexual satisfaction. This shape-changing hag, at once dreadful and comical, steps through the limen of literacy, the doorway between lost oral tradition and fragmentally extant manuscripts, into *The Canterbury Tales*, from a past world long before Freud pivoted the axis of the unconscious around the penis.[18]

The sovereignty hag's prefiguration of the Wife of Bath's hag, then, endorses the sense that although the Wife's hag is problematically compliant to the rapist knight of her choice, she retains a core identity that resists his colonization of her body.[19] We might feel assured that if she chooses to construct a maidenhead for herself to humor her groom, she would be using a trick that belongs to mortal sex-workers, in a tradition of a crafty trade short-change.[20] Such a sham of inexperience would only highlight her expertise. As well as challenging traditional gender stereotypes concerning who seduces whom, and whose pleasure is important, the motif collapses the binary opposites of experience and inexperience, binaries that are critical when women are regarded as objects. Again, the Irish originals set a pattern for how this blurring of the boundaries occurs.

Although the Irish Sovereignty figure is certainly experienced, Níall's tale introduces another key element of some Loathly Lady tales, and thus the motif: a wicked stepmother. Níall's father, a "wondrous and noble king" begets Níall on a young hostage princess, incurring the jealousy of his queen. For Níall, the wicked stepmother is not a second wife, as wicked stepmothers tend to be in fairy tales, but the legitimate queen, angered and threatened by the sexual dalliance of her noble partner. This mother of legitimate sons attempts to kill the unborn baby of her sexual rival by ordering his mother to draw water for the whole household while she is pregnant. When Níall is born, it is beside the well during his mother's work of hauling up water, and, afraid of the queen, she leaves her baby there, unprotected and pestered by birds. Rescued by a male seer and taken away to be raised as a king, Níall particularly incorporates an ability to survive subjugation. There is a psychological realism to the fact that the king's son who has had a hard start in life is stronger than those who have been nurtured at court from birth. At one testing process, pitted against his half-brothers, Níall's selection of an anvil shows that his inception through his mother's tortured labor has endowed him with the quality of endurance. Yet it is also the narrative fate of wicked stepmothers that they exist only to be overcome; their infliction of pain and penalty inevitably strengthens their victims.

Wells in Níall's tale twice measure out the power of women. Níall survives the well-side ordeal of his birth to pass his test with the Sovereignty hag by offering to lie with her in exchange for water from her well.[21] The well controlled by a scheming stepmother, which was to have terminated Níall's life by overtaxing his mother, serves instead to strengthen and bless him, and prepare him for the Loathly Lady's well-side test.

The pattern by which Níall's stepmother's curse eventually enables advantage holds true for the subsequent and analogous subset of tales in which the Loathly Lady is not a quasi-deity, but is a maiden who is ugly because she is bespelled by an evil stepmother.[22] Chaucer's contemporary John Gower opts for a bespelled maiden version of the Loathly Lady in "The Tale of Florent."[23] Despite the fact that these two authors are believed to have shared the source for their tales, there is an inner difference in the two beastly brides: the difference between an independent shape-changer having another fling, and a bona fide maiden seeking to save herself from her wicked stepmother's curse, a curse which has inflicted ugliness upon her.

In the case of the maiden, beauty is her true form, along with all that beauty represents when women are objectified, and she is furthermore a damsel in distress, an acceptable stereotype of femininity. The two very different kinds of Loathly Ladies can be identified as those with authentic intact hymens, and those without. Yet although they are different, they are also surprisingly similar, given the difference in attitude that one might expect between a mortal maiden (proverbially "meeke," as when Chaucer's pilgrim knight is described "as meeke as is a mayde" [GP, line 69]) and an experienced quasi-goddess.

Voice partly distinguishes Gower's and Chaucer's tales. Gower's narrative persona in "The Tale of Florent" is not a strident feminine one like that of the Wife of Bath, but a masculine voice which, nevertheless, has a sexual neutrality, being "softe and faire."[24] Although the speaking priest is in the service of Venus, he is a confessor, a faceless servant, whose stories emerge from a professional performance rather than a personality. Chaucer's Wife is actively sexual, raunchy, aberrant, proud of her own pride. We know that her much-traveled hips are broad and her teeth lasciviously wide-spaced. The Wife and Genius speak from very different rhetorical stances; nonetheless Gower's priest, as the male stripped of pride, somehow matches the inflated feminine Wife. Both their voices, the feminized masculine and the aggressive feminine, are apt for a motif that collapses binary opposites.

Perhaps the most striking contrast between Chaucer's and Gower's versions is that the two protagonists are intrinsically different, casting dissimilar reflection upon the two Loathly Ladies of their tales. The Wife's knight precipitates the action by raping a maiden; Florent is established as "worthi," "chivalerous and amorous" (lines 1408–14), and he is at the onset a victim, seized while he "rod in a pas" (lines 1421–22).[25] The attack on Florent is described with a passive verbal construction masking the identity of those who take him by strength. The story's initiators, who grab Florent, are unnamed workers of the whims of Fortune, that fickle fabricator:

> Fortune, which may every thred
> Tobreke and knette of mannes sped,
> Schop, as this knyght rod in a pas,
> That he be strengthe take was.
>   (lines 1419–22)

The faultlessness of Florent makes his later happy ending unproblematic; he gets a virginal wife because he is more worthy than the rapist knight in

Chaucer's tale. The difference in their Loathly Ladies is evidence of Gower's concern with poetic justice, and his rejection of fleshly excess, compared to Chaucer's penchant for complication and play.

As a hymenated hag, Florent's bride is similar to Dame Ragnelle, another bespelled-maiden type of Loathly Lady, albeit one who is more playfully fleshed out than Gower's. Even though she is not as well-known as Chaucer's and Gower's hags, Ragnelle has a central significance in that "The Wedding of Sir Gawain and Dame Ragnelle" incorporates almost all the elements to be found in medieval Loathly Lady tales. It is Arthurian like Chaucer's "Wife of Bath's Tale," although the Arthurian element is in clearer focus in the "Wedding," in that the male protagonists are named, unlike Chaucer's knight,[26] and behave according to character type. Consideration of property motivates the action of the "Wedding," so that the link with the land of the Irish sovereignty tales is brought into the English set of tales. Specifically, Sir Gromer Somer Joure, the huge carl who instigates the drama (and who later proves to be Ragnelle's brother) launches the action because previously King Arthur wrongfully seized his property and gave it to Sir Gawain. Sir Gromer claims the status of a revenge hero when he grimly says to Arthur, "Thou hast me done wrong many a yere / And woefully I shall quytte the here" (lines 55– 56).[27] The accusation of "wrong" addresses the actual power of the royal court, and its potential for abuse, putting the military elite of knighthood into a less ideal aspect. This slur is comparable to the rape which begins "The Wife of Bath's Tale," except that the abuse of power is sexual in the tale told by the woman, and in the "Wedding" the alleged abuse is land appropriation, a breach of masculine identity and rights rather than of feminine.

Ragnelle proves to be a peace-weaver bride to the rival factions; once her transformation is acknowledged privately and publicly she approaches Arthur to intercede on her brother's behalf: enchanted by her, he agrees to be a good lord to Sir Gromer, for her sake. The transaction shows peace-weaving at its most successful: discordant social intercourse prepares the bed for a sexual intercourse whose jouissance brings social concord. The bespelled maiden, like Níall, grows powerful in social influence through her stepmother's curse. Seeking her own salvation from the spell, she heals social rupture—and in the process she offers her intact maidenhead.

However, Ragnelle's sexual aggression, energy, and ingenuity, and her delight in her groom's discomfort—she tortures him with a very public wedding at which she behaves like a beast—means that she is more similar to the independent shape-shifters than psychological realism allows. Ragnelle insists on a highly public wedding: she will be "made sekry. / In welle and

wo … Before alle thy chyvalry" (lines 527–29). She will be made secure in legal
terms through the marriage vows made before all Arthur's knights. Her desire
for the security of the marriage vows shows shrewd awareness of the legality
of having publicity, but it also includes something like a sneer at all of
Arthur's chivalry, reduced to her witnesses.

She refuses to marry at all, "But there were made a krye in all the shyre"
(line 558): she demands full publicity as part of the bargain. Ragnelle
summons the women to her wedding and into the tale. "Alle of the ladies
nowe of the lond, / She lett kry to com to hand" (lines 560–61); they come,
and they "pitey," with a chorus repeat of "Alas" (lines 568–69). As Russell
Peck notes of Queen Guinevere, the women are as outraged as the men at
having "something so ugly and shameful in their midst."[28] Gaynor pleads for
the wedding to be conducted "As pryvaly as we may" (line 571), intent on
supporting Gawain by minimizing his shame, but Ragnelle insists that "This
daye" is for her "worshypp" (line 585), and that she will "be weddyd alle
openly" (line 575), "In myddys of alle the rowte" (line 580). Then once she has
her party organized, her table manners are also "fulle foulle and nott curteys"
(line 602); "she ete as moche as six" (line 605), with an effective carnivorous
methodology which is offputting: "Her nayles were long ynchys thre; /
Therwith she breke her mete ungoodly" (lines 606–8). A physical isolation of
this bad behavior foregrounds its social unacceptability: "Therfore she ete
alone" (line 609). Now that she has her public wedding feast her guests isolate
her, drawing back from her bestial greed. Full nineteen lines are given to her
behavior at the table, where "she ete tylle mete was done" (line 619). In "The
Wife of Bath's Tale," women toy with the knight. The court of ladies send
him to find the answer to an impossible riddle, and then the Loathly Lady
entraps him in marriage and lies smiling as he tosses and turns on the
wedding night. Ragnelle too seems to enjoy her power to shame Arthur and
his court, so that a sense of something like female solidarity leaks into the
shape-changing motif as a single entity: hags are lively (as well as lovely)
whether they are hymenated or not.

Narrative problems occur when the maidens and experienced hags
behave so similarly, yet these very problems produce a larger-reaching
collapse of objectifying distinctions between types of women. That Ragnelle
is most unmaidenly in her publicity-demanding provocation of Gawain, and
of "alle of Arthoure's chivalry" is entertaining, yet the laughter it invites is
based on confining stereotypes of female beauty and decorum, the beauty-
myth that monstrously menaces the happiness of so many maidens in real life
today. Conversely, in the case of Chaucer's "olde wyf," feminists and others

have felt discomforted by the feminine submission, and the sexual healing of social rift when the knight's heart is bathed in a bath of bliss at the end of the tale.[29] Comedic closure restores the order of romance in "The Wife of Bath's Tale," at least at surface level, with the lady transformed to being young and fair, and with "perfit joye" for the rapist knight, found within the comforting folds of patriarchy. I argue that the inherently unequal power ratios between the quasi-divinity and her unnamed groom destabilize this romance cliché, but here point out that the motif itself seems to encourage the virginal and the nonvirginal to meld in the hag.

Perhaps for Chaucer this subversive melding is one of the motif's attractions. His use of the word *unwemmed* (unspotted, so virginal) in two other tales suggests that the difference between maidens and sexually experienced women is not finally that important.[30] In "The Second Nun's Tale," the saintly and virginal Cecilie is "unwemmed" (SNT, line 137), and in "The Man of Law's Tale," Custance, clearly no virgin with her little son weeping beside her, is, through the grace of God, kept spotless, having tossed her would-be rapist into the sea. The Man of Law, discounting the evidence that one sniveling son provides of Custance's physical lack of virginity, applauds that "thus hath Crist unwemmed kept Custance" (MLT, line 924). That Chaucer should apply this word to both a virgin and a mother entertains the idea that female chastity is independent of the flesh. This disregard for the body as signifier, and specifically the hymen as signifier, aligns with the Loathly Lady motif's narrative effect of making chastity less of an issue than female control. Indeed, perhaps the most compelling thing about the Loathly Lady is that she insists that the female body may be paradoxical, and must be accepted as a text that is "many-shaped."

In Chaucer's use of this motif, female desire and female sovereignty are foregrounded. Whereas the virginal hag's motivation for sexual entrapment is to break the spell that binds her flesh in abjection, and the Irish Sovereignty's motivation is initiating a king-to-be, the unsolved riddle concerning Chaucer's hag is why she bothers to pursue a knight whose only attraction seems to be a "manly voys" (WBT, line 1036). Although it is Dame Ragnelle and not the Wife's hag who states an interest in high testosterone levels by specifying that she wants "the manliest knight," the much married Wife is centrally interested in what is "fresshe abedd" rather than in the knight's moral correctness. Florent gets a virgin because this fits his virtue; his bespelled maiden also gets a virtuous husband.[31] Chaucer, however, is interested in constructing the Wife's voice: male virtue is of little interest to the Wife.[32] She does not take men seriously, except as contestants in the battle of the sexes, or sex objects in their own right, when they have nice legs and gold curls.

What plausibly attracts her to this motif is the sexual politics involved once you shift "sovereignty" as a rightful portfolio of the Loathly Lady into the realm of the personal. The knight is not the hero of "The Wife of Bath's Tale" in the same way that Florent is of his. Chaucer's Loathly Lady stars in the Wife's account, and she gets the husband she inexplicably desires only by patiently reforming him. Since the Wife begins her own prologue by staking her credentials on experience regardless of the *auctoritée* of her day, it is appropriate that the subcategory of Loathly Lady she should feature is the one who is sexually experienced. The Wife has a canny knack of locating chinks in the armor of male subjectivity and her choice here of exactly the best type of shape-changer for her agenda shows just how clever Chaucer is at his literary act of female impersonation.[33]

Considering the precedents, I do not believe that the Wife of Bath's hag has a hymen anywhere in the weft of textual fabrication that conceals this moment of consummation. The command that this Loathly Lady has aligns her with the goddess models; despite her gracious and generous concessions to her groom, there lingers the sense that she retains the final control. Furthermore, the Wife's bid for sovereignty within marriage suggests that Chaucer admits the Loathly Lady to the Wife's tale to make use of the goddess's other-worldly license, and to apply her power to the dynamics of heterosexual relations. It suits the Wife of Bath's agenda that the Loathly Lady's unstable female body scrambles the semiotics of the beauty myth that to this day dictates the female body. And although the Wife admits that "Virginitee is greet perfeccion" (WBP, line 105), she makes it clear through her elaboration of what might tickle the heart's root that maidenheads do not really matter.

NOTES

1. Chaucer's version (ca. 1390) is central for the purposes of this discussion, but the archetype of the Loathly Lady is found in a range of texts from the late medieval period: the poem "Carn Máil" from *The Metrical Dindshenchas*; the *Cóir Anmann*, and "The Adventures of the Sons of Eochaid" (eleventh to twelfth century); John Gower's "The Tale of Florent" (1386–93); several ballads from Francis James Child's collection ("The Marriage of Sir Gawain"; "King Henry"; "Kempy Kay"; "Kemp Owyne"; and "The Knight and the Shepherd's Daughter"); "The Wedding of Sir Gawain and Dame

Ragnelle" (ca. 1450); and arguably "Thomas of Erceldoune" (thirteenth century). In all of these only "The Knight and the Shepherd's Daughter" alludes to the hymen, where a maidenhead reft by rape is the starting point. The shepherd's daughter accuses the knight specifically of stealing her maidenhead. See Lynn M. Wollstadt's consideration of this rape in the present volume. All citations of Chaucer are from Benson, *The Riverside Chaucer*, cited as GP ("General Prologue"), WBP ("The Wife of Bath's Prologue"), WBT ("The Wife of Bath's Tale), MLT ("The Man of Law's Tale"), and SNT ("The Second Nun's Tale").

2. Kathleen Biddick defines gender as "a theory of borders that enables us to talk about the historical construction and maintenance of sexual boundaries, both intra- and intercorporeal" ("Genders," p. 393). I like Biddick's incorporation of "boundaries" in her definition, and that she goes on to include "sex, flesh, body, race, nature, discourse, and culture" (p. 393) in her itemization of the kind of histories that theories of gender involve. Nancy F. Partner calls for a "reality check" (p. 440) on how liberating it is to separate sex and gender, proposing "Gender is not so easily parted from sex" ("No Sex," p. 439). Partner's observation is especially applicable to the way that gender power politics are activated by the Loathly Lady's sexual demands.

3. For example, Priscilla Martin proposes that "The Wife of the *Prologue* and the wife of the *Tale* present an idea of fractured femininity which the transformation attempts to restore to a wholeness of person" (*Chaucer's Women*, p. 61). Mary Carruthers identifies the hag as the Wife's lion, licensed to paint ("The Wife of Bath," pp. 22–53). Closer to my point, Dolores Warwick Frese observes a similarity (based upon active sexuality) between the Wife and the Irish queen, Medb. Frese declares: "Alys of Bath, pursuing her relentless marital agenda of sovereignty, resembles no one so much as Queen Medb, the feminine personification of national sovereignty in Irish tradition, who boasts of her own unbroken succession of Irish kings" ("Chaucer's Hidden Art," p. 163).

4. See Miller, *Chaucer: Sources*, for an itemization of the misogynist sources from which the Wife is at least partially constructed. Some critics find the misogynist material within Chaucer's writing overriding. An example is Sheila Delaney, who moderates her early position—that Chaucer is an "outright misogynist" (p. 110)—to the guarded, and thus highly defensible, opinion that he "both 'is and is not' woman's friend" ("Sex and Gender," p. 111). On the other hand, Margaret Hallissy begins her book by postulating that "if women define a friend as someone who is interested, who listens, and who therefore understands, then this long-dead medieval poet is indeed … all women's friend" (*Clean Maids*, p. xv). Cf. Hansen, *Chaucer and the Fictions of Gender*, and Dinshaw, *Chaucer's Sexual Poetics*. I insist that, regardless of Chaucer's authorial intention, in producing the Wife with her Loathly Lady, he has served women well.

5. I agree with Manuel Aguirre who complains that both Celtic and English scholarship "seem to agree that there is a link, but at that same time they neglect or minimize its value" ("Riddle of Sovereignty," p. 275). This volume goes some way

towards correcting a previous lack of attention to the links between English and Irish tales.

6. Those detectives who chart this terrain—William P. Albrecht, Francis James Child, Arthur C. L. Brown, Sigmund Eisner, Roger Sherman Loomis, G. H. Maynadier, Alfred Nutt, Jessie L. Weston, and Bartlett J. Whiting, et al.—provide the groundwork for my discussion. Scholarly opinion is that all extant works which use the Loathly Lady motif have evolved from earlier oral forms, probably Celtic, pagan, and certainly irretrievable.

7. See Aguirre, "Riddle of Sovereignty," pp. 273–82.

8. See Gwynn, "Carn Máil," pp. 134–43. *Cóir Anmann* is Whitley Stokes's translation: *Cóir Anmann*, pp. 285–444. Cf. O'Donovan, "Appendix A," pp. 67–79.

9. See Whitley Stokes's translation of "The Death of Crimthann Son of Fidach, and the Adventures of the Sons of Eochaid Muigmedon," pp. 172–207.

10. Sigmund Eisner, in *A Tale of Wonder*, itemizes "Nine extant tales ... relevant to the loathly lady theme," noting, however, that in only three is the heroine "the hideous Sovereignty" (p. 17). The shape-changing hag belongs to an interconnected tribe of other quasi-divine Irish figures, some of whom are always beautiful. C. L. Innes supplies an inventory: "Throughout the history of its colonization, Ireland has been represented by British imperialists as well as Irish nationalists as female: she is Hibernia, Eire, Mother Ireland, the Poor Old Woman, the San Van Vocht, Cathleen ni Houlihan, the Dark Rosaleen" (*Woman and Nation*, p. 2). Mary Low lists "Ériu, Étain, Eithne, Mór Muman, Macha Mong-ruad" as "sovereignty motifs" (*Celtic Christianity*, p. 34). Arguably Queen Medb has a place in these lists. Thus the Loathly Lady belongs within a set of similar, but specifically Irish, goddesslike personifications.

11. See Economou, *Goddess Natura*.

12. All quotations are from Gwynn, "Carn Máil."

13. Elizabeth Passmore kindly negotiated the labyrinth of the Old Irish language on my behalf to ensure that the line "lór duib m' esbaid-se m' denor" sustains the translation that provides "lose" through the word *esbaid*. I am indebted to her scholarly guidance with Old Irish.

14. For example, Luke Gernon, in "A Discourse of Ireland" (1620), applies sexual fervor to his colonial interest when he observes, "This Nymph of Ireland, is at all poynts like a yong wench that hath the greene sickness for want of occupying" (qtd. in Falkiner, *Essays*, p. 349).

15. For example, Toni O'Brien Johnson and David Cairns observe that "The notion of using a female figure to embody such contradictory qualities as this sovereignty goddess does is problematic from most feminist points of view" (pp. 3–4). They raise the question of "whether the essentialism of mythically produced figures must inevitably be reductive and have disabling effects on mere historical women" (pp. 4–5), without addressing this problem in their own collection of essays: *Gender in Irish Writing*.

16. Stokes, "The Death of Crimthann," p. 201.

17. Elizabeth Passmore suggested that this is the point when I should mention the tri-goddess connection. See Graves, *White Goddess*.

18. I was bemused by the centrality of the penis in Freud's work before I found Kate Millet's *Sexual Politics*, but endorse her rejection of the penis as a mark of socialization, while acknowledging the usefulness of much Freudian theory.

19. In an otherwise trenchant reading of "The Wife of Bath's Tale," Jill Mann elides the significance of the Irish sovereignty tales and the Loathly Lady motif per se. Mann refers in mortal terms to "the old wife who has been inflicted … as punishment" on the rapist knight, dismissively finding the hag's transformation "no whit more miraculous than the transformation of a rapist into a meekly submissive husband" (*Geoffrey Chaucer*, p. 87). Mann would find her feminist reading of Chaucer considerably reinforced if she also acknowledged his admittance of what the motif brings as cultural baggage.

20. The "Liber Trotuli" (ca. twelfth century) gives a recipe for a fake hymen, useful to one who "wolde be holde for a mayde," showing that this trickery is time-honored. Cited in Barratt, *Women's Writing*, p. 37.

21. Mary Low considers wells with Christian and pagan powers, proposing that "water-deities" were "mostly female," despite the fact that "[m]ost holy wells are nowadays associated with male saints" (*Celtic Christianity*, pp. 66–67).

22. These maidenly Loathly Ladies are not the pure virgins of hagiography, wherein, it might be argued, the only good virgin is a dead one. Howard R. Bloch concludes just this: that "a certain inescapable logic of virginity, most evident in medieval hagiography, leads syllogistically to the conclusion that the only real virgin—that is, the only true virgin—is a dead virgin" (*Medieval Misogyny*, p. 108). In apposition to this, the virginity of bespelled maidens is that of any maiden destined for marriage: designed to be broken.

23. All quotations from "The Tale of Florent" are from *Confessio Amantis*, ed. Peck, pp. 58–71. It is generally accepted that Gower and Chaucer probably shared the same source but that this is unknown. See Hilary, "Wife of Bath's Tale," p. 872, and Eisner, *Tale of Wonder*, p. 9. Maynadier is less willing to commit himself, observing that the questions of whether Chaucer and Gower shared the same source, or one borrowed from the other "cannot be answered definitely" (*"Wife,"* p. 6).

24. "Liber Primus," line 232. A comparison may be made between Genius's soft reasoning voice and the knight's manly voice in which he delivers the answer to the riddle to the court of ladies in "The Wife of Bath's Tale."

25. Kurt Olsson observes that Florent "learns without a teacher," "respects his oaths," "will not be untrue," and "is never witless" (*John Gower*, p. 80). I agree that Florent is a thoroughly decent knight.

26. Angela Jane Weisl identifies the slur implicit in a lack of nomenclature: "Unlike his counterparts, this knight is known for nothing" (*Conquering*, p. 95).

27. Hahn, *Sir Gawain*, pp. 47–80; all quotations of "The Wedding of Sir Gawain and Dame Ragnelle" are from this edition.

28. See Russell Peck's essay, "Folklore and Powerful Women," in the present volume.

29. Lisa M. Bitel categorizes the Loathly Lady as a party to what she terms "sexual healing": "The well-known female symbols of sovereignty who wandered through the pseudohistorical tales of early Ireland were hideous, barren hags until they copulated with the right royal aspirant. At the moment of consummation the loathly ladies turned into beautiful young women and the men became kings.... Whatever the political morals and other symbolic messages of these stories, the vocabulary was sexual healing" (*Land of Women,* p. 70). Her term is not one that I would use, but I note that, significantly, in both the sovereignty tales and "The Wife of Bath's Tale," heterosexual union is restorative. See Van, "False Tests," pp. 179–93. Also see Ellen M. Caldwell's essay in this volume for a contrary reading in which she finds the Loathly Lady completely subdued at the closure of "The Wife of Bath's Tale."

30. I acknowledge thanks to Larry Scanlon for directing me towards this idea.

31. Passmore's identification of the theme of ideal courtly behavior has helped me to locate more precisely what Chaucer does that is different; see Passmore, "Once Upon a Time."

32. See Susan Carter, "The Beastly Bride," pp. 329–45, for my argument that there is something playful about the pillow sermon delivered within the marriage bed. I thus put an emphasis on the old wife's sermon to the knight that is different from Passmore's.

33. Chaucer, a devout Catholic, does not use the sinful Wife of Bath as a spokesperson for his own views on heterosexuality. But he plays so consistently with the construction of gender and of subjectivity that he surely, as Ruth M. Ames notes, "recognised the diversity as clearly as we do ... [and] delighted in multiplicity" (*God's Plenty,* p. 3). H. Marshall Leicester, Jr. gestures towards the convincing sense of the Wife's positive redaction of her history, when he notes that the lines "As help me God, I laughe whan I thynke / How piteously a-nyght I made them swynke!" (WBT, lines 201–2) "catch the way that something that was unpleasant or uncomfortable to live through may not be so to recall" (*Disenchanted Self,* p. 84). Clair C. Olson notes, "We know exactly how the Wife of Bath feels, and that her feelings are not only individualized but strongly held" ("Interludes," p. 164). I agree that there is a real sense of the Wife constructing an autobiography and turning a lived experience into entertainment. I thus disagree with Kathryn L. McKinley who declares that "[i]t is undoubtedly true that the Wife [is] lacking an authentic voice" ("Silenced Knight," p. 360), and concur with Martin Puhvel who argues that "[i]t is a tribute to the psychological meticulousness of Chaucer's art in *The Canterbury Tales* that the tale told by the Wife of Bath should appear so closely tailored to her personality" ("Wife of Bath's Tale," p. 291). Puhvel rehearses the case for "the imprint of Alisoun's personality on the heroine of her tale" (p. 299), while failing to consider that the Loathly Lady motif adds a further dimension to "Alisoun's yearning and striving for 'soverynetee' over her men" (p. 298).

Works Cited

Aguirre, Manuel. "The Riddle of Sovereignty." *MLR* 88 (1993), 273–82.

Albrecht, William P., ed. *The Loathly Lady in "Thomas of Erceldoune": With a Text of the Poem Printed in 1652.* Albuquerque: University of New Mexico Press, 1954.

Ames, Ruth M. *God's Plenty: Chaucer's Christian Humanism.* Chicago: Loyola University Press, 1984.

Barratt, Alexandra. *Women's Writing in Middle English.* Essex: Longman, 1992.

Benson, Larry D., gen. ed. *The Riverside Chaucer.* 3rd ed. Boston: Houghton Mifflin, 1987; repr. Oxford: Oxford University Press, 1988.

Biddick, Kathleen. "Genders, Bodies, Borders: Technologies of the Visible." *Speculum* 68 (1993), 389–418.

Bitel, Lisa M. *Land of Women: Tales of Sex and Gender from Early Ireland.* Ithaca: Cornell University Press, 1996.

Bloch, Howard, R. *Medieval Misogyny and the Invention of Western Romantic Love.* Chicago: Chicago University Press, 1991.

Brown, Arthur C. L. *The Origin of the Grail Legend.* Cambridge, Mass.: Harvard University Press, 1943.

Carruthers, Mary. "The Wife of Bath and the Painting of Lions." In *Feminist Readings in Middle English Literature: The Wife of Bath and All her Sect,* ed. Ruth Evans and Lesley Johnson, pp. 22–53. London: Routledge, 1994.

Carter, Susan. "The Beastly Bride and the Hunter Hunted: What Lies Behind Chaucer's 'Wife of Bath's Tale,'" *CR* 37 (2003), 329–45.

Child, Francis James, ed. *The English and Scottish Popular Ballads.* New York: Pageant, 1882.

Delaney, Sheila. "Sex and Gender in Chaucer's Poetry." In *A Wyf Ther Was,* ed. Dor, pp. 103–11.

Dinshaw, Carolyn. *Chaucer's Sexual Poetics.* Madison: University of Wisconsin Press, 1989.

Dor, Juliette, ed. *A Wyf Ther Was: Essays in Honour of Paule Mertens-Fonck.* Liège: University of Liège Press, 1992.

Economou, George, D. *The Goddess Natura in Medieval Literature.* Cambridge, Mass.: Harvard University Press, 1972.

Eisner, Sigmund. *A Tale of Wonder: A Source Study of "The Wife of Bath's Tale."* Wexford, Ire.: John English, 1957.

Falkiner, Caesar Litton. *Essays Relating to Ireland.* 1909; repr. Port Washington, N.Y.: Kennikat, 1970.

Frese, Dolores Warwick. "The Names of Women in *The Canterbury Tales:* Chaucer's Hidden Art of Involcral Nomenclature." In *A Wyf Ther Was,* ed. Dor, pp. 155–66.

Gower, John. *Confessio Amantis.* Ed. Russell A. Peck. Toronto: University of Toronto Press, 1997.

Graves, Robert. *The White Goddess: A Historical Grammar of Poetic Myth.* London: Faber, 1952.

Gwynn, Edward, trans. "Carn Máil." In *The Metrical Dindschenchas*, pp. 134–43. Dublin: RIA, 1924.

Hahn, Thomas, ed. *Sir Gawain: Eleven Romances and Tales.* Kalamazoo, Mich.: Medieval Institute Publications, 1995.

Hallissy, Margaret. *Clean Maids, True Wives, Steadfast Widows: Chaucer's Women and Medieval Codes of Conduct.* Westport, Conn.: Greenwood, 1993.

Hansen, Elaine Tuttle. *Chaucer and the Fictions of Gender.* Berkeley: University of California Press, 1992.

Hilary, Christine Ryan. "The Wife of Bath's Tale" [notes]. In *The Riverside Chaucer*, pp. 872–74.

Innes, C. L. *Woman and Nation in Irish Literature and Society, 1880–1935.* New York: Harvester, 1993.

Johnson, Toni O'Brien, and David Cairns. *Gender in Irish Writing.* Philadelphia: Open University Press, 1991.

Leicester, Marshall H., Jr. *The Disenchanted Self: Representing the Subject in "The Canterbury Tales."* Berkeley: University of California Press, 1990.

Loomis, Roger Sherman. *Celtic Myth and Arthurian Romance.* New York: Columbia University Press, 1927.

——. *The Grail: From Celtic Myth to Christian Symbol.* Cardiff: University of Wales Press, 1963.

Low, Mary. *Celtic Christianity and Nature: Early Irish and Hebridean Traditions.* Belfast: Blackstaff, 1996.

Mann, Jill. *Geoffrey Chaucer.* New York: Harvester, 1991.

Martin, Priscilla. *Chaucer's Women: Nuns, Wives and Amazons.* Basingstoke: Macmillan, 1990.

Maynadier, Gustavus Howard. *"The Wife of Bath's Tale": Its Sources and Analogues.* London: Nutt, 1901.

McKinley, Kathryn L. "The Silenced Knight: Questions of Power and Reciprocity in the 'Wife of Bath's Tale.'" CR 30 (1996), 359–78.

Miller, Robert P. *Chaucer: Sources and Backgrounds.* New York: Oxford University Press, 1977.

Millet, Kate. *Sexual Politics.* New York: Doubleday, 1970.

O'Donovan, John, trans. "Appendix A to the Genealogy of Corca Laidhe." In *Miscellany of the Celtic Society*, ed. John O'Donovan, pp. 67–79. Dublin: Celtic Soc., 1849.

Olson, Clair C. "The Interludes of the Marriage Group in *The Canterbury Tales*." In *Chaucer and Middle English Studies in Honor of Russell Hope Robbins*, ed. Beryl Rowland, pp. 72–164. London: Allen, 1974.

Olsson, Kurt. *John Gower and the Structures of Conversion: A Reading of the "Confessio Amantis."* Cambridge: Brewer, 1992.

Partner, Nancy F. "No Sex, No Gender." *Speculum* 68 (1993), 419–43.

Passmore, S. Elizabeth. "Once Upon a Time: Introductory Themes in the English and Irish Loathly Lady Tales." International Congress on Medieval Studies. May 2002. Western Michigan University.

Puhvel, Martin. "The Wife of Bath's Tale: Mirror of Her Mind." *NM* 3 (1999), 291–300.

Stokes, Whitley H., and E. Windisch, trans. *Cóir Anmann (Fitness of Names)*. In Vol. 2 of *Irische Texte mit Übersetzungen und Wörterbuch*, ser. 3. Liepzig: Hirzel, 1897, 285–444.

———, trans. "The Death of Crimthann Son of Fidach, and the Adventures of the Sons of Eochaid Muigmedón." *RC* 24 (1903), 172–207.

Van, Thomas A. "False Tests and Disappearing Women in the *Wife of Bath's Prologue and Tale*." *CR* 29 (1994), 179–96.

Weisl, Angela Jane. *Conquering the Reign of Femeny: Gender and Genre in Chaucer's Romance*. Cambridge: Brewer, 1995.

Weston, Jessie L. *From Ritual to Romance*. Cambridge: Cambridge University Press, 1920.

Whiting, Bartlett J. "The Wife of Bath's Tale." In *Sources and Analogues of Chaucer's Canterbury Tales*, ed. W. F. Bryan and Germaine Dempster, pp. 224–64. New York: Humanities, 1958.

Folklore and Powerful Women in Gower's "Tale of Florent"

Russell A. Peck

"Nobody can write a new fairy tale; you can only mix up ... the old, old stories, and put the characters into new dresses." — Andrew Lang

John Gower's "Tale of Florent" is the first sustained Loathly Lady narrative in English literature.[1] Some have speculated that Gower's story and Chaucer's "Wife of Bath's Tale" must have some common source now lost,[2] but it seems more feasible to me that Gower, drawing upon folk materials, put together the basic narrative as we know it. "The Tale of Florent" then functioned as the primary literary source for "The Wife of Bath's Tale" and, along with "The Wife of Bath's Tale," though less exclusively, for the Loathly Lady section of "The Wedding of Sir Gawain and Dame Ragnelle." The subsequent writers, of course, drew upon other materials as well as they reshaped Gower's assemblage for new purposes.

The interface between folktale and literary work is difficult to sort out, especially in the Middle Ages. Usually writers look to literary sources and rhetorical practice in compiling their work.[3] Literary documents take precedence over oral tradition when writers talk about their sources. But given the prominence of oral mediation in pre-print culture, distinctions between folk and literary traditions break down; once a story is performed (read aloud) the text becomes oral property, free to circulate according to the phenomena and praxis of folklore. Professional tale-tellers would most likely be male,[4] while domestic storytelling undoubtedly included women.

Since the recorded word is what survives, the earliest known instances of Loathly Lady folk motifs are, of course, literary. Tales of enchantment are likely to have entered literary contexts from vernacular matriarchal folk traditions, and, in their new context, they are often used subversively against the presumptions of male authority. It is striking to observe how powerful these women tend to be. The earliest work to provide a matrix of loathly women who assail the male hegemony is *The Odyssey*, with its Laistrygonians, Sirens, Circe, and Scylla and Charybdis who, with their admixture of beauty and ugliness, seduce, engulf, and cannibalize male prowess. Loathly Lady stories often pose a threat to the male, reflecting in their power some form of male inadequacy or castration fear, as in Apuleius's *Golden Ass*, with its witches and foul hags who piss all over Aristomenes, cut the throat of Socrates, and threaten to "tie him by his members and so cut them off."[5] Or Loathly Ladies may themselves be caught in an incapacitating enchantment, yearning to regain their lost sovereignty.[6] Either way, the Loathly Lady lurks on the fringe of society, an outsider at the edge of night or the outskirt of the forest, whose marginality has a power unto itself that can challenge, even destroy, complacent male assumptions of normalcy, simply by her monstrosity; conversely, such marginality can bring a great benefit.[7] The hag may have the power of a Medusa to challenge young Perseus who, in his fantasy, would protect the congenial idea of beauty (i.e., his Andromeda) and save his lovely mother Danae from evil enchantment; although he ultimately rescues them both, it is only by appropriating the power of the gorgon's head that he succeeds. The head itself he gives to Athena, where its ugly, petrifying force, not a whit diminished, becomes the protective aegis of the god's potent shield. The power of these strange creatures fascinates and demands consideration.

Loathly Lady stories are as ancient as men and women. Every culture has them; every culture needs them. As in Aeschylus's *The Eumenides*, the gift of the hideous women may provide salvation of the state. Their stories help establish parameters of stability amidst change and provoke audiences to question desire, choice, and boundaries. They query the politics of property and appropriation, the insinuations of jealousy, and the rights of privilege, law, and good rule. Inevitably, because of their strangeness, their stories are bound up with perspective, transformation, enchantment, and other forms of disorientation. Often they reflect coming-of-age and growing-up processes, especially the awkward physical changes that occur during puberty, where animality, sexual insecurity, and a sense of being dirty, deformed, or inadequate haunts the psyche as it tries to protect itself from imagined taboos.[8] Loathly Lady stories focus attention on the unspeakable, on personal deficiency. But they also serve political purposes, from the psychological to the civic.

Although no English writer of the fourteenth century was more intelligently in touch with Ovid and classical narratives than Gower,[9] his "Tale of Florent" seems more attuned to Celtic folk motifs than to classical literary sources, though Ovidian motifs do lurk in the background. Certainly the topics of puberty, matriarchal power, metamorphic enchantment, physical taboos, problems of seeing and understanding what one sees, and the unspeakability of what one encounters along the margins are all there, within the matrix of a folk *mentalité*. Sigmund Eisner has argued that most details of Gower's plot resonate in Irish Loathly Lady tales, like that of Ériu who, having been transformed by enchantment into a monster, is released from her deformity by a kiss, to reveal that she is "the Sovereignty of Ireland."[10]

Parallels with the Irish tale are indeed compelling. There is an "Irishness" about Gower's narrative as it subtly explores oppressions of disenfranchisement. But it is doubtful that Gower or Chaucer could have known the Irish tales, at least not directly. Rather than working from an Irish "source," it seems more likely that Gower is exploring what Coomaraswamy calls "functions of thought,"[11] folk motifs that resonate with each other in particular contexts. Eisner supplies no evidence of how such an Irish tale as Ériu, with its heavily politicized content on the sovereignty of Ireland, might have migrated to England or how Gower or Chaucer could have known it.[12] John K. Bollard argues that "in the case of the transformed hag motif we are lacking the Welsh evidence on which this theory of transmission depends."[13] Stories of women falling into ugliness because of an enchantment that can only be broken by a kiss are the stock and trade of folktales, whether oral or written,[14] particularly tales of humans transformed into grotesque forms that disenfranchise the victim's sovereignty over his/her rightful domain.[15] Bollard insists that the Irish term translated by Eisner and others as "sovereignty," namely *flaithius*, has little to do with "sovereignty in marriage," but is rather a term pertaining to kingship and kingly authority.[16]

For Gower and Chaucer the notion of sovereignty is personal, rather than political in terms of the land as national identity. There is, nonetheless, a political component to Gower's notion of sovereignty in that in his view every person is a king with a kingdom to justify—that is, his own "dom," his judgment or psychological domain[17]—but, even so, this is a different concept of sovereignty from that of the Irish stories and their earth goddess mythology. In "The Wedding of Sir Gawain and Dame Ragnelle" the poet introduces issues of conflict over property rights with connotations akin to *flaithius* in the Irish tales, but that component is only loosely cognate with matters of sovereignty in the Loathly Lady part of the tale, since in the Irish tales there is no riddle to be solved and no double trial of the hero. In "Ragnelle" the notions of *flaithius* and sovereignty have been kept distinct, in that they are divided between Arthur (i.e., the king and sovereignty of property, as in the

Irish) and Gawain (with his personal sense of sovereignty as fealty and marriage, ideas akin to the psychological domain of Gower's story).[18]

There is documentable evidence, however, that Loathly Lady episodes were used in late thirteenth-century England for political advantage in re-claiming sovereignty over land in terms similar to the Irish notion of *flaithius*. Roger Sherman Loomis discusses a Loathly Lady component in a Round Table *spiel* (play) staged by King Edward I (ca. 1299). The event, recounted by the Dutch chronicler Lodewijk van Velthem,[19] tells how Edward ordered his knights to dress as particular Arthurian champions, instructing them "to introduce into the play the wrongs that he had suffered from certain towns so that the chosen knights might be pledged to avenge them."[20] The knights were given the parts of Lancelot, Gawain, Perceval, Aggravaine, Bors, Gareth, Lyonell, Mordred, and Kay, whose saddle was rigged so that he would be hurled to the ground to the laughter of the spectators. At the end of the tournament Edward declared a Round Table feast, with each course interrupted by a stranger who would intrude upon the banquet to make demands upon the company. The first interrupter, a squire splattered with blood, called upon the king and his knights to take vengeance on the Welsh for what he had endured. The king and the Round Table vowed to do so. The second interloper rode in on a sumpter, his hands and feet tied, with a letter from "the king of Irlant," denouncing Lancelot as a traitor and daring him to meet him in battle on the coast of Wales. Lancelot, we are told, seemed overwhelmed by the challenge, but Gawain and the king promised their support:

> After the third course and the customary pause the Loathly Damsel entered, her nose a foot long and a palm in width, her ears like those of an ass, coarse braids hanging down to her girdle, a goitre on her long red neck, two teeth projecting a finger's length from her wry mouth. She rode on a thin limping horse, and of course she addressed her first remarks to "Perchevael" and told him to ride to Licester and win the castle from its lord, who was assailing his neighbors. She bade "Walewein" ride to Cornuaelge and put an end to the strife between commons and lords. The two knights undertook those adventures, and the Loathly Damsel, who, we are informed, was a squire thus disguised at the king's command, slipped away and removed his make up.[21]

The king then proclaimed that his court would be sternly held to their pledges and set the date for the start of his campaigns against Wales and Scotland.[22]

The account of Edward's "Round Table" is instructive in both the nature and uses of folk materials. Folktales are staged folklore. Edward provides a folkloric moment which he uses for a very specific political purpose. The hag appears in a banquet designed to announce the king's next military campaign. His *spiel* entertains, but it also demands a public expression of loyalty as the knights are required to pledge themselves to the upcoming forays. What does it mean that Lancelot is overwhelmed by the challenge? Is the "play" commenting on an Arthurian character or an Edwardian knight who might be reluctant to join the attack on Kenilworth and the Scots? The participants at the feast all know, of course, that the Loathly Lady is a squire acting a comic part. But is it the squire that is hidden in drag or Edward's agenda? The squire can remove his makeup, but the knights are not given the option of putting aside their costumes. Whether they be mythic Gawains or late thirteenth-century knights, Edward sees to it, with plenty of public witnesses, that they have been conscripted for duty.

Edward functions as a kind of play director, a god outside the play who determines the result in the form of covenants and legal contracts. His role is that of what A. J. Greimas calls the *destinateur*.[23] The Arthurian knights, who are more *actants* than characters, convey cultural markers that are read into the occasion, an agenda that Edward I's warriors are expected to be eager to join, given the hope for plunder, retaliation against the proud Scots, and the justice of it all as they get revenge and restore rightful territory to Edward or even make conquest of new, for the glory of his kingdom.

I have dwelt at length on the Edward episode for two reasons, first to emphasize ways in which folk materials may be drawn upon for new purposes, but also to contrast the loathly hag in Edward's play with Gower's use of such folk materials in "The Tale of Florent." Folktales were often performed as popular entertainment, whether in puppet shows, mimes, street scenes, skits, or court masques. But Edward's *spiel,* though one of the first recorded uses of a loathly hag motif in English, scarcely constitutes a story or predecessor to "The Tale of Florent" or "The Wife of Bath's Tale."[24] Edward's entertainment includes only the coming of a hag to Arthur's court to make a demand of Perceval and Gawain to put an end to strife between Commons and Lords. Like Edward, Gower conscripts folk motifs. But that is more or less the extent of the likeness in that Gower works from a different agenda. Gower presents a tale; Edward utilizes a trope. In Edward's *spiel* there are hidden agendas, but they are quite different from those in Gower or Chaucer. In Edward's trope there are no questions to be answered by a wayward knight who is indebted to the hag, no quest for answers, no questions the answer to which can redeem his life or alter his perception of the hag. There is no curse, no plot leading to marriage, no breaking of an enchantment. That is, Edward uses the loathly hag as a suppliant at court, but the device is not cast within the plot lines of a loathly hag narrative such as that of Gower's "Tale of Florent."[25]

All three of the English poets work within a rich tradition of folk motifs that circulated not only in England, Wales, Scotland, and Ireland, but on the continent and beyond as well. But Gower gives us the literary plot whose narratological syntax we recognize as the Middle English Loathly Lady story. That plot is dressed in folktale adornments that, when reconfigured by the poet, provide a compelling English literary narrative that other writers could (and did) spin off from in brilliant ways of their own. Gower's use of folk materials is both calculated and well-informed. It is less determined than Edward's; Gower has no power to commit his audience to binding commitments. He can only attempt to persuade. But his folktales are performative, nonetheless, and in their exemplary mode they are much committed to the staging of ideas.[26] Although he shapes a literary text, he is quite a good folklorist.

Gower and Folk Morphology

Shared motifs within oral traditions, more than any single factor, define folktales, where such figures of thought reappear in what Andrew Lang calls "new dresses." Their new apparel in "The Tale of Florent" is cut from the same literary cloth as other Gower narratives. In *Confessio Amantis* Gower's old stories are tailored in a highly literary, exemplary pattern, and exhibited in a moral frame structure that evokes folktale fashion, as Gower deliberately models his tale-tellings in the "vernacular" of the people. The figures that lurk within Gower's folk-fashion apparel—Loathly Ladies, stepmothers, aspiring youth, powerful uncles, accidental victims with powerful parents, especially female parents—are the cultural stock of ancient stories, whether Irish, English, French, Indian, or even beyond the Indo-European hegemony, who bring with them quirks and dispositions that mark the concerns of Gower's fourteenth-century culture even as much as the individual genius of the author.

There is, in effect, no contradiction between Lang's "Nobody can write a new fairy tale" and the proposition that Gower compiles the English narrative that Chaucer and the "Ragnelle"-poet follow in their Loathly Lady narratives. Both propositions are equally true: Gower loves old tales; he has a keen sense of their power and their cultural insinuations. A superb story-teller, Gower knows what his "poeple" hear best and how they will hear it.

His tale raises questions that must be thought through, a riddling that becomes a part of the narrative's entertainment value. In this regard he is indeed an author, not simply a compiler.[27] The folk motifs of "The Tale of Florent" function like Pirandello's "characters," ancient creatures in search of some "newe" authority (CA, Pro. 6),[28] some genius of "the present time which is now," as Gower puts it (CA, VIII.258),[29] who can give them a fresh presence and a local habitation.[30] That genius is the teller of the tale, but it is also the intelligence of the audience who incepts the story and stages it within its own consciousness. This folk quality is indeed a theater of the people: they are what is being staged.

With Gower, it is always useful to think of plot, the narrative syntax and grammar of tale-telling, in terms of folk morphologies. Folk ideology provides his plain style with a deep resonance, a resonance artfully calculated by the poet. One might argue, in fact, that Gower develops a theory of folklore long before it became a category of academic study. The term *folklore* was coined in 1846 by William Thoms for a discipline that he labeled with "a good Saxon compound, Folklore,—*the Lore of the People*."[31] Although Gower does not use the specific kenning "folklore," Thoms's phrase "lore of the people" sounds very Gowerian in that both sides of the compound—the "folk" and the "lore"—are named hundreds of times in Gower's poem, often as part of the same concept.[32]

Alan Dundes, in his useful introduction to *The Study of Folklore*, defines *folk* as "any group of people whatsoever who share at least one common factor,"[33] a designation that concurs with Gower's recurrent use of that term. The "folk," the "comon poeple," are frequently Gower's sounding board of wisdom in the hundreds of references that he makes to them in the poem. They embody "the comun vois, which mai noght lie" (Pro. 124). The people's voice may not lie because it is the authentic thing itself, a shared value beyond the individual, an evidence upon which to build a folklore, a "science"[34] of the people. Gower's poem is loaded with proverbial lore that serves as "common factor" between plot, character, and audience. The tone of "The Tale of Florent" is that of a folktale, particularly in the way it stages itself. Characters function like *dramatis personae*, rather than as characters in a novel; they are perceived by their function, working within a matrix of performing typologies rather than as beings that accord with some non-diagetic reality. They live within the lexias of folk motifs and types that scholars like Stith Thompson and Antti A. Aarne have concerned them-selves with.[35] Those typologies that Gower explores in Florent are kin to *actants* that lurk within motifs—among women, motifs of maternal supremacy and competition; among men, concepts of prowess, honor, and legal identity, but also male insecurity and fear of the sexuality of women. Both genders are aware of the potency of beauty and revulsion at ugliness, and fear the subversive power of animality. Within the tent of Gower's narrative, characters experience the personal desire for and need of sovereignty; they require dignity and value obedience to one's word. They think of law both as a social mechanism and a phenomenon of nature. Unstable enchantments and transformations of the beautiful into the ugly and of the ugly into the beautiful yield to an interdependency of a people in perpetual need, with tasks and initiation rites that lead on both sides to a participatory selfhood and a community bonding that resides in the lexias of inclusion, incorporation, or embodiment.

The Pre-eminence in English of "The Tale of Florent"

The situation of Gower's "Tale of Florent" as the basic source for other English versions of the story is in some ways akin to that of Boccaccio's "patient Griselda" story, as Francis Lee Utley explains in his discussion of the interlacing of folk and literary motifs in that popular narrative: "Boccaccio's 'Griselda' ... is, so far as I can find, the ultimate source of all modern tales on the subject (Motif H461, Type 887);[36] though Boccaccio's version certainly has links with older classifications like Cupid and Psyche and various tales of the Persecuted Wife."[37] My point is not that "The Tale of Florent" enjoys the popularity or influence of Boccaccio's "Griselda," but only that the narrative syntax of its plot, though somewhat similar to Irish analogues, is, in its literary influence, Gower's, and it defines the principal components that function in all the subsequent English literary versions of the Loathly Lady. These, it seems to me, are the primary components of the tale: 1) a male, under some form of disempowerment, finds himself at the mercy of powerful women who hold his life in their hands; 2) an enchanted hag, who herself is a victim of women, has knowledge that can ultimately help him, providing that he be obedient to her terms of involvement, which to him seems a horrendous threat; 3) the problem of disempowerment and the solution to the threat pertain to a question concerning desire and female sovereignty; 4) for both the male and the female, cultural and personal responses to the relative potency of ugliness and beauty affect their decision-making; and 5) in the narrative resolution each victim helps the other, he by acknowledging her authority, and she by restoring his potency.

Although Gower's folk narrative is fundamentally a subversive exposition on maternal power,[38] let me begin with a look at the masculine syntax embodied in its hero. On the surface, "The Tale of Florent" is an initiation story in which a young knight, full of puberty, sets out to make a name for himself. The education of this somewhat audacious naif has three principal stages.[39]

1. First life exposure: The setting out. Having grown to be a youth of "mochel myhte" (I.1412—for Gower this growth phenomenon is something that just happens to people), Florent presents himself in public in hope of acquiring fame:

> Of armes he was desirous,
> Chivalerous and amorous,
> And for the fame of worldes speche,
> Strange aventures for to seche,
> He rod the marches al about.
>   (I.1413–17)

Florent's exhibitionistic behavior demonstrates a kind of obedience to the processes of nature (*kynde*), an obedience that Genius (the narrator of the story) alleges pertains to love. "Wifles he was" (I.1411), we are told, and that lack seems to be a factor in his desirousness and amorousness. A good comparison with Florent as *actant* in this first setting-out stage might be seen in the young Apollonius, in Book VIII of the *Confessio*, who, in the spirit of adventure, goes forth, vaguely motivated by the amorous disposition of adolescence. Apollonius encounters Antiochus and his daughter, and answers a prenuptial riddle, only to find himself abruptly caught up in the second stage of his growth, namely an entanglement in a perplexing life/death social situation (VIII.374–536). So it is with Florent, who, hoping to impress ladies, enters a tournament only to find himself, in his victory, pursued by women who make demands against his life.

2. Second Life: Social entanglement. When Florent accidentally slays Branchus, who "to the capitain / Was sone and heir" (I.1428–30), his yearned-for encounter with women becomes immediately more threatening than anything he might have anticipated. Instead of some pretty young thing to have and to hold, the first women he encounters are determined to kill him. It is not "the capitain" or a man's world that vows revenge (the men seem to understand the risks of their bravura), but rather it is Branchus's mother and grandmother, who confront him with a question he must answer correctly or forfeit his life. The life/death *demande* requires that he tell what it is that women most desire.

3. *Third life: Discovery.* The third stage of Florent's initiation doubles up on him. He discovers the answer to the question, but then is faced with the consequences of that discovery. The double effect leads to problems of self-definition as well as social definition; he has to answer the old grantdame's question first in a court of law, but then, in a private exchange, he must answer to the hag who supplied him with the answer. What is brought home to Florent in this double bind is first the power of contracts and a sociology of law. But then the amorous youth is also brought face to face with female sexuality in a complex confrontation that is ugly and threatening before it is beautiful.

This discovery state concludes in an epiphany that brings him into an adult male identity based not on conquest, but rather on submission.[40] His epiphany is of a very particular kind. The crux of his trial hinges upon his character, rather than his physical prowess. He must be true to his word, not just once, but twice over: first, he must be willing to sacrifice his life for a question; second, he must be willing to sacrifice himself in what appears to be an unholy marriage. He seems to be trapped in a no-win situation: a naive youth in the machinations of powerful, predatory women. He, who began as a stalker (or, at least, a preening show-off), finds himself to be the one stalked.

The first half of the double bind (answer the question of what women desire or forfeit your life) is determined by Branchus's mother and the grandmother who seem certain of victory, since men never seem capable of understanding women. The second component of the double bind is more complex, in that it has been determined in part by the Loathly Lady, but mainly by a wicked stepmother, a person Florent has never even heard of, who put the curse of ugliness on the princess. Like the women in the first part of Florent's double bind, the stepmother depends on the stupid vanity of men to guarantee her success in maintaining authority over the woman she hates (I.1844).[41] That is, she knows that a man might say he will love a hag in order to save his neck, but it is highly unlikely that any man would ever be true to his word if confronted with marriage to the grotesquery her potent enchantment has made of the princess of Sicily. For all of the powerful women in the tale, the success of their schemes seems certain, given the vain and arrogant indulgences of men. Thus, all the audience can say at this point is "Poor Florent, poor Loathly Lady. Know it or not, the stepmother's got you both in her power."[42]

How Florent manages to get through the double bind is a mystery in itself, given the fact that he has been raised as a male in a chivalric culture that values women as prizes and honors masculine prowess over the understanding of women. Insofar as women may figure into masculine equations at all, they will be evaluated, by both men and women, according to their beauty quotient. The one key factor in Florent's success, however, is the fact that he has, albeit unknowingly, the guidance of a wise woman who, through her carefully timed questions and manipulation of a philosophical dilemma, the dilemma of Buridan's ass,[43] can help the boy to arrive at the right answers at the right time. Timing and patience are crucial features of enchantment narratives. Ruth B. Bottigheimer speaks of "silenced women" as a gender issue in fairy tales.[44] In Gower, there is a kind of silencing of the Loathly Lady (certainly more so than in Chaucer), but the reason is not due to patriarchal oppression; rather, as in many folktales, the woman is oppressed by another woman. Though part of the curse may entail some stricture against the monster's telling what good effects might result if someone were to heed her advice, she still may speak through riddles and questions. Gower's Loathly Lady is more self-controlled and discrete than silenced. She knows when to speak and speaks wisdom when she does. She holds the secrets, knowing that control of her knowledge and the success of her hoped-for freedom are mutual, both for her and for her partner-to-be. She is like Dame Prudence in Chaucer's "Tale of Melibee," who speaks "whan she saugh hir tyme."[45] Keep in mind that Florent has to answer two questions—first, what it is that women most desire, and, then, what it is that *he* most desires—each at the right moment—in order to get out of his double bind; moreover, she too must know enough and be patient enough to supply him with the right questions and answers, in both instances, at the right time.

Genius presents the tale as an exemplum of obedience. An interesting aspect of Gower's version of the loathly hag story is the emphasis placed upon the legality of all proceedings. Obedience and law mirror each other's validation. The mother and grandmother of Branchus are insistent on precise interpretation of the law. Control of the law (*lex positiva*) may usually be thought of as a feature of patriarchy,[46] but, in this instance, it is the women who are determined to use it to their advantage. Florent must not only be true to his word; he must keep his contract with women. When the grantdame and mother get him to agree to answer the question, they "have it under seales write" (I.1474); Florent then must in the presence of witnesses sign his name: "under his seal he wrot his oth" (I.1487). Florent is committed both legally and ethically. It is the legality of the matter that is of primary concern to the two women, who want protection against retaliation by the emperor, Florent's uncle. Law is their constraint against him, their jailer, so to speak.[47] But as far as Florent's initiation is concerned, it will ultimately be through the ethics of his choice, rather than *lex positiva*, that he will be released from all bondage and thereby find a forward-looking freedom.

Florent goes to his uncle the emperor to tell how things stand "upon his aventure" (I.1508), but when the allotted time passes and he still has no answer,[48] he explains that he would rather die "than breke his trowthe and for to lye / In place ther as he was swore" (I.1511–13) and tells his uncle not to intervene, "for that is a point of his oth" (I.1518). Word and contract are for him one. This is, of course, what the Loathly Lady counts on, for it holds the key to their mutual liberation. When Florent encounters the hag, she, like the grantdame, also gets very precise agreements, a pledge of his "trowthe in honde" (I.1559), sealed with a handshake: "Have hier myn hond, I schal thee wedde" (I.1587), a "covenant" that she allows (I.1590). The Loathly Lady, a victim herself, knows that word must be cousin to the deed, as Chaucer says—two separate things which, nonetheless, must be one. Obedience and obligation go hand in hand and their mutual salvation depends upon that coherence.

The legalities of contracts are further delineated when Florent returns to court to give his "full answere" (I.1629):

> Forth with his conseil cam the lord,
> The thinges stoden of record;
> He sende up for the lady sone,
> And forth sche cam, that olde mone.[49]
> In presence of the remenant
> The strengthe of al the covenant
> Tho was rehersed openly.
>   (I.1631–37)

This kind of meticulous legal detail serves to demonstrate a key feature of Florent's initiation into adulthood, demonstrating precisely how Florent, to be completely Florent, must be true to his word even according to the letter of every detail of his contract. In both situations, with the hag as well as with "that olde mone," the hero's obedience becomes as much a challenge to his belief in himself as it is to the keeping of his "forward" in each of the contracts to which he is committed.

But Florent's contract with the Loathly Lady is more subtle than that with the first complement of women. After he meets the demands of the dame and grantdame's contract, he still must fulfill the personal vow about which the others know nothing,[50] a vow for which there were no seals, no public signing, or witnesses to enforce any breach of contract. If Florent fails here he will undefine himself (something only he knows), whereby he would, indeed, destroy himself;[51] in which case he would fulfill the scheme of the Branchus family as a result of something quite outside the plan of the vengeful mothers, without their even knowing it.

The psychological complexity of this second trial, the trial contingent upon a stepmother's scheme of which Florent knows nothing, manifests well Gower's insights into the tenuous nature of humankind, where law merges with ethics: we are creatures who are both social and private, who must simultaneously participate in and fulfill social contracts that few can fully understand. The self definitions that society and the individual psyche demand hinge upon the notion that a "self" exists as a moral state unto itself. In the realm of ethics the individual is always playing with a partial deck; as far as he is concerned, the cards aren't all there. As Gower presents it, this double indemnity is, moreover, as problematic for the Loathly Lady, trapped in a superimposed enchantment, as it is for Florent. Neither has a full deck, but together they do.

Indeed, although the tale is about the coming of Florent's insight into himself, it is also about that other outside himself, the hag to which he finds himself married. The amorous and desirous adventure upon which he set out has become something utterly unexpected: he must begin to understand women, that other half of humanity that nature has made both like and different from himself. The women of "The Tale of Florent" function more as *actants* than as characters, but, beyond that, they provide a setting and determine its subject matter. Women define and control all phases of the plot. In fact, one might argue, if taking a deep structuralist approach to the story, that any discussion of the tale should begin with the stepmother, that folkloric outsider who so often intrudes unwanted into the story, thereby disrupting the patterns of life that would otherwise confine the protagonists to an ungenerative complacence. As audience we know the stepmother from the numberless variants on the jealous outsider that range from Venus in the "Cupid and Psyche" story in Apuleius to the witch in *East of the Sun and West of the Moon* narratives, or the stepmothers who curse the woman in the early Norse and Gaelic winter tales.[52] In most instances the problems arise from competitive situations of women vying among women,[53] as is the case in "The Tale of Florent."

Although the stepmother does not appear until the end of the tale, she is the principal determinant, what might be called (with apologies to Greimas) the *destinateur*[54] of the story, the "why" behind the loathly hag's circumstance. But who exactly is she? After the riddle of what women most desire has been solved (a kind of Oedipus and the Sphinx problem) and the Loathly Lady has been transformed back into her lovely self, she explains how her "destiné" has been "overpassed" (I.1835) and "mi beauté" (I.1837) restored "Til I be take into my grave" (I.1838). She was "the kinges dowhter of Cizile" (I.1841), she says, but her "stepmoder for an hate, / Which toward me sche hath begonne, / Forschop me" (I.1844-46),[55] thereby destroying her beauty and transforming her into the loathly hag. The jealous older woman who would destroy her rivals, so often cast as a stepmother, is the *destinateur* of many a folktale, whether it be some prototype for "Cinderella" stories like "Aschenputtel," "Rushen Coatie," or "Vasillisa"; or the "Snow White," "Sleeping Beauty," or "Beauty and the Beast" narratives that we know so well from childhood.[56] She is the bestower of curses in dozens of animal tales where beautiful youth, both male or female, get transformed into birds, serpents, cats, pigs, frogs, or whatever.[57] Usually, she is jealous—some cranky fairy or hateful elder person who lacks youth, beauty, or paramour; or perhaps she is one who has simply been passed over herself (no invitation? we only know that she acted "for an hate"—I.1844), but who has, nonetheless, the power to dock her enemies of their sovereignty, leaving them in a state of deformity until that sovereignty can be restored.

As we have seen, the problem for the protagonist of the tale, though he does not know it, becomes the disenchanting of the stepmother's victim, upon whom his own salvation depends.[58] The victim is likewise compelled to find some agent who can precipitate the transformation. Both sides are thus involved in a codependent relationship, though only the woman is aware of that. The *actant* in such a scheme is likely to be a virtue figure rather than another power figure, one who can, perhaps with the victim's guidance, solve the riddle and otherwise meet the demands specified by the enchantress. He often works in the dark, quite ignorant of what is at stake for the enchanted creature. The key to what will break the spell, the intelligence behind his success, lies hidden within the victim herself, who may well be under some stipulation of the curse that forbids her from telling all, though this demand for secrecy is not always the case.[59]

Usually, in tales of this kind,[60] the *destinateur*, the power figure who determines the shape of the action, is a woman, a tribute, in its way, perhaps, to the domestic origins of so many of the tales where there is a predominance of women as household storytellers who are the nurturers of the culture itself. Angela Carter, in her essay/tale called "Ashputtle: or, the Mother's Ghost," provides a most thoughtful (and subversive) analysis of maternal power in the Grimm brothers' fairy tale "Aschenputtel,"[61] where, according to Carter, the busiest figure in the tale is the deceased mother (i.e., someone outside the diagetic interior of the story—a *destinateur*) who controls both the plot and the ash girl, indoctrinating the child, even after the mother has died, so that her daughter will grow up to be like her. Although beyond the grave, the mother sees to it that her daughter becomes progressively like herself, providing the girl with a red dress (here the sense seems to suggest menstruation, that red part of maternal acculturation); the ghost inspires the stepmother to mutilate her own daughters as she indoctrinates them into the goals and avenues of success according to the mores of society, just as the mother's ghost does with her daughter as she repeatedly invites the ash girl to join her in her coffin.

Carter's allegory focuses on the pressures of gender behavior embodied in the mother as she indoctrinates the adolescent into customary definitions of the good life—beauty, sexual advantage, marriage, wealth, authority, with a high premium on the sovereignty of desire. In Carter's version of the Aschenputtel narrative, then, the main contest is between two mothers, Aschenputtel's mother and the mother of the stepsisters, both power figures vying for the advancement of their daughters. But in each instance the *destinateur*, in working to advance her daughter, acts mainly to maintain the benefits of power for herself. If necessary she will put a curse on her rival, even if that person is her daughter, though especially if the rival is her stepchild.

In "The Tale of Florent" the hero first comes under the rule of the dame and grantdame. Then, having given his word, he is obliged to the Loathly Lady. Rather than seeking some Cinderella, who will be known by her slipper, he finds himself in a more terrifying situation, bound by wedding contract to a most foul obscenity, what Gower calls "this foule grete coise" (I.1734), which the Middle English Texts Series edition decorously glosses as "ugly woman (rump, *OF cuisse*, 'thigh')." No fairy slipper here: This bride, in her unspeakability, is more like a walking pudendum, with all her masses of uncombable hair,[62] a terrifying prospect to behold—"That myhte a mannes lust destourbe!" (I.1688).

In his detailed description of "this foule grete coise" and Florent's reluctance even to travel with it in public, Gower hints at male fears of woman's sexuality that characterize folklore variants on the *vagina dentata* type,[63] an idea picked up even more graphically by the "Ragnelle"-author. That poet, working from Gower, describes the "lady" three times, each time focusing on the sexual overtones of her horrendous mouth, teeth, and hair:

> Her mowthe was nott to lak
>
> . . . .
>
> Hir tethe hyng over her lyppes,
> Her chekys syde as wemens hippes.
>   (lines 232–36)

It is as if the voracious mouth were between her hips. The second description is more graphic still, as Gaynour and her ladies weep for Gawain:

> "Alas!" then sayde bothe Kyng and knyght,
> That evere he shold wed suche a wyghte,
> She was so fowlle and horyble.
> She had two tethe on every syde
> As borys tuskes, I wolle nott hyde,
> Of lengthe a large handfulle.
> The one tusk went up and the other doun,
> A mowthe fulle wyde and fowlle igrown,
> With grey herys many on.
> Her lyppes laye lumpryd on her chyn.
>   (lines 545–54)

Now the toothsome mouth is itself hairy, the lips lumped on her pelvic chin.[64] But the most disgusting and frightening images are reserved for the wedding feast itself, where Gawain, along with the king, queen, and other marvelling knights ("Ragnelle," line 606), has to witness the unspeakable monstrosity's insatiable appetite[65] as she consumes everything she can get into her mouth—whole capons, curlews, baked meat pies, and so on, using her three-inch-long nails to tear her food as she stuffs herself. Castration complex, indeed. Can he marry—give himself to—something so foul and threatening? When the king and Guinevere approach the wedding bed next morning, "all incerteyn" ("Ragnelle," line 730),[66] they fully expect Gawain to have been devoured by this fiend.[67] My point is not that Gower, or the "Ragnelle"-poet, for that matter, has *vagina dentata* explicitly in mind[68]; rather, that both poets set their dramas within a folk-type that occurs in various forms in a spectrum of cultures in consideration of intimidations, tensions, and debilitations in male/female sexuality.

Gower does not include an account of the wedding feast in his "Tale of Florent" (that is the "Ragnelle"-poet's contribution),[69] but rather sends the "foule grete coise" directly to bed, where Florent, more reluctant than Gawain, must prove himself obedient to his word. Given the circumstances, this is the most difficult task of all. That is, the answering of the question of what it is that women most desire was not the most stringent test, because Florent, in that first trial, came armed with the right answer: the loathly hag had given it to him. But to go "to hire which his trowthe hadde" (I.1667) with a *demande* of marriage—that is the ultimate trial.

As Florent, released from the "old mone," returns to the hag, Genius provides a grotesque description of what he encounters, followed by more legal terminology as she seizes the bridle of his horse "as sche hath ben his warant, / That he hire holde covenant" (I.1695–97). She does get bathed, because, we are told, "it was that time lawe" (I.1746), but "thei were wedded in the nyht," doubtless to avoid the shame of being seen, just as he had brought her to court "as an oule fleth be nyhte / Out of alle othre briddes syhte" (I.1727–28),[70] where "briddes" perhaps suggests, as well as song birds, the courtly standard of lovely women. This kind of legal texture is found throughout the *Confessio* and serves as part of Genius's education of the lover. Though it may tend to mute the folktale quality of the poem,[71] it serves well in maintaining the motif of truth to one's word and in defining Florent's obedience to the contract with the lady that binds him. But the main point is, that the legal bond helps to establish the interdependence of their lives—the trope of mutual need—with which the tale ends. The benefit of re-established sovereignty for both partners, once the needs (conditions) have been met, concludes the tale on a high note, turning the *querelle* to romance. Florent can at last be desirous and amorous and safe.

Gower and Chaucer

The goal of this and the following section is to demonstrate how Chaucer and the "Ragnelle"-poet adapt functions of Gower's "Tale of Florent" to their own literary purposes. I am not attempting to present a definitive reading of either of the two later texts. Rather, I am trying to view Florent as a subtext that helps to identify *actantial* juxtapositions in the new work. All three of the Middle English versions of the Loathly Lady story I am discussing resonate with illusive qualities of folklore that evoke oral traditions of the kind Lang proposes in the epigram, traditions that seem perpetual and yet that give a freshness and aura of mythic relevance to the narrative. Nonetheless, virtually every function of Gower's "Tale of Florent" is present in the subsequent poems.

The substructure of Chaucer's "Wife of Bath's Tale" is Gower's, though the dress of its functions is radically altered.[72] Chaucer's cloth-maker from Bath is a great fabricator, and the texture of her version of the story is, on the surface at least, quite different from Gower's. To begin with, the role of the male protagonist has virtually disappeared.[73] Although he sets the plot in motion through his rape of a woman, thereafter his fate and welfare are completely in the hands of women.[74] Queen Guinevere, rather than a step-mother appended to the conclusion, becomes the *destinateur* figure who sets events in motion while the Loathly Lady becomes multiple *actants*—the hag, but more than hag. She even assumes a crossover identity with her creator.

In the Wife of Bath's scenario the hag has not been placed under a curse; she is simply a person getting old, which is curse enough. But, although some detail from Gower is missing, the substructure adds significance to what has been changed, helping the audience to participate in Chaucer's play with a quickened intelligence. As in Gower, the male who committed the social offense finds himself in a double bind. The functional equivalent of the mother of Branchus and the old grantdame in Gower is now the queen, who takes command over the rapist knight's body. Guinevere poses the question that he must answer within twelve months and a day. Picking up on Gower's legal precision, the Wife's queen spells out the exact terms of the contract: "Thou standest yet ... in swich array / That of thy lyf yet hastow no suretee" (III[D]902–3). If the knight fails to supply "an answere suffisant in this mateere ... suretee wol I han, er that thou pace, / Thy body for to yelden in this place" (lines 910–12). In this narrative, control of the man's body demarcates matriarchal power. When the loathly woman claims him as her prize in marriage, the knight protests, "Taak al my good and lat my body go" (line 1061). But the queen says no. His body, which had been forfeit to the queen, is now given in legal bondage (marriage) to the old lady, a severe challenge indeed to his once potent and amorous view of himself.

A main component of Gower's narrative is the capacity of ugliness to debilitate and the power of beauty to enable. Although the Wife does not describe the intimidation of the male by the unspeakable ugliness of what Gower referred to as "this olde coise," Chaucer has not abandoned that idea. In fact, the *vagina dentata* motif implicit in Gower's story is prominent in

Chaucer. But it has shifted from the tale to the teller. Chaucer, in several places in *The Canterbury Tales*, challenges diagetic boundaries to evoke philosophical propositions about reception theory (e.g., who owns the story, where does it come from, or who is the "author"—the teller? some source? the audience who incepts it?). Can we even know what the boundaries of the story are? For example, the Man of Law protests that he can't tell a "thrifty tale" because Chaucer has told them all. (He is right, of course, since Chaucer, as his maker, supplies him with his voice and whatever story he chooses.) The Merchant, in his tale, breaks diagetic boundaries too as he attempts to interrupt his narrative to warn old Januarie or to scold Damian, neither of whom pay attention to him. Likewise, the Wife of Bath tries to exercise restraint to avoid getting involved in the diagetics of her tale, but, in truth, seldom succeeds in keeping herself out; she can't keep quiet about Midas's wife or all the things that women desire almost as much as sovereignty, and confuses herself with the haggard lady, even as Chaucer deliberately confuses his own authorial voice with the Wife's. Chaucer's appropriation of the *vagina dentata* motif into her voice in the Prologue might be thought of as part of this identity syndrome whereby he makes this compulsion to cross boundaries a feature of the Wife's fecund agility in self creation.[75] Such projection is a central feature of the staging of self, a point upon which Gower and Chaucer agree.

Chaucer uses the *vagina dentata* motif in the Wife's Prologue as an intimidating component of the Wife's demonstration of female power. She uses her private parts to display her potency, not simply as a gender indicator whereby one can tell little girls from little boys. She delights in spelling out the power of her "harneys" (line 136) and the perfection of her "instrument" (line 149) that God generously gave her so that man might "make his paiement" with "his sely instrument" (lines 130–32). Her vagina does indeed have teeth as she uses it to negotiate all men according to her terms. She takes pride in the host of sayings that define her armory: epithets such as her "mille" (line 389), where men may grind their grain (or be masticated); her "bele chose" (lines 447, 510), which she might sell or give when she pleases; her "herte roote" (line 471), that so tickles her when she is properly addressed, whether by eyes or otherwise; her "chambre of Venus" (line 618), which she can scarcely withdraw from any good fellow; that "privee place" (line 620) with the mark of Mars on it where many a battle takes place; that "lanterne" at which innumerable men may "lighte a candle" without diminishing the lantern's light (lines 334–35), etc. She is flattered that Jankyn and her other husbands would tell her that she has "the beste quonyam myghte be" (line 607).[76] But though she might choose to save herself for her husband's "owne tooth" (line 449), if that choice works to her advantage, she certainly knows how to bite, if need be: she can make her "shoo ful bitterly" (line 492) "wring" the one she is mad at, or "soore ... hym twiste" (line 494). It is no wonder that her fourth husband died when she "cam fro Jerusalem" (line 495). It is as if the harness that approaches scares him to death.

The Wife suggests that such a vessel may be sweet, if she chooses to make it so. That is demonstrated in her "Tale," when the knight kept his "nekke-boon from iren" (line 906) by putting himself in her "wise governance" (line 1232), giving her "maistrie" (line 1236), whereby he then took her in his two arms and "his herte bathed in a bath of blisse" (line 1253). Indeed, the Wife tells how the now lovely lady gives him the illusion of power by obeying him "in every thyng / That myghte doon him plesance or likyng" (lines 1255–56); but she makes it clear that the teeth are still there, if she wishes, as she orders Jesus to shorten the lives of all who will not be governed by their wives—"God sende hem soone verray pestilence!" (line 1264). And, it would seem, Jesus is usually obedient to her demands, bestowing plenty of pestilences.[77]

Another instance of the Wife's innovative dressing of the old story from Gower may be seen in the Wife's alteration of the cursed enchantment that befell Gower's Loathly Lady. The old woman in "The Wife of Bath's Tale" has no stepmother to curse her, but the Wife is, nonetheless, concerned with enchantment and appropriates the idea into her tale. She begins by explaining that although enchantments "fulfild of fairye" once were to be found, when "the elf-queene with her joly compaignye / Daunced ful ofte in many a grene mede" (lines 859–61), such behavior has now been displaced by friars, the only "incubus" (line 880) these days to lurk under bushes and dishonor women. But as she proceeds with her tale we see that enchantment has not utterly disappeared. Rather it has been appropriated by women in general—even older ones—to control men. The hag uses the enchantment prowess of female sexuality to trap the knight as she catches his attention with "foure and twenty and yet mo" (line 992) dancing ladies in order to get him to pay attention to the "wyf— / A fouler wight ther may no man devyse" (lines 998–99). And, when in bed with the knight, the old "wyf" enchants him again with her wise discourse on "gentilesse," the merits of poverty, and an assurance of fidelity, rather than cuckoldry, which she combines with a gift that enables him to "knowe [his] delit" and to "fulfille [his] worldly appetit" (lines 1217–18), a kind of beautiful gesture in itself.

We saw in Gower how the Loathly Lady functioned as a wisdom figure, a Dame Prudence to a reluctant Melibee. The Wife's older woman demonstrates a comparable range of sapient disputation as she develops her Boethian argument on "gentilesse," poverty, and old age to become the ultimate wisdom-bringer in the tale. As in Gower, she certainly has the power to help the knight, even though, at first, she seems a threat to his liberties. Although she may not be able to change herself physically to erase years, she, through her wise discourse, can change the knight's mind.[78] The Wife (with and through her surrogate in the tale") is a bit like Bottom in *A Midsummer Night's Dream*, wanting all the parts for herself.[79] The hag is indeed both *actant* and *destinateur*, while the knight becomes, at best, the *destinataire*, as all the oppositions and sendings fall upon him—for better or for worse. As in Gower, the knight is given a choice, and chooses to put himself in her governance: "Cheseth yourself which may be the moost plesance / And moost honour to yow and me also" (lines 1233–34). And, as in Gower's subtext, by giving her "maistrie" he wins his desire.

Chaucer rewrites Gower's notion of obedience, too, though it remains a central feature of the tale, as in Gower, albeit in its new Chaucerian dress. Now the issue is not finding a man who will be true to his word (the Wife and the surrogate ancient in her story know that no such a person may be found); rather, she demands, instead, obedience to herself. It is as if a new feudal order has been established, headed not by King Arthur but by a generous matriarch. The disobedient will be sorely punished by a spate of intimidating tactics—"God sende hem soone verray pestilence!" But the obedient may win rich rewards, which only they can enjoy according to the lady's "genti-lesse"—"gentil dedes," "pryve and apert" (lines 1114–15)—which only she can bestow (see lines 1113–18), deeds made possible by the gifts of the Creator Himself. God gave them, and she, in her own responsive obedience, will use them (see lines 148–50). It is as if she might restore fairy, just as Triamore does in Thomas Chestre's *Sir Launfal*, if only men would obey her and be silent.

The crux of the Wife's tale, is, of course, the question of woman's sovereignty which, as in Gower, is dealt with in two stages. The first question is essentially as it was in Gower—What is it that women most desire? The knight must answer the demand according to the law that has placed him in the hands of the queen (lines 889–98), who, as far as the Wife's tale is concerned, is the power center of the state; but having answered the queen's demand he finds himself still under the sureties of women where, in bed, he must answer with his body to the woman whose agency has just saved his life.[80] Both bondages place demands on his body, which, in the second instance, gives its consent when, in an apocalyptic curtain raiser, he sees before him one who is "so fair ... and so yong" (line 1251) that his potency is restored. Both find release through a kind of parallel pleasure in sex, perhaps even a sense of mutuality, though the Wife is more tentative on that point. Let him think it's mutual.

In Gower, Florent began his coming-out journey by putting himself on exhibit at tournaments. For Chaucer, Gower's simpler narrative has become a showboat for the Wife's creative ingenuity, her "queynte fantasye" (line 516) of what in real life is too often denied to women.[81] As Chaucer redresses Gower's substructure his skillful manipulation of narrative functions provides a wider range of *actants* than Gower had brought into play. The *actants* are so richly bundled that they may be subversive and, in their weird twists, comical all the while that they function in a serious vein. In Gower we are well aware that it is Genius who tells the story, but that narratological function is relatively slight compared to the role that the Wife of Bath plays in her story. For example, in the religious matrix so amusingly generated by the Wife, as she both mocks and affirms through her biblical appropriations, Chaucer foregrounds the central voicing of Christian culture. With her lantern, the Wife can play at being light of the world, the fountain of grace, a revealer of hidden truths through masterful glossing, the wise one who suffers the little children (boys, especially) to come unto her; she can be the bride awaiting the groom ("welcome the sixte" [line 45]), the mistress of the well, guardian of "the beste quonium myght be" and keeper of the sacred utensils, hoping to be the "vas eleccionis" of her lord.[82] Her lamp is well-oiled and ready, a blessed incarnation, indeed, as she works gladly for common profit in the vineyard of her new feudal order. At the same time she controls, even as she manipulates the psyche of the rapist knight, social and philosophical premises drawn mainly from Boethius, that Chaucer himself, throughout his writing, affirms. As in so much folk literature the Wife is less a character than an intratextual vehicle, an "isotopic iterativity,"[83] that enables Chaucer to spark resonances that challenge his voyeuristic, meaning-hungry audience with much to interpret, much to digest as the isotopies are broken down to sustain readerly needs.

Florent and Ragnelle

"The Tale of Florent" provides a literary substructure for only a portion of "The Wedding of Sir Gawain and Dame Ragnelle," the Loathly Lady section of the poem, and it shares a bit of its supporting role with "The Wife of Bath's Tale." "The Wedding of Sir Gawain and Dame Ragnelle" is a poem from the ranks of Middle English Gawain romances that subvert the pseudo-idealism of Arthur's court.[84] The poet has combined several romance tropes: the

hunter who outstrips his domain to find himself in trouble; a heedless king
who unwittingly abuses his privileges and duties as king; a knight who
encounters domestic virtues that divide his loyalties and thereby threaten his
relationship with the court; competition between the Round Table and
outsiders who may be more in the right than the king; an author writing as
a prisoner; and, at the center, the Loathly Lady story, which, with its
emphasis on a woman's desire for sovereignty, is an apt complement to all the
other themes of frustration and dispossession. The heart of the poem is closer
to Gower's telling of the loathly hag story than it is to Chaucer's,[85] as it
returns to several components of Gower's story that Chaucer had altered,
particularly the enchantment of the hag by a stepmother, who, by placing the
spell on Ragnelle, becomes, as in Gower, *destinateur* behind the main portion
of the plot. As in Gower, the narrative includes detailed descriptions of the
hag, recounts the bringing of her to the court, and includes details of the
wedding, more, in fact, than are found in Gower, as we discussed earlier. As
in Gower there is a second powerful woman, but here she is Queen
Guinevere, as in Chaucer. And, most importantly, the principal *acteur* is
again male.

The main differences between Gower's tale and "Ragnelle" are featured
less in the new clothes of the loathly hag story itself than in the tale's
placement within the Arthurian frame. The frame (given Lang's terminology
of new clothes, perhaps we should say "the closet") of the story is entirely
different from the other English versions and is the arena of greatest
innovation that markedly qualifies the inner story. The frame establishes the
political themes of the poem: right rule and proper domain. Like its two
literary predecessors this Loathly Lady story defines feudal law and allegiance,
but it places those concerns more directly in the hemisphere of kingship, with
Arthur functioning more as a target of careless rule than an exemplar of
truth. The king's carelessness is manifested in several ways: 1) As Arthur sets
off on his own to slay the great hart, Gromer Somer Joure catches him off
guard while he is busy butchering his kill; 2) Gromer's grievance against
Arthur is the result of another heedless act by the king, who has given some
of Gromer's land to Sir Gawain (that is, he gave away what was not his to
give);[86] 3) after Arthur has fallen under oath to Gromer, the king breaks his
oath by bringing Gawain in on the problem, then knowingly manipulates
Gawain even though he is aware that he misuses his authority to save his
skin; 4) after Gawain has saved him, the king simply passes over his own role
in the problem, without a second thought about any abuse of privilege; and
5) all of these royal irregularities set up the unexpected conclusion where the

author of the story reveals that he writes from prison, a victim, it would seem, of a ruler who ignores his plight.[87] Such an environment shifts the sovereignty motif from what women most desire and, thus, from Ragnelle's plight, to the rule of Arthur, whose sovereignty Gromer challenges and whose behavior Gawain unwittingly exposes by behaving according to the rules of fealty implicit in the ideal.

If Arthur behaves heedlessly, Gawain is the model of heedfulness. Like Florent Gawain has a keen moral sense and can be counted on not simply by Arthur to get him out of trouble, but by the Loathly Lady as well, who relies on him to break the spell.[88] Such a framework establishes an environment especially well suited to the enclosed narrative on what women most desire in that here women equate with the underprivileged, those dominated by patriarchal rule that abuses its privileges. The narrative begins with the effeminization of Arthur, as he is made subservient to Gromer's command. But unlike other medieval romance narratives (e.g., Chrétien's "Yvain," in which the privileged male is put under constraint until he sees better), there is no evidence that Arthur, as a disadvantaged aristocrat, learns anything from his ordeal. Gawain, on the other hand, guards feudal loyalties selflessly and thus understands how to behave.

But as the narrative proceeds into the Gawain portion of the story we see that we are very much in a realm in which the real power, or at least the balance of moral power, lies with the disadvantaged, the women, albeit somewhat ambiguously in that to some degree the women are filling a vacuum left by the inattentive Arthur. The welfare of the whole state is bound up with its ability to answer the question of what its "women" most desire. In this regard the concern is quite akin to the narratological syntax of Gower's version. The subject shifts from property to sovereignty and how it applies to individuals as well as states.

But in the new context shaped by the "resolutely masculine"[89] politics of the poem, the stumping question on women's desire this time comes from the hag's brother, Gromer Somer Joure, a disadvantaged man, rather than a scheming grantdame or a powerful queen,[90] and it is directed toward the obliviously unjust king, whom Gromer, the victim, hopes to destroy. As in Gower, the challenge of the question hinges upon obedience to personal and social ties. The obedience motif, which originates in Gower and constitutes the very glue that holds the story together, is given new dress. Arthur is more or less true to his word (see lines 115–16) in that he does return to Gromer to answer the question. But mainly it is Gawain who affirms the worth of Arthur's court through his loyalty, self-sacrifice, and obedience to his lord.

But although the focus of concern is centrally masculine, "The Wedding of Sir Gawain and Dame Ragnelle" still has Gower's powerful women in it. We have spoken of the stepmother as *destinateur* here as in Gower. And we have seen how, as in Gower, Ragnelle functions as wise woman as well as the monster. In some ways, however, the most intriguing woman in "Ragnelle" is Guinevere. Unlike Chaucer's queen, she does not have political power. Her force is more akin to that of real queens in a patriarchal realm. Her influence is primarily social, but in this regard she has enormous sway. The king may be a little perturbed that Gawain has gotten stuck with such a beast, but he's glad enough, since she did come up with the answer that saved his life and (at least as far as the public is concerned) his honor. But to Guinevere the marriage is an outrage scarcely to be endured. How can she have an admirable court with something so ugly and shameful in their midst? She tries to obscure the ugliness by having the wedding take place in the wee hours of the morning in a private chapel, but Ragnelle insists on "Highe Masse tyme" and a wedding feast in the great hall "in myddys of alle the rowte" (lines 578–80). One of the funniest lines in the poem is the queen's "I thank God" when she finds out that Ragnelle is beautiful and that the couple is happy; she indicates that her concern has been for Gawain, who might have been harmed, though her relief at not having to deal with an ugly monstrosity in her courtly domain is evident too. It is only after the transformation that the king informs the company, "How did help hym att nede Dame Ragnelle, / 'Or my dethe had bene dyghte'" (lines 760–62).

Perhaps the most striking feature of "Ragnelle" is its conclusion. It is also the most subversive. Up to the morning after the transformation of the hag, the poem has been "resolutely masculine," to return again to Lee Patterson's phrase. Gawain has from the beginning been the wise, loyal, and perfect liegeman. But after the wedding night, Gawain's allegience changes. He is himself transformed even as the "forshapen" Ragnelle is changed and moves beyond Arthur's service to deeper loyalties. It may be that some might call him "coward" in his Ragnelle-centered orientation. That certainly would be the assessment of plenty of political theorists of the day, from Giles of Rome, in his *The Governance of Kings and Princes*, to Gower himself, in his *Vox Clamantis*, where uxoriousness is indeed defined as a cowardly fault. But here, at the end of the poem, Gawain is more like Chrétien's Yvain than Chrétien's Gawain in his domestic affections. One might argue that the dignity of the relationship between Ragnelle and Gawain, so different from the pretentious social relationship of Arthur and Guinevere (who was outraged at having to deal with something as ugly as the hag in her court of lovely ladies), is the culmination of the motif of mutual benefit that was the denouement of "The Tale of Florent." Although Ragnelle was more fiendishly hideous, more animal-like, more voracious in her appetite, and more foul and sexually repulsive than Gower's loathly hag, she becomes not only beautiful and protective of Gawain, but fruitful as well. She gives Gawain a child, a remarkable innovation in romance narrative that has almost Greek resonances—fertility, the ultimate sign of female power. The ugly one has truly become a blessed thing (a Eumenide), whereby the land flourishes.

But the "Ragnelle"-poet concludes with a second innovation, also highly subversive of patriarchal complacence, that protrudes beyond the diagetic boundaries of the romance into the real world of the author. We are told that the poet is in prison, a passage that lends support to P. J. C. Field's speculation on the poem's common features with Malory. How are we as readers to take this quiet, patient assertion? Has the author been wrongly treated by his sovereign? Has his sovereign, like Arthur, been heedless of good governance? Is he victim of faulty political structures that do more harm than good to the people? The passage leaves us wondering about the little faults of government that disenfranchise people like Ragnelle, and even Gawain, though he accepts the constraints without complaint. In fact, Gawain welcomes the hardships with gladness, since they enable him the better to serve Arthur. At least so it is up until the end. Then love and concerns of conscience and a private world lay claim to his attention. In this appreciation of the domestic world, the "Ragnelle"-poet takes the issues of the poem a step beyond its predecessors, though domestic virtue as the fundamental strength of a society is a prominent theme throughout Gower.

Conclusion

I have attempted in this essay to place Gower's "Tale of Florent" at the head of its class as the literary exemplar for the two other Middle English Loathly Lady stories. Gower's mode is folkloristic: it comes across as a tale that is told, "A tale I fynde, as thou schalt hiere."[91] Its voicing is that of a folktale—understated, subversive in its matter-of-factness, as if it were in the local, yet universal, voice of the people. Like all folktales, its grammatology is staged, its action visual, working within a matrix of performance that accords with a nondiagetic reality. Though the syntax of the narrative does not provide fully developed characters, we see *dramatis personae* speaking their roles to occupy their audience with figures of thought that function powerfully within the lexias of cultural linguistics. The configuration of Loathly

Lady motifs which Gower activates are attuned to matriarchal tensions that may be traced back to the most ancient of myths of furies and blessed ones negotiating within an Apollonian world of laws that codependent victims (victims of hatred, chance, ill-will, disenfranchisement) ultimately move beyond. As they proceed they discover a higher ethic, one founded in recognition of the other and the subsequent recovery of personal sovereignty that makes possible mutual love. This reading of the folk motifs is distinctly Gowerian. It is like a quest through hidden forces that support rather than frustrate once the right questions are asked, each at the proper time. The effect is not unlike that in the grail quests, where the naive Perceval learns to see and think feelingly. Both the male and female protagonists learn patience, but they also learn to see with parted eye as each reads as the other might read.

Gower's tale is put in new dress by both Chaucer and the "Ragnelle"-poet, who include in their adaptations every function of Gower's tale, but with fresh variation. The effect sometimes subverts Gower's story, but mainly the subversion is directed at cultural biases within the new situation, what I've referred to as the story's local habitation. The rebellious undertone works mainly through powerful women, in the best of folk traditions, who crack the seams of patriarchal structures. We, as audience to these phenomenal stagings, with their new directors, new settings, new costumes, and altered pathways, can enjoy their versatility and freshness best by looking carefully at what is being performed. Each of the three tales is so well produced that there are no authorial losers in this game.

NOTES

I am grateful to Eve Salisbury, Dana Symons, and Thomas Hahn for many helpful suggestions along the way when I was composing this essay.

Epigraph. Lang, *Lilac Fairy Book*, pp. vii–viii.

1. *Confessio Amantis* was presented to the public in 1390. "The Tale of Florent," which appears in Book I, thus must have been written before 1390, perhaps even as early as 1386 or 1387. Chaucer's "Wife of Bath's Tale" was probably written a few years later, in the early to mid 1390s when Chaucer was reworking the order of *The Canterbury Tales* and rethinking the role of the Wife of Bath. The Wife's Loathly Lady story was most likely not the first tale awarded to Alisoun. That perhaps was what is now "The Shipman's Tale." Her new tale seems to have been part of Chaucer's rethinking of the so-called marriage group (1393–95). With regard to composition of other English Loathly Lady tales, Helaine Newstead, *A Manual of the Writings in*

Middle English, 1:65, suggests that "The Wedding of Sir Gawain and Dame Ragnelle" was composed in the East Midlands about 1450. "The Marriage of Sir Gawain," a ballad, comes from the seventeenth century.

2. For example, G. H. Maynadier, *"Wife of Bath's Tale,"* presumes that "The Tale of Florent," lacking originality, "must have drawn from some source" that Chaucer used for "The Wife of Bath's Tale" (p. 6); Bartlett J. Whiting, "[Sources and Analogues of] The Wife of Bath's Tale," p. 224, asserts that "clearly enough, the English poems have a common ancestor, but their relation to that ancestor is by no means clear," then dodges the issue of priority with a weaselly "Theories, fortunately, do not concern us here, and the poems must speak for themselves," as he praises Chaucer's tale for having more "overwhelming literary power and artistry" than the others; or Sigmund Eisner, who reconstructs a common ancestor for Gower and Chaucer's tales out of Irish tales (*Tale of Wonder*, pp. 70–72).

3. On medieval perceptions of literary composition as compilation see Minnis, "Late-Medieval Discussions," and *Medieval Theory of Authority*; and Olsson, *John Gower and the Structures of Conversion*, pp. 1–15.

4. For example, Captain Cox, who often performed romances and ballads with Coventry players at Kenilworth on court occasions, including the visitation by Queen Elizabeth (1575). See Hahn, *Sir Gawain*, pp. 14–18.

5. Apuleius, *Golden Ass*, p. 23.

6. The English Loathly Lady narratives are all of this kind, as are various Irish versions (see Eisner, *Tale of Wonder*, note 12, below).

7. Carl Lindahl, in "Oral Undertones," observes astutely how this marginal figure "could be viewed as either a threat or a promise" (p. 71). He is speaking directly to the issue of the "magical question" of what women most desire.

8. See Bettelheim, *Uses of Enchantment*, especially the last chapter, "The Animal-Groom Cycle of Fairy Tales," pp. 277–310, on adolescent responses to puberty, especially body odor and menstruation as disturbing phenomenon. On menstruation taboos and loathly women see Coomaraswamy, "On the Loathly Bride," pp. 397–98.

9. For discussion of Gower's extensive uses of Ovid see especially Simpson, *Sciences and the Self*, pp. 134–66; and Salisbury, "Remembering Origins," pp. 159–84.

10. Eisner, *Tale of Wonder*, p. 11. None of the English sovereignty tales look upon the hag-become-beautiful so specifically in terms of geography, though territorial domain in terms of psychology and social and gender politics is a submotif in all three of the English stories. "Ragnelle" comes closest to Eisner's model, where Gromer Somer Joure's property is misappropriated by Arthur and given to Gawain, though that is background to other misappropriations that touch on Arthur's relationship with Gawain and the stepmother's infringements, along with Gromer's, upon Ragnelle. Eisner goes so far as to reconstruct what he thinks the Ur-tale that all the English tales devolve from must have been like (pp. 70–72), speculating that Gower "changed the name of his hero [from Gawain] to Florent because he felt that an Arthurian background would give an element of frivolity to a grave subject" (p. 68).

For other discussions of Celtic treatments of Loathly Ladies, see Coomaraswamy, "Loathly Bride," pp. 391–92; Maynadier, *Wife of Bath's Tale*; Sumner, "Weddynge"; Saul, *Wedding*; Brown, *Origin*, ch. 7 ("The Hateful Fée Who Represents Sovereignty"); Beach's Harvard dissertation on the Loathly Lady (1907); and Loomis, *Celtic Myth*, esp. pp. 221–22 and ch. 29.

11. Coomaraswamy, "Loathly Bride," juxtaposes "figures of thought" with "figures of speech" as a way of talking about functions of folk motifs and typologies that operate within diverse cultures (p. 402).

12. It is easy enough to imagine Welsh or Irish storytellers in the company of Crusaders or perhaps in great households on domestic festive occasions, where loathly hag stories might have been told in earlier times; and Welsh tales appear to have infiltrated English culture during the campaigns of Edward I on the western and northern borders of his kingdom. As we shall see, Edward had a propensity to stage entertainments for the court that combined traditional stories of chivalry with local circumstances. But it is difficult to imagine, let alone authenticate, such transmission as part of English court practices in the time of Richard II. Great households, like that which created the Findern manuscript, were assuredly literate and literary in their entertainments, which included reading and copying poems. Folk entertainments might have occurred—St. George mimes, for example, or perhaps even a Loathly Lady story, but more likely court entertainments would have been drawn from the classics—a tale from Ovid or a heroic event like the siege of Jerusalem. But popular romances and romance motifs were presented at court. Robert Laneham, "A Letter: Wherain part of the entertainment untoo the Queens Maiesty … [1575]" (ed. R. C. Alston. Menston, Eng.: Scolar, 1968), recounts performances by Captain Cox at Kenilworth that used women players as well as men, with Cox blustering about as Gawain, acting, singing, impersonating, with "great oversyht … in matters of storie" (see Hahn, *Sir Gawain*, p. 14, n. 23). But even if there were loathly hag tales being performed, it seems probable to me that Chaucer would have begun his conception of "The Wife of Bath's Tale" with Gower's written narrative and had its functions in mind as he proceeded. This is not to say that Gower or Chaucer would have been deaf to folk stories or the possibilities of what they might add to a literary narrative.

13. Bollard, "Sovereignty," p. 42.

14. The tales of which Eisner speaks survive, of course, only as written texts, which may or may not have had some earlier form. Donnchadh Ó Corráin, in "Textuality and Inter-textuality," observes: "One more point needs to be stressed because of the boring and protracted oral versus written debate which has continued for some years now in Irish studies: early Irish literature is a written literature. True, it finds its plot elements—tale-types, motifs, topoi, call them what you will—wherever they are available. Here are traditional elements which can be used and re-used endlessly" (p. 28).

15. See Coomaraswamy, "Loathly Bride," who discusses stories of enchantment, transformation and redemption from Ireland to India.

16. Bollard, "Sovereignty," pp. 45–47. See also Laura Sumner, "Weddynge," who states that "in the Irish [sovereignty] represents kingly authority; in the English it is used in a somewhat humorous sense to show the advantage of a husband's complete submission to his wife" (p. xv). That is, as Bollard puts it, "we are dealing with two entirely distinct motifs" (p. 47). Rachel Bromwich, "Celtic Dynastic Themes," is even more insistent on the lack of continuity: "Any connection between the *sovereynetee* desired by women and *flaithes na h-Eirenn* may be ruled out as entirely fortuitous. *Flaitheas* denotes kingship or royal rule, and could not possibly be applied to a conception so banal as that intended in the English poems" (p. 453).

17. As Gower puts it: "For conseil passeth alle thing / To him which thenkth to ben a king; / And every man for his partie / A kingdom hath to justefie, / That is to sein his oghne dom. / If he misreule that kingdom, / He lest himself, and that is more / Than if he loste schip and ore / And al the worldes good withal; / For what man that in special / Hath noght himself, he hath noght elles, / No mor the perles than the schelles" (VIII.2109–20). All references to *Confessio Amantis* are taken from Gower, *Confessio Amantis,* ed. Peck, and are cited by book and line number.

18. But see Manuel Aguirre, "Riddle of Sovereignty," who views the woman as an earth figure, "Mother of all life," who, when embraced, can elevate the embracer to kingly status, thus bridging territorial and domestic considerations. The Irish *flaitheas* and the English *sovereynetee* are thus "reduced to a deceptive coincidence of terms" (p. 278). Aguirre is discussing the eleventh-century "Echtra mac n-Echach" ("The Adventure of the Sons of Eochaid"). For a translation of that story see *Silva Gadelica,* ed. and trans. O'Grady.

19. Loomis first discussed the event in "Chivalric and Dramatic Imitations," pp. 91–92, then elaborated on it in "Edward I." Loomis based his summary on a translation of the chronicle supplied to him by Adrian Barnouw.

20. Loomis, "Edward I," p. 118. Loomis enumerates the popularity of "Round Tables" throughout Europe as a means of high-style entertainment for aristocracy, though few were as elaborately staged as Edward's or carried such direct political force where "the poetry of history and the history of poetry are [so] inextricably intertwined" (p. 127).

21. Loomis, "Edward I," p. 119.

22. Loomis, "Edward I," notes that the Dutch chronicler apparently identified Scotia with Ireland ("Irlant"), since there was no expedition against Ireland in Edward's time. "Cornuaelge" likewise shows some confusion between Cornwall and Kenilworth (p. 119). Lodewijk was greatly interested in Edward in that the king's daughter Margaret had married John, son of the Duke of Brabant, whereupon Edward became "une sorte de héros national" for the Brabançons. His second daughter, Eleanor, was subsequently married to the Count of Bar, who was fatally wounded in the Round Table that was staged to celebrate his wedding (pp. 117–18).

23. Greimas, "Réflexions," pp. 172–91. Working from Vladimir Propp's *Morphology* and Étienne Souriau's revision of Propp's analysis of functions, Greimas

reformulates *dramatis personae,* which he calls *actants,* into a matrix structure, a set of symmetrical oppositions, that defines a kind of force field (*forces thématiques*), a taxonomy whose inherent tensions generate the production of narrative. The Subject seeks Object, the Sender (*Destinateur*) seeks the Receiver (*Destinataire*). The Subject is hedged by Helpers (*Adjuvants*) and Opposers (*Opposants*). The semiotics of plot becomes a paradigmatic exercise, with a narratological grammar and syntax. See Greimas, *Structural Semantics.*

24. On possible kinship between Edward's interlude and subsequent Loathly Lady narratives in England, see Hahn, "Old Wives' Tales."

25. Chaucer's hag does share with Edward's a royal hearing at which to make her request, but the parallels end there; her demand presented to the queen has to do with getting a husband rather than some politicized land deal. On the other hand, the fact that Edward uses the Loathly Lady as a device to help settle land disputes does hint at issues in "Ragnelle," where Gromer Somer Joure accuses Arthur of giving Gawain land that belonged to Gromer. But that tale suggests a peaceful solution rather than something like Edward's military display.

26. See *Confessio Amantis,* 2:2–22, on Gower's uses of stagecraft in his presenting of lore.

27. Gower refers to himself as a compiler, but, clearly, by the end of the *Confessio Amantis* he is thinking of himself as author. A. J. Minnis speaks of Gower as "a compiler who tried to present himself as an author" (*Medieval Theory,* p. 210). But Kurt Olsson challenges Minnis's proposition, emphasizing that it "impinges significantly on how [Gower] understands history and organizes moral experience … to energize his authorship" (*John Gower,* p. 5).

28. In Luigi Pirandello's *Six Characters in Search of an Author* (1921), six stock romance characters (a Father, Mother, Stepdaughter, Son, Child, and Madame Pace) interrupt a play rehearsal, insisting that the story be theirs and, after capturing the imagination of the director and cast, take over the production, the way folk motifs and Loathly Ladies are wont to do.

29. See my discussion of Gower's poetic that uses the lore of the past as a means of keeping present time alive, a proposition that lives at the heart of "folklore" as a discipline—in "Gower, Maker of Tales," esp. p. 5.

30. "The Tale of Florent" is not the only tale in the *Confessio Amantis* that, heavy-laden with folktale components, appears in Genius's cadre of exempla with no known source—e.g., "The Tale of the Three Questions" (I.3069–402). As with "The Tale of Florent," the temptation may be to assume that the source has been lost, but the more likely explanation is simply that Gower, his brain filled with people-stories, in these instances wrote without a specific source. Instead, he is working within the cultural parameters of folk narratives that are rich with motifs of the sort Gower uses to design narrative resonances that reverberate at the heart of better-known models within the culture. Many of his most interesting tales, like "The Tale of Medea" or "The Tale of Adrian and Bardus" (V.4837–5174), succeed because such folk materials

add vitality and local color to an already well known story. Gower has a superb sense of what makes a good story, and he understands his audience well.

31. Thoms, *Athenaeum*, p. 862.

32. The *Confessio* locates itself on a "middel weie," "Somewhat of lust [i.e., desire, the private voice], somewhat of lore [i.e., wisdom, the public voice]" (Pro. 17–19). When Gower speaks of "lore" he is talking about learning embedded in the cultural heritage that lives in books that people listen to, to be sure, but also in the voice in people's heads, and in the stories people tell to each other—the "voice of the people" (the *vox populi* so often sounded in Gower's *Vox Clamantis*). This common folk concept is reflected in expressions like "thi lore" (II.80), "the wise mannes lore" (V.7662), one's "ferste lore" (VII.5386), the "wisdom of his lore" (VIII.791), the lore whereby "every man is othres lore" (VIII.256), "the sentence of my lore" (VIII.2923), etc. This mythos of "lore" he refers to dozens of times throughout *Confessio Amantis*.

33. Dundes, *Study of Folklore*, p. 2.

34. *Science*, a knowing, is a favorite term of Gower (forty-three references) to identify the wisdom of a discipline, whereby a people can glue their culture together or think of themselves as a people. It is a function within behavior that fixes the grammatology of being. It enables the *acteur* and the audience to interrelate.

35. See Thompson, *Motif Index* and *Types of the Folktale* (1981). Thompson's *Motif Index* is especially useful in locating like components among diverse tales. So too the functional morphologies of Propp, *Morphology*—all good pointers. I take the term *lexias* from Roland Barthes's *S/Z*, in his excursuses on narrative and its reading. The term complements well Greimas's vocabulary—terms like *actant*, *destinateur*, *destinataire*, *opposant*, and *adjuvant*—to help clarify functions of the *dramatis personae* that populate the plot (see n. 22, above). *Lexias* gets at the fluid, dynamic notion of structuration as texture, a weaving of codes the reader perpetually sorts in provisional ways through a *déja-vu* process of supposition, as if the reader is re-experiencing what s/he has already read/lived and continues to experience within the folk culture. Within tales themselves the lexias assume a local color, the way a word does in any given syntax. Thus I designate the motifs of Florent by operational functions within the story, not necessarily as they correspond to Aarne-Thompson's or Propp's types; I use those indices only as mirrors to shed light on the text-based motifs that Gower's narrative syntax generates.

36. Utley refers to the motif and type classifications of Thompson and Aarne. See Thompson, *Motif-Index* and *Types of the Folktale* (1964). A second revision of the Aarne-Thompson *Types of the Folktale* (1981) has been published since Utley's essay was written. Thompson offers several categories that pertain to the Middle English Loathly Lady tales. See the sections on Disenchantment, especially D730: Disenchantment by submission; D731: Disenchantment by obedience and kindness *Type 431; D732: Loathly Lady, where the disenchantment takes place by an embrace; and D735: Disenchantment by kiss *Type 410; and D735.1: Beauty and the Beast.

37. Utley, "Folk Literature"; see especially pp. 17–18. For a detailed account of the spread of the Griselda story throughout Europe see Raffaele Morabito, "La Diffusione," and his editions *Griselda 1* and *Griselda 2*.

38. Gower is sometimes said to be a friend of women in the *Confessio Amantis*. Much of the effect comes from his use of folk devices that empower women, not simply subversively, but in terms of their wisdom, compassion, desire for sovereignty, and so on. Indeed, Venus, as she scolds Amans for his self-serving cupidity, serves more as a voice of reason than a sex figure who destroys women. In Book VIII, she sends Amans an exemplary sequence of virtuous women, a veritable legend of good women (though very different from Chaucer's), whose emblematic virtue provides a key step in the lover's recovery of his senses. Gower's presentation of positive roles of educated women like Peronelle, in "The Tale of the Three Questions" (I.3067–3402), and Thaise, in "The Tale of Apollonius" (VIII.271–2008), as they teach both young and old and guide men in positions of authority toward more careful reasoning and better judgment and assume dignified positions of authority of their own in society, is a notable feature of his social vision. In the case of more troubled women, like Medea (V.3247–4229), his detailed, even affectionate, presentation exhibits a range of sympathy unique to medieval representations of one who is usually cast as a murderous witch. Other unfortunate women, like Canace (III.143–337), who has been driven by passion and a self-serving brother into incest, is compassionately dealt with by Genius, even though she is forced by her cruel father to commit suicide; Rosemund (I.2459–2646) is likewise presented sympathetically even though she uses sexual blackmail to get the butler to murder her crude husband, Albinus, who publicly humiliated her at table by trapping her into drinking from a cup made from her father's skull. Although these last two tales have bleak conclusions, Gower keeps us keenly aware of the waste of talent caused by the insidious pride of a tyrant. All such stories are part of the woman-friendly vernacular folk matrix where Gower's *actants* function.

39. I am modeling my three-stage initiation formulation on Jerome Griswold's *Audacious Kids*. Griswold's focus is on children's classics like *Huckleberry Finn*, *The Wizard of Oz*, *Toby Tyler*, *Hans Brinker*, *Little Women*, etc., which, though lacking the subtlety of models such as of Northrop Frye's mythic descent and ascent in *Secular Scripture*, serves my purpose for defining folkloric components of the plot of Florent, by virtue of its simplicity.

40. A good parallel may be seen in "The Knightly Tale of Gologras and Gawain," where, in order to win, Gawain voluntarily gives the victory to Gologras. See especially lines 1090–1128.

41. The reason for the stepmother's hatred is not stated. Perhaps she hates the princess because of her youth or her beauty, as in Snow White; or perhaps because she has been slighted in some way, as in Briar Rose. The cause could be as diverse as subsets of what one might desire. It is perhaps worth observing that both victims—Florent and the princess—are victims of hatred.

42. Aguirre, "Riddle," offers a useful summary of stepmother typologies in which her hostility places a "destiny" on her victims, thereby denying them fulfillment in marriage (pp. 277–78). See also MacCana, "Aspects."

43. The problem of Buridan's ass is a favorite in philosophical discourse, from Aristotle to Schopenhauer, namely the problem of a protagonist caught between two equal choices, who, because of the equality, is unable to make up his mind. Buridan poses the dilemma of a donkey, suffering from extreme hunger, positioned equidistant from equally attractive bales of fodder, who starves to death because of the impossibility of making a right choice given the evidence that is before him. See Lynch, *Chaucer's Philosophical Visions*, pp. 90–97; and Rescher, "Choice Without Preference."

44. Bottigheimer, "Silenced Women." See also her "Tale Spinners."

45. CT VIII[B²]979, *2169 (the phrase occurs repeatedly); citations of Chaucer are from *The Riverside Chaucer*, ed. Benson. Compare Gower's adaptation of 3 Esdras 3:4, on the king, wine, and women, where truth is the key addition to the exempla (VII.1883–1984): the wise hag understands the truth and has the discretionary patience to access its power at the right moment. Indeed, if she cannot find the one who will be true to his word, her situation, as well as his, is lost. In her patience, she is not unlike Shakespeare's Viola, who sees herself as "patience on a monument" in *Twelfth Night* (2.4.114), disguised in her "poor monster" form, yet wise enough to wait for time to "untangle this ... too hard a knot for me to untie!" (2.2.34–41); citations of Shakespeare are from *The Riverside Shakespeare*.

46. Positive law may be patriarchal, in that men make the laws and rule the courts; but natural law, though gendered, is without bias, while divine law is beyond gender. Florent's first bind is mainly a matter of positive law; it is in the second bind that he engages the moral issues of higher laws, whether natural or divine.

47. In "Old Wives' Tales," Thomas Hahn comments on the two-pronged trial of Florent and the constraints of law, but sees Gower using the tale to impose "a single answer on an unruly subject" to illustrate "the manly virtue of obedience" (p.100), with "sufficiency and excess defined at first according to notions of law, but ultimately played out through dialectical stereotypes of masculinity and femininity" (p. 102). I would agree with Hahn that the conclusion of the tale is heterosexual and that it "defines generational links, propertied responsibilities, the sense of a socially integrated past and future that constitutes History" (p. 102), but it seems to me that the boundaries of gender are less mechanically explored than "stereotype" implies.

48. Peter G. Beidler, "Transformations," makes the astute observation that in Gower we are not told exactly how much time Florent has for the gathering of information upon which to base his answer. In Chaucer the time is specified as a year and a day, which is perhaps the logic behind Derek Pearsall's "within a twelve-month" (see Beidler, p. 113, n. 6), but Beidler suggests that the old woman, "to make sure that [Florent] does not have much time to pursue his near-impossible quest, ... gives him his freedom for a short period of time .... perhaps as little as a day or two"

(p. 103). So short a duration, as opposed to Pearsall's assertion, is, of course, speculation as well. A year is what folktales usually allow, but Beidler's point is well taken.

49. Genius uses a sexual term to identify the old grantdame, "that olde mone." In my edition of the poem I followed the MED in glossing *mone* as "consort," though that gloss is perhaps too courteous. The word comes from OE *gemaene*, meaning "intercourse"; "old fuck" comes closer to the sense. Genius uses abusive language for an abusive person. The effect is somewhat different from "foule grete coise" (also a sexual term—see the discussion below) for the Loathly Lady (I.1734), in that Florent does not have to marry the "grantdame." "Olde mone" connotes scorn, anger, and insult; "foule grete coise" connotes fear.

50. Although I will discuss Chaucer's adaptation of "The Tale of Florent" in the following section, it should be noted here that in Chaucer the hag's claim on the offending knight is made public and becomes part of the legal control imposed by the queen upon the male. In Gower, however, Florent's truth in and of itself holds sway over royal command (i.e., kings) or women. See n. 45, above.

51. The ethical point here involves conscience, a point shared by other Ricardian writers, where choice affects foremost the chooser and where the individual's self-definition becomes, after the fourth Lateran Council, the *sine qua non* at the Last Judgment. Just as Gawain knows, at the beginning of the fourth fitt of *Sir Gawain and the Green Knight,* that he cannot fool himself by accepting the servant's advice (lines 2091–2159) that he not go to the green chapel, so Florent knows that breaking his oath *does* matter to someone, namely, himself.

52. See the Old Norse *Hrólfr Kraki Saga,* cited by F. J. Child, where a loathly creature begs to come out of the winter and once in, convinces King Helgi that her life depends upon her getting warm in his bed, which he reluctantly agrees to, only to discover that she has transformed into a fair woman who had been under a "weird" imposed upon her by her stepmother which would last until some king invited her into his bed (Torfæus, *Historia Hrolfi Krakii* [1705]); and the Gaelic tale "Nighean Righ fo Thuinn" ("The Daughter of King Under-waves") recorded in Campbell's *Popular Tales of the West Highlands,* no. 86, 3:421–40, as cited by Child (1:297–98), where an ugly creature, hideous, with hair down to her heels, begs admittance to his dwelling, then gets under his blanket, whereupon she is transformed into "the finest drop of blood that ever was, from the beginning of the universe till the end of the world." Child presents these as analogues to the Loathly Lady, a victim of enchantment, in the ballad "King Henry" (1:297–300). In these tales, the male has not been disenfranchised; the king helps the woman without being indebted to her.

53. Bettelheim, *Uses of Enchantment,* especially the last chapter, "The Animal-Groom Cycle of Fairy Tales," pp. 277–310, is perhaps useful in explaining jealousies among women in terms of Freudian theories of rivalry between mothers and daughters and in terms of the child's own fears in maturation processes.

54. See n. 23, above. I am wanting to evoke a notion akin to Greimas's "sender," the cause, "Dieu"; that is, an impetus that effects plot. *Destinateur* has the right

connotations, especially since it is the stepmother who lays what Gower identifies as the lady's "destiné" upon her (I.1835); that is, *destinateur* labels exactly the narrative function of the stepmother as she opposes the Princess of Sicily (the *destinataire*, the victim, recipient, *objet*, *Humanité*) by imposing the loathly destiny upon her. See Griemas's categorizing of such functional relationships, "Réflexions," pp. 180–82.

55. For further examples of this type of tale in which a girl is enchanted into a monstrous form until a lover breaks the enchantment, see Aarne-Thompson, *Types of the Folktale*, Type 405A. That once the curse is "overpassed" (I.1835) the princess will bear her beauty to the grave (I.1838) is a nice folkloristic touch, one the "Ragnelle"-poet picks up on in a sobering way when the restored princess dies young, before age can wither her beauty.

56. For an extensive annotated bibliography on Cinderella tales, analogues, and criticism, in all the arts, see Peck, *Cinderella Bibliography*.

57. For references on animal enchantment in fairy tales and dreams see, in addition to Bettelheim (*Uses of Enchantment*), Leavy, *In Search of the Swan Maiden*; Grosz, "Animal Sex"; and Elwin, '*Vagina Dentata.*'

58. In my discussion I am treating the *adjuvant* (helper) as male and the enchanted one (the *destinataire* or recipient of the curse) as female, because that is the formula of the English Loathly Lady narratives. The gendering might be reversed, with the male the enchanted one and the female the *actant*, as in various "Beauty and the Beast" stories. And, of course, it is reversed in Florent as well, in so far as he is the victim and she his helper. That is, both are *actants* within multiple plots.

59. This demand of secrecy may not be a requirement. In *Mandeville's Travels*, for example, we find the story of the good lady of Lango who was monstrously turned by the goddess Deane (Diana?) into a dragon. She announces that if someone will kiss her she will be returned to her beautiful self and her suitor will not only win her as a lovely, loving bride but will receive enormous wealth as well. As an enticement she even appears to one suitor in her full beauty. But though many vow that they will undertake the task, none succeed because she is so terrifying in her ugliness and with her dragon breath. So she dies, still a dragon, unredeemed of her true nature. For her, there were no risk-takers to be found who were also true to their word. See Seymour, *Mandeville's Travels*, p. 233.

60. Coomaraswamy, "Loathly Bride," argues that in government and marriage, although the man's position may be the authority, "the woman's is the power," and goes on to cite E. Aymonier, *Histoire de l'ancien Cambodge*: "In all the legends, the leading role is the woman's. She is the foundress of the royal race. She, and not the immigrant prince, is the protectress of the realm" (p. 396). So too it is in Aeschylus's *Eumenides*, or even, for that matter, in the story of Medusa, where (according to the ancient authors) the dark, hideous female power, though hidden, is the basis of a generative state. It is important that in both of the Greek stories this force gets bound up with Athena and the laws of Athens.

61. Carter, "Ashputtle," pp. 54–62. Carter lays out her tale/essay in three parts: 1) *The Mutilated Girls*, a reading of Grimms' "Aschenputtel" to suggest a drama between two female families in opposition, animated solely by the wills of the mothers—a story of cutting bits off women so that they will fit in. Were the stepmothers' daughters the father's natural daughters? That would make the speedy marriage and the stepmother's hostility even more probable. Ashputtle is driven by the dove, spirit of her mother, who pecks at her ear to make her dance; the stepmother wields the knife over her daughters—daughters subdued by "both awe and fear at the phenomenon of mother love" (p. 58)—while the dove points out the bloody wounds. The bloody shoe is a hideous receptacle: "Ashputtle's foot, the size of the bound foot of a Chinese woman; a stump. Already an amputee, she put her foot in it." The turtledove triumphs while the mad mother stands by impotently. Ashputtle's foot fits the shoe like a corpse fits a coffin. "See how well I look after you, my darling!" 2) *The Burned Child*, a retelling of the charred, scabbed, and scarred girl, growing fat on the milk of the cow, growing breasts, wanting the man for herself, sucking the cow dry, shedding her mutilated skin, combing her hair with the cat's claws until the cat is maimed but the child clean but stark naked, until the bird in the tree pierces its breast and spills down blood to give the child a red silk dress, and the girl goes into the kitchen, all lovely, catches the eye of the man, who leaves the stepmother behind to stir the ashes while he gives the lovely girl a house and money. "She did all right," and the ghost of the mother sleeps okay. 3) *The Traveling Costume* tells of the stepmother burning the orphan's face with a hot poker for not stirring the ashes enough, the girl weeping over her mother's grave, the mother coming to the girl at night, giving her a red dress—"I had it when I was your age, I used it for traveling" (p. 61). The mother takes worms from her eye sockets which turn to jewels—"sell them as you need to" (p. 62)—and invites the orphan into the coffin, which turns into a coach and horses. "Now go and seek your fortune, darling."

62. "Bot with no craft of combes brode / Thei myhte hire hore lockes schode, / And sche ne wolde noght be schore / For no conseil" (I.1749–52). It is as if she knows, like Samson, that her strength lies in her hair. See Apuleius, *Golden Ass*, pp. 60–65, on the potency of woman's hair and the danger of cutting it.

63. See Thompson, *Motif Index*, vol. 3, F 547.1.1 on the *vagina dentata* motif. The OED refers to it as a motif used to suggest "fear of castration, the dangers of sexual intercourse, of birth or rebirth, etc." The motif is universal. See especially Raitt, "*Vagina Dentata*," and Elwin, "*Vagina Dentata*." Elizabeth Grosz, "Animal Sex," offers the useful summary observation: "The fantasy of the *vagina dentata*, of the non-human status of woman as android, vampire or animal, the identification of female sexuality as voracious, insatiable, enigmatic, invisible and unknowable, cold, calculating, instrumental, castrator/decapitator of the male, dissimulatress or fake, predatory, engulfing mother, preying on male weakness, are all consequences of the ways in which male orgasm has functioned as the measure and representative of all sexualities and all modes of erotic encounter" (p. 293). See also Leavy, *In Search of the*

Swan Maiden, especially ch. 6: "The Animal Bride: Handsome and the Beastess: A Neglected Story Pattern," pp. 196–244. In European lore the motif operates in such stories as the Oedipus and the Sphinx myth; Homer's accounts of Scylla and Charybdis and the Laestrygonians; Virgil's "lovely-breasted" Scylla with her "wolfish groin"; Tertullian's calling "women the gate of hell" (Raitt, p. 421), and, in subsequent medieval art and drama, the vivid portrayals of hell mouth as a fanged monster (*vagina dentata,* indeed; n.b., Eliade, *From Primitives to Zen,* on birth / death / rebirth typologies linked to the motif). For a comic variant on the vagina as hellmouth, see Boccaccio's tenth story on the third day of the *Decameron,* where Rustico teaches a young woman about putting the devil back in hell. In Shakespeare, Lear's disenchanted view of women as centaurs, women above and the fiend's dark hell-pit below, provides yet another extension of the concept: "there's hell, there's darkness, / There is the sulphurous pit—burning, scalding, / Stench, consumption" (4.6.124–29). It is perhaps noteworthy that Ragnelle is a name given a fiend from hell. For discussion of *vagina dentata* motifs in North America see Lowie, "Test-Theme," esp. p. 108; Seligman, "Anthropological Perspective," p. 219; and Ramsey, *Coyote Was Going There,* p. 236, which discusses the trope among the Piaute Indians.

64. Clearly the hairy mouth is meant to be scary. We might recall the ill-fated Absolon, in Chaucer's "Miller's Tale," who, filled with love longing for "my faire bryd, my sweete cynamon," encounters with his mouth no sweetness but "a thyng al rough and long yherd" (*CT* I[A]3699, 3734, 3737). See Elwin, "*Vagina Dentata,*" on various tales about the menace of pubic hairs and the power of long pubic hairs to cause impotence (pp. 439, 452–53).

65. On the voracious appetite of the *vagina dentata* figure see Elwin, "*Vagina Dentata,*" p. 447. But another feature of the phenomenon is political, having to do with the deformative effects of lost sovereignty. The deprived figure is often represented as having a voracious appetite, as if trying to make up for what it has lost. For example, the huge appetite of the loathly hag in "King Henry" (Child, 1:297–300), who eats not only all the "meat" in the house, but the king's "berry-brown steed," his "good gray-hounds," his "gay gos-hawks," and then drinks up his wine. Recall also the folk hero Havelok who, when, as a child, he is taken into exile to be raised by Grimm, has such an appetite that his keeper's whole livelihood can scarce feed the perpetually hungry youth. Such appetite is a common folk motif with a bulemic psychological / political edge, not simply a sexual one. The Loathly Lady's hunger mirrors the consequences of her deformity, whereby she has become unpropertied and thus starved of what is rightfully hers.

66. All citations of the text of "The Wedding of Sir Gawain and Dame Ragnelle" are from Hahn, *Sir Gawain,* pp. 41–80.

67. See the Aarne-Thompson, *Types of the Folktale,* Type 406 of a maiden turned into a cannibal by enchantment until marriage can break the enchantment and return her to her maidenly self.

68. The earliest usage of the term *vagina dentata* cited by the OED is by early twentieth-century American folklorists who describe the motif in American Indian tales, especially of the Northwest. It is then used by British folklorists and anthropologists to identify comparable stories and dreams in India, New Zealand, Samoa, Southeast Asia, Hawaii, and the Ainu of Siberia. But when Kennedy calls Dunbar "cuntbitten" ("The Flyting of Dunbar and Kennedy," line 239), the concept is plainly evident within the medieval English literary provenance. More recently the term has been appropriated by psychologists to describe castration complexes and phobias of men directed toward women. Most recently it has become a category in the discourse of feminist critics, who rather seem to like the idea.

69. See n. 64, above, on voracious appetites, a phenomenon that is akin to the Old Norse and Gaelic Loathly Lady tales, as Child points out.

70. The owl who flies by night is the trope that Chaucer picks up from Gower in his adaptation, a figure that recurs in "Ragnelle" as well.

71. Hahn sees the legal terminology in Florent as part of the elitist, "distinctly male interests" of Gower's tale ("Old Wives," p. 100). Certainly *Confessio Amantis*, with all its academic references and Latin paraphernalia, addresses a literate audience (which I take the sense of Hahn's term "elite" to mean), though it certainly, in this regard, is less elitist than Chaucer's adaptation, with its complex literary rhetoric and Ovidian, biblical, Arthurian, and Boethian allusions. To me, the style of Gower's poem is more populist than academic; its tone is basically that of the folktale against which Chaucer can make a brilliant literary flourish. Legal terminology is not antithetical to popular stories—n.b., the traditions linking loathly hag tales to the margins of law—or to the traditions of exemplary tales like the *Gesta Romanorum*—(Are these elite simply because early versions were in Latin?). The "folk" often learn about the parameters of law through folktales. Law is, in fact, a favorite topic.

72. See Beidler, "Transformations," pp. 100–14, for an excellent laying out of differences between Gower and Chaucer that avoids simplistic value judgments about which poem is better.

73. Carl Lindahl, "Oral Undertones," notes the absence of epithets for the rapist knight in Chaucer. Where in a conventional romance the knight is usually loaded with epithets, in "The Wife of Bath's Tale" he is introduced as a "lusty bacheler" (3.883) and thereafter is simply a "knyght." "There is no male lead in any other romance known to me," Lindahl writes, "who is so unadorned with epithets; the absence of comment is the most effective insult possible" (p. 74).

74. Susan Crane puts the matter well: "The knight-rapist and the king both move from having power to surrendering it, while women throughout the tale move themselves into male purviews" ("Alison's Incapacity," p. 25). See also Lindahl, who comments on all three of the Loathly Lady tales as being "founded on feminine power" ("Oral Undertones," p. 69).

75. I acknowledge that I'm guilty of introducing a kind of anachronism here in that the Wife's "Prologue" must have been written earlier, in the later 1380s, certainly

before Chaucer had decided to give her the Loathly Lady story. But I also acknowledge that the motif is certainly a feature of her prologue and epilogue, and that it also is present, in a more modest way, in Gower.

76. *Quoniam* (because, whereas, since, seeing that) is a scholastic term, a marker of cause, the ground or reason upon which an argument and conclusion may be drawn, that is used to begin the proposition of an argument, as in "because of this, then this." The strength of an argument is contingent upon its *quoniam*.

77. It may be, as Crane argues, that there is incapacity and instability in Alison's "air of tenacious assurance" that suggests uncertainty about just what it is she wants as she resolves "the battle of the sexes into blissful reciprocity," but the important thing is to see that though she gives, she does not give it all away. Her envoy reveals what Crane calls "a still-polarized combativeness" ("Alison's Incapacity," p. 26), though perhaps not exactly as Crane is arguing. I would say, rather, that she simply wants to keep her teeth, even though she is old.

78. See Levy, "Chaucer's Wife." See also Robert J. Meyer, who argues that the knight remains important to the lady's agenda as one in need of education, an education she supplies. He becomes a passive student, and she the aggressive school marm: "The pillow lecture, far from being extraneous, is the immediate cause of his dramatic metamorphosis" ("Chaucer's Tandem Romances," p. 232).

79. It is amusing to think of the Wife of Bath as dramatist/director/*acteur* as she reads and stages her thoughts and desire through the complete cast of *dramatis personae* that Souriau devises to accommodate Propp's plot functions (Greimas labels them *actants*) to get at the subject/object interplay of being and the staging of being. By the end of the tale she is *sujet* (subject: philosopher), *objet* (object: world), *destinateur* (sender: god), *destinataire* (receiver: mankind ["myn housbonde / Sholde lete fader and mooder and take to me," III(D) 30–31]), *opposant* (opponent: matter), and *adjuvant* (helper: mind). See Greimas, "Réflexions," pp. 180–81. It is no wonder that her prologue and tale are so lively: she does it all.

80. The bedroom question differs in the two versions, Gower's question of whether Florent would have the lady be fair by day or fair by night being altered by the Wife to the question of whether he would have her be older and faithful or young and capricious. As Bernard Levy has pointed out ("Chaucer's Wife," pp. 370–73), it may be ambiguous whether the Wife's dame has in fact changed, but certainly there is no doubt but that she, sirenlike, has changed (reformed) the knight's mind, the latter being the significant transformation. In the Wife's solution, the older woman's transformation of the patriarchial rapist's brain takes the burden off the aging female to remain perpetually young and beautiful to survive. This does not imply, of course, that she no longer enjoys the illusion of appearing to be young and fair, a point on which she and her friend Alisoun would doubtless concur.

81. Lee Patterson talks about Alison's verbalizations in the Prologue as remaining "unavoidably dependent, feminine respeakings of a resolutely masculine idiom" ("'For the Wyves love of Bathe'" p. 682); but I don't think that Chaucer and Gower would

conceive of language in exactly that way. It may be true that men have appropriated language and institutions; but women, certainly the Wife of Bath, can reappropriate them, or at least try. It may be that as Alison encounters such language and institutions, her idiom is, as Patterson argues, "resolutely masculine," politically, at least, if one imagines that the society is resolutely patriarchal, which it is not, if viewed from the matriarchal sphere that the Wife embraces.

82. I'm borrowing the term that St. Paul uses for himself in Acts 9:15, where he becomes God's chosen vessel, an idea picked up by Dante in *Inferno* 2.28–32. Chaucer revisions the idea in his juxtaposition of the Wife of Bath and the Clerk, who sits as a bride, in hope of becoming the instrument of God. See Peck, "St. Paul and *The Canterbury Tales.*"

83. I'm using another Greimas-like term to identify isomorphic types of equation that recur iteratively without need to assume specific authorship or psychic substance or natural reference. See Ronald Schleifer's introduction to *Structural Semantics,* pp. xxvi–xxx. Folktales depend for their lightning-quick effects upon such isomorphic iteration, as Gower well knows. But in Chaucer the bundles of isotopies evoke complexes of resonance that carry across from the Prologue to the tale through voicing bound together in the Wife's scriptural glossing philosophic allusion and in the tale's pillow talk sermon and its apocalyptic effect when the wise hag removes the curtain.

84. I am thinking of shorter English Arthurian romances like "Sir Gawain and the Carle of Carlisle," "The Awntyrs off Arthur," "The Knightly Tale of Gologras and Gawain," "The Turke and Sir Gawain," and "Sir Gawain and the Green Knight," where, as in "The Wedding of Sir Gawain and Dame Ragnelle," Gawain approaches perfection in reaffirmation of fealty to the ideal, though Arthur and other members of the court exhibit deficiencies, particularly "surquidry," in their presumptions against people held to be lesser than they.

85. There are a couple of instances, however, in which "Ragnelle" is closer to Chaucer, especially in repetition of the "somme seyde" formula in "Ragnelle" lines 199–204 and "WBT" (III[D]925–34), a use of anaphora not found in Gower. See Field, "Malory," p. 375.

86. See Bromwich, "Celtic Dynastic Themes": "The role of Arthur has encroached upon that of Gawain, who is the real hero of the tale" (p. 452).

87. See Field, "Malory," on parallels between "Ragnelle" and Malory in this regard. It might be useful to consider "The Turke and Sir Gawain" here too, where Gawain's trials seem more like bizarre distractions—tennis matches, feasts which leave him out, beheading games—but which Gawain gets past, with the aid of the Turk, who turns out to be less an enemy than a codependent friend, who, with the aid of Gawain and the Virgin Mary, gets restored to his true, noble nature, Sir Gromer, who, as Hahn points out, "is apparently identical with Sir Gromer Somer Joure of 'Ragnelle' ... and Malory's Sir Gromore Somyr Ioure (*Works,* p. 1164), an ally of Galeron of Galloway (see 'Awntyrs,' line 417)" (Hahn, *Sir Gawain,* p. 358).

88. She is like the Turk/Gromer (her brother), in this regard, who is codependent upon Gawain to get back into his true, noble form. See n. 87.

89. I'm borrowing Patterson's phrase here (see n. 81, above) in that the political milieu is more definitively masculine than in either Gower or Chaucer, even though the patriarchal practices of Arthur and Guinevere's decorous court are ethically subverted. It is the practice, not the system, that is under surveillance here.

90. Field establishes a host of unique details linking "The Wedding of Sir Gawain and Dame Ragnelle" and Malory, so many, in fact, that he speculates whether the "Ragnelle"-poet might not be Malory. Field notes that in Malory, Gromer Somer Joure is three times called Gromersom Erioure ("Malory," p. 375), a detail that might be seen as a link between the English poem and Irish version on the sovereignty of Ireland that Eisner talks about, in that *Erioure* suggests "of Ireland," just as the Loathly Lady in the Irish tale is named Ériu (Ireland).

91. This is the reading in the first recension of the poem, Bodley 902. *Fynde* could mean "invent." In 1393 Gower dignified the sense by naming a source, "In a Cronique as it is write." The revision presumably adds literary authority. See Macaulay, *John Gower's English Works,* note to lines I.1403–6, p. 74.

WORKS CITED

Aguirre, Manuel. "The Riddle of Sovereignty." *MLR* 88 (1993), 273–82.

Apuleius. *The Golden Ass.* Trans. W. Adlington. Loeb Classical Library. Cambridge, Mass.: Harvard University Press, 1977.

Barthes, Roland. *S/Z.* Trans. Richard Miller. Paris: Editions du Seuil, 1970; repr. New York: Hillard Wang, 1974.

Beach, Joseph Warren. "The Loathly Lady." PhD diss., Harvard University, 1907.

Beidler, Peter B. "Transformations in Gower's 'The Tale of Florent' and Chaucer's 'Wife of Bath's Tale.'" In *Chaucer and Gower: Difference, Mutuality, Exchange,* ed. R. F. Yeager, pp. 100–14. Victoria, BC: Victoria University Press, 1991.

Benson, Larry D., gen. ed. *The Riverside Chaucer.* 3rd ed. Boston: Houghton Mifflin, 1987; repr. Oxford: Oxford University Press, 1988.

Bettelheim, Bruno. *Uses of Enchantment.* New York: Vintage Books, 1977.

Bollard, John K. "Sovereignty and the Loathly Lady in English, Welsh and Irish." *LSE* 17 (1986), 41–59.

Bottigheimer, Ruth B. "Silenced Women in the Grimms' Tales: The 'Fit' Between Fairy Tales and Society in Their Historical Context." In *Fairy Tales and Society: Illusion, Allusion, and Paradigm,* ed. Ruth B. Bottigheimer, pp. 115–31. Philadelphia: University of Pennsylvania Press, 1986.

——. "Tale Spinners: Submerged Voices in Grimms' Fairy Tales." *New German Critique* 27 (1982), 141–50.

Bromwich, Rachel. "Celtic Dynastic Themes and the Breton Lays." *EC* 9 (1960–61), 439–74.

Brown, A. C. L. *The Origin of the Grail Legend*. Cambridge, Mass.: Harvard University Press, 1943.

Campbell, J. F. *Popular Tales of the West Highlands*. 4 vols. London: Gardner, 1890–93.

Carter, Angela. "Ashputtle: or, the Mother's Ghost." In *Disorderly Conduct: The "VLS" [Voice Literary Supplement] Fiction Reader*, ed. M. Mark, pp. 54–62. New York: Serpent's Tail, 1991.

Child, Francis James, ed. *The English and Scottish Popular Ballads*. 5 vols. New York: Dover Publications, 1965. First published Boston: Houghton Mifflin, 1882–98.

Coomaraswamy, Ananda K. "On the Loathly Bride." *Speculum* 20 (1945), 391–404.

Crane, Susan. "Alison's Incapacity and Poetic Instability in 'The Wife of Bath's Tale.'" *PMLA* 102 (1987), 20–27.

Dundes, Alan. *The Study of Folklore*. Englewood Cliffs, N.J.: Prentice-Hall, 1965.

Eisner, Sigmund. *A Tale of Wonder: A Source Study of "The Wife of Bath's Tale."* Wexford, Ire.: John English, 1957.

Eliade, Mircea. *From Primitives to Zen*. New York: Harper and Row, 1967.

Elwin, Verrier. "The *Vagina Dentata* Legend." *British Journal of Medical Psychology* 19 (1943), 439–53.

Field, P. J. C. "Malory and 'The Wedding of Sir Gawain and Dame Ragnell,'" *Archiv* 219 (1982), 374–81.

Frye, Northrop. *The Secular Scripture: A Study of Romance*. Cambridge, Mass.: Harvard University Press, 1976.

Gower, John. *Confessio Amantis*. Ed. Russell A. Peck. 3 vols. Kalamazoo, Mich.: Medieval Institute Publications, 2003–2006.

Greimas, A. J. "Réflexions sur les Modèles Actantiels." *Sémantique Structurale: Recherche de Méthode* (1966), 172–91.

——. *Structural Semantics: An Attempt at a Method*. Trans. Daniele McDowell, Ronald Schlieffer, and Alan Velie. Lincoln: University of Nebraska Press, 1983.

Griswold, Jerome. *Audacious Kids: Coming of Age in America's Classic Children's Books*. London: Oxford University Press, 1992.

Grosz, Elizabeth. "Animal Sex: Libido as Desire and Death." In *Sexy Bodies: The Strange Carnalities of Feminism*, ed. Elizabeth Grosz and Elspeth Probyn, pp. 278–99. New York: Routledge, 1995.

Hahn, Thomas. "Old Wives' Tales and Masculine Intuition." In *Retelling Tales: Essays in Honor of Russell Peck*, ed. Thomas Hahn and Alan Lupack, pp. 91–108. Cambridge: Brewer, 1997.

——, ed. *Sir Gawain: Eleven Romances and Tales*. Kalamazoo, Mich.: Medieval Institute Publications, 1995.

Lang, Andrew. *The Lilac Fairy Book*. London: Longmans, Green, 1910.

Leavy, Barbara Fass. *In Search of the Swan Maiden: A Narrative on Folklore and Gender*. New York: New York University Press, 1994.

Levy, Bernard S. "Chaucer's Wife of Bath, the Loathly Lady, and Dante's Siren." *Symposium* 19 (1965), 357–73.

Lindahl, Carl. "The Oral Undertones of Late Medieval Romance." In *Oral Traditions in the Middle Ages*, ed. W. F. N. Nicolaisen, pp. 59–75. Binghamton, N.Y.: MRTS, 1995.

Loomis, Roger Sherman. *Celtic Myth and Arthurian Romance*. New York: Columbia University Press, 1927.

——. "Chivalric and Dramatic Imitations of Arthurian Romance." In *Medieval Studies in Memory of A. Kingsley Porter*, ed. Wilhelm Koehler, pp. 91–92. Cambridge: Cambridge University Press, 1939.

——. "Edward I, Arthurian Enthusiast." *Speculum* 23 (1953), 114–27.

Lowie, R. H. "The Test-Theme in North American Mythology." *Journal of American Folklore* 21 (1908), 97–148.

Lynch, Kathryn L. *Chaucer's Philosophical Visions*. Rochester, N.Y.: Boydell and Brewer, 2000.

Mac Cana, Proinsias. "Aspects of the Theme of King and Goddess in Irish Literature." Parts 1–3. *EC* 7 (1955–56), 76–114, and 356–413; *EC* 8 (1958–59), 59–65.

Macaulay, G. C., ed. *John Gower's English Works*. 2 vols. Oxford: Oxford University Press, 1901.

Maynadier, G. H. *"The Wife of Bath's Tale": Its Sources and Analogues*. London: Nutt, 1901.

Meyer, Robert J. "Chaucer's Tandem Romances: A Generic Approach to the 'Wife of Bath's Tale' as Palinode." *CR* 18 (1984), 221–38.

Minnis, Alastair J. "Late-Medieval Discussions of *Compilatio* and the Role of the Compilator." *Beiträge zur Geschichte der deutschen Sprache und Literatur* 101 (1979), 385–91.

——. *Medieval Theory of Authorship: Scholastic Literary Attitudes in the Later Middle Ages*. 2nd ed. Philadelphia: University of Pennsylvania Press, 1988.

Morabito, Raffaele. "La Diffusione della Storia di Griselda dal XIV as XX Secolo." *Studi sul Boccaccio* 17 (1989), 237–85.

——, ed. *Griselda 1: La Circolazione Dei Temi e Degli Intrecci Narrativi: Il Caso Griselda*. Rome: Japadre Editore l'Aquila, 1988.

——, ed. *Griselda 2: La Storia di Griselda in Europa*. Rome: Japadre Editore L'Aquila, 1990.

Newstead, Helaine. *A Manual of the Writings in Middle English 1050–1500*. Ed. J. Burke Severs. New Haven: Connecticut Academy of Arts and Sciences, 1937.

Ó Corráin, Donnchadh. "Textuality and Inter-textuality: Early Medieval Irish Literature." In *Griselda 2*, ed. Morabito, pp. 21–32.

Olsson, Kurt. *John Gower and the Structures of Conversion: A Reading of the "Confessio Amantis."* Cambridge: Brewer, 1992.

Patterson, Lee. "'For the Wyves love of Bathe': Feminine Rhetoric and Poetic Resolution in the 'Roman de la Rose' and *The Canterbury Tales*." *Speculum* 58 (1983), 656–95.

Peck, Russell A. "Gower, Maker of Tales." In *Confessio Amantis*, ed. Peck, 1:1–7.
———. "St. Paul and *The Canterbury Tales.*" *Mediaevalia* 7 (1981), 91–131.
———. *The Cinderella Bibliography*, http://www.lib.rochester.edu/camelot/cinder/cinintr.htm.
Pirandello, Luigi. *Six Characters in Search of an Author: A Comedy in the Making.* Trans. Frederick May. London: Heinemann, 1954.
Propp, Vladimir. *Morphology of the Folktale.* Trans. L. Scott. Austin: University of Texas Press, 1968.
Raitt, Jill. "The *Vagina Dentata* and the *Immaculatus Uterus Vivini Fontis.*" *Journal of the American Academy of Religion* 48 (1980), 415–31.
Ramsey, Jarold. *Coyote Was Going There.* Seattle: University of Washington Press, 1977.
Rescher, Nicholas. "Choice Without Preference: A Study of the History and the Logic of the Problem of 'Buridan's Ass.'" *Kant-Studien* 51 (1959–60), 146–51.
The Riverside Shakespeare. 2nd ed. Boston: Houghton Mifflin, 1997.
Salisbury, Eve. "Remembering Origins: Gower's Monstrous Body's Poetic." In *Re-Visioning Gower*, ed. R. F. Yeager, pp. 159–84. Asheville, N.C.: Pegasus, 1998.
Saul, George Brandon. *The Wedding of Sir Gawain and Dame Ragnell.* New York: Prentice-Hall, 1934.
Schleifer, Ronald. Introduction to *Structural Semantics*, by A.-J. Greimas. Trans. Daniele McDowell, Ronald Schleifer, and Alan Velie, pp. xxvi-xxx. Lincoln: University of Nebraska Press, 1983.
Seligman, C. G. "Anthropological Perspective and Psychological Theory." *Journal of the Royal Anthropological Institute* 62 (1932), 219.
Seymour, M. C., ed. *Mandeville's Travels.* Oxford: Clarendon Press, 1967.
Silva Gadelica. Ed. and trans. Standish O'Grady, pp. 368–73. London: Williams and Northgate, 1892.
Simpson, James. *Sciences and the Self in Medieval Poetry: Alan of Lille's "Anticlaudianus" and John Gower's "Confessio Amantis."* Cambridge: Cambridge University Press, 1995.
Sumner, Laura, ed. *The Weddynge of Sir Gawen and Dame Ragnell.* Smith College Studies in Modern Languages 5.4. Northampton, Mass.: Department of Modern Languages of Smith College, 1924; repr. Folcroft, Penn.: Folcroft, 1974.
Thompson, Stith. *Motif Index of Folk Literature: A Classification of Narrative Elements in Folk Tales, Ballads, Myths, Fables, Mediaeval Romances, Exempla, Fabliaux, Jest-Books, and Local Legends.* 6 vols. Bloomington: Indiana University Press, 1966.
———, and Antti A. Aarne. *The Types of the Folktale: A Classification and Bibliography.* Folklore Fellows Communications 184. Rev. ed. Helsinki: Soumalainenen Tiedeakatemia, 1964; 2nd rev. ed., 1981.
Thoms, William. "Folk-Lore." *Athenaeum* 982 (22 August 1846), 862–63.
Utley, Francis Lee. "Folk Literature: An Operational Definition." In *The Study of Folklore*, ed. Dundes, pp. 7–24.

Whiting, Bartlett J. "[Sources and Analogues of] The Wife of Bath's Tale." In *Sources and Analogues of Chaucer's Canterbury Tales*, ed. W. F. Bryan and Germaine Dempster, pp. 224–64. London: Routledge and Kegan Paul, 1958.

Controlling the Loathly Lady, or What Really Frees Dame Ragnelle

Paul Gaffney

"The Wedding of Sir Gawain and Dame Ragnelle" exemplifies the traditional stream of the Loathly Lady tale, little influenced by bookish traditions. The form preserved in Bodleian Library MS 11951 is an instance of an orally derived story that is likely much older than any of the written versions that survive.[1] As such, the "Wedding" is well situated to show the particular strengths of a simpler, less artful tale compared to its more literary cousins, namely John Gower's "Tale of Florent" and Geoffrey Chaucer's "Wife of Bath's Tale." Scholarship has generally traced the origins of the Loathly Lady narratives to Irish sovereignty tales, the versions of which survive are dated to the eleventh and twelfth centuries. In these we see some of the mythic headwaters of this narrative stream, sources that supply much of the inherent[2] power still found in these later instances.

Carl Lindahl's comments on the Loathly Lady motif in his essay "The Oral Undertones of Late Medieval Romance" prompted this inquiry; his episodic analysis of these three tales illustrates his argument about the strengths of what John Miles Foley calls "orally-derived" tales,[3] such as the "Wedding."[4] Although he stresses the "common ground of elite and folk cultures,"[5] arguing that surviving texts show the marks of both, he goes on to discuss how the oral style is characteristically unglossed: "By letting each member of the audience assign her or his own meaning to an unexplained symbol or action, the teller allows many diverse readings of the performance."[6] "Elite" style, in contrast, is marked by glossing: "Vinaver argues that this juxtaposition of the story with its *sens* [treatment or theme] was rooted in the monastic technique of interlinear and marginal glosses."[7] Scholarship has interpreted medieval works overwhelmingly in terms of elite culture, largely because manuscript culture overwhelmingly represents it. Folk, or popular, culture is not as easily detected or dissected, yet it should be acknowledged and appreciated on its own terms.[8] This essay shares Lindahl's conclusions, but presses them further with terminology provided by narratology, specifically that of Roland Barthes.

The tale "The Wedding of Gawain and Dame Ragnelle" is what Roland Barthes calls a *discours,* the particular embodiment of a *histoire,* or bare story line. Barthes's narratological approach is certainly not the only one—in fact, narratology suffers under an excess of competing terminologies—but he presents perhaps the most widely used system of terms, from which I will just make use of the most basic: *histoire* and *discours.* In Saussurean terms they are the *langue* and *parole* of narrative. Barthes follows earlier narratologists, notably Vladimir Propp, in postulating a deep structure for narrative—the *histoire*—corresponding to, and extending, the syntactic deep structure of generative linguistics. He writes, "A discours is a long 'sentence ... just as a sentence is a short 'discours.'"[9] The *histoire* is a sort of deep structure, an abstracted skeleton of the basic elements of a story: essential characters, events and perhaps settings, whereas the *discours* is an embodiment of its *histoire,* necessarily set apart by its style, emphasis, and details. This sort of approach has justifiably been criticized for its shortcomings; no one claims that a postulated *histoire* is necessarily prior to a *discours,* a realized account, and it is often difficult to agree on what element constitutes the core of a narrative, so the process is not rigorously scientific. I would hesitate to apply it to a single text, for then the core elements are more difficult to isolate convincingly. However, this sort of narratology is strongest when used to compare differing *discourses* of a particular *histoire,* in the manner of this essay. In this case there is little question that these tales share a common historical background, so a shared abstract source should be easily granted.

Briefly, my thesis is that the less fixed the meaning of a *discours,* the more evocative it can be. As authors extrapolate their *histoire,* providing background, characters' thoughts, psychological detail, designated meaning, and the like, their *discours* becomes by some measures richer, but at the same time more determined. The more concrete, exterior, unexcavated, the *discours* is (the closer to the *histoire*), the more is left to the audience. This suggests that the seemingly rougher, "orally derived" romances are a different species of story, one in which the audience participates more in the construction of meaning. I will show how "The Wedding of Sir Gawain and Dame Ragnelle" exemplifies the difference in this species, and some of its special strengths.

John Miles Foley addresses the issue of meaning in orally derived narrative in "The Implications of Oral Tradition":

> In the modern, literary work of art, we place the highest priority on a writer's personal manipulation of original or inherited materials, rewarding the work that strikes out boldly in a new direction by providing a perspective uniquely its own, memorable because it is new, fresh, or, best of all, inimitable. In such a case the work is praised for the finesse with which an author (not a tradition) *confers* meaning on his creation…. In contrast, a traditional work depends primarily on elements and strategies that were in place long before the execution of the present version or text, long before the present nominal author learned the inherited craft. Because the idiom is metonymic, summoning conventional connotations to conventional structures, we may say that the meaning it conveys is principally *inherent*.[10]

This distinction between "conferred" and "inherent" meaning harmonizes well with Lindahl's characterization of medieval elite (or bookish) culture as marked by glossing, for glossing is a prominent medieval means of conferring meaning.

At the end of the "General Prologue" to *The Canterbury Tales*, Chaucer promises "tales of best sentence and moost solaas";[11] *sentence* is "content, meaning, signification," so he is announcing his intention to manage the *sentence* of the tales. Since *sentence* is generally seen as inscribed by an *auctor*, Chaucer is claiming the *auctoritas* of a poet who instructs as well as delights. The elite culture was well aware that there are many ways to interpret the *sentence* of a work, even a vernacular tale: Dante, in his *Convivio*, outlines the reading of vernacular texts through the fourfold interpretive method usually applied to Scripture,[12] and medieval writers often use the same *histoire* toward very different ends. In *The Rise of Romance*, Eugene Vinaver discusses how the application of methods of interpretation to vernacular stories began in the eleventh and twelfth centuries, and that this contributed to the shift in learning from monasteries to universities.[13] The bookish world became increasingly interested in all manner of storytelling, and clerkly practice expressed interest through definition, assessment and other means of control. In *Chaucer's Sexual Poetics*, Carolyn Dinshaw discusses glossing at length, specifically in reference to the Wife of Bath. She writes: "Glossing is a gesture of appropriation; the *glossa* undertakes to speak the text, to assert authority over it, to provide an interpretation, finally to limit or close it to the possibility of heterodox or unlimited significance."[14] As they multiplied, glosses could multiply interpretations; well-glossed manuscripts often contain contradictory glosses on the same page. Larry Benson points out that "[f]or Chaucer 'glose' is usually pejorative"[15] and in her "Prologue" the Wife disparages (with Chaucerian irony, perhaps) men who "may devyne and glosen up and doun" (line 26). Perhaps Chaucer and Gower sought to exercise some control of *sentence* in order to resist later exegesis, although manuscript glosses on these very tales witness that such a strategy could not be entirely effective.[16]

Glosses are technically exterior to the text, attached to it in some way, but the function of glossing, specifying or fixing meaning, can be accomplished in various ways within the text as well. Other strategies for controlling *sentence* included the assigning of morals for retold tales, particularly in such collections as Fulgentius's *De continentia Virgiliana* and many versions of the *Ovide moralisé*. Geoffrey of Vinsauf's *Poetria nova*, a well-known treatise in the fourteenth century, stresses the craft of assembling poetry to best carry meaning.[17] O. B. Hardison, Jr. writes that the theme running throughout the *Poetria* is "the primacy of the intellectual conception of the work over its materials."[18] Chrétien de Troyes writes in the prologue to his *Erec and Enide* that he "tret d'un conte d'avanture/ une molt bele conjointure" ("makes from an adventure tale a very beautiful composition").[19] This is "composition" in the sense of arranging things; in Chrétien's case, he arranges his *matière* (source material) to fit his *sens* ("authorial intent," as Donald Howard translates it).[20] John Miles Foley's "conferred meaning" can function as a variety of internal or implicit glosses as the author includes direct commentary, reports of characters' thoughts and feelings, and (above all) explanation for events in the plot. Material, concrete images are forthrightly explained or fleshed out though further narration. The idea is that *sens* and *sentence* must control *matière* and *solaas*, for the multiplicity of interpretative strategies makes obvious how unglossed (internally or externally) narrative remains so much more open, vulnerable to innumerable audience interpretations or misinterpretations.

Though they are both clearly interested in storytelling as an art, this is Chaucer and Gower's cultural context, and they both worked to establish vernacular poetry as a viable product of elite culture, like the *auctores* of the Latin corpus. Textual authority, *auctoritas*, was long located exclusively in Latin works, usually ones long established and sanctioned by the church. Larry Scanlon links the beginnings of vernacular *auctoritas* in English to the courtly Richardian poets, mainly Chaucer and Gower, who established authority through connection to the king instead of the church.[21] Dante and Petrarch surely contributed to the establishment of vernacular *auctoritas*, but Chaucer is rightly considered the primary founder of vernacular literary *auctoritas* in England, and Gower shared in that creation.[22]

For both Gower and Chaucer, the job of defining the meaning of their tales begins with a framing conceit, a narrator who forthrightly states what principle the story is meant to illustrate and then returns at the end to reiterate the message. Larry Scanlon categorizes "The Wife of Bath's Tale" as an exemplum "on the grounds of its exemplary relation to the parodic sermon that constitutes its prologue."[23] The control of *sentence*, however, is not simply imposed from outside the stories, but is also carried on throughout the narratives. In their *discourses*, Chaucer mainly uses commentary—remarks not part of the *histoire*—whereas Gower relies almost entirely on elements within the *histoire*. Chaucer is the most controlling of his narrative; "The Wife of Bath's Tale" may be the most glossed of all his works. Gower uses the *histoire* also, in a different manner, and to a lesser degree.

Of course, meaning is not so easily contained, and certainly both literary versions have meaning that overflows their function as exempla.[24] Some of this is due to the residue of meaning inherent in their source materials: had they tried, they could not have wholly buried meaning long infused into the tale. Several critics have argued that Chaucer and Gower both complicate (in different ways) the tale that they retell, but the extent to which that may be true cannot erase the already suggestive, allusive nature of their material. Did they strive to cast doubt on their professed meaning through the use of unreliable narrators, ironic commentary, or other literary techniques, or does vigorous meaning simply seep through or bubble up of its own accord? The texts of their tales, compared to that of the "Wedding," show literary craft used to control meaning, particularly in Chaucer's case. If they did complicate the *histoire*, it was a clerkly complication, a multiplication of details that serve to corral and channel *sentence* rather than disperse it.

Much of twentieth-century philosophy and literary theory has dwelt on the "problem of language": Stanley Fish, Jacques Derrida, and many others have explored how meaning in language is "always already" out of the control of its user, whether one prefers to think of it as overdetermined or under-determined. Deconstruction has shown that language is so full of possible meaning, perhaps infinite possibilities, that meaning is always deferred, that an author and his audience both live inside language and play inside the inevitable gap between signified and signifier. Reader-response critics show that the reception of communication can never be fully anticipated, even when the author belongs to the same "interpretive community" as an audience. Stanley Fish is opposed to "the assumption that there *is* a sense, that it is imbedded or encoded in the text."[25] Instead, he looks to the audience to create meaning through interpretation: "meanings are not extracted but made and made not by encoding forms but by interpretive strategies that call forms into being."[26] In *Social Chaucer*, Paul Strohm compromises this seemingly one-sided formulation: "the text is not transmitted from the author to the reader, but it is constructed between them as a kind of ideological bridge."[27] I find all of this quite valid in the larger picture. Ultimately, a narrative is not bound by its author's intentions; it can be read (or interpreted) in an infinite number of ways. Even if they sought to fix a meaning for their narratives, Chaucer and Gower could not do so.

Yet some narratives, some *discourses*, open up interpretive possibilities, and others try to close them. Medieval bookish culture focused on the glossing of texts, trying to govern *sentence*; after all, the essential purpose of writing was to impart moral instruction.[28] J. A. Burrow argues that

> it is not surprising to find [the Ricardian] poets exercising strict control over the moral bearings of a story.... Hence we might expect to find a preponderance of single-episode stories, given the relative ease with which the moral bearing of such tales can be controlled and limited. Like the authors of clerical *exempla*, these poets are governed by a principle of selection which requires them to pick out individual episodes from existing cycles and series.[29]

In contrast, folk narrative tends to be underdetermined, even ambiguous in its *sentence*; it is more a space of evocative images than of specific morals. In folk narrative, the inner world of thought and emotion are not well-developed because the entire world of the romance is an interior landscape—the characters do not think so much as they embody thought, just as the places and things are part of a sort of socially and psychologically metonymic landscape. Carl Lindahl says that most of the anonymous English romancers "let at least part of the story speak for itself, retaining a certain imagistic magic.... [They] tended to observe one of the fundamental laws of oral esthetic, which holds that the most concrete images are the most powerful because they are the most suggestive."[30] Certainly folk literature is often didactic in some sense—often quite explicitly—while some, like "The Wedding of Sir Gawain and Dame Ragnelle," seems to have an aim beyond *solaas*, yet show only a diffuse *sentence* that resists exclusive interpretation. While not strictly folk literature, the "Wedding" shows much more influence from folk traditions than from bookish traditions, and this *histoire* doubtless derives from folk sources. Gower and Chaucer use the *histoire* in more bookish ways, adapting the folk source to learned culture.

John Gower's "Tale of Florent" represents a species of literary storytelling. Apart from the frame, it presents the story fairly directly, with few narratorial comments. Gower instead uses literary technique to try to direct readers' responses to the story. He inserts very little commentary into the *discours,* but stresses what the characters *think,* and works to direct how they should be perceived. The word *thoght* and its synonyms appear more than ten times in the 468 lines of "The Tale of Florent": "in his thoght was curious" (line 1524), "Tho fell this knyht in mochel thoght" (line 1568), "And thoghte, as he rod to and fro" (line 1571), "Him thoghte he scholde taken hiede" (line 1720), "as of thoght and of memoire" (line 1775), "caste his thoght" (line 1815), and so on.[31] In Gower, we are given direct commentary from the narrator, indirect reports of Florent's thoughts and feelings, and direct internal monologue. As with Chaucer, the tale is told by a literary narrator, whose authority is not unchallenged. Larry Scanlon notes, "as many commentators have observed, the poem's exempla frequently fail to fit the sententiae Genius assigns to them."[32] If this is the case with "The Tale of Florent," then the *sentence* is about "trowthe" or keeping one's word, which is not so different from "Obedience in love availeth, / Wher al a mannes strengthe faileth" (lines 1401–2); the obedience may not truly be "in love" (despite Branchus's granddame's disingenuous "on love it hongeth" in line 1479), but Florent is dutiful as well as discreet. In any case, Gower certainly has shaped the *discours* to serve as an exemplum, as the Latin gloss at line 1407 clearly states: "Hic contra amori inobedientes ad commendacionem Obediencie Confessor super eodem exemplum ponit."[33]

Gower immediately makes his *discours* more clerkly by giving it a classical setting and by giving characters Latin names: Florent, Branchus, and Claudius. This brings the tale into the bookish realm, where meaning is more mapped than in the folk realm; the tale may be an orally derived narrative told in the vernacular, but Gower has claimed authority over it. The tale is told simply enough, with only one brief passage of narratorial comment: lines 1703–13, an aside about doing what one must, which is punctuated by a direct statement of *sentence:* "He wolde algate his trowthe holde, / As every knyht therto is holde, / What happ so evere him is befalle" (lines 1715–17). This echoes a narratorial statement about Florent near the beginning of the tale: "This knyht hath levere forto dye / Than breke his trowthe and forto lye" (lines 1511–12). A heavy narratorial presence hardly seems necessary in order for this *sentence* to permeate the tale, particularly since the narrator frames the telling with statements that the story exemplifies obedience. Throughout the narrative the audience is reminded, through description of his thoughts, how careful Florent is to do what is right.

The emphasis in "The Tale of Florent" is on the interior life, how the characters think and feel. The audience hears Florent pondering what to do with the Loathly Lady's offer and is reminded several times how downhearted he is at the prospect of spending his life with her. Even some of the dialogue consists of expressed thoughts and feelings. This constant and relatively detailed focus on thought more than action strives to direct the *audience's* thought as much as possible, for the action is interpreted through the thoughts. In the case of Florent, he is clearly concerned with his "trowthe" and doing what is best: "And in his thoght was curious / To wite what was best to do" (lines 1524–25), "He wot noght what is best to sein, / And thoghte, as he rod to and fro" (lines 1570–71), "Thus wot he noght what is the best" (lines 1626), "Bot for al that yit cowthe he noght / Devise himself which was the beste" (lines 1816–17). Being privy to Florent's thoughts also invites the audience into his emotional life, which Gower skillfully uses to make him a sympathetic as well as admirable figure. The overall effect is calculated to draw in the audience and keep its attention on the *sentence* that Gower has fixed for the *discours*.

Chaucer, through the Wife of Bath, works to control *sentence* very explicitly, as well as in more subtle ways. "The Wife of Bath's Tale" punctuates the Wife's "Prologue," and the lecture continues to bubble up to the surface even within the tale, which is less than half as long as its "Prologue." Alisoun fills the "Prologue" with allusions to and exempla from *auctores*, though her glossing usually misappropriates them. She promises in line 179: "I shal telle ensamples mo than ten."[34] It could easily be argued that the tale is little more than another "ensample," albeit one that has yet another exemplary tale embedded within it (the story of Midas)! This is not to say that it is not masterfully told; many critics have argued that Chaucer develops his *matière* into a tale far more graceful, concise, and meaningful than its likely predecessor. Chaucer has his Loathly Lady demand the traditional unnamed boon, rather than offering an explicit bargain, and even then the audience is not privy to the Loathly Lady's answer, for "Tho rowned she a pistel in his ere" (line 1021). Chaucer also waits until the very end, after all the dialogue is done, to reveal with a flourish the lady's transformation: "Cast up the curtyn, looke how that it is" the lady finally says (1249). These sorts of changes to the *discours* show a master storyteller, one in full command of the *histoire*.

Chaucer simplifies his *discours* and includes a few folktale elements not found in the analogues, making his *discours* appear at first glance more like a fairy tale or even a fable. The Wife's tale excises the king/nephew relationship that plays a significant part in other *discourses* and eliminates the Gromer Somer figure and the stepmother role. Limiting the cast of characters focuses the tale and allows for a simplification of the plot, since less action is required with only two essential characters rather than three in "Florent" and four in the "Wedding." (I do not count the poor "mayde" who was the victim of the rape, as I do not count Branchus in "The Tale of Florent"—their victimization leads to the central action of the plot, but they take no part in that action.) The opening lines, which describe—tongue in cheek—how England was so different in King Arthur's time, set the stage for a seemingly simple anecdote with a straightforward moral. Rape makes the central conflict unambiguous, unlike killing in fair combat (as in "Florent") or making land claims (as in the "Wedding"). The knight must answer to Guinevere and the other ladies, who do not begrudge his answer, "But seyden he was worthy han his lyf" (line 1045). Guinevere's challenge is a reprieve rather than a trap; unlike Gromer Somer or Branchus's granddame, she has no special animus toward the protagonist.

Chaucer's Loathly Lady is easily the most mysterious of the three in these *discourses*: she appears under a tree after twenty-four (plus) ladies who had been dancing at the edge of a forest suddenly vanish. This seems to suggest that she is "the elf-queene" mentioned in the fourth line of the tale, particularly since she has the power to transform herself, rather than being the victim of a malicious stepmother as in the other *discourses*. She is not named, not described, and we hear no explanation for her loathly appearance. All of this makes her a commanding figure—she controls her appearance and is a master rhetoritician, like the narrator, the Wife of Bath. Not only is there no description of the Loathly Lady, there is very little descriptive language at all in the tale; concrete images are set aside for abstract figures and lengthy dialogue.

This simplification of the *histoire* also leaves Chaucer free to insert much commentary by the Wife of Bath, including clerkly allusions. He highlights the fairy-tale nature of his exemplum, rather than trying to invite the reader into the characters' heads, as Gower does. There is no "thoght" in "The Wife of Bath's Tale," but much speech. Of the 408 lines in the tale, 227 are quotations, and another 68 are asides by the narrator, including the story of Midas. That leaves only 113 for direct narration, so the commentary outweighs the tale. Although Chaucer has his Wife of Bath disparage the "auctoritee" of *auctorites*, he thoroughly establishes his own "auctoritee" over "The Wife of Bath's Tale," masterfully controlling its *sentence* as much as is possible.

"The Wedding of Sir Gawain and Dame Ragnelle" represents the story-telling of folk culture. Its virtues are found largely in its concrete, unglossed, exterior narration; this sort of straightforward narration can be elaborate in description, dialogue, and account of action, but its meaning, its *sentence*, is less determined than in the bookish versions. Andrew Taylor, in his investigation of the original audience for these romances, writes that the anonymous Middle English romances "are a transitional literature; written for readers, they deliberately evoke an oral heritage, a pervasive, concurrent, but now largely irrecoverable oral culture."[35] The "Wedding" seems to have been textually produced, but it surely shows less influence from "elite" culture and less concern by its author to establish control and *auctoritas*. John Miles Foley's phrase, "orally derived literature," is useful here: "a text which has reached us in written form but which has roots in oral tradition."[36]

The insistence on concrete images accounts for the fact that "The Wedding of Gawain and Dame Ragnelle" is the only one of these *discourses* in which all of the characters are named. Surely the names Gromer Somer Jouer and Ragnelle meant more to a fourteenth- or fifteenth-century English audience than they do to us, but their meaning was evocative and ambiguous, not specific. Gromer Somer Jouer, or some folk cousin of his, turns up not only in several other romances, but seems closely connected with the Green Knight (of *Sir Gawain and the Green Knight* and other stories), the Wild Men of the Wood and similar folk figures featured in summer festivals. Ragnelle is the name given to a devil in line 188 of *Patience*, and in the Chester mystery play *Antichrist*, among other places, so her name apparently is intended to convey significant menace. Sir Gawain himself is a complicated figure in Middle English literature, surely the most popular character in surviving Middle English romances. Chaucer retains the Arthurian connection for its setting, but leaves the knight unnamed, while Gower gives him the not particularly meaningful name Florent. The figures in "The Wedding of Sir Gawain the Dame Ragnelle" resonate with "inherent" intertextual dimensions as much as dimensions inscribed by a specific *auctor*.

Inevitably the "inherent" meaning is more prominent in this *discours* than in the others, since the "conferred" meaning is so sparse. There is the conventional opening refrain praising Arthur and his knights, which Chaucer invokes rather mockingly, but because it is such a romance convention, the audience of the "Wedding" should not necessarily take it too seriously as a comment on the *sentence* of the tale. The only other direct comment by the author is at the end, where he attaches an appeal to God that has no apparent connection to the tale. Perhaps the author of this *discours* slyly discounts the bookish collecting and fixing of *sentence* by having Arthur and Gawain vainly collect in books their answers to Gromer Somer's question. We could also interpret Dame Ragnelle as referring allegorically to narratives when talking about what women want; rather than approach women (and narratives) "With flatryng and glosyng and quaynt gyn" (line 416), women (and narratives)

> desyren of men above all maner thyng
> To have the sovereynté, withoute lesyng,
> Of alle, bothe hyghe and lowe.
> For where we have sovereynté, alle is ourys.
> (lines 422–25)[37]

When the story itself is sovereign, rather than its author (the particular user of the *histoire*), then it is more free to evoke many things for many audiences. It can be interpreted variously, but does not surrender its *sentence* to a particular *sentence*.

The narrative does not point convincingly to just one *sentence* for this tale; the narratorial voice gives no instruction on the matter anywhere. In fact, he does not even comment on the events, he merely reports action and speech, with very few exceptions. When Arthur returns home after first meeting Dame Ragnelle, we are told, "Hys hartt was wonder hevy. / In this hevynesse he dyd abyde" (lines 134–35). Nowhere else is the poem as descriptive about a character's state of mind. Speaking of Ragnelle's death, the poet writes, "That grevid Gawen alle his lyfe," and adds "I telle you securely" (lines 821–22) to assure us that he is quite certain about Gawain's state of mind in this one case. On a couple of occasions characters report feelings in the barest of terms: Arthur says of Dame Ragnelle's offer, "I nott whate I do may" (line 308), not even thinking, as in the other *discourses*, to offer money or land instead. The poet does not report Arthur's feelings again, but does allow him to say "Thus in my hartt I make my mone" (line 341). The word *thoght*, which features so prominently in "The Tale of Florent," appears only three times in the 852 lines of the "Wedding," and those all in dialogue: "Thys thynkythe me nowe best" (line 218), "Butt me wold thynk more honour" (line 582), and "I wenyd, Sir Gawen, she wold the have myscaryed" (line 754). What limited thoughts the audience perceived in the characters are expressed through simple speech. Otherwise the *sentence* of the tale must be sought in the action of the plot, which is perilously open to manifold interpretations.

"The Wife of Bath's Tale" is claimed to be about women's sovereignty, and Genius declares that "The Tale of Florent" is about obedience in love (or being true to one's word); each tale tells us its *sentence* and whether or not the declarations are completely accurate, the tales consistently direct the reader to the *sentence*. We are not told, or even directed, toward an answer to what "The Wedding of Sir Gawain and Dame Ragnelle" is about, so it is what we make of it. Either of the meanings attributed to its analogues could serve; certainly both Arthur and Gawain are mastered by Dame Ragnelle, and Gawain finds reward and contentment through obedience in love and "trowthe." Gawain also shows outstanding obedience toward his liege-lord, Arthur. I could easily argue that its *sentence* has to do with honor, courtesy, or loyalty. Perhaps the "Wedding" is an exemplum for how a liege should behave, perhaps it is simply a glorification of the ideal knight, Sir Gawain: Arthur relies on him, and both Gromer Somer and Dame Ragnelle desire him and/or his possessions. Ellen Caldwell points out that much of the story is about a rivalry between Gromer Somer, apparently a lord from the fairy realm, and King Arthur, who is lord of the earthly, Christian realm.[38] The tale could be seen as an indictment of weak royalty—which certainly Arthur is here—or even, as some have suggested, a critique of the ruling class as a whole. Mary Leech says that there is no lesson to be learned from this *discours* because "the faults are constantly in flux within the social structure itself."[39] Is Arthur's killing of the hart shameful, as Martha Fleming suggests?[40] What are we to make of the enchantment of Ragnelle and Gromer Somer by a stepmother who is otherwise outside the *discours*? Who is even the central figure in this romance?

So the audience of the "Wedding" is not told or directed toward *sentence*—audience members see what happens and must draw their own conclusions, and those conclusions are bound to be plural. What does it mean that this tale does not try to control its *sentence* as do "The Wife of Bath" and "Florent"? On an online storytellers' forum, Alan Irvine, a well-known storyteller, writes that he has developed a dislike for the Dame Ragnelle story, which seems to be the version preferred by storytellers in the United States.[41] He complains that it is told too often, is difficult to tell well, and that it is "a flawed story, poorly constructed." Nevertheless, he hears it told more than any other tale. There is a reason that storytellers continue to tell the tale of Dame Ragnelle. Like all good mythology and folk narrative, it remains a well of meaning, highly flexible and open to recasting in manifold ways for manifold situations. To return to Carl Lindahl: "By letting each member of the audience assign her or his own meaning to an unexplained symbol or action, the teller allows many diverse readings of the performance.... Whatever the causes of the symbolic mode so characteristic of folk performance, its greatest effect is freedom of interpretation. While elite glosses limit meaning to support authoritarian dicta, folk communications remain unfinished, open-ended, and relatively free."[42]

I do not read Chaucer or Gower as supporting "authoritarian *dicta*," nor am I trying to establish a dialogic opposition between them as elite narratives and the "Wedding" as folk narrative, but these authors who worked to establish *auctoritas* for vernacular texts in England treated their *discourses* as exempla. The fact that Gower's and Chaucer's exempla may not be the best vessels for the principles they purport to illustrate does not detract from their status as exempla; indeed, many medieval sermons (not to mention the Wife of Bath's "Prologue") show how often exempla were used inappropriately. They are intended, whether by their authors or their fictional narrators, to illustrate a point, and as such their authors seek to establish control over their *sentence*. This control is exercised through all manner of means: plot, style, characterization, and commentary. There is no indication, internal or external, that the "Wedding" carried such intent. Still, these works are not opposites, but sit at different places along a scale, none of them wholly elite nor wholly folk. All are *discourses* of the same *histoire*. Yet most of the strengths of "The Wife of Bath's Tale" and "The Tale of Florent" are the strengths of good elite culture literature, while most of the strengths of "The Wedding of Sir Gawain and Dame Ragnelle" are the strengths of folk literature. The "Wedding" simply is constructed to do something rather different than these other *discourses*; Dame Ragnelle's anonymous poet frees her to take many shapes.

NOTES

1. All of the source-studies of the tale have concluded this. See Maynadier, *"Wife of Bath's Tale,"* and Eisner, *Tale of Wonder*.
2. "Inherent" as discussed by Foley, "Implications," pp. 31–57.
3. Foley, "Implications," p. 32.
4. Lindahl, "Oral Undertones," pp. 59–75.
5. Lindahl, "Oral Undertones," p. 64.

6. Lindahl, "Oral Undertones," p. 67.

7. Lindahl, "Oral Undertones," p. 66.

8. "Jacque Le Goff speaks of two cultures in medieval society: the culture of the clergy or 'learned' culture, and popular or 'folkloric culture'" (Gurevich, *Medieval Popular Culture*, p. xvi).

9. Barthes, "Introduction to the Structural Analysis," p. 83.

10. Foley, "Implications," pp. 34–35.

11. Benson, *Riverside Chaucer*, line 798; all citations of Chaucer are from this edition.

12. Dante, "Convivio," 2.1.2–12.

13. Vinaver, *Rise of Romance*, pp. 17–24.

14. Dinshaw, *Chaucer's Sexual Poetics*, p. 120. Following Alisoun's (the Wife's) statement in the epilogue to "The Man of Law's Tale," "My joly body schal a tale telle," Dinshaw associates the female body and the text, as opposed to gloss, which is a patriarchal method of control. She argues that Chaucer, through Alisoun, "mimics patriarchal discourse ... not in order to 'thwart' it altogether, to subvert it entirely, but to reform it, to keep it in place while making it accommodate feminine desire" (p. 114).

15. Benson, *Riverside Chaucer*, p. 877.

16. See Caie, "Significance of the Early Chaucer," pp. 350–60; Echard, "With Carmen's Help," pp. 1–40.

17. Geoffrey of Vinsauf, *Poetria nova*, p. 128–31.

18. Hardison, "Geoffrey of Vinsauf: Introduction," pp. 123–28, esp. p. 126. Though it may not have been highly respected by the Ricardian period, over fifty surviving manuscript copies of the *Poetria nova* demonstrate its widespread influence.

19. Kelly, "Chrétien de Troyes," p. 14.

20. Howard, *Three Temptations*, p. 233. The meaning of *sens*, or *sen*, covers a "semantic spectrum," as Vinaver discusses (pp. 16–17).

21. Scanlon, *Narrative*. Although traditionally lay authorities were the seat of *potestas* and spiritual authorities the seat of *auctoritas*, Scanlon argues that secular narrative developed a reciprocal relationship with the Crown and that, "It is precisely because [Chaucer's] explorations of narrative are so thorough that he is able to reclaim it as a medium of lay authority" (p. 244). This is also true of Gower, according to Scanlon: "he [Gower] demonstrates the capacity of lay poetry to generate from within its own limitations an authority that transcends them" (p. 277).

22. Axton, "Gower—Chaucer's Heir?" and Scanlon, *Narrative*, among others, argue that Chaucer and Gower influenced each other more than has often been acknowledged.

23. Scanlon, *Narrative*, p. 137. Also see Miller, "'Wife of Bath's Tale.'"

24. Echard, "With Carmen's Help," perceives the *histoire's* inherent power in "The Wife of Bath's Tale," but also the attempt to control its meaning: "It is as if the tale has a life and voice of its own, one which refuses to be constrained to any single meaning, no matter how many levels of hermeneutic guardianship are provided for it" (p. 34).

25. Fish, *Is There a Text?*, p. 158.

26. Fish, *Is There a Text?*, pp. 172–73.

27. Strohm, *Social Chaucer*, p. 49.

28. See Hugh of St. Victor, *Didascalicon*, pp. 60–74.

29. Burrow, *Ricardian Poetry*, pp. 82–83.

30. Lindahl, "Oral Undertones," p. 68.

31. Gower, *Confessio Amantis*, ed. Peck; all citations of the text are from this edition.

32. Scanlon, *Narrative*, p. 249.

33. "Here the Confessor presents another *exemplum* on the same topic, against those who are disobedient in love, to the commendation of obedience." Quoted and translated in Echard, "With Carmen's Help," p. 33.

34. Chaucer, "The Wife of Bath's Prologue and Tale," *The Riverside Chaucer*, ed. Benson; all citations of the text are from this edition.

35. Taylor, "Fragmentation, Corruption," p. 54.

36. Foley, "Implications," p. 32.

37. "The Wedding of Sir Gawain and Dame Ragnelle," *Sir Gawain: Eleven Romances and Tales*, ed. Hahn; all citations of the text are from this edition.

38. See Ellen Caldwell's essay, "Brains or Beauty," in the present volume.

39. See Mary Leech's essay, "Why Dame Ragnell Had to Die," in the present volume.

40. Fleming, "Repetition and Design," p. 157.

41. Irvine, "Why I Hate Lady Ragnell."

42. Lindahl, "Oral Undertones," p. 67.

WORKS CITED

Axton, Richard. "Gower—Chaucer's Heir?" In *Chaucer Traditions: Studies in Honour of Derek Brewer*, ed. Ruth Morris and Barry Windeatt, pp. 21–38. Cambridge: Cambridge University Press, 1990.

Barthes, Roland. "Introduction to the Structural Analysis of Narrative." In *Image-Music-Text*, pp. 79–124. London: Fontana, 1977.

Benson, Larry D., ed. *The Riverside Chaucer*. 3rd ed. Boston: Houghton Mifflin, 1987.

Burrow, J. A. *Ricardian Poetry: Chaucer, Gower, Langland and the "Gawain" Poet*. London: Routledge and Kegan Paul, 1971.

Caie, Graham D. "The Significance of the Early Chaucer Manuscript Glosses (with Special Reference to the Wife of Bath's Prologue)." *CR* 10 (1975–76), 350–60.

Dante Alighieri. *Il Convivio* [The Banquet]. Trans. Richard H. Lansing. Garland Library of Medieval Literature 65, series B. New York: Garland, 1990.

Dinshaw, Carolyn. *Chaucer's Sexual Poetics*. Madison: Wisconsin University Press, 1989.

Echard, Siân. "With Carmen's Help: Latin Authorities in the *Confessio Amantis*." *SP* 95 (1998), 1–40.

Eisner, Sigmund. *A Tale of Wonder: A Source Study of "The Wife of Bath's Tale."* Wexford, Ire.: John English, 1957.

Fish, Stanley. *Is There a Text in This Class? The Authority of Interpretive Communities.* Cambridge, Mass.: Harvard University Press, 1980.

Fleming, Martha. "Repetition and Design in 'The Wife of Bath's Tale.'" In *Chaucer in the Eighties*, ed. Julian N. Wasserman and Robert J. Blanch, pp. 151–61. Syracuse, N.Y.: Syracuse University Press, 1986.

Foley, John Miles. "The Implications of Oral Tradition." In *Oral Tradition in the Middle Ages*, ed. Nicolaisen, pp. 31–57.

Geoffrey of Vinsauf, *Poetria nova*. Trans. Margaret F. Nims. In Hardison et al., *Medieval Literary Criticism*, pp. 128–44.

Gower, John. *Confessio Amantis*. Ed. Russell A. Peck. New York: Holt, Rinehart and Winston, 1968.

Gurevich, Aron. *Medieval Popular Culture: Problems of Belief and Perception*. Trans. János M. Bak and Paul A. Hollingsworth. Cambridge: Cambridge University Press, 1988.

Hahn, Thomas, ed. *Sir Gawain: Eleven Romances and Tales*. Kalamazoo, Mich.: Medieval Institute Publications, 1995.

Hardison, Jr., O. B. "Geoffrey of Vinsauf: Introduction." In *Medieval Literary Criticism: Translations and Interpretations*, ed. Hardison, Jr., O. B., Alex Preminger, Kevin Kerrane, and Leon Golden, pp. 123–28. New York: Unger, 1974.

Howard, Donald. *The Three Temptations*. Princeton: Princeton University Press, 1966.

Hugh of St. Victor. *The Didascalicon of Hugh of St. Victor*. Trans. Jerome Taylor. New York: Columbia University Press, 1961.

Irvine, Alan. "Why I Hate Lady Ragnell." *Works In Progress: The Journal of the Art and Business of Storytelling*, http://www.midatlanticstorytell.org/wipsite/home.htm (16 April 2003).

Kelly, Douglas. "Chrétien de Troyes: Narrator and His Art." In *Romances of Chrétien de Troyes Symposium*, ed. Douglas Kelly, pp. 13–47. Kentucky: French Forum Publishers, 1985.

Lindahl, Carl. "The Oral Undertones of Late Medieval Romance." In *Oral Tradition in the Middle Ages*, ed. Nicolaisen, pp. 59–75.

Maynadier, G. H. *"The Wife of Bath's Tale": Its Sources and Analogues*. London: Nutt, 1901.

Miller, Robert P. "'The Wife of Bath's Tale' and Medieval Exempla." *ELH* 32 (1965), 442–56.

Nicolaisen, W. F. H., ed. *Oral Tradition in the Middle Ages*. Binghamton, N.Y.: MRTS, 1995.

Scanlon, Larry. *Narrative, Authority and Power: The Medieval Exemplum and the Chaucerian Tradition*. Cambridge: Cambridge University Press, 1994.

Strohm, Paul. *Social Chaucer*. Cambridge, Mass.: Harvard University Press, 1989.
Taylor, Andrew. "Fragmentation, Corruption, and Minstrel Narration: The Question of the Middle English Romances." *YES* 22 (1992), 38–62.
Vinaver, Eugene. *The Rise of Romance*. Oxford: Clarendon Press, 1971.

"The Marriage of Sir Gawain"
Piecing the Fragments Together

Stephanie Hollis

"The Marriage of Sir Gawain" is incompletely preserved in the Percy Folio (ca. 1650). The bottom half of each page of the text had been torn off before Bishop Percy acquired the manuscript.[1] Like "The Wedding of Sir Gawain and Dame Ragnelle," the "Marriage" is dated, on linguistic grounds, to the mid- or late fifteenth century.[2] Unlike "Ragnelle," the "Marriage" is usually categorized as a ballad; I follow this conventional terminology. The two works are noticeably similar in plot. They differ most obviously from the Loathly Lady tales of Chaucer and Gower in their employment of a hostile knight (subsequently revealed to be the brother of the Loathly Lady) as the originator of the quest to discover what it is that women most desire, and also in their "splitting" of the protagonist; whereas the tales of Chaucer and Gower have a single protagonist whose life is at risk and who marries the Loathly Lady in return for the answer to his antagonist's question, in the "Marriage" and in "Ragnelle," it is Arthur whose life is in jeopardy and Gawain who marries the Loathly Lady.

Since the appearance of Sigmund Eisner's study, it has been generally accepted that the "Marriage" and "Ragnelle" derived independently from a common ancestor (which, Eisner argued, derived ultimately from the same source as the common ancestor underlying the tales of Chaucer and Gower).[3] Opinions continue to differ, however, on whether or not the ballad originated earlier than the romance.[4] Stemmatic and chronological questions are outside the scope of my reconsideration of the missing text of the "Marriage." It is, however, worth observing at the outset that, although Thomas Hahn and Thomas J. Garbáty echo the generally held belief that there is no direct link between the "Marriage" and "Ragnelle," their reconstructions, based on the assumption that the missing text of the "Marriage" invariably bore a close resemblance to the parallel sections of "Ragnelle," seem to be more consistent with a belief that the "Marriage" derived directly from "Ragnelle."[5]

It goes almost without saying that any attempt to reconstruct the action of lost passages of a text is, of course, speculative. The surviving passages of the "Marriage" are, nevertheless, component parts of an originally complete whole. Unless we are to engage in a near-impossible (and surely unprofitable) attempt to "read" the surviving passages, in the purely literal sense of the word, as isolated fragments, we are bound to construct their meaning in terms of the assumptions we make about their relationship to the narrative as a whole, and this inevitably involves some degree of hypothetical reconstruction of the missing action. My hypothetical reconstructions are incidental to my argument. My central concern is to argue, on the basis of a close consideration of the surviving passages of the "Marriage," that it is not, as Hahn and Garbáty assume, a simplified and inferior version of "Ragnelle," but an economical and original recasting of the plot. From this it follows that I think they are mistaken in assuming that the missing action of the "Marriage" invariably bore a close resemblance to that of the analogous episodes in "Ragnelle." The speculative reconstructions of the missing action which inevitably occur in the course of the reading of the "Marriage" that I offer here are based, instead, on the assumption that the general nature of the missing action can be deduced from a consideration of the narrative and thematic relationship of the surviving passages.

Both the "Marriage" and "Ragnelle" are commonly described as "popular." Although advances in the understanding of popular literature have enhanced our appreciation of "Ragnelle," the "Marriage" has been largely ignored[6] and it continues to suffer at the hands of commentators for whom "popular" literature is synonymous with inferior and substandard quality. As Jane Gilbert explains:

> According to this view the artistic conception motivating popular culture is crude and its execution incompetent, while the conceptual value is negligible: popular culture presents simple ideas in a simple way.... Quality cultural products are viewed as aesthetically sophisticated and skilfully executed, conceptually subtle and far-sighted, often politically exploratory or liberal (in contrast to the supposed unimaginative conservatism of popular culture). Despite being purportedly apolitical, the distinction between popular and quality culture centrally incorporates an element of social class; by definition, "popular culture" is enjoyed primarily by "the people," while quality culture is the preserve of an intellectual and social elite.... In this first, "substandard"

version, then, "popular culture" is a nexus in which the inferior aesthetic standard of the work reflects and reinforces the low social and cultural status of the audience.[7]

Hahn characterizes the "Marriage" almost entirely in terms of what it lacks by comparison with the Loathly Lady tales of Chaucer and Gower:

> "Marriage" presents a retelling bolder and balder than any of the others. The characters play exaggerated parts: Arthur's antagonist is not knightly, but a threatening thug "With a great club upon his backe"; the lady "in red scarlett" is simply monstrous; Kay at first is totally disgusted, and at the end filled with brotherly congratulation; Gawain is impeccably courteous.... As a proper ballad, "Marriage" maintains the fundamental simplicity of the plot. There are none of the literary touches that Gower adds, or the learned allusions to Ovid, Dante, and Boethius of Chaucer's version. Likewise, "Marriage" forgoes the narrative replications and thematic and verbal repetitions that mark "Ragnelle" as a popular romance and complicate its possible meanings. The interlocking sets of masculine social relations held in place through "Ragnelle"'s plot do not surface in "Marriage;" indeed, the nameless antagonist calls his nameless sister "a misshappen hore" and promises to burn her "in a fyer" if he catches her.[8]

Hahn's conception of the audience of the work matches his low estimation of its aesthetic and literary qualities and is dubiously authenticated by reference to Howard Pyle's *Merry Adventures of Robin Hood* (1883), which includes a fictional performance of the "Marriage" by a tinker-minstrel: "Pyle's portrayal of this impromptu performance before a tavern audience at the edge of Sherwood Forest likely corresponds to the sort of setting in which the complier of the Percy Folio Manuscript heard the version of 'Marriage' that he wrote down."[9]

Garbáty, somewhat similarly, in comparing "Ragnelle" and the "Marriage" as a means of enforcing his argument that the ballad, as a genre, was a chronologically later development than the romance, regards "Ragnelle" as superior by virtue of its "courtly" character, which in his view is synonymous with the logic and coherence of the narrative. "Ragnelle," he writes,

> though humorous and unheroic, is a courtly tale of *gentilesse* both on Arthur's part and Gawain's. I would not count this one among the debased Gawain romances of the fifteenth century. To the contrary, the story is logically told, very consistent within itself as to characterization and action, and at times

even surprisingly poignant and moving…. Admittedly [the author] dwells at
length on the loathliness of the lady …, but in general there is a controlled
elegance to the whole and real pathos at the end. In contrast, the ballad
consciously moves toward the burlesque and definite degradation of Arthur,
with a tendency toward bawdiness shown in the puns of the ballad riddle
answer: "A woman will have her will and that is her chief desire."[10]

As Gilbert observes, "Constructing the meaning of a text depends on a
certain presumption of competence."[11] The fragmentary state in which the
"Marriage" is preserved does nothing to dispel the view that it is a "debased"
composition. Hahn's reconstruction of the missing action is handicapped
by his assumption that the "Marriage" is merely a simplified, and inferior,
version of "Ragnelle;" he assumes a greater degree of similarity than the
surviving text warrants. Garbáty, for his part, constructs his primary example
of the illogicality of the "Marriage" on the basis of his own misapprehensions
and his willingness to assume that the author did not understand the source
he was working from. Both in "Ragnelle" and the "Marriage," he observes,
Arthur first offers a collection of written answers to the knight whose
question he must answer in order to save his life and gives the answer he
received from the Loathly Lady only when the knight spurns the written
compilation. Garbáty regards this as consistent with the characterization of
Arthur in the romance—although Arthur has obtained Gawain's willing
consent to marriage with the Lady as the price she asks for giving him the
"correct" answer, Garbáty explains, it is in keeping with Arthur's reluctance
to grant her Gawain as a husband that he makes an attempt to save him by
offering first the written answers. In the "Marriage," however, Arthur
responds to the Lady's claim that she can help him by immediately offering
her marriage to Gawain as an inducement. In Garbáty's view, it is inconsis-
tent for Arthur in the "Marriage" to offer first the written answers to the
knight because, having voluntarily granted the lady marriage to Gawain,
Arthur has been deprived of any motive for attempting to save him. Arthur's
offer of marriage to Gawain, however, is immediately followed by a hiatus in
the text; I suggest below that his offer gives a misleading impression of the
missing conversation. But, even if we take this offer at face value, *does* it
logically preclude an attempt by Arthur to offer first the written answers in
the hope of averting marriage to the lady? Instead of considering the
possibility that the dialogue missing from the "Marriage" may have differed
in kind from the parallel episode in "Ragnelle," Garbáty assumes that the
author of the ballad was following his source uncomprehendingly: "The

ballad maker, by including an irrelevant incident, shows that he did not understand his source or used a corrupt one some distance removed from it."[12]

I want first to outline the distinctive and original aspects of the "Marriage" author's handling of the plot, and then to discuss the meaning and values it embodies. Whereas the "Marriage" is unique among the Loathly Lady stories in its demonic conception of the enchantment of the lady, its universalizing conception of courtesy demands her social inclusion, and this is reflected also in the ballad's unique handling of the episode in which she is disenchanted.

In her wedding-night speech to Gawain following her disenchantment, the Loathly Lady explains (in contrast to all other extant versions) that both she *and* her brother have been enchanted by her stepmother: "She witched my brother to a carlish B" (line 183). As in "Ragnelle," the Loathly Lady's brother gains power over Arthur when he strays alone into a wilderness[13] and threatens Arthur with death if he does not return with the answer to the question "What do women most desire?" His characterization as a Wild Man is enhanced in the "Marriage" by the mighty club he carries on his back. In the "Marriage," however, the brother is not motivated by a seemingly legitimate grievance as he is in "Ragnelle" (that Arthur has taken his lands and given them to Gawain). But when Arthur returns to him, he reveals that he is not a mere Foe of Chivalry,[14] as his location in the wilderness and mighty club might suggest, but a rebellious baron, who draws a sword to stake a rival claim to the throne:

> And then he puld out a good browne sword,
>   And cryd himselfe a king.
> And he sayd, "I have thee and thy land, Arthur,
>   To doe as it pleaseth me,
> For this is not thy ransome sure:
>   Therfore yeeld thee to me.
>
>   (lines 90–96)

The pattern-making of the "Marriage" author thus sharpens the moral and symbolic polarization of Arthur and his challenger, the wilderness and the court, which is modified in "Ragnelle" by the motivating grievance of the lady's brother; in the "Marriage," the survival of legitimate order is threatened by a villainous usurper and potential regicide. The shared bewitchment of the lady and her brother creates an identity between them which is, however, developed in terms of contrast and antagonism—unlike the Loathly Lady, her brother reveals that he is a more dangerous and hostile foe than his appearance suggests, and his violent abuse of his sister when he realizes that she has given Arthur the correct answer is in keeping with the villainously uncourtly conception of his character. He declares her "a misshappen hore," and vows that, if he can catch her, he personally will burn her to death (lines 111–15).

In "Ragnelle," the Loathly Lady's brother denounces her, more temperately, as an "old scott," and, rather than threatening to burn her himself, he hopes to God that he "maye se her bren on a fyre" (lines 474–76).[15] In the "Marriage," this threat of burning harmonizes with the Loathly Lady's associations with witchcraft and the demonic, which are virtually absent from other versions. As the lady explains her stepmother's action to Gawain in the "Marriage":

Shee witched me, being a faire young lady,
    To the greene forrest to dwell,
And there I must walke in womans liknesse,
    Most like a feeind of hell.
                    (lines 179–83)

In Gower's "Tale of Florent" the Loathly Lady is described by the narrator as a "vecke,"[16] but there is nothing witchlike about her appearance, or her explanation of her transformation. She says only that her stepmother "forschop" her "for an hate" (lines 1844–46) and, although the stepmother's counterpart in this tale (the malign old grandmother who entraps Florent) may appear witchlike, the worst the narrator has to say of her is that she was "an old Mone" (line 1634). Just as, for Gower, the desirability of the bride is epitomized by her transformation into an eighteen-year-old, the sexually off-putting loathsomeness of the lady is primarily defined by her aged characteristics (wrinkles, hoary locks, bleary eyes, and so on).[17] In "Ragnelle," the lady explains that she has been "shapen by nygramancy ... and by enchauntement" (lines 691–93).[18] The linking of necromancy to enchantment serves to neutralize its potentially demonic suggestions, and the lady's appearance is characterized entirely within the conventional romance discourse of faery enchantment. Her monstrosity is an artefact of the inversion of conventional portraiture of feminine beauty and refinement, though there is also a distinctly uncourtly, carnivalesque touch in the conjunction of her buttocks and cheeks ("Her chekys syde as wemens hippes" [line 236]). This literary inversion prefigures the lady's subsequent ability to regain her original form, further underlined by the lack of congruity between her bodily appearance and the resplendently caparisoned palfrey she rides, which betokens her association with faery enchantment (since palfreys adorned with gold and gems are the chief identifying attribute of the faery women in "Sir Launfal" and "Thomas of Erceldoune").[19]

In the "Marriage," only the setting in which the Loathly Lady is located is faerylike—she is seated on a moor between an oak and a holly tree (although whereas encounters with the faery traditionally take place beneath a single tree, this conjunction of a deciduous and an evergreen tree is suggestive of the way in which her enchantment suspends her between permanent loathliness and the potential for change). But she is dressed in "red scarlett" (line 56), which, as Stephen Shepherd notes, "is a sign of nobility or an aspiration thereto."[20] Here, the incongruous finery of the lady's clothing associates her with the court (or even the fires of hell) rather than with faery enchantment. (It hints, too, at the discrepancy between her physical appearance and inner nature which is shortly to be demonstrated—which is absent from "Ragnelle"'s conception of the Loathly Lady, though less conspicuously so than any mention of a stitch of clothing to cover her grotesque body.)[21] Having shrouded the Loathly Lady in rich array, then, the author of the "Marriage" focuses entirely on her face—she does not bear witness to an act of transformation which inverts her to an opposite state (whether age, as in Gower, or monstrous bestiality as in "Ragnelle") but to an act of sudden and deliberate perversion. Her monstrousness is conceived as a literal deformity—it is as if a malign hand has wrenched and twisted her facial features sideways:

Then there as shold have stood her mouth,
    Then there was sett her eye;
The other was in her forhead fast,
    The way that she might see.
Her nose was crooked and turnd outward,
    Her mouth stood foule awry;
A worse formed lady than shee was,
    Never man saw with his eye.
                                        (lines 57–64)

This is not the misshaping transformation of faery enchantment but the perverse twisting awry of witchcraft and diabolic powers. But whereas the bewitchment of the lady's brother has transformed him, both in appearance and in character to a "carlish B," the lady's more radically malign appearance is immediately shown by her words to belie her character, as she reproves Arthur for his failure to reciprocate her courteous greeting because he is misled by mere appearances:

> To halch upon him, King Arthur,
>   This lady was full faine,
> But King Arthur had forgott his lesson,
>   What he shold say againe.
> "What knight art thou," the lady sayd,
>   "That will not speak to me?
> Of me be thou nothing dismayd
>   Tho I be ugly to see.
> For I have halched you curteouslye,
>   And you will not me againe;
> Yett I may happen, Sir Knight," shee said,
>   "To ease thee of thy paine."
>   (lines 65–76)

In contrast to her brother, the lady's bewitchment affects only her superficial appearance, creating a discrepancy between her outer and inner nature. Unlike the Loathly Lady in "Ragnelle," this lady is neither aggressive nor transgressive in her approach to Arthur; she merely insists that, deformed and outcast though she is, she has a right to a courteous response, and she offers her help. As in "Ragnelle," the denizens of the wilderness in the "Marriage" expose Arthur's falling short of the ideal chivalric and courtly values purportedly upheld by the Round Table. But it would be more accurate to regard the characterization of Arthur in "Ragnelle" as a "burlesque degradation."[22] In both narratives, the lady's brother exposes his lack of courage but, as Arthur describes himself in the "Marriage," there is nothing craven in his refusal to fight—his explanation represents a humorously sardonic and sophisticated awareness of the way in which the proponents of upper-class *politesse* cover their lapses by claiming the sanction of an alternative, but undefined, canon of appropriateness:

> To fight with him I saw noe cause,
>   Methought it was not meet,
> For he was stiffe and strong withall,
>   His strokes were nothing sweete.
>   (lines 40–44)

Such is Arthur's haste to avail himself of her offer of help when the lady rebukes him for his lack of courtesy that he immediately offers her marriage to Gawain as her reward. In this, as Garbáty observes, the "Marriage" diverges from "Ragnelle," where the Loathly Lady demands marriage to Gawain as the price of her help and Arthur protests that he must first ask Gawain's consent; this then gives rise to a scene in which Gawain's chivalric values are lampooned in the comic extravagance of his loyalty to Arthur—for his sake he is willing to marry the lady "Thowghe she were a fend; / Thowghe she were as foulle as Belsabub" (lines 344–45), just as he is later willing to consummate the marriage when the lady calls on him to do it for Arthur's sake (line 635).

Arthur's exchange with the Loathly Lady in the "Marriage," from the point at which he offers her marriage to Gawain as her reward, is missing from the manuscript. Noticeably, Arthur's offer violates the spirit of a story which is, at least ostensibly, an affirmation of the mutual benefits of volition and choice in marriage; to a reader familiar with "Ragnelle," Arthur gives the impression that he already knows this story and is in a hurry to cut it short in order to save his life. I want to suggest, however, that this divergence from "Ragnelle" is not an ill-conceived abridgement; it represents a reconception of the way in which the narrative embodies the theme of marital choice, which is reflected in the author's later, and most substantive departure from the plot of "Ragnelle." The account of Arthur's return to court after his escape from the Loathly Lady's brother is also missing. But it is evident, from lines 116–50, that Arthur has returned to the Loathly Lady, bringing with him all his knights.[23] This encounter is the site of an even more radical exposure of the court's lack of courtesy, since Sir Kay makes derogatory remarks about the lady and asserts that he would rather die than marry her. Gawain attempts to silence him by pointing out that "there is a knight amongst us all / That must marry her to his wife" (lines 138–39). The scene breaks off with the knights beating a hasty retreat (snatching up their hawks and hounds) while Arthur (again demonstrating his ability to gloss things over) attempts to persuade them not to scorn the Lady just because she's a bit ugly: "For a litle foule sight and misliking" (line 150).

Hahn's reconstruction of the lines missing before and after the encounter between Arthur's knights and the Loathly Lady preserved in lines 116–50 posits that Arthur "returns to the lady in the forest, though he appears to have informed Gawain alone of his marriage pact," and that "after Arthur's speech, Gawain announces his intention to marry the lady."[24] Rather, I suggest, the conclusion to be drawn from Gawain's words to Kay is that the lady rejected Arthur's attempt to deny both her and Gawain an exercise of choice in marriage and required him to bring his knights to her so she could choose for herself whom she would marry (thus exemplifying her insistence on having what she wants by publicly demonstrating the imposition of her will upon the court, in somewhat the same manner as the Loathly Lady in "Ragnelle" insists on a public wedding against the wishes of the court).[25] In the event, it appears, her choice was determined by the fact that only Gawain chose to remain, thereby proving himself, presumably, the worthiest of all (since, both in "Ragnelle" and in Gower's "Tale of Florent," the supreme worthiness of the knight who marries the Loathly Lady is one of the conditions of her disenchantment).

It is symptomatic of the "Marriage"'s lack of interest in the courtly love dimensions of the question that lies at the center of the story that the answer is not "wommen desiren to have sovereynetee" (variously elaborated) but a plain English statement: "And she says, 'A woman will have her will, / And this is all her cheef desire'" (lines 104–5). "The tendency towards bawdiness found in the puns," which Garbáty discerns in this answer is not made manifest in the extant lines.[26] In Hahn's view, the answer "turns out to be a tautology, for 'a woman will have her will': she wants what she wants."[27] It might, more aptly, be described as a witty enigma, which simultaneously encapsulates the all-encompassing nature of female desire and affirms its inscrutability; it is an apt answer to a question which is intended to be unanswerable. The "Marriage" is also unique in its handling of the lady's disenchantment through the knight's decision to let her make the choice that she offers him. Gawain first responds, artfully, by testing out the waters under cover of expressing the difficulty of the choice—what he would say, he explains, is that he wishes her to be fair by day, although, if he could, he would rather have her fair by night.[28] Gawain, in other words, wishes to assert the primacy of his own desires—private pleasure with the lady by night—but is uncertain whether this will accord with her wishes; he attempts, in effect, to discover the specific meaning of "a woman will have her will" in the situation in which he finds himself. He says:

"Well I know what I wold say—
    God grant it may be good!
To have thee fowle in the night
    When I with thee shold play;

> Yet I had rather, if I might,
> > Have thee fowle in the day."
> > > (lines 157–62)

The lady objects that, if she is to be fair by night, she will be excluded by day from communal enjoyment in his company:

> "What! When lords goe with ther feires," shee said,
> > "Both to the ale and wine?
> Alas! Then I must hyde my selfe,
> > I must not goe withinne."
> > > (lines 163–66)

Gawain responds that he was just kidding and (speaking more truly than he knows) leaves it to her to choose:

> Said, "Lady, thats but a skill:
> And because thou art my owne lady,
> > Thou shalt have all thy will."
> > > (lines 168–70)

In the "Marriage," then, the knight is not presented with a test which he must pass, unaided, by surrendering to the lady the right to choose for herself her existential identity, thereby enacting the subordination of his wishes to hers. The disenchantment of the lady in the "Marriage" is the result of a co-operative decision negotiated between equals. It is an enactment of mutual respect for the other's wishes, as Gawain responds to a question about what he wants, not by simply giving up, but by attempting to find out what she wants and coming to the conclusion that she must decide that for herself. This negotiation—and the concomitant absence of the knight's subordination to the "sovereignty" of the lady—makes it unlikely that the lady, in this version, subsequently surrendered the supremacy granted to her by promising to be obedient to his wishes, as she so disappointingly does in the other three versions.

It is intrinsic to the "Marriage"'s handling of the lady's disenchantment, where Gawain is shown to grapple with the actuality of the lady's wishes, that it is the only version in which it is given to her to guide him to the right choice, which she does by voicing the unhappy consequences for her of a wrong choice on his part.[29] Unlike Arthur, whom she rebukes for failing to reciprocate her courteous greeting, "gentle Gawain" reciprocates the freedom to choose that she offers him. In both of these scenes, the lady objects to her social exclusion; just as she asserts that her deformed appearance does not place her outside the conventions of courtesy, so she protests against her exclusion from the communal festivities of the court. The conclusion of the ballad images her incorporation into the society of the Round Table—arm-in-arm with Sir Gawain and Sir Kay, she is led off to be welcomed by the king, the queen, and all the knights of the Round Table. But the lady is also depicted as a creator of social bonds; she is made central to the forgiveness of Sir Kay's earlier discourtesy and his reconciliation with Sir Gawain, and appears (in marked contrast to her counterpart in "Ragnelle") as the consolidator of the bonds of brotherhood between knights.[30] Gawain invites Kay to kiss his bride, and Kay, savoring the kiss, congratulates Gawain on his good fortune. Then, thus united in their appreciation of the bride's attractions,

> Sir Gawaine tooke the lady by the one arme,
>   Sir Kay tooke her by the tother;
> They led her straight to King Arthur
>   As they were brother and brother.
>   (lines 202–5)

The "Marriage" ends in communal rejoicing in the good fortune of Gawain and his lady; Gawain expresses his appreciation of the part played by Arthur, and Arthur remembers to express his thanks for the part played by Gawain:

> King Arthur beheld that lady faire
>   That was soe faire and bright.
> He thanked Christ in Trinity
>   For Sir Gawaine that gentle knight.
> Soe did the knights, both more and lesse,
>   Rejoyced all that day,
> For the good chance that hapened was
>   To Sir Gawaine and his lady gay.
>   (lines 210–17)

Basically, it couldn't have happened to a nicer couple. Contemporary documentation reveals the presence of minstrels at weddings.[31] If we want to imagine the characteristic milieu for the oral performance of the "Marriage," we would do better, I suggest, to replace the tavern on the edge of Sherwood Forest with the celebration of a wedding—though this does not, of course, bring us any closer to identifying the social constitution of its audience(s), not, at any rate, if we do not share the belief that minstrel performance invariably took place in low-life settings.[32] Performance at Christmas celebrations, another traditional site of minstrel entertainments, is also a possibility, in view of the Christmas setting of the "Marriage."

In strictly literal terms, the "Marriage" may be a "bolder and balder" version of the Loathly Lady story than "Ragnelle," but this gives a misleading impression of its quality. It is not a mere abridgement of "Ragnelle," but an original and economic recasting of the plot. In essence, the constituting actions of the plot are the same up until the point at which Arthur offers the lady marriage to Gawain. That the reader familiar with "Ragnelle" feels that Arthur already knows this story and is attempting to cut short his encounter with the lady is not, perhaps, beside the point. Stephen H. A. Shepherd found in "Ragnelle" a form of deliberate intertextuality which, he suggested, served as an encouragement to a comparative reading on the part of the audience and therefore drew attention to the author's novelty and impudent burlesque.[33] Arthur's unhesitating offer of marriage to Gawain in the "Marriage" conceivably functioned in a similar way, alerting an audience familiar with the traditional story to the novelty of its recasting.

This new twist to the plot dispenses with the need to have Arthur ride off to obtain Gawain's permission and return to the lady with his answer. Gawain, however (according to my reconstruction), is given the opportunity to demonstrate his worthiness and willingness in the "Marriage" by the invention of a new episode, Arthur's summoning of his knights to the lady, which replaces "Ragnelle"'s account of the lady's discomfiture of the court (the embarrassment Arthur suffers as her escort, her insistence on a public wedding despite the appeals of the queen, and her bestial table manners at the wedding feast). Dame Ragnelle's imposition of her wishes upon the court is, certainly, a good deal funnier than the episode in the "Marriage" which replaces it, but the "Marriage"'s negotiation is not without humor, and it accomplishes a good deal in a short space. The hasty departure of the knights from the lady's presence dramatizes her social exclusion, which is under-scored by the insulting mockery of Sir Kay; Gawain, by contrast, in asserting her right to respect as the future wife of one of the knights of the Round Table, includes her within the operative range of social convention.

The greater complexity of "Ragnelle"'s plot is chiefly to be found in the narration that follows the achievement of wedded bliss which forms the ending of the story as told by Chaucer and Gower. Following a rather long-winded and repetitive explanation of the disenchantment to Arthur and his court, the author relates that Dame Ragnelle removed Gawain from the fellowship of the Round Table and prevailed upon Arthur, for her sake, to readmit her brother to his favor (lines 805–16). This sudden opening up of the possibility of an underlying conspiracy between Ragnelle and her brother finds no echo in the "Marriage," but its framing of the post-wedding-night narrative is, again, strikingly coherent and economical. The employment of an encounter between Kay and the happy couple as a means of uniting them with the court, in place of the arrival of the court at the bedchamber door in "Ragnelle," anxious to discover Gawain's fate, forms the basis for the concluding images of her social incorporation as she is led, arm-in-arm with Kay and Gawain, to Arthur and his court, and also for the reconciliation of Kay and Gawain in which she is given a pivotal role.[34]

Bishop Percy, in his reconstruction of the "Marriage" (more in the nature of an attempted re-creation of what he believed to be the underlying source of other Loathly Lady tales, particularly Chaucer's), postulated that the Loathly Lady, in revealing that her stepmother had bewitched both her and her brother, also announced that Gawain's "correct" reply had simultaneously removed the spell from her brother.[35] This would, certainly, fit well with the concluding developments of the "Marriage"; a happy ending, even for the villainous Baron, would be in keeping with the inclusive thrust of the ballad. It would, too, provide a foreshadowing, an underlying magical rationale even, for the transformation and reconciliation with Kay, who likewise makes the lady the butt of his villainous discourtesy. There is, unfortunately, nothing in the surviving fragments to support the view that this formed part of the "Marriage" author's unique recasting of the plot.

Nor is the meaning expressed by the "Marriage" a crude simplification of "Ragnelle." Its equation of faery magic and enchantment with witchcraft and the demonic may appear to suggest a lack of intellectual sophistication characteristic of "popular" culture in its most derogatory sense. What is, indeed, remarkable about medieval literary representations of the faery otherworld is that medieval authors found it possible to make creative use of this particular form of the non-Christian supernatural, despite the fact that Christian hegemonic thinking regarded all forms of the supernatural which had not been assimilated to Christian belief as opposed to it, and therefore diabolical.

The Loathly Lady in "Ragnelle," as I have mentioned, describes herself as having been "shapen by nygramancy … and by enchauntement" (lines 691–93), but the depiction of the Loathly Lady is unaffected by the potentially diabolic connotations of "nygramancy." The author appears to be conscious of a potential identification of the two forms of non-Christian supernatural but untroubled by it.[36] Gawain asserts his willingness to wed the lady time and again for Arthur's sake, "Thowghe she were a fend; / Thowghe she were as foulle as Belsabub" (lines 344–45), and Arthur, leading the court to the bridal chamber to find out whether Gawain has survived the night, explains: "I am fulle ferde of Syr Gawen / Nowe lest the fende have hym slayn" (lines 724–25). Arthur makes actual Gawain's purely subjunctive identification of the lady with the fiend, but, significant as these remarks are in terms of cultural conceptions of women, the comic extravagance of the speakers precludes any seriously intended suggestion that Dame Ragnelle is either a demon or an agent of the devil.[37]

Chaucer, in "The Wife of Bath's Tale" appears more comprehensively untroubled by Christian hegemonic equations of the faery supernatural with diabolism. The opening lines of "The Wife of Bath's Tale" explicitly voice the hegemonic view by explaining that the friars have exorcised "the elf-queene, with hir joly compaignye," in consequence whereof there now remains "noon oother incubus" except the friar (lines 860–81).[38] Yet, as the Loathly Lady here (and only here) is not a mere victim of enchantment but appears to be an otherworldly being capable of changing shape at will, she is, in the terms advanced at the beginning of the tale, a succubus, and the knight's consummation of his marriage to her is therefore tantamount to engaging in intercourse with evil spirits, an act prohibited by ecclesiastical law and regarded by later witch-hunters as a characteristic activity of practitioners of black magic.[39]

A greater degree of anxiety is expressed by the fifteenth-century romance of "Thomas of Erceldoune," where the faery is carefully distinguished from the diabolical when the faery mistress who spirits Thomas away to her kingdom points out to him the five separate (though adjacent) paths that lead, respectively, to heaven and paradise, to hell and purgatory, and to the faery otherworld (lines 200–22). Paralleling this careful distinction is her assurance to Thomas, in their initial encounter, that she is not, as he thinks, the Queen of Heaven (lines 87–96), and her subsequent assurance—when Thomas, finding that his insistence on possessing her has transformed her shining beauty to leaden black, attempts to exorcise her—that she is not, as he thinks, a fiend from hell.[40] As Ellen M. Caldwell shows, this generates an ambivalent reading of the lady's role: "Is she a temptress or a saviour of her courtly lover?"[41] But, set against the increasing demonization of the non-Christian supernatural, reflected in the growing number of witchcraft trials in the sixteenth century, "Thomas of Erceldoune" appears to be staking a claim to an area of literary license that Chaucer, Gower, and the author of "Ragnelle" were able to take as given.[42] This lends a particular significance to the fact that, in "Thomas of Erceldoune," the faery otherworld, being obliged to pay a tithe to hell, has to some extent fallen under its sway. It is only in ballads recorded in the eighteenth and nineteenth century that the faery otherworld is fully assimilated to a Christian hegemonic worldview and its inhabitants appear as demons, witches, and ghosts. In the analogous Loathly Lady ballad of "King Henry," for instance, the narrator describes the monstrous apparition who appears to the king as a "griesely ghost," and exclaims: "I ken naething she 'peard to be, / But the fiend that wons in hell."[43]

Given that the author of the "Marriage" has gone to such extremes in locating the Loathly Lady beyond the limits of social acceptability by associating her enchantment and her resulting appearance with diabolical power, it is all the more striking that she insists, in her rebuke to Arthur, on her right to inclusion within the reciprocal conventions of courtesy, and that the narrative likewise moves to affirm her social inclusion. Whereas "Ragnelle" undercuts and burlesques the courtesy of Arthur's court, particularly in the characterization of Gawain, the "Marriage" extends the range and meaning of courtesy, redefining it, not as an exclusive aristocratic code, but as a universally applicable form of mutual respect and good-natured kindness, which encompasses even a woman whose appearance manifests alterity of an extreme and prohibited kind.

This universalizing redefinition of courtesy is reminiscent of the Wife of Bath's anti-elitist sermon on true "gentilesse," which is regarded by Caldwell as characteristic of the way in which the appearance of the Loathly Lady "ushers in values that compete with the conventional ones of courtly romance," and by S. Elizabeth Passmore as illustrative of the consistent centrality of the Loathly Lady's role as advisor and educator, particularly to the ruling class.[44] Superficially, the Loathly Lady in Chaucer's tale is a more apt mouthpiece for this democratization of aristocratic virtue than her richly arrayed counterpart in the "Marriage," since, like Gower's Loathly Lady, Chaucer's is characterized as poor, as well as old and ugly.[45] But her sermon, like her poverty, is not embodied in the tale, and its import is undercut, both by the part it plays in the Loathly Lady's manipulation of the knight and by the characterization of the Wife-narrator as a highly status-conscious member of the merchant class.

Just as Dame Ragnelle functions as an expression of the author's enjoyment of his own transgressions against courtliness, so the Loathly Lady of the "Marriage," in her rebuke to Arthur, may be regarded as emblematic of the author's redefinition of courtesy. It is, of course, tempting to see, in the "Marriage"'s claims for the inclusion of an ugly and marginalized woman—easily construed as representative of the women most liable to be shunned (or worse) as witches—an instance of the shaping influence of women as transmitters of ballads, which Lynn Wollstadt demonstrates.[46] It is Gawain, however, famed in romance for his aristocratically conceived "courtesy" who exemplifies this redefinition, in a novel rewriting of the disenchantment scene which replaces renegotiation of the female sovereignty postulated by the conventions of "courtly love" with an enactment of a co-operative decision which accommodates the lady's wishes.

Notes

1. London, British Library MS Add. 27879, pp. 46–52; described by Rogers, "Percy Folio Revisited," pp. 39–64. Bishop Percy acquired the manuscript from Sir Humphrey Pitt of Shiffnal in Shropshire in about 1757. A number of texts in the manuscript are incomplete; Bishop Percy recorded in a note on the flyleaf that, when he discovered it, it was lying on the floor under a bureau in the parlor and was being used by the maids to light the fire. My quotations from the "Marriage" are from Hahn, *Sir Gawain*, pp. 359–71. The "Marriage" has also recently been edited by Shepherd, *Middle English Romances*, pp. 380–87. Citations of editorial reconstructions, commentary, and notes in these two editions take the form of editor's surname followed by "Marriage" and a page number.

2. "Ragnelle" is preserved in a manuscript dated to the late fifteenth or early sixteenth century (Oxford, Bodleian Library MS 11951 [formerly Rawlinson C. 86], fols. 129^r-140^r). For the dating of the "Marriage" and "Ragnelle," see Garbáty, "Rhyme, Ballad, Burlesque," p. 292. My quotations from "Ragnelle" are from Hahn, *Sir Gawain*, pp. 47–70.

3. Eisner, *Tale of Wonder*, pp. 73–90. He argued that the common ancestor of the "Marriage" and "Ragnelle" differed from the common ancestor of the tales of Chaucer and Gower because it had been influenced by "a form of the ford-combat" tale, as represented by the eleventh-century Welsh story, *Pwyll*, which "is based on the eternal combat between summer and winter" (pp. 84–85). Prince Pwyll, while out hunting, encounters King Arawn, who has been recently defeated by King Hafgan. They exchange identities; at the end of the year Pwyll defeats Hafgan (Summer-White), and they resume their identities. Eisner considered that this accounted for the action involving Arthur and an antagonist and the surrogacy of Gawain, as well as more minor features such as the Christmas setting of the "Marriage" and the name of Arthur's antagonist in "Ragnelle," Gromer Somer Joure (Man of the Summer Day).

4. Garbáty, "Rhyme, Ballad, Burlesque," in arguing that the romance is earlier than the ballad, takes issue with Sumner, "The Weddynge of Sir Gawain and Dame

Ragnell," pp. xxiii–xxiv, who argues for the priority of the ballad. Hahn, "Marriage," p. 360, on the other hand, appears to regard the "Marriage" as much older than "Ragnelle," since he states: "The Percy Folio poem may well be the record of one more retelling of a story that had been popular at least from the time of King Edward I, and that, in addition to giving rise of a group of literary renditions, must have circulated widely in oral performances throughout the Middle Ages and the Renaissance."

5. Hahn, "Marriage," pp. 362–71; Garbáty, "Rhyme, Ballad, Burlesque," pp. 293–97. The editorial reconstruction of Shepherd, "Marriage," pp. 380–87, is generally more cautious; see further below. Bishop Percy, in his edition of the manuscript (1765) included a fanciful reconstruction of the "Marriage" based on his belief that the "Marriage" represented the underlying source of Chaucer's version: see Percy, *Reliques*, 3:11–24; and Lupack, "The Marriage of Sir Gawain," pp. 108–18. Cf. Bollard, "Sovereignty and the Loathly Lady," pp. 41–60, who, in his re-examination of Eisner's conclusions, warns against "taking too simplistic a view of the transmission problem" and points out that the "marked differences in approach in each of these [four Middle English] tales demonstrates the wide range of style and theme within which an author or redactor can work when retelling a traditional tale" (p. 56).

6. Garbáty, "Rhyme, Ballad, Burlesque," is the only study to have appeared in the last fifty years that focuses attention on the "Marriage." It has, however, received passing attention in analogue and comparative studies.

7. Gilbert, "Theoretical Introduction," p. 17.

8. Hahn, "Marriage," p. 359.

9. Hahn, "Marriage," p. 360.

10. Garbáty, "Rhyme, Ballad, Burlesque," pp. 293–94. Garbáty assumes an audience more socially elevated than the one envisaged by Hahn, i.e., an Anglicized audience, not exclusively consisting of members of "the upper levels of society," whose tastes, however, were less elevated than those of the Francophone nobility of the later fourteenth century for whom Chaucer and the romance authors wrote: "The whole evolution of *courtoisie* and gentilesse to a matter-of-factness, even a kind of prosaic view of things, was an ongoing process of Anglicization" (p. 297). Garbáty's view of the "courtly" character of "Ragnelle" is not widely shared; cf. Shepherd, "No Poet Has His Travesty Alone," pp. 112–13.

11. Gilbert, "Theoretical Introduction," p. 29.

12. Garbáty, "Rhyme, Ballad, Burlesque," p. 297. He finds a further illogicality in Arthur's possession of a collection of written answers in his meeting with the Baron in the "Marriage": "Why would Arthur have collected these at all when the implication is that the king, having granted the hag's wish, received her answer immediately?" But in "Ragnelle," Arthur (and Gawain) collect the written answers *before* Arthur meets with the Loathly Lady. In this case it is reasonable to assume (as do Hahn, "Marriage," p. 363, and Shepherd, "Marriage," p. 383, n. 6) that the action in the missing text of the "Marriage" (between lines 83 and 84) paralleled that of

"Ragnelle." In other words, Arthur's possession of written answers in his encounter with his antagonist is no less logical in the "Marriage" than it is in "Ragnelle."

13. The surviving fragments offer no support for the hypothesis that in the "Marriage," as in "Ragnelle," Arthur encountered the Baron while he was hunting; see Hahn, "Marriage," p. 362. The hunting motif does appear in Arthur's second meeting with the Loathly Lady; whether this represents a displacement or a replication of the setting of the opening episode is impossible to determine.

14. For the Wild Man and the churlish Foe of Chivalry, see Benson, *Art and Tradition*, pp. 72–90. By contrast, Sir Gromer Somer Joure in "Ragnelle," dressed as a knight and armed with a sword, has only a generalized resemblance to these stereotypical opponents of the representatives of chivalry; but cf. Hahn, "Ragnelle," p. 73, note to line 62, who suggests that his name associates him with giants.

15. This resembles the response of the malignant grandmother who occupies the role of antagonist in Gower's "Tale of Florent," I.1662 ("I wolde that thou were afire"). Quotations are from Gower, *Confessio Amantis*, ed. Peck.

16. Peck glosses *vecke* (line 1675) as "hag." Also appearing as *wekke*, its etymology is uncertain; cf. OE, "wicce" (f.) and "wicca" (m.): "witch."

17. "Tale of Florent," lines 1678–97, 1803–5. Gower's ageism here mirrors the conclusion to *Confessio Amantis*, VIII.2820–2970, where Venus compels his dream persona to confront the fact that he is old and therefore unsuited to love. Gower's thematization of age is reflected in his construction of Florent's antagonist as an aged crone. Surprisingly, he does not characterize the Loathly Lady's stepmother as old; cf. the "Marriage" which describes the stepmother as the young wife of an old knight (lines 175–79).

18. For Gawain and Arthur's association of the Loathly Lady with the fiend ("Ragnelle," lines 344–45 and 725), see below.

19. "Sir Launfal," lines 949–60 (Shepherd, *Middle English Romances*, pp. 190–218); "Thomas of Erceldoune," lines 49–64 (Murray, *Romances and Prophecies*). In both these romances, however, the trappings of the palfrey include bells, which also feature in the depiction of the Green Knight's horse in *Sir Gawain and the Green Knight*, line 195. Ironically, at any rate, the "lute she bare upon her bak," "Ragnelle," line 237 (glossed as "hump" by both Hahn and Shepherd), recalls the association of the faery with the harp; cf. "Sir Orfeo, line 344, "And henge his harp opon his bac" (Shepherd, *Middle English Romances*, pp. 174–90).

20. Shepherd, "Marriage," p. 382, n. 9. "Scarlet" originally denoted the quality of the cloth, not the color, but because of the tendency to dye the highest quality fabric with the most expensive dye (kermes), by the fourteenth century, "scarlet" denoted the dye and soon thereafter became a color word: Ball, *Bright Earth*, pp. 229–30.

21. *Sir Gawain and the Green Knight* notwithstanding, shining radiance and rich array appear to be more consistently characteristic and prominent in the depiction of faery beings than the wearing of green (and gold)—indeed, even in *SGGK*, the ladies of the castle are colored white; cf. the white clothing and horses of the faery women

in "Sir Orfeo" (lines 144–46). In "Sir Launfal," the maidservants of Dame Tryamour wear mantels of "grene felwet" (line 235), matching the saddle cloth of her horse (line 950), but their kertels are of indigo silk (line 232), and she herself wears "purpere palle" (line 943). Like "scarlet," "purpere" was as much a synonym for royal clothing as a color word; as a color word it encompassed deep red as well as a range of blues (Ball, *Bright Earth*, pp. 222–26, 230). In "Thomas of Erceldoune," the Faery Queen is initially described only as shining (line 48); her clothing (termed "riche," though only in one manuscript [Thornton, line 133]) is not mentioned until Thomas insists on possessing her, at which point her clothing vanishes (or disintegrates) as her body turns dark. Mary Leech, in her essay "Why Dame Ragnell Had to Die" in the present collection, may therefore be right in assuming that Dame Ragnell is "at least as well dressed as the horse"; the description may, equally, be an invitation to imagine her naked as a Wild Woman. Whereas the depiction of the Loathly Lady in the "Marriage" and "Ragnelle" echoes the depiction of faery women by virtue of her fine trappings (whether her own or her palfrey's), Gower, like Chaucer (who courteously eschews all description of the Loathly Lady), conceives his Loathly Lady (who is in actuality a princess [line 1841]), as "old and ugly and poor," although her tattered rags are not mentioned until later, when an attempt to transform her by dressing her in fine clothing proves unsuccessful [lines 1745–59]).

22. Garbáty, "Rhyme, Ballad, Burlesque," p. 294.

23. Arthur's first meeting with the Loathly Lady takes place on a moor, where she is seated between an oak and a holly tree. In the second meeting she is in "the greene forrest, / Underneath a greene holly tree" (lines 124–25). Readers who expect that, as in "Ragnelle," Arthur will return to "the same place and stede" (line 496), are likely to see this as a further inconsistency in the "Marriage." Pragmatically, the hunting subterfuge employed by Arthur to convey his knights to the Loathly Lady requires this shift in setting, but, whether or not the author made this "logical" by having Arthur arrange to meet the lady again in the forest, the change from barren wasteland to green woods represents a unique extension of the lady's transformation. Like the midwinter setting, this may be a reflex of a seasonal myth.

24. Hahn, "Marriage," p. 366; Shepherd, "Marriage," p. 384, n. 5, reads the text more carefully: "The text evidently related how Arthur returned to Carlisle and told his knights that a bride awaited one of them in the forest (it seems that Gawain was not approached directly)."

25. See Hahn, "Marriage," p. 365: "The lady agrees to the 'Marriage' bargain and tells Arthur what women most desire." Shepherd, "Marriage," p. 381, n. 2, postulates that Arthur's first offer "was uttered with the same kind of mocking contempt with which the King first greets Dame Ragnell in the *Weddyng*.... Contempt soon turns to desperate compliance, nevertheless, as it is revealed later that Arthur has indeed made a compact with the hag."

26. Garbáty, "Rhyme, Ballad, Burlesque," p. 294.

27. Hahn, "Marriage," p. 359.

28. What Gawain means by "Well I know what I wold say," I assume, is that he feels the force of a moral code which dictates the renunciation of his own libidinal desires.

29. My reading of this scene differs from that of Elizabeth Passmore, in her essay "Through the Counsel of a Lady" in the present volume, who regards the lady as coercing Gawain into arriving at the "correct" answer.

30. See the essays by Mary Leech, "Why Dame Ragnell Had to Die," and Ellen M. Caldwell, "Brains or Beauty," in the present volume.

31. Southworth, *English Medieval Minstrel*, p. 84.

32. This is not to deny the evidence of an association between traditional oral performers and "the common people" in the sixteenth century, e.g., George Puttenham, *Arte of English Poesie* (ca. 1560): "blind harpers or such like taverne minstrels that give a fit of mirth for a groat, and their matters being for the most part stories of old time, as the tale of Sir Thopas, the reportes of Bevis of Southampton, Guy of Warwicke, Adam Bell, and Clymme and such other old Romances or historicall rimes, made purposely for the recreation of the common people at Christmasse diners and brideales, and in taverns and alehouses and other such places of base resort" (qtd. in Burrow, "Sir Thopas," p. 78).

33. Shepherd, "No Poet Has His Travesty Alone," pp. 117–20.

34. Cf. Hahn, "Marriage," p. 368 (again assuming close adherence to "Ragnelle"): "In the morning Kay comes to check on Gawain's welfare"; Shepherd, "Marriage," p. 386, n. 1 (again more cautious and attentive to the surviving text): "Gawain then escorts his wife into the presence of an amazed court."

35. Percy, *Reliques*, 3:24.

36. Gower's description of his Loathly Lady as a "vecke" may perhaps have been suggestive of witchcraft (see n. 16, above); but, in his remarkably relaxed description of the enchantment performed by Medea (V.3945–4186) through her "art magique" (line 3947) and with the aid of Hecate "goddesse of Sorcerie" (line 3982), he makes no allusion to witchcraft or diabolic arts—his only contemporary reference is to faery magic ("In sondri wise hir forme changeth, / Sche semeth faie and no woman" [lines 4105–6]).

37. Hahn, "Ragnelle," pp. 75–76, note to line 319, instances several fifteenth- and sixteenth-century uses of "Ragnel" as the name of a pagan god or demon. The demonic connotations of the name, if known to the author of "Ragnelle" and its earliest audiences (though it may have been of folk, ultimately pagan, derivation) were, presumably, in keeping with the comic extravagance of Arthur and Gawain's diabolic references.

38. Benson, *Riverside Chaucer*, pp. 116–22 (pp. 116–17).

39. See *Dives and Pauper* (ca. 1410), which says that the fiends who take the form of men or women in order to tempt people to lechery are popularly called "elves," but in Latin are called "incubi" and "succuby" (Barnum, *Dives and Pauper*, p. 118).

40. This episode is preserved only in one of the four surviving manuscripts (Lansdowne, lines 141–56).

41. See Caldwell, "Brains or Beauty," in the present volume. Cf. *Sir Gawain and the Green Knight*—only Gawain discerns a diabolic atmosphere clinging to the Green Chapel (lines 2189–96), an evidently subjective projection, provoked by the guide's description of the Green Knight as a enemy of the religious orders (lines 2107–9), and undercut by its usefulness as a justification for escaping from his appointment with the Green Knight. The narrator, by contrast, appears bent on disassociating Morgan from witchcraft and the demonic. She is a practitioner of learned ("white") magic; having learnt from Merlyn "that conable clerk," she exercises "koyntyse of clergye, bi craftes wel lerned" (lines 2447–50): Tolkien and Gordon, *Sir Gawain*, p. 67. Cf. Malory (I.2), who relates that Morgan "was put to scole in a nonnery, and ther she learned so moche that she was a grete clerke of nygromancye": Vinaver, *Works*, 1:10.

42. Cf. the absence of demonic suggestion in "Sir Launfal" and in "Sir Orfeo" (although, in "Sir Orfeo," lines 387–94, the timeless suffering of some who have been "taken" is suggestive of the torments of hell). The *Malleus Maleficarum*, seminal to the development of diabolism and the persecution of witches, first appeared in 1486.

43. Child, *English and Scottish Popular Ballads*, 1:298–99.

44. See Caldwell, "Brains or Beauty," and Passmore, "Through the Counsel of a Lady," in the present volume.

45. For the tattered rags of Gower's Loathly Lady, see "The Tale of Florent," lines 1745–59.

46. See the essay by Lynn Wollstadt, "Re-Painting the Lion," in the present volume, who suggests that evidence of women as transmitters of ballads prior to the sixteenth century is elusive, as is evidence of female minstrels. Southworth, *English Medieval Minstrel*, for instance, found reference to only one woman harper (who was blind), remunerated by Henry VIII in 1531 (p. 164).

WORKS CITED

Ball, Phillip. *Bright Earth: The Invention of Colour*. London: Penguin, 2002.

Barnum, Priscilla Heath, ed. *Dives and Pauper*. Vol. 1, part 2. EETS, 280. Oxford: Oxford University Press, 1980.

Benson, Larry D. *Art and Tradition in Sir Gawain and the Green Knight*. New Brunswick, N.J.: Rutgers University Press, 1965.

Benson, Larry D., gen. ed. *The Riverside Chaucer*. 3rd ed. Boston: Houghton Mifflin, 1987; repr. Oxford: Oxford University Press, 1988.

Bollard, J. K. "Sovereignty and the Loathly Lady in English, Welsh and Irish." *LSE* 17 (1986), 41–59.

Burrow, J. A. "Sir Thopas in the Sixteenth Century." In *Middle English Studies Presented to Norman Davis*, ed. Douglas Gray and E. G. Stanley, pp. 69–92. Oxford: Clarendon Press, 1983.

Child, Francis James, ed. *The English and Scottish Popular Ballads*. 5 vols. 1857–59; repr. 5 vols. in 3, New York: Folklore, 1957.

Eisner, Sigmund. *A Tale of Wonder: A Source Study of "The Wife of Bath's Tale."* Wexford, Ire.: John English, 1957.

Garbáty, Thomas J. "Rhyme, Ballad, Burlesque, and the Confluence of Form." In *Fifteenth-Century Studies: Recent Essays*, ed. R. F. Yeager, pp. 283–301. Hamden, Conn.: Archon, 1984.

Gilbert, Jane. "A Theoretical Introduction." In *The Spirit of Medieval Popular Romance*, ed. Ad Putter and Jane Gilbert, pp. 15–38. Longman: Harlow, 2000.

Gower, John. *Confessio Amantis*. Ed. Russell A. Peck. New York: Holt, Rinehart and Winston, 1968.

Hahn, Thomas, ed. *Sir Gawain: Eleven Romances and Tales*. Kalamazoo, Mich.: Medieval Institute Publications, 1995.

Lupack, Alan. "The Marriage of Sir Gawain." In *Modern Arthurian Literature: An Anthology of English and American Arthuriana from the Renaissance to the Present*, ed. Alan Lupack, pp. 108–18. New York: Garland, 1992.

Murray, James A. H., ed. *The Romance and Prophecies of "Thomas of Erceldoune."* EETS 61. London: Trübner, 1875.

Percy, Thomas, ed. *Reliques of Ancient English Poetry*. 3 vols. 1765; repr. with a new introduction by Nick Groom. London: Routledge, 1996.

Rogers, Gillian. "The Percy Folio Manuscript Revisited." In *Romance in Medieval England*, ed. Maldwyn Mills, Jennifer Fellows, and Carole Meale, pp. 39–46. Cambridge: Brewer, 1991.

Shepherd, Stephen H. A., ed. *Middle English Romances*. New York: Norton, 1995.

——. "No Poet Has His Travesty Alone: 'The Weddynge of Sir Gawen and Dame Ragnell.'" In *Reading Romance on the Book: Essays on Medieval Narrative Presented to Maldwyn Mills*, ed. J. Fellows, Rosalind Field, Gillian Rogers, and Judith Weiss, pp. 112–28. Cardiff: University of Wales Press, 1996.

Southworth, John. *The English Medieval Minstrel*. Woodbridge: Boydell, 1989.

Sumner, Laura, ed. "The Weddyng of Sir Gawen and Dame Ragnell." *Smith College Studies in Modern Languages* 5. Northampton, Mass.: Paris Press, 1924.

Tolkien, J. R. R., and E. V. Gordon, eds. *Sir Gawain and the Green Knight*. 2nd rev. ed. by Norman Davis. Oxford: Clarendon Press, 1967.

Vinaver, E. V., ed. *The Works of Sir Thomas Malory*. 3rd ed. 3 vols. Revised by P. J. C. Fields. Oxford: Oxford University Press, 1990.

A Jungian Approach
to the Ballad "King Henry"

Mary Edwards Shaner

The ballad "King Henry" is from the Jamieson-Brown manuscript that was owned by William Tytler and which contained ballads sung by his daughter, Mrs. Brown of Falkland. She had learned these ballads from an aunt, Mrs. Farquhar. On the basis of this manuscript, Robert Jamieson, Matthew Gregory Lewis, and Sir Walter Scott each edited a version of "King Henry" for collections of Scottish folk stories and songs. The Brown manuscript disappeared before Francis James Child made his notable edition, and all three of those previous editions differ from each other. Lewis rewrote the Brown version as "Courteous King Jamie." Jamieson expanded the Brown version to thirty-four stanzas by considerable interpolation. Scott claimed to have added four stanzas received in oral recitation from Mrs. Brown, but his edition does not specify which stanzas they are, and Scott's well-known habit of freely amplifying and revising his sources from aesthetic as much as scholarly motives makes his edition not altogether trustworthy. This article is based primarily upon Child's edition because it is the most scholarly, but I recognize that there may be authentic additions from oral tradition in any one of the early published editions. The texts of orally transmitted material are necessarily more slippery than most work transmitted by manuscript or print. I will not attempt to trace the evolution of the text of "King Henry," nor will I venture to guess at its age. Again, our clues to a time of origin are slippery; the archaisms in vocabulary went on being used in rural Scotland well into the nineteenth century, so the fact that they were in common use in the fourteenth or fifteenth century does not prove a medieval origin for the ballad. No internal evidence points toward a specific and real King Henry who inspired the ballad, although the temptation to speculate has seduced not merely Lewis with his "Courteous King Jamie" (above) but even a modern

retelling by Jane Yolen in which she chooses Henry VIII as the particular
Henry who undergoes the adventure.[1] The most we can say is that the central
supernatural event of the story, the transformation of the "Loathly Lady"
into "the fairest lady that ever was seen," was in circulation during the Middle
Ages, and, as that motif is certainly medieval or earlier, we can justifiably
study "King Henry" as either a surviving medieval ballad or a more modern
preservation of medieval material. Although apparently not widely known
prior to the nineteenth century, this ballad has enjoyed considerable
popularity in the twentieth century. More than one folk artist or group has
recorded it, although the best-known recording is probably the one by
Steeleye Span on the album "Below the Salt."

Like fairy tales, most ballads were orally transmitted and, with some
brilliant exceptions such as "The Twa Corbies" or "The Wife of Usher's
Well," lack the qualities we generally seek in literary productions. The settings
are usually conventional and described briefly if at all. The characters are
two-dimensional and sometimes nameless. The events of the plots are
repetitive and incremental. The poetry of the ballads, except in inspired
instances, is not notable, the rhythms being strong but uneven, the meter
extended or contracted to meet the needs of the narrative. Rhyme may be
inexact, possibly due to aural errors creeping in during oral transmission. The
diction of speech is more colloquial than elegant, even in the mouths of dukes
and kings. Imagery, again with inspired exceptions, is usually formulaic. Even
the plots, which are clearly the heart of this genre, may be formulaic and
derivative. Why, then, do the ballads continue to have appeal for us? Because,
like fairy tales, they often speak to deep internal issues in the human psyche.
Marie-Luise von Franz, Jung's disciple who focused her studies on fairy tales,
said, "In interpreting fairy tales ... we try to bring out a new approach or
understanding of age-old words which have always been told and understood
in some form in their essential wisdom.... I feel, with this clue of Jungian
psychology, that it is possible to renew such a story so that it again has the
living meaning which people had always formerly felt in it."[2] Although by no
means a professional Jungian analyst myself, I have chosen a Jungian critical
strategy to approach "King Henry," finding that a more useful perspective on
the ballad than a formalist reading. There are many ways in which Jungian
principles may be applied to literature, from Northrop Frye's archetypal
criticism[3] to Von Franz's more clinical analysis using story as a vehicle to
analyze psychological ills and point toward healing. I will attempt to utilize
Jungian ideas in a fashion more imitative of Von Franz than of Frye, but
with, I hope, a more literary and less clinical application.

The essential quality of Jungian criticism that I choose to emphasize is its integrative nature. Jungian criticism sees the characters and events of story as disparate and scattered parts of the human personality which need and desire (usually) to become whole. To greatly oversimplify, the *animus* is the masculine principle in every human; the *anima* is the feminine principle; and the *shadow* is that part of our unconscious that is not accessible to us and which can belong to either the anima or the animus if either of those is uncontrolled, or be a complex mix of the most negative and fearsome parts of ourselves. Men tend to project the anima in themselves outward onto the world and women around them. Women tend to project the animus similarly onto men. All three of these—animus, anima, and shadow—are free in story to stand apart and act out their natures in such a way that the ego may recognize and perhaps reconcile them. Of course, these mighty figures are disguised in story, but they will behave according to their natures, and we the audience need only to see their behaviors and icons with understanding to know them. I believe they are identifiable in "King Henry," and their resolution of their mutual and fearsome needs is an integrative process.

The plot of the ballad "King Henry" is simpler than those of the literary versions of the Loathly Lady story. It is especially notable that no motivation is given explicitly for any action, and little emotional direction for the audience is expressed in the text. To illustrate my meaning, let us consider one of the most sophisticated versions of the Loathly Lady motif, Chaucer's "The Wife of Bath's Tale,"[4] which provides a number of clear motives for the action that eventually brings the knight and the Loathly Lady together: the knight commits a rape (presumed motive: lust) and is brought before the king for judgment (motive: justice); the king is about to sentence him to death when the ladies of the court beg mercy for him (motive: pity) and the king turns him over to the queen for judgment (motive: mercy). And so forth. All major events are clearly, sometimes explicitly, motivated. But when we look at the ballad "King Henry," the plot of which has at least one strong analogy to "The Wife of Bath's Tale," we see action without explanation. The story is not hard to follow, but reasons for the actions and events are primarily inferential. King Henry has gone to a hunting lodge seven miles from any town, where he enjoys a day's successful hunting. That night, an ogress enters the lodge and he gives her his mantle to cover her nakedness. She demands meat and orders him to kill his horse, his hounds, and his goshawks, all of which she consumes down to hide and hair or feathers. She then demands drink and orders him to sew up the horse's hide to hold drink for her. He does this and fills the hide with wine, which she drinks in one draft. She then commands him to make a bed for her by pulling up heather. He does so and spreads his mantle over it for her bed. She next orders him to lie down by her side. He protests at this but evidently does sleep with her. The next morning, she has become "the fairest lady that ever was seen"[5] and he cries out, "How lang'll this last wi me?" (line 84). She replies that it will last until he dies. She says many men have given her her fill, but none before him ever gave her all her will.

For my purposes, the lack of explicit statement of motives is helpful. It not merely encourages the practice of inferring the causative goals and emotions behind events, it virtually requires it. The first stanza of the ballad gives advice for courtship:

> Lat never a man a wooing wend
>> That lacketh thingis three:
> A routh o gold, an open heart,
>> Ay fu o charity.
>>> (lines 1–4)

The count of three "thingis" seems wrong here, since the "open heart" full "o charity" would appear to be a single item. Clearly we are intended to take the charity as a separate item, a thing in itself, not just a quality of the heart. That is a properly medieval idea, that *caritas* may be held in the heart, but that it is more than the heart. The gist of the courtship advice, then, is that one must have something to give (abundance of gold, the shelter of an open heart) and the will to give it (charity). Whether King Henry is so equipped remains to be seen. Certainly, his present intention is not, consciously, courtship. The second stanza tells us that he has in fact gone hunting:

> As this I speak of King Henry,
>> For he lay burd-alone;
> An he's doen him to a jelly hunt's ha,
>> Was seven miles frae a town.
>>> (lines 5–8)

This stanza is our actual introduction to King Henry, and it provides a number of details that are, from a Jungian perspective, suggestive. The first line of the stanza, "As this I speak of King Henry," can mean either that King Henry possesses the requisite "thingis three" for courtship or that it is true that he will need them, or it may have both meanings at once. What is really being spoken of King Henry we will have to learn over the course of the ballad, as King Henry himself does.

The sequence of stanzas, from courtship advice to the hunting hall, implies an intimate relationship between hunting and courtship. Such a relationship is, of course, widely accepted in our society, as is apparent from the use of hunting metaphors in love poetry and song, such as Sir Thomas Wyatt's "Whoso list to hunt, I know where is an hinde."[6] This correspondence between loving and hunting is explicit in the dual meanings of "venery,"[7] both the act of hunting and the pursuit of sexual pleasure. King Henry's pursuit of game is successful, as the third verse states; his unstated but implied prey of the lady is something that he does not even realize he's hunting: a woman and the anima with all its great power and horror. This second hunt is conducted not in the woods and vales, but in the isolation of a lodge "seven miles frae a town." King Henry's isolation from all companionship has important implications. (Perhaps I should mention at this point that in Scott's version of the ballad, King Henry's huntsmen are at the lodge with him but flee the hall at the advent of the ogress, a companionship that would partially invalidate my reading, but since it also contradicts the "burd-alone" of the second stanza, it is therefore unlikely. As I have said before, Scott's emendations of ballads make it difficult to determine an authoritative reading.)[8] Von Franz says that "loneliness invites the powers of the Beyond, either evil or good. The natural explanation would be that the amount of energy normally used in relating to one's surroundings is dammed back into oneself and activates the unconscious, loads up the unconscious part of the psyche, so that if for a long time one is alone, one's unconscious will come alive, and then you are caught for better or worse; either the devil will get you or you will find greater inner realization."[9] King Henry is not in isolation for any great period of time, but it would appear that the dangers of loneliness manifest to him all the same. His unconscious need is shown in the fact that his distance from people is specifically seven miles; Von Franz says that in Jungian terms eight as a "double of four points to the inner totality, to psychic completeness."[10] Therefore, seven connotes incompleteness, an emptiness that needs to be filled. The shadow hunt of courtship, in which Henry does not even know he is engaged, implies that what is missing is the feminine, the anima aspect of the subconscious. The second line of stanza 2 also points to the missing anima in its use of *burd-alone*, a term meaning "solitary" made from "burd.""Burd" can mean "bird" or "damsel," which permits us to pun upon Henry's solitary state as both lonely and sexually deprived.

The second stanza, in conjunction with the third, introduces the animus aspect of King Henry most emphatically. First, he is a king, an archetype which in Jung's thought is "embodiment of the dominant of collective consciousness."[11] He has the power of a ruler of a community, and the responsibility. Yet we see him only alone until his grim visitor arrives. Verse 3 does demonstrate his masculine animus through his hunting, but he has abandoned, at least temporarily, the society over which he rules:

> He chas'd the deer now him before
>   An the roe down by the den,
> Till the fattest buck in a' the flock
>   King Henry he has slain.
>
> O he has doen him to his ha,
>   To make him beerly cheer,
> An in it came a griesly ghost,
>   Steed stappen i the fleer.
>   (lines 9–16)

King Henry has no shortage of masculine energy, as the outcome of his hunting shows: he kills the fattest buck (male deer) in the deer herd and goes back to the hunting lodge for an evening of "beerly cheer." But the successful hunt in itself suggests that Henry has a troubled unconscious. Von Franz says that killing in dreams signifies total repression of the element which the slain creature represents;[12] following this thought, we may find the killing of the buck, a symbol of male virility, to be an outward representation of Henry's total repression of his sexual needs.

Into Henry's isolation stamps "a griesly ghost," a grisly spirit, just as he is enjoying his "beerly cheer." She is the anima, the subconscious made manifest, and she is *huge*. Her head strikes the roof-tree, her teeth and nose are enormous, and she is naked. Henry tosses her his cloak and tells her to cover up her body, an action that seems to confirm that he is repressing sexual need which he finds ugly and threatening, possibly even evil, but certainly overwhelming. She appears to be a fiend come from hell, the devil that Von Franz warns can come to us in loneliness. And King Henry has created her in this image. As a male who has given himself over to the animus entirely, he has projected the anima onto women not as the loved and desired model of mother and wife, but as the unappeasable devourer, the giant whose appetite is insatiable, like love or death. This grim visitor is a giant, and giants have played some very interesting symbolic roles in fairy tales. Von Franz tells us,

Giants in Germanic mythology are mostly characterized by their enormous strength and, in general, by their outstanding stupidity.… But in older, pre-Christian Nordic mythology, giants are also very clever.… Giants are mostly responsible for the weather; they create mist.… There are thunder giants, lightning giants, and giants responsible for landslides.… From these associations we can see that they represent the brute, untamed power of nature, a psychological dynamism mostly of an emotional character that is stronger than man. Therefore we could associate them with overwhelming emotional impulses which overcome the humanity of man as does a giant.[13]

Von Franz probably never heard of the ballad "King Henry," but her reading of giants seems strikingly apt for his gigantic guest. Although the Loathly Lady makes no direct threat toward Henry, her vast presence is clearly powerful and there is no question of Henry's resisting her will at first. In Scott's version of the ballad, her coming is heralded by a mighty storm and an earthquake. Those details may be authentic or may originate with Scott, but they suit the associations Von Franz tells us most cultures make with giants.

The ballad's narrative voice, which speaks in the first person only this once, in the sixth stanza offers a seeming identification of the horrid visitor: "And I ken naething she 'peard to be, / But the fiend that wons in hell" (lines 23–24). The assertion that she seems to be the fiend that dwells in hell may point us toward a specific identity for her. Again in Von Franz we find a relevant reading: In many Germanic fairy tales, there is said to be a female companion to the devil in hell. In some stories, like "The King's Son and the Devil's Daughter" collected by the brothers Grimm, for instance, this female companion is the Devil's daughter; in other stories, she is his grandmother. According to Von Franz, "The word grandmother does not imply kinship … but means that [the Devil] lives with the Great Mother, the earth goddess, the mother of all life."[14] The Great Mother is the embodiment of the feminine principle, and in Western Christian culture as represented by the fairy tales, "a part of the feminine principle is repressed, together with the devil, into the underworld. It waits only for an opportunity to come up again and take its ruling place on the surface."[15] The Great Mother as Devil's companion is more friendly to humanity than the devil, often working to thwart the devil's plans for mortals. She has, however, her dark and fearsome side. As we see her in "King Henry" come up like a storm or earthquake to shake this solitary man, she is a manifestation of the shadow, "a moral problem that challenges the whole ego personality, for no one can become conscious of the shadow without considerable moral effort. To become conscious of it involves recognizing the dark aspects of the personality as present and real."[16] The implications of Jung's thoughts for "King Henry" are, first, that Henry has projected the anima upon women as a dangerous monster because he perceives women (and sexual desire) as a moral problem; second, he has gone through a moral struggle (hence, perhaps, his self-imposed isolation) or the ogress would not have appeared. Her shadow aspect is as a devourer, and she's hungry. She demands meat from King Henry. He, apparently forgetting that he's killed a buck that day, says, "What meat's in this house, lady, / An what ha I to gie?" The obvious answer is that *he* is in the house and it's himself he has to give. But the ogress works her way to that answer slowly, consuming all his extraneous holdings until only his own body is left.

The animals that King Henry must slay to feed the anima/shadow projection have many possible symbolic meanings. The horse is a traditional symbol of male virility, although Jung also points out that a horse could represent "the mother within us," intuitive understanding. Hounds can represent loyalty and faithfulness to friends, and the hawk may have a dark meaning as predatory sin getting its claws into the human soul, or, what seems more likely here, it may stand for vision or perception. It seems to me most useful to read the assorted animals as representations of earthly senses that must be subjugated and absorbed by the anima in order to get past the defenses of the animus.

The object of human psychological development is wholeness which, according to Jung, requires an integration of the masculine principle of the animus and the feminine principle of the anima, what Jung calls "syzygy," or union. Each of these principles can be dangerous if out of control, but recognition and acknowledgment of the shadow is a necessary precursor to syzygy. Jung says, "I should like to emphasize that the integration of the shadow, or the realization of the personal unconscious, marks the first stage in the analytic process, and without it a recognition of anima and animus is impossible. The shadow can be realized only through a relation to a partner, and anima and animus only through a relation to the opposite sex, because only in such a relation do their projections become operative."[17] Obviously, King Henry is not undergoing formal Jungian analysis. But his situation appears to be one that he has instinctively arrived at in an intuitive search for health. It is as dangerous a situation as a major surgical procedure, but it may have similarly restorative results.

Hitherto, Henry has been thoroughly masculine: the lone male hunter surrounded by the accouterments of the chase. What he has done most successfully is kill. But among his equipment for hunting (in the sense of

courting) is the charity which fills his open heart. This generosity of heart
means that even a fearsome "fiend that dwells in hell" will receive from him
what he has to give. His first action after the giant appears is to give her his
cloak. She then demands of him that he kill *for* her. His compliance is not
without cost: after the death of each creature the ballad repeats the only line
in the entire song, to this point, that denotes emotion: "Wow but his heart
was sair!" Each of these deaths is a wrench, and his heartsoreness reinforces
the impression that these animals are parts of himself, the instincts and senses
that have protected his innermost self from the intrusions of emotion. After
King Henry has killed every creature at his disposal but himself, the monster
asks for drink. Furthermore, she orders King Henry, "O ye sew up your
horse's hide, / An bring in a drink to me"(lines 59–60). This action may be
more powerfully symbolic than its surface appears. As I have said, the horse
can be a symbol of male virility. Turning its hide into a cup, a common
symbol of female sexuality, seems to be an indication that the integrative
union of anima and animus has begun, as indeed Henry's courteous
acquiescence to the gigantic female's every request has also signified. It
remains for the process to be completed by actual physical union.

At last the bed is made and the cloak once more given as a coverlet; now
the hunter must yield himself up as prey. At this point Henry makes his one
protest:

"O God forbid," says King Henry,
    "That ever the like betide;
That ever the fiend that wons in hell
    Should streak down by my side."
                    (lines 75–78)

Nonetheless, he does lie with her, although the ballad does not say so
explicitly. Between stanzas 17 and 18 of the ballad, both Child and Scott used
a line of asterisks without explanation. This is precisely the point at which
one would expect some account, however euphemistic, of what transpires in
the bed. But there is only this starry line, the purpose of which is unexplained
(certainly Child shows no tendency to censor explicitly sexual scenes
elsewhere; perhaps the asterisks indicate a belief that a verse or so have been
lost). Whatever transpires between stanza 17 and stanza 18, it does not
happen without a struggle on Henry's part, and this is evidently what Jung
would expect. Jung says, "Although, with insight and good will, the shadow
can to some extent be assimilated into the conscious personality, experience
shows that there are certain features which offer the most obstinate resistance

to moral control and prove almost impossible to influence. These resistances are usually bound up with *projections*, which are not recognized as such, and their recognition is a moral achievement beyond the ordinary."[18] In the ballad, the resistance comes not from the projection, the ogress, but from the projector, King Henry. But clearly, whatever his objections, Henry goes to bed with the "griesly ghost." There is nothing left for King Henry to "gie" but himself, so that is what he gives, and it is an act of great moral courage. And it proves to be the solution to loneliness and fragmentation.

Let us now turn to Henry as the animus, the masculine principle. We have said that his actions have been masculine-assertive in the beginning of the ballad, but the results of them have been repressive. He has successfully hunted and slain the buck, a possible symbol of male virility. He has placed himself seven miles from all human contact, far from any temptation of emotional impulse. As an embodiment of the animus, King Henry is organized, powerful, active, and self-contained. Speaking of a king in another story, Von Franz says, "The disease of the ruler … must have to do with a loss of contact with the anima, the feminine psychic principle."[19] Henry may have become too intellectual, controlled, and ordered for his own psychic health. He needs the balance of the anima, and he needs to acknowledge frankly strong feelings and strong symbolism. Von Franz sums up Jungian thought on kings: "[I]n order to be renewed, the king first has to be trans-formed into his chthonic nature … the earth aspect of king. When he dies he goes into the earth.… Because the king represents the dominant of collective consciousness, … every dominant of collective consciousness, every central image of the Self which dominates in a cultural setup, has to fall back from time to time into the unconscious and be renewed there."[20] We have not seen King Henry in his role as ruler of a court or regulator of a society; but we do see him enter a symbolic death when he lies down with the "fiend that dwells in hell." Both sleep and the sex act have sometimes been called "little deaths." Through the symbolic descent into death by way of the embrace of the anima / shadow and sleep, King Henry undergoes renewal during that night. He awakens not merely to a new and lovely form of the anima; he awakens as a new self:

> Whan night was gane, and day was come,
>   An the sun shone throw the ha,
> The fairest lady that ever was seen
>   Lay atween him an the wa.
>   (lines 79–82)

With the coming of the sun and light, the dark night of simulated death is over. Resurrection and revelation come with the morning. In this stanza, the great transformation of the monster to the lovely and beloved woman is announced. The Loathly Lady has become both fair and accessible, between Henry and the wall. What was hideous and fearsome, a shadow from the subconscious, is now conscious and known as the beautiful and desirable. She is not the only one transformed:

> "O well is me!" says King Henry,
>   "How lang'll this last wi me?"
> Then out it spake that fair lady,
>   "Even till the day you dee."
>   (lines 83–86)

Earlier in the ballad, we have seen King Henry celebrate with "beerly cheer" the slaying of the buck. That happy occasion was observed in isolation and silence. Now Henry cries out, "O well is me!" an inversion of the more common "woe is me." It means that what has come to him is well, good, happy, fortunate; and it means that he is well, healed of the psychic wound caused by his monstrous projection of the anima. He has clearly been made whole by his union with the loathly, now lovely, lady. In Jungian terms, the animus and anima have been reconciled and individuation has been achieved. In metaphoric terms, the hunt has been completed, that which was needed and sought has been found.

That King Henry can scarcely believe his new condition is implied in the question, "How lang'll this last wi me?" The reassurance from the lady that it will last until he dies means that this is a real and permanent renewal of his life and self. He will not unknow what he knows, unlearn what he has learned. She explains the reason for this wonderful new state of being in the final stanza:

> For I've met wi mony a gentle knight
>   That's gien me sic a fill.
> But never before wi a courteous knight
>   That ga me a' my will.
>   (lines 87–90)

The lady is beautiful now that she has been accepted by King Henry in the bed he made for her. We could read "gave me all my will" as expressing sexual satisfaction, but good sex alone is not enough to make a divided personality whole. It is King Henry's acceptance of the anima that heals them both, him into joy, her into beauty. The animus has acknowledged the existence of the anima, thus giving it permission to be its most beautiful self, no longer a creature to be feared. This transformation has not been achieved by passivity on the part of the anima. She has not merely appeared to King Henry as a terrifying projection but has used both that projection and its terror to push the resisting King Henry into the union of a symbolic marriage bed. Henry's own gentility and charity bring him to the verge of this union, but the demanding "fiend from hell" pushes him into it. In this respect, this Loathly Lady has some resemblance to others of her genre, since her advice, couched as a demand, proves good for Henry, as several of the Loathly Ladies while in their loathsome form give wise advice to their partners.

None of these readings should be seen as absolute and certain. They are drawn from hints in the ballad more than from explicit words or deeds, and in Jungian thought as in much medieval thought, most elements have both a good and a bad meaning, depending on context. Nevertheless, I think that the *clue* of Jungian thought, as Von Franz calls it, leads us deeper into the maze of folk story/ballad than many critical strategies might, and gives us useful matter to bring back out.

NOTES

An earlier version of the article was delivered at the International Medieval Congress in Kalamazoo, Michigan, in May 2003.

1. Yolen, "King Henry."

2. Von Franz, *Shadow*, pp. 168–69.

3. Frye, *Anatomy of Criticism*.

4. Benson, *Riverside Chaucer*.

5. Child, *English and Scottish Popular Ballads*, ballad 32, line 81; unless otherwise noted, all quotations from the text of "King Henry" are from this edition, cited by line number.

6. Wyatt, *Essential Wyatt*.

7. I am indebted to the gentleman in the audience at the International Medieval Congress at Kalamazoo (May 2003) who drew these parallel meanings to my attention; I regret that I did not get his name.

8. Scott, *Minstrelsy of the Scottish Border*, pp. 382–86.

9. Von Franz, *Shadow*, pp. 150–51.

10. Von Franz, *Shadow*, p. 206.

11. Von Franz, *Individuation*, p. 45.
12. Von Franz, *Individuation*, p. 14.
13. Von Franz, *Shadow*, pp. 206–7.
14. Von Franz, *Shadow*, p. 265.
15. Von Franz, *Shadow*, p. 266.
16. Jung, *Psyche and Symbol*, p. 7.
17. Jung, *Psyche and Symbol*, p. 21.
18. Jung, *Psyche and Symbol*, p. 7.
19. Von Franz, *Individuation*, p. 171.
20. Von Franz, *Individuation*, p. 45.

WORKS CITED

Benson, Larry D., gen. ed. *The Riverside Chaucer*. 3rd ed. Boston: Houghton Mifflin, 1987.

Child, Francis James, ed. *The English and Scottish Popular Ballads*. Vol. 1. Boston: Houghton Mifflin, 1884; repr. New York: Dover, 1965.

Frye, Northrop. *Anatomy of Criticism: Four Essays*. Princeton: Princeton University Press, 1957.

Jung, Carl G. *Psyche and Symbol: A Selection from the Writings of C. G. Jung*. Ed. Violet S. de Laszlo. Garden City, N.Y.: Doubleday, 1958.

Scott, Sir Walter. *Minstrelsy of the Scottish Border*. Glasgow: Grand Colosseum Warehouse, 1868.

Steeleye Span. "Below the Salt." Chrysalis Records 1008, 1972.

Von Franz, Marie-Luise. *Individuation in Fairy Tales*. Boston: Shambala, 1977.

——. *Shadow and Evil in Fairytales*. Dallas: Spring Publ., 1987.

Wyatt, Thomas. *The Essential Wyatt*. Selected and with an introduction by W. S. Merwin. New York: Ecco, 1989.

Yolen, Jane. "King Henry." In *Ballads*, ed. and illus. Charles Vess. n.p.: Green Man, 1997.

Repainting the Lion
"The Wife of Bath's Tale" and
a Traditional British Ballad

Lynn M. Wollstadt

Though the similarities between the traditional British ballad "The Knight and the Shepherd's Daughter" and Chaucer's "Wife of Bath's Tale" have long been acknowledged, the specific nature of the relationship has yet to be examined.[1] Both narratives are built upon rape, punishment, and reward surrounding a woman who is not what she appears. The ballad, which was quite well-known in the late eighteenth and early nineteenth centuries, tells of a shepherdess who is accosted and apparently raped by a young knight. Though the young woman in "The Knight and the Shepherd's Daughter" is not a literal shape-shifter, the plot clearly aligns the narrative with the body of Loathly Lady tales: a knight is forced to marry a seemingly undesirable woman, but he then finds her ultimately transformed into a desirable one. Interestingly, however, this ballad echoes "The Wife of Bath's Tale" much more closely both in substance and message than any other Loathly Lady analogue, even those far more contemporary to the ballad.[2]

In "The Knight and the Shepherd's Daughter," the knight's victim takes matters into her own hands, asking the knight's name and following him back to court, where she complains that the knight has robbed her of her virginity. The king (or queen, in some versions) promises the maiden that if the offending knight is married, he will be put to death, but if he is single, he must marry her. The knight is devastated by this sentence and tries to buy off the woman, but she insists on her right to the marriage. In the end, however, the knight is delighted to learn that the apparent shepherdess is really a wealthy noblewoman. They all, apparently, live happily ever after.

"The Wife of Bath's Tale" is, of course, the only other British Loathly Lady tale to begin the story with a rape, making its protagonist a criminal

rather than a hero.[3] As feminist scholars have long noted, this modification
complicates that tale's ending, especially since the tale is told by the Wife
of Bath. While the Wife professes independence and a love of female
"sovereigntee," she tells a tale in which a knight is ultimately rewarded for
violence against a woman. The tale's closing lines assure the reader that the
Loathly Lady, now a beautiful young woman, "obeyed [the knight] in every
thyng / That myghte doon hym plesance or likyng," allowing them to live the
rest of their lives "[i]n parfit joye."[4] Indeed, many recent readings of the tale
suggest that these lines completely negate the narrative's ostensible message,
its illustration of woman's wish for authority over men, as well as cancel out
the pillow sermon's message that true "gentillesse" comes from God alone
rather than the external trappings of appearance, money, and class. Brian
Lee, for example, argues that the tale's initial rape is shocking primarily
"because it is ultimately rewarded, not just by good luck but as a matter of
deliberate judicial policy.... If the tale is designed to show that women desire
sovereignty, it succeeds rather in demonstrating that women serve for men's
delight both by chance and by policy."[5] Lynne Dickson likewise sees the tale's
out-come as "a strange affirmation of masculine desire," arguing that it
"rewards the concession of masculine 'maistrie' with the very thing patriarchy
wants to begin with."[6] Similarly, Ellen Caldwell, in her article in this volume,
sees little, if any, true female sovereignty in "The Wife of Bath's Tale." She
notes that any power the Loathly Lady holds is linked specifically to her
loathsome, and unfeminine, state: "Generally, it is only when she is loathsome
and "ungendered" (i.e., freed from her female role), that the Loathly Lady is
beyond male control and is sought after, not as a sexual object but as the
source of special powers."[7] The task facing scholars trying to evaluate the
tale's ultimate messages regarding gender and power is to decide which aspect
of the text holds more sway. The bulk of the narrative shows the erring
knight in a position of powerlessness, suffering for the actions he has taken,
and finally giving up his own power to the very class of person he had
victimized. Is that aspect trumped by the final few stanzas of the poem, in
which the woman voluntarily gives up her position of power and the knight
indeed gets every-thing he wants?

These contradictory messages and ambiguity are preserved in "The Knight
and the Shepherd's Daughter," and this connection becomes even more
intriguing when one takes into account the oral nature of the ballad tradition.
The content of traditional ballads was ultimately controlled by those who
sang them. Listeners who heard and remembered ballads became authors

when they repeated them; they ultimately had textual authority over the texts they passed on. Furthermore, for any individual ballad to stay alive in a culture of oral transmission, someone must want to repeat it, or else it will die out.[8] A song that did not appeal to enough singers simply did not survive, in the same way a joke that few people find funny simply disappears.[9] Though the extent to which these performers might alter a ballad would be constrained by audience expectations, the fact that individual singers did alter ballad texts (both consciously and subconsciously) is clear, and small textual changes could ultimately create a very different narrative.[10]

In her Prologue, the Wife of Bath ponders the issue of textual authority, pointedly asking, "Who peynted the leon, tel me who?" (line 692). Complaining of the "wikked wives" chronicled in the writings of men, she asserts, "By God, if wommen hadde writen stories.… They wolde han writen of men moore wikkednesse / Than all the mark of Adam may redresse" (lines 685, 693–96). In the years before the advent of general female literacy in Great Britain, orally transmitted ballads did, in fact, function as women's stories. The tradition was by no means the sole providence of women, but women singers have played a vital role in passing down these texts since at least the sixteenth century.[11] Thus, the fact that the ballad "The Knight and the Shepherd's Daughter" should so closely resemble "The Wife of Bath's Tale" is provocative. What might women singers have found appealing in a tale offering such a message? On the other hand, the narrative is indeed a tale of the male "wikkedness" that Alisoun claims women authors would recount; it is the story of a man who commits a crime. As is true in the Wife's tale, most of the ballad's narrative focuses on relating the knight's punishment. But just as Alisoun's tale was actually authored by a male whose attitudes toward his female storyteller were clearly mixed, this ballad evolved for generations within a patriarchy that also accepted the ballad tradition as its own. To have survived in popular tradition, the song must have appealed to male singers as well as female ones, a fact that could well explain the knight's reward at the ballad's end. As is the case in "The Wife of Bath's Tale," the punishment is important, but only temporary. This turnaround allows different audiences (and singers) the space to hear (or relate) different messages.

Some scholars have seen traditional balladry as an aspect of folk culture that provided the opportunity for communicating hidden messages among women. For example, in her essay "Wishful Willful Wily Women: Lessons for Female Success in the Child Ballads," Polly Stewart argues: "Just as women in ballads might on occasion circumvent oppressive situations by means of verbal or other mental agility, so might women ballad singers use these songs to send coded messages to women audiences—an agile use of traditional material, message within message."[12] While I agree that women certainly might have done so, talking specifically about coding leads to the problem of authorial intention. Many ballads may have been sung by men before they were sung by women, and there is no way to say that the women singers themselves actually recognized the codes that today's feminist critics see. As Dianne Dugaw points out in her study of ballads that portray female warriors (women who disguised themselves as men and fought in the military), gender issues are particularly difficult to see outside of our own twentieth-century perspective: "We tend to assume (of course without realizing it) that seventeenth- and eighteenth-century people—and their 'archaic' counterparts in the folk culture of our own time—were more repressed and restrictive on matters of sex and gender than we in modern times."[13] Therefore, what seems far more interesting to me than simply trying to "decode" ballad images, in a search for some ultimate meaning, is seeing these images as spaces in which multiple, even contradictory, interpretations are simultaneously possible.

The lack of explanatory detail in ballads, the preference for, as Buchan puts it, "the concrete rather than the abstract," provides a particularly large space for multiple readings that are superficially incompatible, particularly when the narrative is heard rather than read.[14] Hearing a ballad sung or recited requires one to make immediate and unconscious decisions about what is happening in the narrative and how one feels about it. That interpretive space might have allowed women listeners and singers to see in ballads a "wild zone" of female experience that could be quite at odds with the ideology of the dominant segment of Scottish society. I use the term *female experience* here simply as a matter of convenience. We must take care not to think of this zone as outlining a single "female" interpretation, however, but rather a multitude of different meanings that may have been more likely to be identified by female than by male listener-performers. Within this protective space was room for various interpretations—different meanings for different women.[15] The contradictory messages that "The Knight and the Shepherd's Daughter" sends illustrate this situation aptly.

Furthermore, the fact that ballad singers did alter the songs they sang means that the apparent desirability of the marriage at the end of "The Knight and the Shepherd's Daughter" varies with different versions of the ballad. Perhaps not surprisingly, the version whose ending most unambiguously embraces the union between the seeming shepherdess and the errant knight is not a version collected directly from a female singer, but rather is a seventeenth-century broadside titled "The Beautifull Shepherdesse of Arcadia." While the canon of orally transmitted ballads has stood the test of time, selected and distilled by generations of singers who learned and passed on only those texts that they found meaningful, broadsides were always a for-profit endeavor, earning money for the printers, the authors, and the sellers.[16] A product of the cheap printing first available in the sixteenth century, the broadside ballad was printed on a single sheet of paper, usually on one side only, often illustrated with a woodcut and usually indicating a popular tune to which the ballad should be sung. Most were original compositions, but many publishers apparently found it profitable to print their own versions of ballads and other folk songs that were already popular. The authors and printers who did so, of course, would have had complete license to alter such texts in any way they saw fit in order to appeal to the greatest segment of the purchasing market, making the ballad more profitable. Given the low rates of female literacy in Great Britain throughout the seventeenth and eighteenth centuries, the heyday of the broadside ballad, it is likely that the majority of ballad-buyers were men.[17]

The number of surviving broadside texts of "The Knight and the Shepherd's Daughter," as well as the number of oral versions collected a century or so later, suggests that this ballad was one that existed in popular tradition before it was published, rather than vice versa.[18] The broadside ballad text, then, is the only version of the ballad that is almost certainly male-authored. Regardless of the ballad's evolution among a largely female population of ballad singers, the man or men who rewrote it for publication had complete editorial license, a fact that may explain the intriguing differences between the broadside and the versions that were collected orally. One of the most striking is the broadside's presentation of the initial sexual encounter. While every version originally collected from an oral source makes it clear that this encounter is nonconsensual, "The Beautifull Shepherdesse of Arcadia" describes the woman apparently giving the knight permission to have sex with her. "O I shall dye this day," the knight tells her, "If I have not my will of thee," to which the maiden replies, "The Lord forbid … That such a thing should be, / That ever such a courteous yong knight / Should dye for love of me" (Child 110A). Moreover, the broadside ends with an unambiguously happy union, as the ballad addresses the economics of marriage negotiation in the language of romantic love. When the woman reveals her true position as a duke's daughter, the knight bemoans his close call, praising the woman for being "true" to him despite his attempt to get out of the deal:

"Accursed be the gold," he said,
   "If thou hadst not bin true,
That should have parted thee from me,
   To have chang'd thee for a new."

Of course, in cursing the "gold" that almost parted him from his newly beloved, the knight is worried primarily about his economic situation, not the loss of romantic love. He is concerned not only with the gold he would have lost in paying her off but also the money he now stands to gain with a wealthy and well-born wife. The primacy of financial issues to the knight, as well as his concern with re-establishing his sexual and social dominance, are confirmed in the final stanza, which unambiguously affirms the knight's romantic and economic good luck:

Their hearts being then so linked fast,
   And joyning hand in hand,
He had both purse and person too,
   And all at his command.

In adopting such a clearly one-sided point of view—the text unambiguously invites the reader to identify with the knight rather than the shepherd-ess—the broadside version of "The Knight and the Shepherd's Daughter" simply does not invite the complexities of interpretation that the orally transmitted versions of the ballad do. Its final lines clearly and heartily celebrate the reconfirmation of the knight's social and financial dominance over the woman who has tricked him.

The more complex issues of authority and victimization in "The Wife of Bath's Tale" are much more evident, however, in the oral versions of the ballad, which were initially collected from individual singers in the late eighteenth and early nineteenth centuries (though the ballad remains in circulation even today). First of all, these versions make it much clearer that the sexual encounter that opens the narrative is not consensual. In the broadside version, the knight "has his will" of the lady in the fourth stanza, after three stanzas of mutual flirting. Of the eight oral versions published by Child that are not fragmentary, on the other hand, seven begin abruptly with what looks like a rape:

There was a shepherd's dochter
   Kept sheep upon yon hill,
And by cam a gay braw gentleman,

> And wad hae had his will.
> He took her by the milk-white hand,
> And laid her on the ground,
> And whan he got his will o her
> He lift her up again.
>
> (Child 110B)

The eighth version presents the rape in an even more alarming way, offering no fewer than thirteen stanzas in which the knight propositions the young woman only to have her rebuff him at every turn. After she refuses his offer of ships, mills, cows, steeds, and gold in return for her maidenhead, he takes her by force:

> He caught her by the milk-white hand,
> And by the grass-green sleeve,
> And there has taken his will of her,
> Wholly without her leave.
>
> (Child 110E)

That this rape, which does not exist in any other version of the Loathly Lady tale analogues except "The Wife of Bath's Tale," should be so clearly emphasized in the traditional versions of the ballad implies that singers found this element of the narrative important. Most traditional British ballads do seem to recognize a cultural system of male hegemony; they often depict female characters as victims of situations that they cannot control. However, many of these ballads also demonstrate ways of circumventing that lack of power; they show women taking control in whatever circumscribed ways they can.

This is what happens in "The Knight and the Shepherd's Daughter." The ballad conflates Chaucer's rape victim, a nameless and silent figure who barely figures into Chaucer's text, with the powerful Loathly Lady who intercedes to both punish and educate the knight to create one powerless/powerful character. In "The Wife of Bath's Tale," the knight's punishment is twofold: first he must carry out the errand that is his official sentence, and then he must marry the seeming hag who helps him carry out that sentence. His education, of course, comes in the form of the pillow lecture on "gentillesse." In the ballad, the knight's punishment is similar: he must marry a woman who appears to be an undesirable (lowborn) mate. It is, however, the young victim herself who forces these consequences. She learns his name (even in the versions in which he tries to mislead her) and follows him to court, where she officially charges him with taking her virginity. Intriguingly, it is specifically the woman's powerlessness at the narrative's beginning that affords her authority later. Her initial victimization leads to her later position of dominance over the knight as she insists on the marriage that the king or queen has imposed. From her apparent lack of power comes sovereignty, an idea that may well have appealed to women leading lives that often may have been circumscribed by their own genders.

Even more fascinating is the fact that the oral versions of the ballad all show that the young woman relishes the knight's predicament, and she does all that she can to heighten his discomfort and shame. As the loathly hag in "The Wife of Bath's Tale" subjects the knight to the pillow lecture, the ballad's maiden increases the "punishment" element of the ballad by exaggerating her supposed common traits specifically to horrify the knight. Every one of the complete oral versions contains at least two and as many as ten stanzas in which the maiden mentions her preference for rough clothing, coarse bedding, or humble food. In many versions, for example, the couple passes a thicket of nettles either right before or after the marriage, and the maiden pretends to reminisce about how her mother loved to eat the coarse plant:

> She wad boil ye weill, and butter ye weill,
>   And sup till she war fu,
> And lay her head upon her dish-doup,
>   And sleep like onie sow.
>   (Child 110C)

This evidence of his new wife's coarse nature causes the knight to despair of what is happening to him, and each of these complaints is met with a stern rebuke. In the version of the ballad quoted above, for example, the knight snaps, "Hold your tongue, ye beggar's brat, / My heart will brak in three." The maiden replies, "And sae did mine on yon bonnie hillside, / Whan ye wadna lat me be." In other versions, the woman more directly reminds the knight that he is to blame for his own unhappiness, telling him, "you might hae ridden on your ways, / And hae let me alane" (Child 110B). These lines, in fact, become a refrain of sorts in several versions, as the maiden repeatedly chastises the knight.

The extent to which either the knight in "The Wife of Bath's Tale" or the ballad is actually educated is debatable. Some scholars, such as Kathryn McKinley and Susan Crane, put great stock in the ultimate transformation of Chaucer's knight. Crane argues, for example, that only "by accepting that the knight has listened to his wife and been changed by her words can we explain the difference between 'My love? ... nay, my dampnacioun' and 'my lady and my love, and wyf so deere, / I put me in youre wise governance' [III 1067, 1230–31]."[19] It is equally possible, however, that the knight is simply saying what he knows the Loathly Lady wants to hear. In "The Knight and the Shepherd's Daughter," the knight's transformation is equally ambiguous. In almost all versions, including the printed broadside, the knight laments the drunkenness that contributed to his raping the maiden:

> O an I had drank the wan water
>   Whan I did drink the wine,
>   That eer a shepherd's dochter
>   Should hae been a love o min!
>   (Child 110B)

This remorse is not quite the moral transformation that is arguably in evidence in "The Wife of Bath's Tale," since the knight seems primarily upset by the cause (drunkenness) and the consequences of his behavior rather than the behavior itself. As a result of the young woman's words and actions, he nonetheless regrets what he has done and envisions the alternative course he might have taken.

As in Chaucer's tale, however, the revelation of the woman's true status at the ballad's ending appears to contradict the message embedded in the tale itself. While the bulk of the ballad narrative is devoted to the knight's punishment, as he is essentially under the control of his own victim, the ending reveals an ultimate reward for his crime: he now has a wife who is even richer and higher born than he. The orally transmitted versions of the ballad do not, however, seem to celebrate this fact so unreservedly as does the broadside. The broadside's triumphant declaration that "[h]e had both purse and person too / And all at his command" does not appear in a single one of these oral versions. Most oral versions end simply with the revelation itself (which comes on the heels of the reminder that he might have let her alone):

> But yet I think a fitter match
>   Could scarcely gang thegither
>   Than the King of France's auld dochter
>   And the Queen of Scotland's brither.
>   (Child 110B)

Of the nine complete (or nearly so) versions in Child's collection, four end abruptly with this revelation. Two other versions add a stanza depicting the knight's response to this news, both of which imply that the knight had long wanted to marry this very woman. This modification changes the tenor of the tale slightly, lending some element of credibility to the claim that the match is a "fitting" one. In four versions, however, the maiden herself never reveals her true identity; the knight only learns of it accidentally through an old man or overheard conversation. In one version, the woman is actually furious that her true station has been revealed. She curses the blind man who let the cat out of the bag, telling him that she'd planned to keep the knight in the dark for at least seven years:

> Wae but worth you, Billy-Blin,
>   An ill death may ye die!
> My bed-fellow he'd been for seven years
>   Or he'd kend sae muckle frae me.
>   (Child 110F)

The woman's motivation for withholding the truth from the knight for so long is not spelled out, of course. Her desire to do so, however, heightens the importance of the errant knight's "punishment." Since keeping her wealth and status secret would have required that she, as well as the knight, would have to live as if she were a peasant, this version of the ballad implies that the woman's position of authority over the knight is more desirable to her than her true social and economic status, which seem to offer considerably less "sovereignty" than her temporary position as a victimized woman claiming the retribution awarded her. This version of the ballad also has further implications for the other versions of the ballad in which the woman's true identity is revealed by someone else, since it clearly acknowledges that the woman might well be displeased by the revelation.

Of course, the ending of most versions of "The Knight and the Shepherd's Daughter" is meant to be a happy one, leaving the knight with the same satisfying reward for his original crime that "The Wife of Bath's Tale" does. Negotiating the apparent contradictions within each text is a difficult, and perhaps impossible, task. The fact that the ballad does exist in these different versions, however, suggests that women singers may well have recognized the same contradictions that modern literary critics do. The emphasis in all of the oral versions on punishing and chastising the knight, together with the fact that half of the orally transmitted versions do not depict the young woman choosing to reveal her own identity, implies that some singers (and audiences) might not have been convinced that the ballad's heroine would have been thrilled with the final union, but rather considered it the price of her time in power. The differences between the oral and broadside texts further suggest that male and female singers, authors, and audiences might have considered the basic tale quite differently. Ultimately, both "The Knight and the Shepherd's Daughter" and "The Wife of Bath's Tale" reflect dual sensibilities, offering narratives of male subjugation to female authority while seeming to reinforce a system of cultural male hegemony. Regardless of the stories' endings, however, the bulk of each text focuses on the punishment of men who abuse the power afforded them by their class and sex. This focus may well explain the ballad's appeal to generations of women singers, just as it explains the relish with which the Wife of Bath tells her tale.

NOTES

1. The early ballad collector William Motherwell first remarked on the similarities between "The Knight and the Shepherd's Daughter" and "The Marriage of Sir Gawain" in his *Minstrelsy* (p. 378). In his exhaustive ballad compilation, *The English and Scottish Popular Ballads*, Child repeats Motherwell's observation, comparing the plots of his collected versions of "The Knight and the Shepherd's Daughter" (vol. 2, ballad 110) with "The Wife of Bath's Tale," "The Wedding of Sir Gawain and Dame Ragnelle," Gower's "Tale of Florent," and "The Marriage of Sir Gawain." Maynadier has given the closest look at the relationship between these texts in "*The Wife of Bath's Tale.*" Maynadier's discussion of the ballad is primarily devoted to the consideration of a Scandinavian ballad called "Ebbe Galt" as a possible historical source (pp. 111–18).

2. For instance, "The Marriage of Sir Gawain," which is a derivative of the earlier "The Wedding of Sir Gawain and Dame Ragnelle" (ca. 1500), is contemporary with the earliest extant version of "The Knight and the Shepherd's Daughter." Both date from the seventeenth century.

3. The three closest analogues, "The Tale of Florent," "The Wedding of Sir Gawain and Dame Ragnelle," and "The Marriage of Sir Gawain," all offer male protagonists who must find the answer to what a woman desires. All find Loathly Ladies who give them the answer in exchange for marriage and see the woman become beautiful. All are offered the choice of a wife who is ugly by day and lovely by night, or vice versa, and leave the choice up to their wives, to be rewarded with a permanently beautiful wife. These protagonists, however, are clear heroes. They are not punished as is the Wife of Bath's knight. Florent is simply unlucky, having been

captured by enemies who are looking for a legitimate reason to execute him. The protagonist is even more unambiguously heroic in both "The Marriage of Sir Gawain" and "The Wedding of Sir Gawain and Dame Ragnelle." In both narratives, Gawain actually offers himself in place of King Arthur, who was the one given the task in the first place when he comes across an angry knight after killing a deer.

4. Lines 1255–56, 1258; quotations from "The Wife of Bath's Tale" are from Benson, *Riverside Chaucer*.

5. Lee, "Exploitation," p. 17.

6. Dickson, "Deflection," p. 89. See McKinley, "Silenced Knight," pp. 359–73, for a more complete summing-up of arguments in this vein.

7. See Ellen M. Caldwell's essay in the present volume, "Brains or Beauty," p. 236.

8. Of course, ballads have not existed in a completely nonliterate world in Great Britain for several hundred years. David Buchan and, to a lesser extent, David Fowler (see Fowler, *A Literary History*) have written extensively on the complicated nature of ballad transmission in the semiliterate Scotland of the eighteenth and nineteenth centuries. Ballads might exist solely as oral texts in a nonliterate segment of the population (Buchan hypothesizes that women maintained a purely oral tradition longer than men did because women were more poorly educated), ballads might be written down and then re-enter the oral tradition as oral texts, and ballads might be learned as oral texts by literate singers. Studies of earlier singers (see, for example, Buchan, Brown, and McCarthy) as well as the recording archives of the University of Edinburgh's School of Scottish Studies indicate that the majority of singers recorded from the late eighteenth through the twentieth century learned most of their repertoires orally, though many were actually literate.

9. I am indebted to Toelken for this analogy, which he uses in "Context and Meaning," p. 32.

10. We see evidence of this not only in the tremendous variation that exists between different versions of the same ballad but also in the repertoires of individual singers, who might sing a ballad differently on different occasions.

11. Though men have been until recently the primary collectors of ballads, their sources have been largely women. For example, the oldest and most famous recorded repertoire of one singer is that of Anna Gordon Brown (1747–1810), commonly known as "Mrs. Brown." The daughter of Thomas Gordon, a professor at King's College, Aberdeen, Mrs. Brown was herself educated (or at least literate) and learned most of her ballads at an early age. All of her sources were women: her mother, a maidservant, and, primarily, her maternal aunt, Anne Forbes (Mrs. Farquherson). Mrs. Farquherson also had female sources: "the nurses and old women ... in that neighborhood" (letter from Thomas Gordon to Alexander Fraser Tytler, qtd. in Buchan, *Ballad*, p. 63). Buchan lists several other sources for Scottish ballads, most a little later than Mrs. Brown but all women: Margaret Paterson (Widow Michael), Mrs. Amelia Harris, who learned her ballads from "an old nurse Jannie Scott," Mary Barr, and Mrs. Gibb (pp. 66–67). There were male sources from this period as well, but Buchan claims

"certainly women outnumber men as recorded sources in the transitional period between general orality and general literacy" (p. 76). Also see Brown, "Old Singing Women," for a more recent synthesis of these early women singers.

12. Stewart, "Wishful Willful Wily Women, " p. 55.

13. Dugaw, "Popular Marketing of Old Ballads," p. 144.

14. Buchan, *Ballad*, p. 82.

15. These interpretive "spaces" within ballad narratives would, of course, have allowed men to find various alternative meanings as well.

16. See Würzbach, *Rise*, pp. 13–23, for a discussion of the business of ballad printing and selling.

17. Studies have estimated that the rates of female illiteracy in England were at least as high as 90 percent in the seventeenth century; even a century later the rates (in Scotland) are nearly this high for women of the servant, laboring, and farming classes. Eighty-eight percent of female servants in lowland Scotland were illiterate, as were 90 percent of the wives, daughters, and widows of laborers, and 86 percent of the wives, daughters, and widows of tenant farmers (Houston, *Scottish Literacy*, p. 57).

18. At least eight extant editions of the broadside version of this ballad exist today, printed in the late seventeenth and early eighteenth centuries; it had been licensed as a broadside in 1624 and 1656. Child offers eleven versions that were originally collected from oral sources, most from the late eighteenth and early nineteenth centuries. Three of these are fragments.

19. Crane, *Gender and Romance*, p. 37. Also see McKinley, "Silenced Knight," pp. 359–73.

Works Cited

Benson, Larry D., gen. ed. *The Riverside Chaucer*. 3rd ed. Boston: Houghton Mifflin, 1987.

Brown, Mary Ellen. "Old Singing Women and the Canons of Scottish Balladry and Song." In *A History of Scottish Women's Writing*, ed. Douglas Gifford and Dorothy McMillan, pp. 44–57. Edinburgh: Edinburgh University Press, 1997.

Buchan, David. *The Ballad and the Folk*. London: Routledge and Kegan Paul, 1972.

Child, Francis James, ed. *The English and Scottish Popular Ballads*. 5 vols. Boston: Houghton Mifflin, 1882–1898.

Crane, Susan. *Gender and Romance in Chaucer's Canterbury Tales*. Princeton: Princeton University Press, 1994.

Dickson, Lynne. "Deflection in the Mirror: Feminine Discourse in the 'Wife of Bath's Prologue and Tale.'" SAC 15 (1993), 61–90.

Dugaw, Dianne. "The Popular Marketing of 'Old Ballads': The Ballad Revival and Eighteenth-Century Antiquarianism Reconsidered." *Eighteenth-Century Studies* 21 (1987), 71–90.

Fowler, David C. *A Literary History of the Popular Ballad*. Durham: Duke University Press, 1968.

Houston, R. A. *Scottish Literacy and the Scottish Identity*. Cambridge: Cambridge University Press, 1985.

Lee, Brian S. "Exploitation and Excommunication in 'The Wife of Bath's Tale.'" *PQ* 74 (Winter 1995), 17–35.

Maynadier, G. H. *"The Wife of Bath's Tale": Its Sources and Analogues*. London: Nutt, 1901.

McCarthy, William Bernard. *The Ballad Matrix: Personality, Milieu, and the Oral Tradition*. Bloomington: Indiana University Press, 1990.

McKinley, Kathryn L. "The Silenced Knight: Questions of Power and Reciprocity in 'The Wife of Bath's Tale.'" *CR* 4 (1996), 359–78.

Motherwell, William. *Minstrelsy, Ancient and Modern, With an Historical Introduction and Notes*. Glasgow: J. Wylie, 1827.

Stewart, Polly. "Wishful Willful Wily Women: Lessons for Female Success in the Child Ballads." In *Feminist Messages: Coding in Women's Folk Culture*, ed. Joann Newlon Radner, pp. 54–73. Urbana: University of Illinois Press, 1993.

Toelken, Barre. "Context and Meaning in the Anglo-American Ballad." In *The Ballad and the Scholars*, ed. D. K. Wilgus, pp. 29–52. Los Angeles: Clark Memorial Library, 1986.

Würzbach, Natascha. *The Rise of the English Street Ballad 1550–1650*. Trans. Gayna Walls. Cambridge: Cambridge University Press, 1990.

Why Dame Ragnell Had to Die
Feminine Usurpation of Masculine Authority in "The Wedding of Sir Gawain and Dame Ragnell"

Mary Leech

Dame Ragnell is a unique character within the Loathly Lady tales. Unlike other Loathly Ladies who are transformed into beautiful women, such as the ugly woman in "The Wife of Bath's Tale," the hag of "The Tale of Florent," or the loathly bride of "The Marriage of Sir Gawain," Dame Ragnell, the Loathly Lady from "The Wedding of Sir Gawain and Dame Ragnell," continues to exert unladylike power once she becomes beautiful until she dies and is, in a sense, transformed again through death. There are several elements in the Dame Ragnell story that do not appear in other Loathly Lady tales. Besides the brief continuation of her story after her transformation and the description of her death, Dame Ragnell is the only Loathly Lady who is named; she is also the only Loathly Lady whose physicality is related in lengthy and graphic detail, along with her voracious appetite and appalling table manners.

Gawain as well is unusual in this story. Unlike the other knights in the Loathly Lady tales, Gawain has no obvious flaw. Gawain never acts un-chivalrously; he is never discourteous to anyone, not even the hideous Dame Ragnell; he never argues with Arthur, nor does he ever sway from his duty to his king. Gawain searches for answers to Arthur's problems just as willingly as he accepts the solution of having to marry Dame Ragnell. The great contrast between the beastlike Dame Ragnell and the perfect chivalrous knight in Gawain points to two seemingly contradictory natures forced together within a community that must accept them both as part of their social identity. Even when the Loathly Lady transforms into a beautiful woman, the contrast in natures remains. Only when the disruptive facet of feminine authority is stripped of its agency is the community once again at ease with itself.

The supposed danger that this "other" facet represents to the established, idealized social order is not necessarily a defined defect that can be overcome. Through theories of social order and disorder, particularly in the works of literary theorist Mikhail Bahktin and anthropologist Mary Douglas, I will explore the contradiction in the ideal world of Arthur that the extended ending of "The Wedding of Sir Gawain and Dame Ragnell" may represent and will demonstrate how this ending may be understood as a commentary on the tenuous nature of civilized manners and authority.

With the detailed portrayal of her "mouthe fulle wide and foulle y-grown," and her "yallowe teethe" that are "as boris tuskes" and "hing overe her lippes,"[1] Dame Ragnell presents the gaping orifices described by Bahktin in his work on the grotesque. Bahktin refers to grotesque bodies as bodies "in the act of becoming" which reflect part of "a cosmic hierarchy."[2] The misshapen and sagging body of the Bahktinian grotesque displays what is usually hidden in the body—its interior—and in so doing challenges the boundaries of the body and the society from which that body emerges. The classical body is contained, confined and hidden; the grotesque body defiantly revealed, and revealing.

Bahktin's grotesque challenges the society that creates it. By presenting those parts of the body that are normally enclosed, the grotesque body forces a culture to observe images (and the ideas those images represent) that are usually unseen. As Bahktin states, "the grotesque ignores the impenetrable surface that closes and limits the body as a separate and completed phenomenon. The grotesque image displays not only the outward but also the inner features of the body.... The outward and inward features are often merged into one."[3] The grotesque body becomes its own entity, one that is both inward and outward, life-giving and life-taking, cosmic and earthbound. It eliminates the differentiation between what is acceptable to a particular culture and what is not.[4] The "act of becoming" and the revelatory nature of the grotesque body point to the uncontrolled or the feared aspects of the world outside the societal order. Because of this fear of the unknown, these liminal grotesque figures inspire distrust and unease at what may lie beyond regulated space, particularly if such characters represent aspects of the culture that it would rather not be forced to acknowledge.[5]

In most cases, however, particularly in the similar stories of "The Wedding of Sir Gawain and Dame Ragnell," "The Marriage of Sir Gawain," "The Wife of Bath's Tale," and "The Tale of Florent," the Loathly Lady works to help the knight.[6] Though she has ulterior motives, the motives are not to destroy or injure the knight, but more often to return herself to her normally beautiful (and therefore closed and nonthreatening) body. Still, the existence of figures that draw attention to the shadowy places of a culture's values and morals is initially disturbing. The reinforcement of the social values at the end of the tales restores some comfort to a culture that has been confronted with its deepest fears and shown that there is a potential threat to social order.

Dame Ragnell's face, body, and manners, by far the most vivid in all the Loathly Lady tales, materialize the Bahktinian threat. While Chaucer and Gower both describe their Loathly Ladies in general terms,[7] Dame Ragnell's physical ugliness is given in great detail.[8] Even in "The Marriage of Sir Gawain," the description of the hag is not nearly as detailed as the description of Dame Ragnell.[9] With her "boris tuskes" and "pappis" that hang like "an hors lode," the beastlike appearance of this woman harkens back to female monsters of mythological literature, creatures like the dog-monster Scylla or the serpentine Medusa, monsters that threatened to annihilate the civilized nature of men. Manuel Aguirre compares such disruptive women to Circe,[10] who is "forever welcoming new men into her palace only to turn them into beasts."[11] During the Middle Ages, the metaphoric dynamics of mythology are remodeled into views that substantiate prevalent notions of feminine inferiority. With what Aguirre calls the concept of "Sovereignty of Reason,"[12] the patriarchal values of the Middle Ages are reinforced, so that "woman's 'proper' role more and more becomes that of submissive lover, faithful wife, unassuming servant. And if she does not comply with this injunction, she will be typecast as the shrewish, malevolent woman whose purpose seems to be to wreak havoc in an otherwise well-ordered society."[13] Dame Ragnell's appearance at court overrides concerted social outrage, horror, and failed attempts to curb her will. Although she is greeted with sighs and curses, she succeeds in her orchestrated public display of herself, and she attains clear authority within the masculine culture of King Arthur's court.

The Loathly Lady is not just ugly; she is deformed. Since she cannot be a viable commodity for marriage, she is not marketable. Because she is disgusting, she is not subject to the same regulatory standards as beautiful women. The Loathly Lady is therefore accorded a certain amount of freedom not otherwise permitted to a woman. This usurped authority is considered at least as loathsome and obscene as the lady herself. The Loathly Lady seeks reintegration to the very society that she disrupts: her influence, which comes from her transformed state and not her original state, is normally limited once again when she returns to her beautiful form.[14]

The surest method of controlling feminine agency and sexuality in the Middle Ages was through marriage, particularly within the context of a romance. Normally, after a woman marries in a romance, her identity is all but erased.[15] She is taken out of the public realm and relegated to a private sphere within the home.[16] Georges Duby explains this separation of space in terms of the desire for social control through marriage: "[T]he institution of marriage, by its very position and by the role in which it assumes, enclosed in a rigid framework of rituals and prohibitions—rituals because it involves publishing, that is, making public, and thereby socializing and legalizing a private act, and prohibitions because it involves setting boundaries between the norm and the marginal, the licit and the illicit, the pure and the unpure."[17] Women in the home were safe, private, and conventionalized. Women outside this sphere, especially those who did not have the potential or the desire to be normalized, presented a tangible threat as they cross the boundary between "the licit and the illicit," and in doing so challenge the rigors of such a social order.

Rigid social order, Mary Douglas points out, especially in societies that hold to strong gender distinctions and restrictions on sexual behavior, often leads to strident beliefs concerning what is sexually dirty or polluted: "Another kind of sex pollution arises from the desire to keep straight the internal lines of the social system.... A third type may arise from the conflict in the aims which can be proposed in the same culture."[18] If the body of the Loathly Lady, particularly the appallingly deformed body of Dame Ragnell, is outside of controlled sexual politics, then its very existence menaces not just sexuality controlled through marriage but the community that seeks to exert such control.[19] Yet the unusual image of Dame Ragnell may indicate a flaw (or flaws) within the Arthurian court unrelated to her intrusion.

Deformed or hideous figures may serve a protective function in a society, but these figures are still placed outside the borders of a culture and are viewed as part of the margins they guard against. In an article relating Celtic mythology and Arthurian lore, Lorraine Kochanske Stock compares the Loathly Lady to representations of Celtic Sheela-na-gigs. These figures, found primarily on religious and civic structures, emphasize femininity through exaggerated portrayals of female genitalia. Though Stock draws her comparison between the Sheela figures and Morgan le Fay of *Sir Gawain and the Green Knight*, much of what she describes relates to Dame Ragnell as well. The dominant physical features of the Sheela-na-gig include "disfigured facial features; pulled up shoulders; small, flat, or lopsided breasts; long arms and prominent hands; and diminutive, foreshortened legs emerging from an oversized buttocks."[20] Stock describes clawlike hands that form "spaces suggesting the toothy 'mouth' of the *vagina dentata*, which mirrors the toothy grin or grimace of her hideous face."[21] The emphasis on Dame Ragnell's yellow teeth and boarlike tusks relate to this type of threatening sexual imagery, yet a disruptive sexual nature is associated with all women as fallen daughters of Eve. The sexuality of Dame Ragnell, and of Loathly Ladies in general, is no more or less disturbing than her presence in civilized society. The transgressive act of the Loathly Lady, while sexual in part, transcends sex and points instead towards social functions of gendered roles.

Stock further claims that the "apotropaic function of the Sheela—guarding castles or towns; warding off threats by brazen vulvic exhibition ... endowed these figures with a power parallel to and perhaps derived from, the force attributed to various Celtic goddess figures, foremost among which is the war goddess Morrigain."[22] Associated with Sheela figures, then, is a feminine incursion over a primarily masculine realm.[23] Despite the images of Sheelas being used for protection, they seem to have associations with a great and dangerous essence that is being directed outside of the castle or town, or that is being prevented from entering. These images, then, ostensibly used for protection, are threatening enough that they must remain outside the social boundaries.

Yet the Loathly Lady must be invited into the community from the outside because of a vital service she can give: the answer to the riddle that will save the knight's life. Despite the public horror at her, she is needed within the closed structure of the court to preserve the ideals of the society that are represented in the endangered knight. Again there is a contradiction presented within the goals of the society: to preserve the ideals of the culture, it must open itself up to something that it fears as contaminative of its central values.

In this case, the boundary crossing is initiated by the masculine, and not restricted to the feminine protagonist. In all the English Loathly Lady tales, a knight (or king) has been given a quest, the seemingly impossible task of discovering what women want. Each of the knights has crossed the moral boundaries of society.[24] To atone for this transgression, authority is taken away from the knight and put in the hands of another. If the knight and/or king is to regain that authority, he must solve the riddle or forfeit his life.[25] Even before the Loathly Lady arrives on the scene, the highest representative of the masculine world has been taken outside the safety of ordered society and faced with a lethal threat. The circumstances that permit the Loathly

Lady to gain her authority originate from a masculine breach of boundaries rather than a feminine intrusion into the ordered society.

The danger that these open and revealing women represent in these tales is situated away from the recognized social structure. Dame Ragnell and the ugly old women of "The Wife of Bath's Tale," "The Marriage of Sir Gawain," and "The Tale of Florent" are all found in the woods,[26] a traditionally marginal place with unknown forces at work. As Douglas notes, "To have been in the margins is to have been in contact with danger, to have been at a source of power."[27] The margins are not governable; there is no control there, no comforting order. Anything or anyone who lives outside the community in the liminal spaces has survived the unknown, controlled the uncontrollable, and faced what is feared. In this experience of knowing what should not be known comes power.[28] In the case of the Loathly Lady, that power is in knowing the answer to the riddle that saves the knight's life.[29]

The perversion of the male/female relationship represented by the Loathly Lady mirrors other challenges to social order as well, including class structure. In both "The Wife of Bath's Tale" and "Florent," the Loathly Lady is seen as noble only after she becomes beautiful. Part of the tradition of the Loathly Lady holds that she is common.[30] The Loathly Lady in "The Wife of Bath's Tale" is "low-bred." Her clothes and wedding garments are not mentioned. The hag in "Florent" is "in ragges" and "tortore" (lines 1721–22). At the wedding, her rags are taken off, and "She hadde bath, sche hadde reste, / And was arraied to the beste" (lines 1747–48). However, "with no craft of combes brode / Thei myhte hire hore lockes schode" (lines 1749–50). Though she has the clothes of a noble woman and has washed away some of the common dirt on her, the tale emphasizes that while she is loathly, her lower status remains, as seen in the inability to comb or tame her hair. The Loathly Lady in "The Marriage of Sir Gawain" is clad "in red scarlet," rather than the tattered rags of other Loathly Ladies. No definitive identification of her status is given, but she chastises Arthur for his lack of courtesy in greeting her. While these characteristics may not confirm a noble status, they do demonstrate that she expects to be treated like a lady despite the fact that Arthur does not see her as noble and barely sees her as human.

In contrast to her hideous appearance, Dame Ragnell "sat on a palfray was gay begon, / With gold beset and many a precious stone" (lines 246–47). At her wedding, "She was arrayd in the riches maner, / More fresher than Dame Gaynour; / Her arrayment was worthe three thousand mark" (lines 590–93): she is not only dressed well, but her clothes are better than Guinevere's. Just as Dame Ragnell's foulness is described in more detail than in any other story, so her clothes are described as more costly than in any other tale. Even in the woods she has a richly arrayed horse (and presumably she is as well dressed as the horse), indicating a noble station. Clothing was important sign of social rank, used to signal, maintain, control, and transform social identity[31] based on class distinction. From the first appearance of Dame Ragnell, she posits herself as noble and insists on the treatment and public display befitting a noblewoman. She even appropriates the place of the feminine pinnacle of the male society: the queen.

In the scenes before her marriage, the disruptive force of Dame Ragnell becomes more and more apparent. Dame Ragnell arrives in fine clothes and with an entourage, which includes Arthur. Upon entering, she passes him, which "liked the king fulle ille" (line 520). Though Arthur does not like her presumption, Dame Ragnell, by passing Arthur, refuses to remain inconspicuous. At no point is Dame Ragnell subject to the will of the court: she rides in as she wishes, she is married when and where she wishes, she marries whom she wishes, she is dressed as she wishes, and she eats where and how she wishes. Her will prevails at all times because of the debt of honor Arthur owes her. She is a "foule unswete," a form of social pollution, but to refuse her entry to the court would deny the very precepts of chivalry that define the court of Arthur.

Forms of social pollution, according to Douglas, can be divided into categories: threats from outside the social system, threats from the inside, threats from the margins, and, lastly, "internal contradiction, when some of the basic postulates are denied by other basic postulates, so that at certain points the system seems to be at war with itself."[32] Dame Ragnell, whose grotesqueness is the most vividly described, is also the best dressed, both in the woods and at court. She is not a typical incursive figure, one attempting to bring lower class pollution into the noble community, nor is she pollution from within the community as she comes from outside the social structure. Her knowledge, gained on the margins of society, enables her to permanently tie herself to the model of chivalric society: Gawain. Dame Ragnell's ability to enter Arthurian society presents a myriad of contradictions and reveals a social system at odds with itself.

Even before she becomes beautiful, Dame Ragnell has begun to transform herself into something socially acceptable.[33] Once she enters court she has adopted all the outer trappings of a noble, and the other nobles are forced to accept her in this role, no matter how repulsed they are by her. The courtiers recognize that she does not belong, but they have no power to reject her, demonstrating that the contradiction she represents is not within her but within the society that allows her performance to succeed as it does.

Unlike the other tales, this one emphasizes the public nature of Dame Ragnell's entrance to court. Duby's discussion about the public ritualizing of marriage as a method of socially legitimizing a private act is relevant here as well.[34] A private marriage early in the day will not place Dame Ragnell in the social position she desires. That this public display is necessary to break the curse inflicted on her by her stepmother makes the stepmother oddly complicitous in the usurpation of masculine culture. Feminine agency in performance, then, and not the masculine regulation of that performance, becomes a central part of the Dame Ragnell tale.[35]

Often the public display of a woman, particularly a beautiful woman, denotes control of her, a turning of the woman into an object of desire and pleasure.[36] Here, the roles of object and objectifier are reversed, as Dame Ragnell insists on being made an object of pleasure and desire, but her hideous appearance and appalling table manners would seem to defeat this purpose: everyone is horrified by her, yet they all must respond to her in the way she intends. The reaction to her is not as important as the fact that she controls her own public display by her very insistence on it. Rather than being controlled or diminished by her assumed role as an object, Dame Ragnell shows power by being able to place herself in the position of desired object when she clearly is not desirable in any way.

Later, once she is beautiful, she again fills the role of desired object when Arthur enters Gawain's and her bedroom: "She stood in her smock alle by that fire; / her here was to her knees as red as gold wire" (lines 742–43). As she supervised her own placement and performance at her wedding, Dame Ragnell controls her role as desired object by voluntarily placing herself in that part rather than being placed there by either Gawain or Arthur. In this way, she usurps the power of the objectifier and places it within the purview of the objectified, once again upsetting the normal balance of power. Social order has been disrupted, not just by her appalling physical appearance, but also by her manipulation of the power structures within the established social order, both before and after her transformation.

Yet this subversion begins before she enters the tale. From the beginning of the Dame Ragnell tale, the credibility of masculine authority is called into question. In many ways, Arthur acts in a manner that is not entirely kingly. First, he insists on hunting the deer alone. In other tales, hunting is an activity that indicated knightly fellowship. The Green Knight of *Sir Gawain and the Green Knight* hunts each day with his men, and all participate in the hunt together. The Green Knight only goes after the boar alone when it becomes clear the boar will hurt or even kill his men if he does not take action. Even so, the men ride with him as they chase the boar and witness his killing of it. In *Erec and Enide,* one of the activities Erec forgoes to be with his new wife is hunting, which again is presented as a homosocial group activity. Gawain himself is chastised after his marriage to Dame Ragnell for not hunting or jousting with the other knights. Hunting was, as John Cummins explains, a sport of noble pageantry: "In the eyes of the late Middle Ages kings and noblemen are not as other men are; the structure of society which sets them apart is divinely ordained, and their superiority must be made clear by pomp, pageant, ceremony, procession, and other physical glories."[37] The hunt was part of this noble pageantry, as the "dead boar or deer was often brought home with fanfares and triumph."[38] The hunt clearly had social functions of establishing the higher station of the nobility, establishing camaraderie among knights and honing skills necessary for combat.

In the Dame Ragnell tale, though, Arthur appears to want to hunt this spectacular animal alone in order to show his prowess: "Hold you stille, every man, / And I wille go myself, if I can / With crafte of stalking" (lines 28–30). He forgoes the unity of the hunt and attempts to enter combat on his own to satisfy his desire to test his individual "crafte." His subsequent humiliation at being taken prisoner by Sir Gromer warns against the foolishness of abandoning one's comrades while outside of the societal order. Arthur's performance here as king is less convincing than Dame Ragnell's later performance as an honored member of the court, despite his place and status within proper court society.

When he meets Sir Gromer, Gromer appears to have a legitimate grievance with Arthur, as he says to Arthur: "Thou hast gevin my landes in certain / With great wrong unto Sir Gawen" (lines 58–59). Arthur never contests this charge, nor does the poem ever indicate that Sir Gromer's accusation is unfounded. Instead, Arthur is able to put off Gromer by saying "To slee me here honour getist thou no delle" (line 65). He does not challenge Gromer to fair combat[39] or defend himself verbally. His tactic is to manipulate Gromer by appealing to his honor.[40] That Gromer capitulates to Arthur's speech about honor may also imply that Gromer is indeed an honorable knight who has been wronged somehow, or at least feels he has been wronged, and that the alleged wrong has not been addressed.[41] Throughout this scene, Arthur does not act with any kingly authority or with any of the qualities one might expect in an honorable and noble knight.

The question of honor is pertinent to the Loathly Lady tales. In "The Wife of Bath's Tale," the knight has raped a maiden and therefore must make amends. The knight who once imposed his will on an unwilling maiden is forced to relinquish control to his wife and be a better man for it. In "The Tale of Florent," Florent must learn humility after killing the son of a military captain. After he hands decision-making over to his wife, he is absolved of the sin of pride by a priest. In both of these tales,[42] the riddle has a clear relationship to a moral transgression, and the choice given to the knight by the Loathly Lady demonstrates that each knight has developed the virtues he lacked at the beginning of the story.

In "The Wedding of Sir Gawain and Dame Ragnell," Gawain has not acted immorally at any time. Arthur is the one who was given the riddle, so he is the one who supposedly committed the moral transgression, yet Gawain is the one who surrenders authority to his wife. Of course Arthur cannot marry the Loathly Lady because of Guinevere, but normally a king would take moral responsibility for a subject, not the other way around. Here Gawain appears to take on whatever moral responsibility comes with the riddle. Because the lesson of the riddle is not apparent, there is no clear triumph in the surrender of sovereignty, although Gawain is rewarded for his loyalty to Arthur. There is no repentance demonstrated, nor is there any spiritual growth. The disruption and the lessons or warnings within the riddle may be more usefully explored through Dame Ragnell herself and not in the patriarchal traditions of morality and masculine virtue.

As a symbol,[43] the Loathly Lady would seem to represent a needed change within the social structure, as seen in "The Wife of Bath's Tale" when the Loathly Lady lectures the knight on what true nobility and wealth are, and in "The Tale of Florent" when Florent repents of his pride and learns humility.[44] Dame Ragnell, though, does not function in exactly the same way. While her presence challenges the accepted social structure, she also insists on acceptance by using conventions of the very culture that recoils from her. She is a figure of grotesque revelation and sexual perversion garbed in the outer trappings of a lady, one who is married in full ceremony at High Mass, who seeks to release her voracious sexual appetite within the bonds of matrimony. As a grotesque figure, Dame Ragnell challenges norms and reveals fears. With her body in a state of continual fluctuation and formation, she acts as a regenerative signifier of problems within the social structure that are also in a process of continual flux and reformation. There is no specific lesson to be learned because the faults are constantly in flux within the social structure itself.

The mutability of the danger Dame Ragnell represents is most clear after she transforms. When Gawain does not appear at court, Arthur becomes concerned, as he says, "I am fulle ferd of Sir Gawen, / Nowe lest the fende have him slain; / Nowe wold I fain preve" (lines 725–27). After Arthur has seen the transformed Dame Ragnell, he again says "I wenid, Sir Gawen, she wold thee have miscaried; / Therefore in my hart I was sore agrevid; / But the contrary is here seen" (lines 754–56). Here, Arthur fears the usurpation of power she displayed at the wedding and at the feast. Gawain, as Arthur's champion and defender, represents the main source of masculine power at the court of Arthur, both physically and morally. Whether he fears that Dame Ragnell has devoured Gawain vaginally as she devoured food at the feast (her "boris tuskes" as the *vagina dentata*), or just exhausted him through excessive sex,[45] is not clear or important. Arthur's concern clearly shows that he believes she has the potential to control and even destroy Gawain, and in turn the very essence of Arthurian masculine power.

The sexual politics of marriage, especially medieval marriage, were arranged to benefit the male more than the female, and to address masculine fears about feminine sexuality.[46] Foucault, in *The Uses of Pleasure,* discusses the importance of the economic and political factors concerning sexual roles and sexual behavior within marriage. Monogamy for men had a different meaning than it did for women: "In the case of the woman, it was insofar as she was under the authority of her husband that this obligation was imposed on her. In the man's case, it was because he exercised authority and because he was expected to exhibit self-mastery in the use of this authority by limiting his sexual options. For the wife, having sexual relations only with her husband was a consequence of the fact that she was under his control. For the husband, having sexual relations only with his wife was the most elegant way of exercising his control."[47] Monogamous sexual activity within marriage, then, is supposed to be a sign that the man is in control of not only his wife, but the household as well. Duby's discussion on medieval marriage and sexual politics would indicate the same sort of concerns seen in the methods of governance over women both inside and outside of marriage.

Dame Ragnell's behavior and influence over Gawain indicate otherwise. Once they are alone, Dame Ragnell is the one who initiates sex by urging Gawain to show her "cortesy in bed." She is the one who directs every aspect of the marriage, from its inception to its consummation; there is no time that she is ever made to act against her will by any male figure in the story, not even by her husband or the king. Her monogamy, then, does not indicate Gawain's control over her so much as it demonstrates her power over him.

Ragnell's reformed beauty is even more threatening to patriarchal hierarchy than her breach of social codes. Gawain is more affected by his wife when she is beautiful than he ever is when she is ugly. Unlike the knights in "The Wife of Bath's Tale" and "The Tale of Florent," Gawain never complains about nor resists Dame Ragnell. He readily agrees to the marriage, saying he would "wed her and wed her again … Though she were as foulle as Belsabub" (lines 343, 354) even before he has seen the creature Arthur calls "the foulist lady / That evere I sawe sertenly" (lines 336–37). Gawain gives no reaction upon seeing Dame Ragnell for the first time, even when everyone else at court is horrified by her entrance and appearance. In the bedroom, when she asks him for a kiss, he responds by saying "I wolle do more / Then for to kisse, and God before!" (lines 638–39). Gawain acts out of loyalty to Arthur, and therefore as a loyal knight he is bound by honor to fulfill his word. Nevertheless, there is no reaction from him until Dame Ragnell becomes beautiful, when he asks her, "whate are ye?"[48] Though he quickly rejoices at his good fortune, he seems more alarmed at the danger of a beautiful woman than an ugly one. While Dame Ragnell was ugly, she was not a sexual creature to Gawain: he married her out of obligation and was about to consummate the marriage out of the same obligation to his king. The dynamic here was masculine and within the social performance of male hierarchy. Once Dame Ragnell transforms, she becomes a sexual temptress, a daughter of Eve that leads men away from spiritual purity (seen as part of masculine nature). Gawain's quick capitulation to her temptation and his forsaking of masculine society reveals an inherent weakness in the male hierarchy of Arthur's court.

After she becomes beautiful, Dame Ragnell again takes control of the situation by giving Gawain the choice of whether to have her beautiful during the day and ugly by night, or ugly by day and beautiful by night. Gawain is in effect being offered control over Dame Ragnell's body. When Gawain gives the decision back to Dame Ragnell, he returns control of her body to her, and in doing this re-establishes the power she has wielded up to this point. With no moral transgression to correct, Gawain, by giving the decision to Dame Ragnell, hands over his sexual control and marital authority as well. Gawain's reluctance to leave his bed and go to his king demonstrates the depth of his wife's sexual power over him.

Dame Ragnell is made beautiful, as "She was recovered of that that she was defoiled" (line 710); the couple "made mirthe" until day, "And than wold rise that faire maye" (line 716). She explains that she was cursed by her stepmother,[49] who "defoiled" her:

And shold have bene oderwise understond,
Evin tille the best of Englond
Had wedded me verament
And also he shold geve me the sovereinté
Of alle his body and goodes, sicurly.

(lines 694–98)

When the work of her stepmother has been overcome, Dame Ragnell is made whole again, yet the stipulation attached to her return to wholeness (a closed, proper, submissive body) is for Gawain to surrender himself, in body and spirit, to the will of Dame Ragnell. Here, the breaking of the feminine curse by male sexuality (i.e., power) should signal Dame Ragnell's submission to the male hierarchy and the return to social stability. Instead, Dame Ragnell once again becomes a figure that follows the surface rules of the culture, but the contradiction in her appearance and behavior points to inconsistencies within these social expectations.

On the surface, she performs all the acts of a dutiful wife: she promises to never "wrathe thee" and to be always "obaisaunt"; her beauty wins the approval of the court and the queen; and she goes to all the feasts where she "bare away the bewtye," bringing honor to her husband as a wife should. While she does keep her husband in bed with her "bothe day and night," Dame Ragnell also does other things that are possibly far more dangerous than just weakening Gawain's performance as a knight. Her sphere of influence goes beyond Gawain, as she exerts power over her brother, Sir Gromer, and even Arthur, and this power does not disappear when she becomes beautiful.

Even after her marriage, Dame Ragnell performs the role of ideal courtly woman, yet in doing so she reshapes the masculine court of Arthur to conform to her specifications; in other words, as she has done before, Dame Ragnell places herself in the role she wants to perform. Arthur's formal presentation of Dame Ragnell in her socially acceptable form, the public acceptance of the marriage, and Dame Ragnell's own personal vows to be "obaisaunt," should take away her last remnants of independence. The culturally sanctioned role of a conventional woman and wife, however, is not the part Dame Ragnell chooses to play. Though "Gawen lovid that lady Dame Ragnell, / In alle his life he lovid none so welle" (lines 805–6), he takes this love too far: "As a coward he lay by her bothe day and night. / Nevere would he haunt justing arighte" (lines 809–10). Dame Ragnell's ability to control Gawain through excessive sex shows that the feminine ability to tempt is stronger than the masculine ability to control feminine agency.

As for her behavior towards Arthur, Dame Ragnell uses the obligations of chivalry to her advantage.[50] When Dame Ragnell makes the request to Arthur to "be good lord" to her brother, Sir Gromer, "She praid the king for his gentilnes" (line 811). Just as Arthur did with Gromer, Dame Ragnell uses the notion of knightly honor to coerce someone who presumably has power over her to her will. By prefacing her request with a reminder of his obligation to her as a chivalrous lord and knight (not to mention her saving of his life), Dame Ragnell ensures the answer she desires. Arthur responds "that shalle I nowe for your sake," thereby acknowledging his obligation to grant her request.

Dame Ragnell's request also places her brother under her control, though her ability to undermine his trap for Arthur already shows her mastery over him. The image that she presented from the start has not really altered. When ugly, she wore the clothes of a noble; as a beautiful woman, she retains the authority she had when she was ugly. She cannot be governed by any of the conventional methods of society, and so she must be transformed again in a way that allows the culture, or, more specifically, the masculine culture, to reclaim control over her. Dame Ragnell is the only Loathly Lady to die after she becomes beautiful. How, then, does Ragnell's death transform her into a malleable figure that no longer presents a challenge to any of the culture's masculine virtues or authority?

Part of the answer may be seen in the formation of Christian icons as a means of controlling beliefs of the Christian people. Peter Brown explains that icons could "be heightened by the capacity of the silent portrait of the dead to take an even heavier charge of urgency and idealization without answering back."[51] As the Church came to realize in its presentation of icons such as Mary, icons and ideals were much easier to control than living persons.

This same theory works with the ideal lady of romances as well, for if the lady (in the image of Mary) is ideally chaste, she is perfect only for so long as she is unattainable. Once she is attained, as Dame Ragnell eagerly is, the ideal is gone. In this case, even in an ideal form and married, Dame Ragnell still presents a threat to masculine purity, order, and identity. In her loathly state, though Arthur, Gawain, and the court of nobles must acknowledge her place among them, her actions at court distance her from the other nobles. She is seen as a repugnant creature. After her change, her power, her forceful nature, her ability to exert influence has not gone away, despite the fact that she now has the physical appearance of a lady and claims that she wants to behave like a good wife. If anything, her authority is more subversive, as she is able to control the men around her in a less obvious and more insidious way.

Once Dame Ragnell dies, however, she can be molded into what is necessary to reinforce the social structure and identity already established, rather than challenging it as she did while alive. Gawain is said to grieve for Ragnell for the rest of his life, since, "In her life she grevid him nevere; / Therfor as nevere woman to him lever" (lines 823–24).[52] Yet, not even ten lines earlier, he is called a coward because he stays in bed with her all day and ignores his hunting and jousting. As a dead wife, one who no longer keeps him from the company of the other knights, she becomes the perfect wife just as she had promised. Her status as an iconic figure is emphasized just a few lines later: "Gawen was wedded oft in his days; / But so welle he nevere lovid woman always, / As I have hard men sayn" (lines 832–34). Out of all the wives Gawain has after her, she becomes the best loved, the favorite, the penultimate ideal.

In death, she can be made compliant. Gawain idolizes her for the rest of his life, just as a Christian knight of romance was supposed to worship the unattainable lady. In this scenario, though, Gawain can reconfigure her in his memories. In life, her physical presence cannot be ignored or manipulated. Whether ugly or beautiful, she exerts influence over the men and events around her, which makes her dangerous in too many ways. As an icon, she is reduced to her orthodox exterior that can be resignified into a more acceptable role by those she once dominated. Her interior motives, power, and control are gone, and only the conventional outer shell remains.

Arthur as well is able to reclaim his authority. Dame Ragnell is no longer physically there to remind him of his debt to her, and he is able to reshape her in the same way Gawain does. Arthur publicly confirms her iconic status: "She was the fairest lady of alle Englond, / When she was on live, I understand; / So said Arthoure the king" (lines 826–28). When she was alive, it was the queen who validated her beauty, as Arthur could not honorably praise a living woman's beauty over his wife's. In death, she poses no threat to Arthur's loyalty to his wife, so he can praise her as he would praise any other iconic or ideal figure. Alive, she was a constant reminder of how she saved Arthur's life and the debt he owed her. In death, she becomes an almost saintly patron—one that can be praised and flattered, but cannot demand anything in return.

As a Loathly Lady tale, "The Wedding of Sir Gawain and Dame Ragnell" offers several twists to the normal signification of the shape-shifter. Dame Ragnell's purpose is not to reinforce knightly virtue or correct serious moral faults, but rather to point out the flaws within the masculine social identity itself. Like the Sheela door guardians, she must be placed outside again, where her threat and influence can no longer disrupt cultural values and may even work to reinforce them. Masculine authority is reaffirmed and the troublesome female grotesque is transmuted into an iconic ideal of patriarchal womanhood. For this final transformation, Dame Ragnell must die.

Notes

1. All quotations from "The Wedding of Sir Gawain and Dame Ragnell" are taken from Donald Sands's edition, *Middle English Verse Romances*.

2. See Bahktin, *Rabelais and His World*, pp. 316–19.

3. Bahktin, *Rabelais and His World*, p. 318.

4. Bahktin details the relationships within medieval carnival figures to laughter, hierarchy, and idealism in the introduction to *Rabelais and His World*, pp. 1–58. See particularly pp. 4–17.

5. The suspicion of liminal spaces and the fear of what may exist beyond the boundaries of social structure are discussed in detail by Mary Douglas in her work *Purity and Danger*. Marginal figures "are somehow left out in the patterning of society [and so] are placeless. They may be doing nothing morally wrong, but their status is indefinable." Douglas, *Purity and Danger*, p. 95.

6. Even a figure such as Morgan le Fay in *SGGK*, though she sets out to humiliate Guinevere, eventually ends up verifying the exemplary traits of Arthur's best knight, and therefore Arthur himself.

7. Chaucer states about the hag: "A fouler wight ther may no man devyse" ("WBT," line 999); Chaucer quotations are taken from Benson, *The Riverside Chaucer*. Gower describes his hag as "A lothly wommannysch figure, / That for to speke of fleisch and bon / So foul yit syh he nevere non" (lines 1530–33). Quotations of "The Tale of Florent" are taken from Peck's 1968 edition of the *Confessio Amantis*.

8. The descriptions of Loathly Ladies do not tend to dwell on physical details as much as the implications of social intrusion. G. H. Maynadier mentions that in the ballad "Kempy Kay," the "deformity of a woman as well as that of her lover, is given in nauseating detail; and this is almost all there is to the story" ("*Wife of Bath's Tale*," p. 143). Maynadier also claims that this ballad may be related to the Loathly Lady tales. For a full version of the ballad, see Child's *English and Scottish Popular Ballads*, ballad 33. For a fuller discussion of the parallels between the Loathly Lady motif in tales and ballads, see Mary Shaner's article, "A Jungian Approach to the Ballad 'King Henry,'" included in the present volume.

9. In this tale, the Loathly Lady is described as having an eye "there as shold have stood her mouth" (line 57) and another "was in her forhead fast" (line 59). Further, "Her nose was crooked and turnd outward, / Her mouth stood foule awry" (lines 61–62). Other than that, "A worse formed lady than shee was, / Never man saw with his eye" (lines 63–64), and later she is described as "misshapen." All quotations of "The Marriage of Sir Gawain" are taken from Thomas Hahn's *Sir Gawain*.

10. Circe is the sorceress in *The Odyssey* who turned Odysseus's men into swine.

11. Aguirre, "Roots of the Symbolic Role," p. 62.

12. Aguirre uses this term to refer to the reduction of the sovereignty of women in ancient and medieval literary traditions. In ancient Irish and Germanic mythology, women drew power and "sovereignty" from their representation of the power of earth, as seen in the process of life and death. In medieval literature, particularly with the image of the Loathly Lady, women are seen "as fickle, as variable, as subject to irrational moods and changes.... In so far as she is still credited with a certain power or sovereignty, she is rejected as evil, unreasonable, or silly." As the concept of "reason" gained strength over this notion of feminine variability, the "sovereignty of reason," associated with the more reasonable male, became the source of power and authority in literature ("Roots of the Symbolic Role," pp. 62–63).

13. Aguirre, "Roots of the Symbolic Role," p. 63.

14. Ellen Caldwell discusses the issue of female ugliness and its relationship to a limited role of power in her article, "Brains or Beauty," included in the present volume. Her argument that the Loathly Lady's hideousness allows her a temporary ingress to the world of masculine authority and negotiation dovetails nicely with my discussion of the threat posed by the Loathly Lady and of why Dame Ragnell presents a different type of threat than the Loathly Ladies of other tales.

15. This has been widely noted, though a quotation from Marina Warner seems appropriate here: "A woman might be the lord of her troubadour, but she remained the vassal of her husband" (*Alone*, p. 139).

16. Barbara Hanawalt writes of the conscious effort by medieval men to keep women in their appropriate place, stating that, "Since [medieval men] regarded women as by their very nature unruly, the best way to control them was to enclose them." Despite this attempt at control, "[f]emale challenges to male spatial domination occurred continually throughout the Middle Ages." See *Of Good and Ill Repute*, p. 83. Hanawalt also discusses how women in religious orders were considered particularly threatening, as they were often self-sufficient and not under any clear male authority.

17. Duby, *Love and Marriage*, pp. 3–4.

18. Douglas, *Purity and Danger*, p. 140.

19. See Duby's discussion on the relationship between marriage and religious and social order, *Love and Marriage*, p. 11.

20. Stock, "Hag of Castle Hautdesert," p. 123.

21. Stock, "Hag of Castle Hautdesert," p. 124.

22. Stock, "Hag of Castle Hautdesert," p. 129.

23. Morrigain is sometimes linked with the valkries of Norse mythology—female figures who chose who would die on the battlefield. This association is interesting in that the fate of warriors is placed outside the control of male order and given to a monstrous female figure. This monstrous female figure would seem to be associated with the fear of those parts of masculine culture that are beyond society's ability to regulate.

24. This crossing of boundaries is literal as well as metaphoric. Arthur, Florent, and the rapist-knight are all outside ordered society (either hunting, fighting, or traveling) when they commit or are accused of a crime. These accusations point to a metaphoric crossing of boundaries as well, resulting in the need for penance before they can fully rejoin the society and clarification of what it is meant to represent (order, law, civilization).

25. This is a fairly common motif, the so-called "neck riddle," in which a person has to answer a riddle or lose his (or her) life. The most famous neck riddle is probably that of the Sphinx, which Oedipus answered and was therefore given kingship.

26. The Loathly Lady of "The Marriage of Sir Gawain" is found "Betwixt an oke and a greene hollen" (lines 55–56), traditionally a place where magic was to be found. Perhaps this points to the Irish origins of the Loathly Lady that Maynadier discusses in his book on "The Wife of Bath's Tale."

27. Douglas, *Purity and Danger*, p. 97. Douglas's notion here is part of the Jungian structure of society in terms of reactions towards social boundaries and marginal figures, as well as of other theories of taboo in culture. See in particular Jung's *Man and His Symbols*; and Hutton Webster, *Taboo: A Sociological Study*, both interesting works on this topic.

28. This point is made particularly clear in "The Wedding of Sir Gawain and Dame Ragnell" in that Gromer and Dame Ragnell, both marginal figures found in the woods, share the knowledge/power of the riddle. Gromer, a disgruntled knight, uses his knowledge to gain mastery over his king. Dame Ragnell uses this same knowledge to gain mastery over both Arthur and Gawain, but also to usurp her brother's power.

29. It is interesting to note here that the answer to the neck riddle in the Loathly Lady tales is *given* to the one who must answer the riddle and does not come from any knowledge the victim himself has. This transference of knowledge is another aspect of the Loathly Lady and is perhaps part of the advisory role of the Loathly Lady that S. Elizabeth Passmore discusses in her article "Through the Counsel of a Lady," in the present volume.

30. Since these romances were normally presented to noble audiences, making the threatening figure part of an experience outside of their own ensures her marginal nature. The threat of an increasingly well-to-do peasant class intruding into noble society was no doubt also being manifested in the Loathly Lady.

31. Several works are good references for the details of sumptuary laws and their enactment, the standard still being Frances Elizabeth Baldwin's seminal work *Sumptuary Legislation*. The basis for sumptuary laws in the Middle Ages was to

preserve class distinctions that were being blurred by the rising wealth of the lower classes. As peasants became able to buy clothing that once only the nobility could afford, sumptuary laws sought to control what clothing could, and sometimes should, be worn by what classes. This attempt at regulating the presentation of social identity relates well to the actions of the Loathly Lady in both "The Marriage of Sir Gawain" and "The Tale of Florent" in which the ladies' attempts to present themselves in the garb of nobility while still ugly are unsuccessful. Dame Ragnell's successful intrusion into the noble class while still ugly marks another unique aspect of her character.

32. Douglas, *Purity and Danger*, p. 122.

33. Burns discusses the distinction between the innate majesty of Christ and the performed majesty of kings, proposing that earthly kingship had to be made through the public receipt of the proper clothes. In other words, public display of clothing creates status. Thus nobles feared that peasants would think themselves equal to their betters because they could afford "noble" clothes. *Courtly Love Undressed*, pp. 31–32.

34. See Duby, *Love and Marriage*, pp. 3–8.

35. Performance in regard to gender, power, and agency are discussed in many places, but Judith Butler's theories on gender identity seem most appropriate here. Butler states that performance constitutes "the identity it is purported to be.... There is no gender identity behind the expressions of gender; that identity is performatively constituted by the very 'expressions' that are said to be its results.... Without an agent … there can be no agency and hence no potential to initiate a transformation of relations of domination within society" (*Gender Trouble*, p. 25). While Ragnell's transformation is a gendered performance, as she places herself in the role of a desirable and noble woman, her performance is just as much social. By effecting her own transformation in the social arena before her actual physical transformation, Dame Ragnell assumes agency for her reception and placement within the order of society.

36. Much has been written about this theory. Most of the terminology I use comes from Laura Mulvey's seminal article on "Visual Pleasure and the Narrative Cinema."

37. Cummins, *Medieval Art*, p. 5. Cummins places this pageantry within the aristocratic amusement of hunting, which helped to build moral character and prepared knights for war.

38. Cummins, *Medieval Art*, p. 7.

39. In other tales, knights, such as Erec and Lancelot, fought foes unarmed as an indication of their skill, strength, courage, and moral virtue.

40. Dame Ragnell uses this same tactic later with Arthur. An appeal to honor rather than a triumph in combat is a more feminine approach to chivalric authority, and therefore not befitting a king.

41. For more details on the intricacies of chivalric honor and courtesy between knights, see Leon Gautier's definitive book *La Chevalerie*.

42. In "The Marriage of Sir Gawain," the details of why Arthur is given the riddle by the Baron are lost in a missing half page of the manuscript. The lady's claim that

her stepmother made her ugly and "witched my brother into a churlish B[aron]" would imply that the Baron's actions are dictated by a transformation and not by anything Arthur has done. Arthur demonstrates his worthiness as a king and knight by giving his pledge to the Baron by raising his hand, a sign of chivalric honor and a binding oath. For details on the significance of this as a method of oath-swearing, see Gautier, *Chivalry*, pp. 79–83. The Loathly Lady also says that her father, an old knight, married a young woman, the wicked stepmother who curses the lady and the Baron. The transgression may well be that of the old knight, who, like January in "The Merchant's Tale," makes an improper marriage which instigates dishonor. If this is the case, Arthur, like a good medieval king, may be objecting to the sin of a subject, since he (as king) was responsible for the moral as well as the social well-being of his subjects.

43. The function of symbols in any mode of storytelling is contingent on meanings and values portrayed not only in the stories, but also within the community that produced the story. In distinguishing between the nature of sign and symbol, Julia Kristeva asserts that the meanings of symbols are less arbitrary than the meanings of signs. Once a sign "is more or less free from its dependence on the 'universal' (the concept, the idea in itself), it becomes a potential mutation, a constant transformation which, despite being tied to one signified, is capable of many regenerations. The ideologeme of the sign can therefore suggest what is not, but *will be*, or rather *can be*." (*Reader*, p. 71).

44. In "The Marriage of Sir Gawain," missing leaves make an exact analysis of social concerns difficult, but there does seem to be an emphasis on the inability of Kay to accept the ugly woman as Gawain's wife, even after Gawain and Arthur have consented to the marriage. Here, Kay is the one who rushes to Gawain's room when he does not appear the next day, and the triumph of the tale is Kay and Gawain's presentation of the now beautiful wife to Arthur and Guinevere. The social disruption would seem to be between the knights, and the lady serves to reunite the masculine fellowship of knighthood rather than to point out any significant flaw in it.

45. According to medieval medical beliefs, having too much sex would disrupt the balance of a man's humors and therefore make him weak and less manly. It might even be possible for the man to become seriously ill. Gawain's later refusal to take part in knightly activities attests to the weakness he sustains from too much sexual activity with his wife. For a detailed discussion on medieval perceptions of humors and health, see Thomas Laqueur's *Making Sex*, particularly Chapters 1 and 2.

46. Duby discusses masculine concerns about feminine sexuality and ways men tried to regulate female sexuality through marriage (*Love and Marriage*, pp. 7–13).

47. Foucault, *Use of Pleasure*, p. 151.

48. Gawain undoubtedly believes that his wife is a magical creature of some sort, or perhaps even an evil spirit. He never expresses this fear while she is ugly, even though she is found in the woods and knows the answer to the riddle.

49. Regina Barreca puts curses such as this one in the realm of the feminine: "The

skillful and effective curse is a power belonging to the vanquished, not the victor. In part this power depends on the subterfuge of the vanquished, the camouflage offered by perceived insignificance.... These figures are able to catalyze the liminality of their inscription within the larger social order to draw upon forces and mechanisms outside the orthodox belief systems" ("Writing as Voodoo," p. 177). The stepmother who curses Dame Ragnell has no presence or motives within the tale. Yet although no man ever has control over Dame Ragnell's body, even after marriage, the only one who ever overpowers her, or "defiles" her, is the phantom stepmother. As Ragnell gains control over Gawain and Arthur, it appears that the stepmother has given her an inroad to power rather than the terrible punishment the curse was presumably meant to be.

50. In *Erec and Enide*, this obligation is shown in its extreme form with the knight in the garden. After being defeated by Erec, the knight tells Erec he only fought because his lady made him promise never to leave the garden until someone defeated him. The knight admits to Erec that he should not have made the oath, but declares that it was right that he fulfilled it. In this incident, breaking an oath to a lady was more dishonorable than keeping a bad oath. Again, Gautier's book *Chivalry* covers this topic quite thoroughly.

51. Brown, "Dark Age Crisis," p. 15.

52. The trope of the absent female as the ideal in romance literature has been widely discussed. For a discussion of how the absent female ties into the goals of the troubadour as lover and the structure of Augustinian rhetoric, see Spence, *Rhetoric of Reason*, pp. 111–15.

WORKS CITED

Aguirre, Manuel. "The Roots and Symbolic Role of Woman in Gothic Literature." In *Exhibited by Candlelight: Sources and Developments in the Gothic Tradition,* ed. Valeria Tinkler-Villani and Peter Davidson, with Jane Stevenson, pp. 57–64. Amsterdam: Rodopi, 1995.

Bahktin, Mikhail. *Rabelais and His World.* Trans. Hélène Iswolsky. Bloomington: Indiana University Press, 1984.

Baldwin, Frances Elizabeth. *Sumptuary Legislation and Personal Regulation in England.* Baltimore: Johns Hopkins University Press, 1926.

Barreca, Regina. "Writing as Voodoo: Sorcery, Hysteria, and Art." In *Death and Representation,* ed. Sarah Webster Goodwin and Elisabeth Bronfen, pp. 174–91. Baltimore: Johns Hopkins University Press, 1993.

Benson, Larry D., gen. ed. *The Riverside Chaucer.* 3rd ed. Boston: Houghton Mifflin, 1987.

Brown, Peter. "A Dark Age Crisis: Aspects of the Iconoclastic Controversy." *EHR* 346 (1973), 1–34.

Burns, E. Jane. *Courtly Love Undressed: Reading Through Clothes in Medieval French Culture*. Philadelphia: University of Pennsylvania Press, 2002.

Butler, Judith. *Gender Trouble: Feminism and the Subversion of Identity*. New York: Routledge, 1999.

Child, Francis James, ed. *The English and Scottish Popular Ballads*. 5 vols. New York: Dover Publications, 1965. First published Boston: Houghton Mifflin, 1882–98.

Cummins, John. *The Medieval Art of Hunting: The Hound and the Hawk*. New York: St. Martin's, 1988.

Douglas, Mary. *Purity and Danger: An Analysis of Concepts of Pollution and Taboo*. London: Routledge and Paul, 1966.

Duby, Georges. *Love and Marriage in the Middle Ages*. Trans. Jane Dunnett. Chicago: University of Chicago Press, 1994.

Foucault, Michel. *The Use of Pleasure*. Vol. 2 of *The History of Sexuality*. Trans. Robert Hurley. New York: Vintage Books, 1985.

Gautier, Leon. *Chivalry*. Trans. Henry Frith. London: Routledge and Sons, 1891.

Gower, John. *Confessio Amantis*. Ed. Russell A. Peck. New York: Holt, Rinehart and Winston, 1968.

Hahn, Thomas, ed. *Sir Gawain: Eleven Romances and Tales*. Kalamazoo, Mich.: Medieval Institute Publications, 1995.

Hanawalt, Barbara. *Of Good and Ill Repute: Gender and Social Control in Medieval England*. New York: Oxford University Press, 1998.

Jung, Carl G. *Man and His Symbols*. New York: Dell, 1969.

Kristeva, Julia. *The Kristeva Reader*. Ed. Toril Moi. New York: Columbia University Press, 1986.

Laqueur, Thomas. *Making Sex: Body and Gender from the Greeks to Freud*. Cambridge, Mass.: Harvard University Press, 1990.

Maynadier, G. H. *"The Wife of Bath's Tale": Its Sources and Analogues*. New York: AMS, 1901.

Mulvey, Laura. "Visual Pleasure and Narrative Cinema." In *Gender and Gaze*. Ed. Anthony Easthope, pp. 111–23. New York: Longman, 1993.

Sands, Donald, ed. *Middle English Verse Romances*. York: Holt, Rinehart, and Winston, 1966.

Spence, Sarah. *Rhetorics of Reason and Desire: Virgil, Augustine, and the Troubadours*. Ithaca: Cornell University Press, 1988.

Stock, Lorraine Kochanske. "The Hag of Castle Hautdesert: The Celtic Sheela-na-gig and the *Auncian* in *Sir Gawain and the Green Knight*." In *On Arthurian Women: Essays in Memory of Maureen Fries*, ed. Bonnie Wheeler and Fiona Tolhurst, pp. 121–48. Dallas: Scriptorium, 2001.

Warner, Marina. *Alone of All Her Sex: The Myth and the Cult of the Virgin Mary*. New York: Knopf, 1976.

Webster, Hutton. *Taboo: A Sociological Study*. Stanford: Stanford University Press, 1942.

Brains or Beauty

Limited Sovereignty in the Loathly Lady Tales
"The Wife of Bath's Tale," "Thomas of Erceldoune,"
and "The Wedding of Sir Gawain and Dame Ragnelle"

Ellen M. Caldwell

"King Henry," the ballad version of the Loathly Lady story collected in
F. J. Child's *English and Scottish Ballads*,[1] offers most of the familiar elements
in the tradition: the sudden appearance of a hideous woman who makes
difficult demands upon a man—in this case, food and drink and sexual favors
to satisfy her prodigious appetite. When the man complies with her requests,
he is rewarded with the transformation of the loathly hag into a beautiful
lady. In the ballad the lady compliments King Henry as the only "courteous
knight / That ga' me a' my will," revealing another feature of the medieval
Loathly Lady tradition—the affirmation of the woman's sovereign will.

Yet the Loathly Ladies of English medieval romances generally do not
exercise as much power as the ballad offers this old hag. Greek myth describes
females like Hecate and Demeter who are able at will to transform from
beautiful to loathsome—and back again—to serve their own purposes.[2] But
the ladies of medieval romances are punished with ugliness, or else their
loathsomeness is simply unexplained. Dame Ragnelle of "The Wedding of Sir
Gawain and Dame Ragnelle" (ca. 1450) is turned into a hideous creature by
her stepmother, while the lady in the first fytte of "Thomas of Erceldoune"
(ca. 1388–1401) loses her beauty when she loses her chastity to Thomas, her
suitor. In *The Canterbury Tales* (ca. 1386–1400) Chaucer's Wife of Bath, a
Loathly Lady herself, tells the story of an old hag who inexplicably regains
her beauty. Misogynist explanations for the Loathly Lady's characterization
abound, including folk traditions that describe woman as alternately desirable
and loathsome according to her position in the menstrual cycle. Other critics
have established a connection between the Loathly Lady who demands

sovereignty in her marriage with the Irish Loathly Lady who personifies the rule of Ireland.[3] In recent times hope springs among some feminist critics that these Loathly Lady stories might offer a message of empowerment.

Indeed, the Loathly Lady initially may appear to exercise female sovereignty. Like Dame Ragnelle or the hag in "The Wife of Bath's Tale," she may demand that her passion be satisfied in a shotgun marriage or, as in the case of "Thomas of Erceldoune," she may abduct her lover to the underworld. And yet the three Middle English variations on the Loathly Lady theme considered here ultimately curtail female sovereignty. In the private sphere of marriage defined in "The Wife of Bath's Tale," as well as in the public spheres of poetic prophecy and social governance in "Thomas of Erceldoune" and "The Wedding of Sir Gawain and Dame Ragnelle," no woman, ugly or beautiful, may successfully challenge the male authority of medieval society or literary romance. Thus, the old hag in Chaucer's "Wife of Bath's Tale," Thomas of Erceldoune's lady, and Dame Ragnelle initially enjoy their roles as masters in their marital, linguistic, and political spheres, assuming "masculine" powers to make demands of powerless men who are gendered "feminine." But when they become beautiful, the women revert to their conventional roles. Generally, it is only when she is loathsome and "ungendered" (i.e., freed from her female role), that the Loathly Lady is beyond male control and is sought after, not as a sexual object but as the source of special powers.

The terms *gendered masculine* and *gendered feminine* are informed by Judith Butler's suggestion that "gender is performatively constituted."[4] Individuals may be biologically defined as male or female, but their masculine or feminine qualities are far more fluid and are socially determined. Thus, men may be "gendered" female if they occupy a subordinate, nurturing, or marginal social position such as that commonly held by women. Similarly, women who assume authoritative roles or mannerisms are gendered "masculine." I use the term *ungendering* to suggest a suspension of the conventionally gendered ways in which society classifies behavior. An old hag, for example, unmarried or widowed, ugly, and poor, is not so much gendered masculine as she is "ungendered"—that is, her contradictory or ambiguously gendered appearance and behavior make her social or even biological status unclear.[5] The Loathly Lady tales reveal the consequences for women of such transgressive behavior that is described as "masculine" or which defies classification.

Despite the warnings delivered in the poems about the consequences of a hag's transgressive behavior, loathsomeness has its advantages. In "The Wife of Bath's Tale," the old hag wins the riddling contest and a husband—but only when she is old and poor. As soon as she turns beautiful, she reverts to the traditional role of wife, who never again demands sovereignty. The lady of "Thomas of Erceldoune" loses both her chastity and her beauty as soon as she gives in to Thomas's demands for sex, but she also gains, or retains, her extraordinary powers of prophecy. It seems, by contrast, that by surrendering her ugliness, Dame Ragnelle gains everything: her beauty, a loving husband and even some share of marital sovereignty. Yet in five years Ragnelle is dead, and her husband Gawain has returned to his former role, wedded to the desires of his king rather than his wife. In each instance, then, the Loathly Lady enjoys more power when she is flawed rather than flawless. Like her sister Dame Sirith, the clever panderer of the first Middle English fabliau, the Loathly Lady can bargain with men without beauty as an impediment. In fact, her haglike features may be less significant than the "masculine" behavior of shrewd negotiation that characterizes the ugly lady. But when beauty enters the picture, that is, when her appropriate gendering is recovered, her powers abate.

In exercising inappropriate power, the Loathly Lady in medieval romances often challenges courtly romance conventions. The elitist attitudes of the Arthurian knight in "The Wife of Bath's Tale," the sexual aggression of Thomas of Erceldoune, and the chilly reception the ugly Ragnelle receives at Arthur's court all undergo critique. Housed in her ambiguous portrayal, then, the Loathly Lady challenges the chivalric code by invoking a mercantile or exchange system in which she controls the outcome. However, the consequences of these negotiations are dire, leaving us to wonder if power is ever fully secured by loathly or lovely women in these texts.

"The Wife of Bath's Tale": Loathly Sovereignty in Marriage

Each of these Loathly Ladies shares a similar management style. First, the lady violates conventional behavior, appropriating male authority by making demands and conducting negotiations both marital and economic. Second, she utilizes the female power of speech to offer a critique of romance ideals or of male behavior or attitudes. Through these actions, the Loathly Lady threatens or actually breaks (albeit temporarily) the homosocial bond between men, her third violation of the norm. Finally, for these displays of powers, she is "punished"—usually through a form of confinement, such as marriage, which reasserts the sovereignty of a husband. "The Wife of Bath's Tale" exemplifies the Loathly Lady's challenge to the romance tradition, her appropriation of power over men, and ultimately, the disenfranchising consequences.

Stories that link the marriage of the Loathly Lady to the claiming of the Irish kingdom consistently portray the lady with divine, shape-shifting powers. She magically transforms herself; she tests her suitors and ultimately confers the kingship upon the rightful ruler. Dame Alisoun, however, spends no time on the old hag's transformative powers in her tale, preferring to address issues common to the fourteenth century and *The Canterbury Tales:* competition and class consciousness. The Loathly Lady's powers in this tale are not so much magical as mercantile. She is the negotiator who wins two rewards: one is the "quyting" of Guinevere and the ladies of the court who set the riddle for the knight; the other is the knight himself in marriage. When the knight encounters the old hag near the end of his year's search, he still has no answer to the queen's riddle. The old hag prompts him:

> "Sire knyght, heer forth ne lyth no wey.
> Tel me what that ye seken, by youre fey!
> Paraventure it may the bettre be:
> Thise olde folk kan muchel thyng," quod she.
>
> (lines 1001–4)

There is no way through this dilemma, in other words, except through a canny intermediary: the Loathly Lady. The language promptly takes on the coloring of a pragmatic business arrangement with the knight announcing, "I nam but deed but if that I can seyn / What thyng it is that wommen moost desire. / Koude ye me wisse, I wolde wel *quite youre hire*" (lines 1005–7; my emphasis).[6] Perhaps the knight has promised payment to others he has asked, but the text is silent on this point. Here, however, a bargain is quickly struck: though money is proffered, the hag instead makes her own shrewd bargain for something far dearer: the knight's hand in marriage. In her intermediary position between knight and the ladies judging him at court, the old hag functions like Dame Sirith, another "wif" whose assistance is sought by a beleaguered suitor. The shrewdness of the seller and the negotiations of the arrangement suggest that the Arthurian chivalric code has met its match in the marketplace from a savvy representative of the merchant class. And the old hag emphasizes her triumph by suggesting that her knowledge is at least equal to that of her royal "sister" Guinevere:

> Upon my lyf the queen wol seye as I.
> Lat see which is the proudeste of hem alle
> That wereth on a coverchief or a calle
> That dar seye nay of that I shal thee teche.
>
> (lines 1016–19)

The old hag reduces class differences to a matter of headdress—and asserts that, in fact, there is no privilege afforded the woman who wears a crown, as opposed to the one who wears a kerchief, or even Dame Alisoun the tale-teller, who wears "an hat / As brood as is a bokeler or a targe," complete with "coverchiefs ful fyne weren of ground … / That on a Sonday weren upon [the Wife of Bath's own] heed" (I, lines 470–71, 453–55).[7]

Having proven her ability to solve the riddle of the most aristocratic of ladies, the old hag further demonstrates her rhetorical abilities with her wedding-night harangue that wins her sovereignty over her husband. She justifies her loathsomeness, her age, and her lower class as not only Christian virtues but practical advantages in marriage in an explicit critique of aristocratic (and romance) values.[8] In effect, when the knight tolerates the old hag's argument about the universal access to "gentillesse" and her praise of poverty and ugliness, he surrenders his allegiance to the Arthurian Round Table, breaks from the bond of men, and weds the woman to whom he owes not only his life but the marriage debt. "Thanne have I gete of yow maistrie" (line 1236), crows the old hag, but her transformation to a beautiful and faithful wife at the moment of her triumph is immediately undercut by the reassertion of marital conventions: "And she obeyed hym in everythyng / That myghte doon hym pleasance or likyng" (lines 1255–57), an echo of the "romance" ending of the Dame Alisoun's stormy marriage to Jankyn:

> After that day we hadden never debaat.
> God helpe me so, I was to hym as kynde
> As any wyf from Denmark unto Ynde,
> And also trewe, and so was he to me.
>   (lines 822–25)

The power so shrewdly won is eventually surrendered.

The appropriation of male authority begins early in "The Wife of Bath's Tale" with the account of Guinevere's supervision of the rapist knight's trial and sentencing. R. J. Blanch suggests that both the sovereignty of Guinevere and of the loathly hag must be overturned at the end of the tale in favor of "true freedom and order," when the knight and his transformed wife "reject the desire for mastery," an interpretation that differs from more recent feminist readings of the tale.[9] Perhaps some anxiety over the romantic nature of her own tale drives the Wife of Bath to her final outrageous requests for "Housbondes meeke, yonge, and fresh abedde" (line 1259), for "grace t'overbyde hem that we wedde" and for death or the pestilence to those husbands who are ungovernable or miserly. But the return of this sovereign voice does not quite dispel the tale's conventional sentiments uttered by the fair young wife: "I prey to God that I moote sterven wood, / But I to yow be also good and trewe / As evere was wyf, syn that the world was newe" (lines 1242–44).[10]

Manuel Aguirre notes that from the twelfth to the fifteenth centuries, the woman in the romances seems increasingly unable to maintain control over either lands or love; moreover, she is often characterized by "her wiles, her wantonness, her almost incomprehensible perversity."[11] In Chaucer's permutation of the loathly/lovely lady motif, the wantonness is borne principally by the loathly tale-teller, while the old hag, now a lovely lady, agrees to be subject to her husband's authority. Furthermore, the challenge to authority in the tale is not only to men's sovereignty in marriage, but to aristocratic women's superiority. The old hag's "quyting" of Guinevere and her court undercuts the authority of a royal female by a lower-class female. The private domestic bliss of the married couple, thus, is allowed to stand, cast in the balanced phrases of the lines "I was to hym ... kynde / ... And also trewe, and so was he to me" (lines 822–25), while the loathly tale-teller is vilified as the harridan no man will have. If sovereignty can be shared in the idealized marriage, its practice is surely questioned in Guinevere's court and in the Wife of Bath's marketplace.

"Thomas of Erceldoune": Negotiating Linguistic Sovereignty

From the domestic sphere of Chaucer's tale, we move to the literary sphere and a challenge over who controls not marital but linguistic negotiations. The fickle, inconstant nature of woman is particularly developed in the next romance, which sympathetically portrays the courtly lover at the mercy of his devilish mistress. A perplexing version of the Loathly Lady motif, "Thomas of Erceldoune" supplements the Loathly Lady story with two sections recounting the lady's prophecies before she returns to the underworld. This romance also reverses the typical order in the Loathly Lady transformation story by presenting the lady initially as fair and beautiful, only to become foul and loathly when she accedes to Thomas's requests to sleep with him. The punishing marks of illicit sex are borne solely by the woman. All four manuscripts of the poem—Thornton, Cotton, Lansdowne, and Cambridge—record that Thomas initially mistakes the lady for the "Qwene of heuene" (Thorn., line 88). She corrects him, "ne am j noghte, / ffor j tuke

neuer so heghe degree" (lines 91–92), and answers his request for sex with a
warning:

> [T]hou mane, that ware folye,
> I praye the, Thomas, thou late me bee;
> ffor j saye the full sekirlye,
> That synne will for-doo all my beaute.
>   (lines 101–4)

All four manuscripts describe Thomas's enthusiastic lovemaking and the
lady's protestations:

> [M]ane, the lykes thy playe:
> Whate byrde in boure maye delle with the?
> Thou merrys me all this longe daye,
> I praye the, Thomas, late me bee!
>   (Thorn., lines 125–28)

The word *merrys* in Thornton is clarified in Lansdowne as *marrest*. The
damage has been done.

All four manuscripts similarly describe the loathsome transformation:

> Hir hare it hange all ouer hir hede,
> His eghne semede owte, thatare were graye.
> And alle the riche clothynge was a-waye,
> That he by-fore sawe in that stede;
> Hir a schanke blake, hir other graye,
> And all hir body lyke the lede.
>   (Thorn., lines 131–36)

Thomas's explanation for her transformation, offered only in the Lansdowne
manuscript, associates the lady with the devil:

> On euery syde he lokyde abowete,
> he sau he myght no whare fle;
> Sche woxe so grym and so stowte,
> The Dewyll he wende she had be.
>   (Lans., lines 141–44)

Although she assures him that she is not the devil, the lady nevertheless
requires Thomas to accompany her to the underworld. At this point in both

Thornton and Cambridge manuscripts, Thomas turns to the Virgin Queen, whom he calls the "lufly lady," for help when he hears of the upcoming journey with the Loathly Lady before him:

"[L]ufly lady! rewe on mee,
Mylde qwene of heuene, als thou beste maye.
Allas!" he sayd, "& wa es mee!
I trowe my dedis wyll wirke me care."
                              (Thorn., lines 163–66)

The contrast between the homage he should pay the heavenly queen and the worship he offers this lady is firmly noted, with Thomas kneeling to pray to the Virgin in the very spot where the passionate lovemaking has occurred. And yet the three years in the underworld pass without any complaint from Thomas, whose confinement is mitigated when the lady miraculously recovers her beauty, an occurrence noted in all four manuscripts, but explained by the lady only in the Lansdowne manuscript as a guise to escape detection by her jealous husband:

My lorde is so fers and fell,
That is king of this contre,
And fulle sone he wolde haue ye smell,
Of the defaute I did with the.
                              (Lans., lines 249–52)

Her loathsomeness has protected both of them, since it prevents the husband from sniffing out her lover. Is she, then, a temptress or a generous courtly lady? Although she exercises power over Thomas, she is also subject to the wills of both husband and lover. Her nature, like her behavior, resists classification, a mark of the Loathly (as well, sometimes, of the courtly) Lady.

The return of Thomas to middle earth at the beginning of the second fytte marks the end of the lady's sovereignty over Thomas. In the underworld kingdom, she pledges him to silence:

When thou commes to yone castelle gaye,
I pray the curtase mane to bee;
And whate so any mane to the saye,
Luke thou answere none bott mee.
                              (Thorn., lines 225–28)

But when she returns Thomas to his own world, he uses his reacquired speech to coerce the lady into prophesying for him.[12] When Thomas asks for a love token from her, "Gyff me a tokynynge, lady gaye, / That j may saye j spake with the" (Thorn., lines 311–12), she gives him the gift of words, or tale-telling, with a stipulation:

> If thou will spelle, or tales telle,
> Thomas, thou sall neuer lesynge lye,
> Whare euer thou fare, by frythe or felle,
> I praye the, speke none euyll of me!
> (Thorn., lines 317–20)

At the end of the third fytte, the lady agrees to meet Thomas again, if he heeds her caveat:

> [I sa]ll the kenne whare euer thou gaa,
> [To ber]e the pryce of curtaysye;
> [For tu]nge es wele, & tunge es waa,
> [And tun]ge es chefe of Mynstrallsye.
> (Thorn., lines 685–88)

By regaining his voice as well as the power of minstrelsy, Thomas wrests control over language and curtails the lady's authority. Now that she is again beautiful, she becomes subject to the demands of her lover and a jealous husband. Yet the lady warns that she will expect Thomas "[To ber]e the pryce of curtaysye" (line 686). The Cotton manuscript offers additional evidence of the strings attached to this gift of minstrelsy:

> [T]ong is weke & tong is woe of mynstralsy
> tong is water & tong is wyne
> [Tong is che]fe of melody
> & tong is thyng that fast wil bynd.
> (lines 689–92)

In both the Thornton version "tunge es wele, & tunge es waa" (line 687) and Cotton's "tong is water & tong is wyne" (line 689), the tongue or the gift of speech produces both wele and woe, the good and the bad, the miraculous and the ordinary. And the Cotton manuscript further warns that the gift itself, the tongue, can bind or imprison the speaker—perhaps in the very way that the lady, bound by her powers of prophecy, is caught between the words of two worlds, her vow to her underworld husband and her devotion to her poet. The gift, a mixed blessing, readjusts our reading of the nature of sovereignty in this text.

The lady is not simply the unwilling victim of Thomas's lust, nor is she either merely a temptress or a savior for her courtly lover. Rather, she is a negotiator, who offers the gift of tale-telling in order to assuage her lover, but also to retain power over him. Mastery in this romance is negotiated not over one's lover or spouse but over the power of language. In this relationship of compromise, Thomas gains both the benefits and the responsibilities of "possessing" the lady's art. Unlike "Thomas the Rhymer," the ballad version of this story, "Thomas of Erceldoune" includes the Loathly Lady material to serve in this poem as an allegory for the poet's art—and his tenuous control over language.[13] Just as "The Wife of Bath's Tale" seems to negotiate a compromise between the "good" bride of the tale and the transgressive hag Dame Alisoun, the struggle for sovereignty also ends in a draw for Thomas of Erceldoune and the lady. While he gains his gift of storytelling and the use of several prophecies to publish, the lady returns to her privileged liminal state, between the fairy world and middle earth, and between her roles as wife and lover, underworld queen and poetic muse.

Homosocial Bonds and "The Wedding of Sir Gawain and Dame Ragnelle"

At least fifty years after the composition of "The Wife of Bath's Tale" and "Thomas of Erceldoune," the anonymous author of "The Wedding of Sir Gawain and Dame Ragnelle" returns to the Loathly Lady theme in order to examine political sovereignty and the male bonds that sustain it. In this romance version Arthur must answer the riddle about what women desire and procure Gawain as a husband for Dame Ragnelle in order to gain that answer demanded by Sir Gromer Somer Joure. Arthur's position becomes gradually feminized in this romance,[14] beginning with his subordination to Sir Gromer, his reliance on assistance from his nephew Gawain, and his final endebtedness and submission to the will of Dame Ragnelle. By the end of the poem, however, the hag is forced to surrender her position of loathly authority over Arthur and assume her properly gendered role in her marriage to Gawain.[15] Again, the surrender of power corresponds to her transformation from ugly hag to beautiful maiden. At stake here is not the marital sovereignty disputed in "The Wife of Bath's Tale," or linguistic sovereignty debated in "Thomas of Erceldoune," but male authority contested in the home and in the kingdom.[16] This loathly hag challenges the authority of her brother, Sir Gromer, as well as of her king.

While another Loathly Lady, Morgan le Fay, tests the ethics of the Round Table in *Sir Gawain and the Green Knight*, the challenge in the "Wedding" is more specifically directed against Arthur's abuse of kingly power.[17] Claiming that the king has taken his lands and given them to the king's favorite, Sir Gawain (lines 54–60), Sir Gromer sentences Arthur to death unless in one year he can determine "whate wemen love best" (line 91).[18] After nearly an entire year of fruitless searching, Arthur meets Dame Ragnelle, whose loathly description by now is familiar:

> Her face was red, her nose snotyd withalle,
> Her mowithe wyde, her teethe yalowe over alle,
> With bleryd eyen gretter then a balle;
> Her mowithe was nott to lak;
> Her tethe hung over her lyppes;
> Her cheekys syde as wemens hyppes;
> A lute she bare upon her bak.
>
> . . . .
>
> And lyke a barrelle she was made;
> And to reherse the foulnesse of that lady,
> Ther is no tung may telle, securly;
> Of lothynesse inowghe she had.
>
> (lines 231–45)

Although Arthur is reluctant to promise his knight in marriage, Gawain is eager to undertake any trial to save Arthur's life: "I shalle wed her and wed her agayn, / Thoughe she were a fend; / Thoughe she were as foulle as Belsabub" (lines 343–45). Gawain promises, "For your love I wolle nott spare" (line 371), and Arthur extravagantly praises his loyal kinsman, promising love that will last as long as his reign (line 377). The marriage arrangement, then, is created explicitly for the benefit of Arthur, and the betrothal, rather than pulling Gawain from this male bond with his king, solidifies it. At the moment that Gawain steps forward to meet his bride, he addresses himself first to the bond he honors with his king: "Then cam forth Sir Gawen the knyghte: / 'Syr, I am ready of that I you hyghte, / Alle forwardes to fulfylle'" (lines 533–35).

Much of the story of the "Wedding" is not about Ragnelle at all, but about men: the bond between kinsmen, Arthur and Gawain; and the bond between rivals, Ragnelle's brother, Sir Gromer, and Arthur, the representative of the

Round Table. And rather than the woman being a point of rivalry, it seems to be land, or Gawain himself, the possessor of Sir Gromer's lands. Eve Sedgwick's theory that the homosocial bond among men is more significant than any relationship with women seems clearly reflected in this text.[19] To some degree, the major concern of the romance is making sure that Gawain (with his lands) remains with Arthur, rather than being taken away by Sir Gromer or his kin. Sibling rivalry further threatens the romance's male bonds. When Sir Gromer learns Arthur's answer to the riddle of what women want most, he knows immediately that he has been bested by his sister. In failing to tame Arthur, Sir Gromer loses his knight, while his sister "wins" her knight, Sir Gawain. Eventually, she arranges an uneasy alliance between her brother and Arthur, offering Arthur a chance to pardon Sir Gromer's insubordination for Ragnelle's sake (lines 811–16).[20] Perhaps the rift will mend as the lands are "returned" to the family with Ragnelle's marriage.[21]

But to sort out exactly who tames whom in this story is more complicated. Arthur gains his sovereignty over Sir Gromer, with the help of Ragnelle's answer. But the female challenge to male authority is doubled in this text: first by a woman, Ragnelle, and second, by one who is gendered feminine, Arthur. Sir Gromer had initially exercised his authority over Arthur in their meeting in the forest, where Arthur, isolated and vulnerable, lacked the might or the wit to withstand the challenge. But now Sir Gromer must admit that this king, whom Sir Gromer had characterized as weak, sly, and slippery (even womanly?), has indeed triumphed.

In delivering the answer that Dame Ragnelle has given him, Arthur places himself before Sir Gromer in the very position that is gendered feminine in the poem:

> Wemen desyre sovereynte, for that is theyr lykyng,
> And that is theyr moste desyre:
> To have the rewlle of the manlyest men,
> And then ar they welle; thus they me dyd ken:
> To rule thee, Gromer Syre.
>
> (lines 468–72)

Arthur's claim that women most desire "the rewlle of the manlyest men" is proven in the rule that Arthur himself has gained over this tyrant. Dame Ragnelle instructs Arthur, "Of the moste manlyest is oure desire; / To have the sovereynte of such a syre, / Such is oure crafte and gynne [conniving]" (lines 428–30). Arthur, thus, wins sovereignty over Sir Gromer with women's advice, but also with womanly tactics. Sir Gromer has already insinuated

Arthur's "feminine" qualities at their first meeting. When Arthur reminds the knight that it would not be honorable to kill a king, especially one inappropriately attired for combat, and further promises to amend any wrongful seizure of lands, Sir Gromer retorts,

> I have thee nowe att avaylle;
> Yf I shold lett thee thus goo withe mokery,
> Anoder tyme thou wolt me defye;
> Of that I shalle nott faille.
>
> (lines 75–78)

He makes Arthur swear to return with the riddle's answer or to answer with his life and threatens, finally, "Looke nott today thou me beguile, / And kepe alle thyng in close" (lines 110–11). Sir Gromer treats Arthur as if he has an established reputation as a liar and beguiler, as one who wheedles his way out of difficult situations with easy banter (line 76). And, as is proven fifty lines after Arthur's meeting with Sir Gromer, Arthur (just like a woman?) can't keep a secret, but must, explicitly against Sir Gromer's order, tell Gawain of his dilemma. Later, Arthur's own rhetorical powers will help him convince Gawain to wed the Loathly Lady and save the life of his king. Although he is essentially subject to Sir Gromer, Arthur wins sovereignty over his challenger not by a manly show of force, but by the wiliness offered him by a woman and by mimicking her language and behavior ("craft and gynne").

The inversions of conventional sovereignty and gender continue. Dame Ragnelle demands a lavish wedding and public entry to Carlyle, escorted by Arthur:

> The kyng of her had greatt shame;
> Butt forthe she rood, thoughe he were grevyd;
> Tylle they cam to Karlyle forth they mevyd.
> . . . .
> Itt likyd the kyng fulle ylle.
>
> (lines 515–20)

Until this point, Ragnelle has enjoyed clear sovereignty—over her brother, whom she defeated in the riddling game, over Arthur, and over her future husband, Gawain. When she requests a kiss in the bridal chamber later that evening, he is dutiful in granting it, but only when Ragnelle asks, "Yett for Arthours sake kysse me att the leste" (line 635). True to his bond with Arthur, Gawain prepares to fulfill the marital debt with his loathly bride.

Furthermore, he borrows language from the marketplace, in linguistic deference to the old hag, when he is asked to decide whether she will be fair by day or by night:

I putt the choyse in you;
Bothe body and goodes, hartt, and every dele
Ys alle your own, for to buy and selle—
That make I God avowe!

(lines 681–84)[22]

Just at the moment that Ragnelle has achieved this sovereignty, she abruptly returns authority in this marriage to the "weaker sex," in much the same way that Sir Gromer was forced to defer to the puny Arthur.[23] Gawain and his lands are initially gendered female, to be possessed by his sovereign wife. She then surrenders sovereignty to take up her appropriately gendered roles as wife and mother.

Buried at the heart of this happy story rests some jealous rivalry that has always threatened Ragnelle's power. After giving birth to Gawain's son Gyngolyn, Ragnelle becomes a liability at court because her husband dotes on her: "As a coward he lay by her bothe day and nyghte: / Nevere wold he haunt justyng aryghte / Ther-att mervalyed Arthoure the kyng" (lines 808–10). The narrator signals another rewriting of the sovereignty code when he comments, "Now for to make you a short conclusyon, / I cast me for to make an end fulle soone, / Of this gentylle lady" (lines 817–19). In the next line, five years have passed and Ragnelle is dead, with Arthur rather than her husband asserting the epitaph: "She was the fayrest lady of alle Englond / When she was on lyve, I understand, / So sayd Arthoure the kyng" (lines 826–28).

Why must Dame Ragnelle die? The answer is in the word *coward* (line 808; translated as "lazy lover" by editor James Wilhelm [p. 486]) and in Arthur's astonishment that Gawain cares more for his wife than for jousting tournaments. The text ends the rivalry, "Here endythe the weddyng of / Syr Gawen and Dame Ragnelle / For helpyng of Kyng Arthoure" (lines 853–55). That is, the marriage must end in order to reassert the more significant bond between men. Ragnelle's death allows Gawain to return to his rakish reputation and reinstates Gaynour as "the fairest ... in the halle" (line 794), a title Ragnelle had also threatened to usurp. The author notes "Gawen was weddyd oft in his days, / Butt so welle he nevere lovyd woman always, / As I have heard men sayn" (lines 832–34). His subsequent marriages never jeopardize the primary bond that Gawain shares with his king. Thus, the poem reasserts the male bonds of the Round Table over the subversive claims of women, whether ugly or beautiful. What might be read as a tale of a woman's shrewd manipulation of men, her successful escape from the curse of loathsomeness, and happy marriage, actually is a tale of punishment of the lady who threatens the bond between men. The Loathly Lady may be beautiful, but she is also just as surely dead for all her efforts.

Whether it is an old hag's homiletic discourse on the merits of the lower class, a lady's prophecy, or Dame Ragnelle's folk wisdom, Loathly Ladies seem to have the upper hand in the oral tradition, whereas men are portrayed as those who transcribe the prophecies, as Thomas of Erceldoune, or collect others' tales. In "The Wedding of Sir Gawain and Dame Ragnelle," a woman knows the answer to the riddle, leaving Arthur, Gawain, and even the author with roles as recorders or compilers of stories. The king and his loyal retainer not only spend nearly a year searching for an answer to the riddle, but carefully note down and compare the answers they receive:

> Syr Gawen has goten answerys so many
> That had made a boke greatt, wytterly;
> To the courte he cam agayn.
> By that was the kyng comyn withe hys boke,
> And eyther on others pamplett dyd loke.
>   (lines 207–11)

After Sir Gromer dismisses the contents of these journals, Arthur counters with the answer provided him by Dame Ragnelle. While Arthur and Gawain are responsible for the narratives, indeed for the manuscripts, Ragnelle relies on the spoken word as bond, offering to "make warrauntyng" (line 268) and "suche covenaunt I wolle make thee" (line 282).

Framing the story of a woman who knows how to manipulate language for her purposes is a poet's request that his audience listen to his "spelle" (line 18). "Lythe and listenythe," begins the poem, followed by "Nowe wylle ye lyst a whyle to my talkyng" (line 13) and "Nowe herken to my spelle" (line 18). At the end of the romance, the author closes this frame, noting that some elements of the story are what "I have heard men sayn" or "telle" (lines 834, 837), but also claiming that he is the one "that this tale dyd devyne" (line 842) and "that made this tale" (line 848). Another curious feature of this frame is the narrator's admission of his imprisonment, "beset withe gaylours many / That kepen hym fulle sewerly, / With wyles wrong and wraste" (lines 844–46). He asks God to "Help hym oute of daunger that made this tale, / For therin he hathe bene long" (lines 848–49). The syntax allows the suggestion that the poet has been trapped both in prison and in the poem, with the plea for release becoming, perhaps, both literal and aesthetic. As Arthur, by procuring a husband for Ragnelle, guaranteed his release from the threat of death, and as Ragnelle negotiated her release from the prison of her loathsomeness, the author hopes to end his own incarceration. The plea places the narrator in a subordinate, powerless position—another feminine gendering of the male—with the readers of the poem promoted to positions of power over him. While Ragnelle seems to exert control as both loathly and lovely lady, her triumph spans five years. Indeed, Ragnelle's power was always limited by males: Arthur appropriates her answer to the riddle to assure his safety; her husband Gawain gains her wifely obedience and a male heir, and then the narrator makes an abrupt end of her.

If a beautiful woman uses sexual charms to manipulate a man, the Loathly Lady uses her wits, not only shrewdly bargaining for what she wants, but overcoming the male's disgust with her ugliness. In fact, she is confronting a virulent misogyny that argues men must conquer their sexual desires or else be subject to intercourse with corrupted female flesh. Patricia Ingham suggests that by being forced to agree to a union with the Loathly Lady, the male learns to forgo his libidinal desire in order to achieve a higher purpose, such as the fulfillment of a pledge, for Chaucer's knight, or the rescue of a king, for Sir Gawain. The Loathly Lady is used first as punishment and then, with her transformation, as prize for the man who has mastered his desire for beauty—and is thus rewarded with a beautiful bride.[24]

Finally, to erase the potential threat of this hideous hag, the Loathly Lady is returned to the conventional role of wife or property, a position from which her ugliness had, temporarily, liberated her. One might say that she is "lucky" to regain her beauty, but she also immediately forfeits her power by becoming a wife, or in Ragnelle's case, she forfeits her very life. Loathly Ladies threaten to subvert male authority because, by nature of their ambiguous gendering, they threaten to stand outside the conventional institutions of sovereignty that might tame them. Eventually, because these Loathly Ladies are transformed, they may be returned to conventional social roles, and the male bonds of the romance genre, of medieval society, and particularly of Arthur's court, may be reasserted. The Loathly Lady's unattractive powers are dispelled, proving that relationships in these romances "between men" will withstand the brains or beauty of any woman.

NOTES

1. Child, *English and Scottish Popular Ballads*, 1:64–67. See Mary Shaner's essay on the "King Henry" ballad in the present volume.

2. In "Chaucer, Gower, and the Unknown Minstrel," Vasta notes that the Loathly Lady "loses her power at the moment she is rescued from the curse of ugliness by demonstrating her use or value to a man" (p. 397).

3. For a discussion of the Loathly Lady and the menstrual cycle see Coomaraswamy, "On the Loathly Bride," especially p. 397. Early discussions of the Irish sovereignty motif are offered by Stokes, "Marriage of Sir Gawain," and Nutt, "Marriage of Sir Gawain and the Loathly Damsel." In *Tale of Wonder*, nine extant tales of Irish sovereignty are examined by Sigmund Eisner. In three of them a Loathly Lady is transformed into a beauty when she is kissed by the future heir of the Irish kingdom. See Eisner's chapters "Tales of Eriu" and "The Irish Loathly Lady," pp. 17–44. See also Albrecht, *Loathly Lady*, and Bollard, "Sovereignty."

4. Butler, *Gender Trouble*, p. 25. In her introduction to *Speaking of Gender*, Elaine Showalter notes that "within Anglo-American feminist discourse, the term 'gender' has been used … to stand for the social, cultural, and psychological meaning imposed upon biological sexual identity" (pp. 1–2).

5. "Ungendering," like Lady Macbeth's "unsexing" (1.5.37) or the beards of the weird sisters noticed by Banquo (1.3.46), upsets normative definitions of gender, hinting perhaps at the creation of a third gender that combines characteristics from both male and female. Loathly Lady stories seem to demonstrate that transgressive behavior by women is intolerable, whereas in the religious realm a certain degree of gender flexibility seems to be encouraged. Caroline Walker Bynum argues that pious men and women of the Middle Ages used female symbols in different ways: "Where women used gender as image they usually spoke of themselves as female to a male God or as *androgynous*" (my emphasis) (p. 291). In the writings of medieval male mystics, "[m]an became woman metaphorically or symbolically to express his renunciation or loss of "male" power, authority, and status" (p. 284); see Bynum, *Holy Feast and Holy Fast*.

6. Quotations of "The Wife of Bath's Tale" are from *Canterbury Tales*, ed. Benson.

7. Rivalry is also suggested in Queen Gaynour's dislike and then grudging acceptance of Dame Ragnelle. The "competition" between Guinevere and the old hag in "The Wife of Bath's Tale" might be further evidence of misogyny—women will always try to outdo each other and in their pettiness or incompetence, they are all alike. Arthur Lindley argues that "The hag knows what the Queen will accept. After all, they are aspects of the same personality" ("'Vanysshed was this Daunce,'" p. 15). However, in the world of men, ladies have no power unless men give it to them, as Arthur gives the Queen mastery over the fate of the rapist knight. Even when the old hag "chooses" to be fair and faithful, Lindley claims that her choice is determined by "the 'worldly appetit' (line 1218) of the other. To control him by his desire she must be controlled, literally shaped, by that desire" (p. 16).

8. For example, the old hag argues that "gentillesse" comes from God, not from one's aristocratic bloodlines (lines 1151–52). Her life of poverty, furthermore, follows the example of "Jhesus, hevene kyng, / [who] Ne wolde nat chese a vicious lyvyng" (lines 1181–82). Contrary to this reading of the old hag as a social critic, Penn R. Szittya suggests that the Friar makes his devilish yeoman into a parody of the Wife's old hag to ridicule women's vices. See Szittya, "Green Yeoman as Loathly Lady," which offers evidence for the fluidity of gender in the characterization of the old hag, who appears submissive or humbly ingratiating at the very moment that she wields her greatest power.

9. See Blanch, "'Al was this land fulfild of fayerye,'" p. 48. Mann, *Geoffrey Chaucer*, pp. 82–83, and Dinshaw, *Chaucer's Sexual Poetics*, p. 9, discuss the violence against women in the tale and the unsatisfactory conclusion (the Wife's surrender of authority to the rapist knight). A more positive view of the knight's reformation is offered by Corrine Saunders in *The Forest of Medieval Romance*, p. 161. If Dame Alisoun assumes the role of Loathly Lady, the character in her tale may safely be the lovely damsel of the romance tradition.

10. An alternative reading to this passage is provided by Potkay and Evitt, *Minding the Body*, who find that Chaucer's act of "gender ventriloquism" in the Wife of Bath's prologue and tale presents an image of prelapsarian perfection as well as postlapsarian "commodification of women to be possessed or exchanged" (pp. 164–65). Straus, "Subversive Discourse," also discusses the power of language: Straus argues that the Wife "upsets phallocentric discourse [that is] grounded in a sexual economy based on deficit and domination" (p. 535). Although elsewhere Straus suggests that the Wife is a "woman speaking as if a man" (p. 538), she also claims that the Wife uses her woman's sense of language (the ability to lie) to retain her options, if not her sovereignty, by promising to treat her husband as women have treated men "syn that the world was newe" (line 1244). Given the example of Eve, this may not be a marker of marital fidelity.

11. Aguirre, "Riddle of Sovereignty," esp. pp. 280–81.

12. While clearly the lady is the one with prophetic powers, it is Thomas who extracts them from her, despite her reluctance, expressed as "ffare wele, Thomas, j wend my waye" (line 305) at the end of the first fytte and in second fytte in the repeated expression, "Fare wele, Thomas, j wend my waye, / I may no lengare stande with the!" (lines 309–10, 337–38, 357–58, 365–66). Thomas counters her refusals with the request, "telle thou me of some ferly" (lines 324, 340, 372). Quotations are taken from Murray, *Romance and Prophecies of "Thomas of Erceldoune."*

13. In "Relationship between 'Thomas the Rhymer' and 'Thomas of Erceldoune,'" E. B. Lyle notes the omission of Loathly Lady material in the ballad.

14. A ballad version of the story, "The Marriage of Sir Gawain" (Child, *Ballads*, vol. 1, no. 31), offers substantive differences in characterization, making Arthur more typically the brusque leader than the weaker and more sensitive character of the romance. See Garbáty, "Rhyme, Romance, Ballad," esp. pp. 296–97, and the essay in the present volume by Stephanie Hollis.

15. Mary Leech's essay in the present volume, "Why Dame Ragnell Had to Die," demonstrates that Dame Ragnelle exercises authority over the men of the romance as both loathly and lovely lady. While Ragnelle initially is employed to solidify the bonds between men, she ultimately must suffer death because she is an impediment to the devotion of Gawain to Arthur.

16. A number of critics emphasize the positive portrayals of these romance characters. For example, Laura Sumner suggests that the romance "makes Arthur the flower of chivalry" in her introduction to the text (*Weddynge*). In "Liberation of the 'Loathly Lady,'" Robert Shenk offers a similarly complimentary reading of Ragnelle and Gawain: "Instead of bondage to a domineering mate, Gawain has the greater freedom of husband to a gentle and obedient lady. Both have submitted, and both have become free" (p. 73). A version closer to the one I propose here is offered by Stephen Shepherd: "while the *Weddyng*, just like other "testing" poems, questions the integrity of Arthurian excellence it does so ... at the antithetical and ridiculous level of such things as bumbling and furtive breaches of contract (for example, lines 279–90), opportunistic deal-making and manipulation (for example, lines 279–335), the dismissal of a woman on the basis of her appearance (for example, lines 2252–84), and begrudging bravado (for example, lines 485–90, and 814–16)" (*Middle English Romances*, p. 379). Davis, "More Evidence for Intertextuality," suggests that the poem "is a parody of elements familiar to the poem's target audience" (p. 431).

17. Sir Gromer Somer Joure is frequently glossed as part of the "forces of wildness and incivility" associated with "the licensed anarchy of Midsummer's Day, as Hahn suggests in his introduction to the text (*Sir Gawain*, pp. 41–42). A compelling counter-argument that the name derives from a knight named Goumerés sans Mesure in the French verse romance *L'Âtre périlleux* (ca. 1250–75) is offered by Trimnell, "And shold have been oderwyse understond.'"

18. Quotations of "The Wedding of Sir Gawain and Dame Ragnelle" are from Wilhelm, *Romance of Arthur*, pp. 467–87. According to Davenport, *Chaucer and his English Contemporaries*, "Ragnel is a name given to a devil in Patience and in the Chester Cycle," a sign for Davenport that the tale is borrowing from the ballad tradition (p. 147). In the behavior of Arthur and Gawain, Davenport sees a burlesquing of the romance tradition, particularly "their joint conduct [sic] of a sort of social survey and the compilation of a book of answers" (p. 147). The burlesquing seems to be a satiric feature in all three of the romances.

19. See Sedgwick, *Between Men*. I am applying Sedgwick's idea of "male homosocial desire within the structural context of triangular, heterosexual desire" (p. 16) to the Middle Ages, though her study examines this phenomenon only in nineteenth-century fiction. See Dinshaw's application to arranged marriages in Chaucer in *Chaucer's Sexual Poetics*, pp. 3–27. Dinshaw cites the work of Gayle Rubin, "The Traffic in Women," in *Toward an Anthropology of Women*, ed. R. R. Reiter (New York: Monthly Review Press, 1975), pp. 157–210.

20. "She prayd the kyng for his gentilness, / 'To be good lord to Sir Gromer, i-wysse ...' / 'Yes, lady, that shalle I nowe for your sake, / for I wott welle he may nott

amendes make; / He dyd to me fulle unhend'" (lines 811–16). It is tempting to see this admission as Ragnelle's coup, but it, of course, serves masculine interests, protecting the life of Sir Gromer and the face of King Arthur. In accordance with Sedgwick's argument, a woman here again negotiates between the desire of men. See Sedgwick, *Between Men*, pp. 21–27.

21. In *Sovereign Fantasies*, Patricia Clare Ingham explores the connection between land, sovereignty, and the Loathly Lady, which in John Gower's "Tale of Florent" "stakes the lady's ugliness against her landed wealth, contrasting her sexual undesirability with her economic power and prestige" (p. 181). By contrast, the possession of both the land and of Gawain's body seems to be the goal for Dame Ragnelle or perhaps a dual goal for brother and sister (pp. 180–81). See also Forste-Grupp, "Woman Circumvents," who argues that Arthur, according to English inheritance law, has a right to give unclaimed lands as gifts and that Ragnelle achieves "a small, significant victory in the patriarchal world of Arthur's court" by acquiring the lands through marriage to Gawain, the legitimate landholder and by producing an heir, Gyngolen, to secure those lands for the next generation (p. 122). This shrewd manipulator sounds quite unlike Robert Shenk's characterization of a lady "who 'never yet begilid man'" ("Liberation of the 'Loathly Lady,'" p. 320). Even Forste-Grupp, however, must acknowledge Ragnelle's pyrrhic victory: "Ragnell relinquishes her newly won sovereignty over Gawain and her family's lands, thereby winning her husband's love and thus becoming a conventional heroine of medieval romance—silent, passive, and beautiful" ("Woman Circumvents," p. 118). In her essay "A Hymenation of Hags" in the present volume, Susan Carter shrewdly counters the argument of powerlessness with her contention that hags may control heterosexual relations and may even assert some female solidarity among the various women who control men in "The Wife of Bath's Tale" and the "Wedding."

22. Ragnelle further notes that not her brother, but another (jealous?) woman, her stepmother, enchanted and "disformyd" her until the worthiest of knights marries her and surrenders all "his body and goodes" to her (line 698). The language of Ragnelle repeats the "body and goodes … to buy and selle" that Gawain offers her (lines 682–83) and counters conventional romance rhetoric with the language of the marketplace.

23. See Ingham, *Sovereign Fantasies*, p. 142.

24. While this is Sedgwick's concept, the bond between men is frequently asserted in the romances, particularly the "Wedding." Sumner, *Weddynge*, concurs with earlier critics that "the loathly lady story was attached to Gawain to picture the loving relationship between nephew and uncle" (p. xxv). It is true that more often than not, the contest for sovereignty ends in a draw between male and female, but there is also ample evidence to suggest that the Loathly Lady is often found serving not her own interests, but those of men. For example, Hahn notes that Gawain's willingness to marry Ragnelle for Arthur's sake demonstrates that "male chivalric loyalty" gains precedence "over romantic personal love, and makes clear how women operate in romance as the intermediate term in the bonds between men" (*Sir Gawain*, p. 76).

Works Cited

Aguirre, Manuel. "The Riddle of Sovereignty." *MLR* 88 (1993), 273–82.

Albrecht, William P. *The Loathly Lady in "Thomas of Erceldoune": With a Text of the Poem Printed in 1652.* Albuquerque: University of New Mexico Press, 1954.

Blanch, Robert J. "'Al was this land fulfild of fayerye': The Thematic Employment of Force, Willfulness, and Legal Conventions in Chaucer's 'Wife of Bath's Tale.'" *SN* 57 (1985), 41–51.

Bollard, J. K. "Sovereignty and the Loathly Lady in English, Welsh and Irish." *LSE* 17 (1986), 41–59.

Butler, Judith. *Gender Trouble: Feminism and the Subversion of Identity.* New York: Routledge, 1990.

Bynum, Caroline Walker. *Holy Feast and Holy Fast.* Berkeley: University of California Press, 1987.

Chaucer, Geoffrey. *The Canterbury Tales.* Ed. Larry D. Benson. Boston: Houghton Mifflin, 2000.

Child, Francis James, ed. *The English and Scottish Popular Ballads.* 5 vols. New York: Cooper Square, 1962.

Coomaraswamy, Ananda K. "On the Loathly Bride." *Speculum* 20 (1945), 391–404.

Davenport, W. A. *The Art of the Gawain-Poet.* London: Athlone, 1978.

Davis, Rebecca. "More Evidence for Intertextuality and Humorous Intent in 'The Weddynge of Syr Gawen and Dame Ragnell.'" *CR* 35 (2001), 430–39.

Dinshaw, Carolyn. *Chaucer's Sexual Poetics.* Madison: University of Wisconsin Press, 1989.

Eisner, Sigmund. *A Tale of Wonder: A Source Study of "The Wife of Bath's Tale."* Wexford, Ire.: John English, 1957.

Forste-Grupp, Sheryl. "A Woman Circumvents the Laws of Primogeniture in 'The Weddynge of Sir Gawen and Dame Ragnell.'" *SP* 99 (2002), 105–22.

Garbáty, Thomas J. "Rhyme, Romance, Ballad, Burlesque, and the Confluence of Form." In *Fifteenth-Century Studies: Recent Essays,* ed. Robert F. Yeager, pp. 283–301. Hamden, Conn.: Archon, 1984.

Hahn, Thomas, ed. *Sir Gawain: Eleven Romances and Tales.* Kalamazoo, Mich.: Medieval Institute Publications, 1995.

Ingham, Patricia Clare. *Sovereign Fantasies: Arthurian Romance and the Making of Britain.* Philadelphia: University of Pennsylvania Press, 2001.

Lindley, Arthur. "'Vanysshed was this Daunce, He Nyste Where': Alisoun's Absence in the Wife of Bath's Prologue and Tale." *ELH* 59 (1992), 1–21.

Lyle, E. B. "The Relationship between 'Thomas the Rhymer' and 'Thomas of Erceldoune.'" *LSE* 4 (1970), 232–30.

Mann, Jill. *Geoffrey Chaucer.* London: Hemel Hempstead, 1991.

Murray, James A., ed. *The Romance and Prophecies of "Thomas of Erceldoune." Printed from five manuscripts.* EETS 61. London: Trübner, 1875.

Nutt, Alfred. "The Marriage of Sir Gawain and the Loathly Damsel." *Academy* 41 (30 April 1892), 425.

Potkay, Monica Brzezinski, and Regula Meyer Evitt. *Minding the Body: Women and Literature in the Middle Ages, 800–1500*. New York: Macmillan; London: Twayne, 1997.

Saunders, Corrine. *The Forest of Medieval Romance*. Cambridge: Brewer, 1993.

Sedgwick, Eve Kosofsky. *Between Men: English Literature and Male Homosocial Desire*. New York: Columbia University Press, 1985.

Shenk, Robert. "The Liberation of the 'Loathly Lady' of Medieval Romance." *JRMMRA* 2 (1981), 69–77.

Shepherd, Stephen H. A. "Introduction: 'The Weddyng of Syr Gawen and Dame Ragnell for Helpyng of Kyng Athoure.'" In *Middle English Romances*, ed. Stephen H. A. Shepherd, pp. 378–87. New York: Norton, 1995.

Showalter, Elaine. "Introduction: The Rise of Gender." In *Speaking of Gender*, ed. Elaine Showalter, pp. 1–16. New York: Routledge, 1989.

Stokes, Whitley. "The Marriage of Sir Gawain." *Academy* 41 (23 April 1892), 399.

Straus, Barrie Ruth. "The Subversive Discourse of the Wife of Bath: Phallocentric Discourse and the Imprisonment of Criticism." *ELH* 55 (1988), 527–54.

Sumner, Laura, ed. *The Weddynge of Sir Gawen and Dame Ragnell*. Smith College Studies in Modern Languages 5.4. Northampton, Mass.: Department of Modern Languages of Smith College, 1924; repr. Folcroft, Penn.: Folcroft, 1974.

Szittya, Penn R. "The Green Yeoman as Loathly Lady: The Friar's Parody of the 'Wife of Bath's Tale.'" *PMLA* 90 (1975), 386–94.

Trimnell, Karen Hunter. "'And shold have been oderwyse understond': The Disenchanting of Sir Gromer Somer Joure." *MAE* 71 (2002), 294–301.

Wilhelm, James, ed. *The Romance of Arthur*. New York: Garland, 1994.

Vasta, Edward. "Chaucer, Gower, and the Unknown Minstrel: The Literary Liberation of the Loathly Lady." *Exemplaria* 7 (1995), 395–418.

CONTRIBUTORS

Elizabeth Biebel-Stanley earned a BA at the University of
Pittsburgh, an MA at Villanova University, and a PhD at
Lehigh University. She is currently an Associate Professor at
Delaware County Community College in Media, Pennsylvania,
where she teaches composition and a variety of literature
courses, including children's literature and Shakespeare. She
has published articles on Chaucer and coauthored *Chaucer's
"Wife of Bath's Prologue" and "Tale": An Annotated Bibliography,
1900–1995* with Peter G. Beidler.

Ellen M. Caldwell earned a BA at the University of Southern
California and an MA and PhD at UCLA. She taught at
Vanderbilt University and Kalamazoo College before accepting
a position at California State University, Fullerton, in 2001,
where she teaches graduate and undergraduate courses on
Chaucer, medieval literature, Shakespeare, Shakespeare and
film, and gender theory. She has published on the medieval
mystics, Lyly's *Gallathea*, Shakespeare's *The Winter's Tale*, and
Webster's *Duchess of Malfi*. Forthcoming articles are on female
heroism in the medieval romance "Sir Orfeo" and iconoclasm
in Shakespeare's *I Henry IV*. Current research interests are
Renaissance emblems and medieval distinctions between word
and "entente."

Susan Carter completed her BA and MA at the University of
Auckland, and her English literature PhD at the University of
Toronto in 2001, her dissertation topic being "Willing Shape-
shifters: The Loathly Lady from Irish Sovranty to Spenser's
Duessa." She has published on Chaucer's "Wife of Bath's
Tale" (2003); the Green Knight and Ragnelle as monstrous

testers of Sir Gawain (2005); Spenser's Loathly Lady Duessa
(2005); Galadriel and Morgan le Fey (2007); a pedagogy method
SHNID (2006); and more mundanely, on mnemonics (2007)
and punctuation (2007). She now coordinates the Doctoral
Program at the University of Auckland Student Learning
Centre, while convening an extramural course, "Mythology
and Fantasy," for Massey University, Palmerston North.
Current research interests include higher education and
learning advisor support among mnemonics, medieval
constructions of identity, and the Mary Magdalene.

Paul Gaffney teaches medieval and Renaissance literature and
linguistics at Hiram College in Ohio. He received his BA from
Western Washington University and his PhD from the
University of Virginia. His dissertation explores how the
corpus of Middle English romances functions as an intricate
network of inter-referentiality. His research interests include
anonymous Middle English romances, the Arthurian chronicle
tradition, Renaissance chapbooks, and electronic textual
editing.

Stephanie Hollis is Director of the Centre for Medieval and Early
Modern European Studies at the University of Auckland. She
teaches Old and Middle English literature and a course on
Tolkien's Lord of the Rings. Her publications include articles on
Chaucer, Middle English romance, cycle drama, and Old
English literature. Her principal research interest is women in
England in the Anglo-Saxon and post-conquest periods, and
she is the editor of Writing the Wilton Women: Goscelin's Legend
of Edith and Liber Confortatorius. She is currently working on a
sequel to her Anglo-Saxon Women and the Church: Sharing a
Common Fate as well as a study of Goscelin of Saint-Bertin's
writings for the Barking community.

Mary Leech received her PhD from the University of Cincinnati
in 2002. Her dissertation is entitled "The Rhetoric of the Body:
A Study of Body Imagery and Rhetorical Structure in Medieval
Literature," in which she discusses body metaphor as it is
informed by the medieval understanding of medical science.

After participating in an NEH seminar on the Old French Fabliaux, she contributed to a volume based on the themes from the seminar. She was a founding member of the Société Fableors and currently serves as president of that society.

S. Elizabeth Passmore is an Assistant Professor of English at the University of Southern Indiana, Evansville, where she teaches courses on Chaucer, Ricardian Literature, medieval surveys, and the History of the English Language. She completed her PhD in Medieval Studies from the University of Connecticut in 2005 and is currently revising her dissertation, "The Loathly Lady Transformed: A Literary and Cultural Analysis of the Medieval Irish and English Hag-Beauty Tales," for publication. She has published articles on late medieval English narratives and early Irish texts. Her research interests include Middle English romance, Celtic studies, text-image relationships, and literary fairy tales.

Russell A. Peck, the John Hall Deane Professor of English at the University of Rochester, is the creator and general editor of the Middle English Texts Series. He has published two editions of Gower's *Confessio Amantis* (the most recent in three volumes) as well as numerous other scholarly books and articles ranging from Gower and Chaucer to Middle English romance, fairy tales, theory of structure, aesthetics, and drama. He has been the recipient of numerous teaching awards.

Mary Edwards Shaner is Professor Emeritus of Medieval Literature at the University of Massachusetts, Boston, where she taught a variety of medieval English and children's literature courses for over thirty years. She edited Chaucer's "Legend of Good Women" for *The Riverside Chaucer* and the Advocates manuscript of Sir Gowther for *Medieval Literature for Children* and has published articles on medieval and children's literature. Her interests include fourteenth-century poetry, early English drama, and the history of childhood.

Lynn M. Wollstadt is a tenured Instructor of English at South Suburban College in the Chicago suburbs. She received her BA

at Wellesley College and her MA and PhD at the University of
California, Davis, with a dissertation entitled "Women and
Ballads and Ballad Women: Gender and the History of
Scottish Balladry." Her research interests and publications
focus on the traditional ballads of England and Scotland,
especially concerning ballad origins and issues of gender.

R. F. Yeager is Professor and Chair of the Department of English
and Foreign Languages at the University of West Florida. In
addition to editing several books and *JGN: The John Gower
Newsletter*, he is the author of numerous articles on Chaucer,
Gower, Hoccleve, and others, and has written *John Gower's
Poetic: The Search for a New Arion* and most recently, with Terry
Jones, Terry Dolan, Alan Fletcher, and Juliette D'Or, *Who
Murdered Chaucer? A Medieval Mystery*. He has been president
of the John Gower Society since 1981.

INDEX

Medieval Institute Publications is a program
of The Medieval Institute, College of Arts
and Sciences, Western Michigan University

Typeset in 10/13 LTC Goudy Oldstyle
with LTC Ornaments Three
Designed by Linda K. Judy
Composed by Heather M. Padgen
Manufactured by Sheridan Books, Inc.

Medieval Institute Publications
College of Arts and Sciences
Western Michigan University
1903 W. Michigan Avenue
Kalamazoo, MI 49008-5432
http://www.wmich.edu/medieval/mip

 WESTERN MICHIGAN UNIVERSITY